Contents

CHANCE SCOUT

Chapter 1

Americans: The Only People Who Have Walked On Another Planet.

MAKE AMERICA GREAT AGAIN. MAKE AMERICA STRAIGHT AGAIN. MAKE AMERICA WHITE AGAIN. MAKE AMERICA RIGHT AGAIN.

While debating hatred is a fool's errand, arguing with ignorance can prove a more fruitful endeavor, so here's a retort to the first words of this chapter.

"If it's the blacks, browns, immigrants, Jews, LGBTQ+, and woke liberals causing all your problems, then please explain something to me. Back in the 1600s, early settlers, possibly including your forebears, came over from Europe into a 'whites-only' America. The slave colony in the south would have been of no concern to them unless they were benefiting from it. Then, for the next two hundred and fifty years, America was wide open and free for the taking, with the only competition coming from other straight white Anglo-Saxons.

By the 1860s, across the West, the United States Army had kindly wiped out most of the pesky brown people—whose civilization was here first—to steal their land. Had your relatives homesteaded there, Uncle Sam would have gifted them one hundred and sixty acres of that land, which would be worth over two million dollars today.

The even more adventurous of your kin could have headed to California to strike gold. Or, if 'black gold' were their thing, they could have scooped up scrubland in Texas to become oil barons. Always remember, throughout this time, straight, white men reigned supreme, with no black, brown, Jewish, or LGBTQ+ folks allowed to compete with your great-grandparents.

But perhaps your forefathers came here too late to take advantage of all the free land and gold? No problem. During the boom years following the end of the Second World War, they could have started any business and cleaned up, almost completely untroubled by challenges from any marginalized people.

So, given all these infinite possibilities and endless opportunities for creating generational wealth, what the hell were your people doing back then for you not to be a multimillionaire today?"

Maybe some on the other side genuinely don't know, or maybe they do. Someone less kind-hearted might use the same line conservatives use on poor black folks; that their ancestors were too lazy or too weak to succeed. But I'm not that person, and this is not one of those books.

I understand that the system is functioning exactly as planned and that the outcomes are precisely as intended. That system, which secured the votes of working-and lower-middle class white folks, was never intended to educate them, nor were their ancestors ever meant to ascend to positions of influence, wealth, or power.

Instead, they were indentured servants in the 1700s, deceived by their bosses and denied their promised hundred acres after fulfilling their obligations. They were coal miners in the 1900s, striking for their rights, whose bosses ordered them beaten by the Pinkertons and shot by the police. They were soldiers sent off to war, while the bosses' kids stayed home. Then, on coming home, shattered from the horrors of seeing things no human should ever see and from doing things no human should ever do, they found themselves thrown away.

This is the design because this is who they always were: the disposable, the malleable, and the replaceable, but allowed the slight advantage of feeling superior to people of color.

In 1865, 1954, 1964, 2008, and 2020, Americans may have thought they had overcome hate and division. However, many never saw the demonic force, once beaten—but whose ideas were never vanquished and therefore never vanished—feeding and stoking the fires of fury.

What you may know as MAGA, I call the Confederate Taliban. They are the gun-wielding, freedom-hating, race-baiting, Russia-loving, women-hating, planet-heating Americans. They exist within a coalition of Scared, (fake) Christian, Angry, Rich and Insane (SCARI) people. In them, we find an unyielding need to subdue, dominate, and control anyone who will not conform to their dogma. Theirs is a world where they demand the right to do anything without having to take responsibility for anything they do.

That being said, it was F. Scott Fitzgerald, borrowing from the ancient Greek philosopher Aristotle, who wrote;

> The test of a first-rate intelligence is the ability to hold two opposing ideas in the mind at the same time and still retain the ability to function.[1]

To prove the point, what has happened in America over the past four hundred years would be amazing if it were a country in Europe. But this is a country younger than some European homes.

America is the first nation to have institutionalized slavery and fought a civil war to end it. It's the first nation to create a legal apartheid state within its borders and then peacefully dismantle it, and it's the only nation whose citizens have walked on another planet.

As far as people go, it's the nation that gave us Robert Edward Lee and Frederick Douglass, Donald Trump and Dr. Martin Luther King Jr., and Phyllis Schlafly and Harriet Tubman. In a nutshell, America is the most exciting, diverse, and powerful society that humanity has ever produced.

If there is a single focus of light that could illuminate what an American can be, it is the ability of someone to dream the impossible and turn it into the possible, regardless of where they come from, what they look like, or who their parents are. Maybe that's what a kid from Wapakoneta, Ohio, thought when, just thirty-nine years into his life, he became the first human to set foot on another planet. Conceivably, it may also have been in the mind of the skinny son of a single mom from Honolulu, who, forty-seven years into his time here on Earth, would become the 44th President of the United States.

The progress we have made should be an immense source of pride. America has evolved from a place where, just ninety-nine years ago, President Woodrow Wilson was screening the KKK promo video, "Birth of a Nation," in the White House[2]. Yet, showing how two things can be true at once, Wilson's own grandson marched for civil rights[3] and was proud to be alive to see a black man stand for president.

Nevertheless, as we progress, we challenge interests that are adept at stoking fear in order to preserve their power. That can lead to regress; thus, Trump followed both Obama and Biden. Still, despite huge headwinds from the Confederate Taliban, this nation of over three hundred million people is moving relatively peacefully from a majority European ethnic culture to a majority non-European American culture, with white, black, and brown people learning together, working together, loving together, and living together.

Through the chapters, I hope to take you on an incredible journey. There are four recurring themes that will come up again and again, even though I won't specifically reference them: Self-interest, status, class, and race. It is impossible to understand America's past, present, or future without understanding these four characteristics. There's a fifth theme called 'courage.' Sometimes, I may point it out, but if you're reading this, you'll be smart enough to recognize it.

There are enough explanations and solutions within the chapters—not just from me, but, more importantly, from many other brilliant people—that by the end of the book, you will be energized to fight the fear and help build an astonishing American future.

I have to acknowledge some of the many sources and inspirations that have led to this. Without the books of Kurt Andersen, Amy Chua, Thomas Frank, Adam Serwer, Ty Siedule, David Corn, David Pepper, Jill Lepore, and so many others, it wouldn't have been possible. But also, it's a modern age, and brilliant, insightful American exemplars are using podcasts to drill down into the issues of today. John Fugelsang, Andy Levy, Danielle Moody, Wajahat Ali, Bob Cesca, Allison Gill, Jared Yates Sexton, F. P. Wellman, Mary Trump (the polar opposite of the rest of that family), and many others can help to make you much smarter.

At the end of the book, there will be a reading and listening list for you to get a deeper dive into that which I can only scratch the surface of here.

Finally, thank you for reading. That alone means it was worth all the hours of effort.

James Mahadevan
December 2024

Chapter 2

Raped, Robbed And Murdered, Yet The 'Red Indian' Still Wants To Help You.

There are only three types of people in America. The indigenous, the immigrant, and the stolen. Some had their land stolen, some arrived by choice, and some were stolen from their lands. Of the first group, there were six tribal nations that made up the inhabitants of Turtle Island: the Mohawk, Oneida, Onondaga, Cayuga, Seneca, and Tuscarora. They had lived here for a hundred thousand years before anyone had even heard the name Christopher Columbus.

I wanted to see the journey that got us here, but also how crucial Native Americans are to solving some of the greatest problems of the 21st century.

Over the next few pages, we are going to discover some stories that history would not have taught you and how relevant they are today. By the end of this chapter, apart from learning how non-Christians are more useful to us than fake-Christians, you may actually question who the more sophisticated people actually are. But before that, a brief foray to explain the fake Christianity that got us here. Just to note, in writing, I may switch between the terms 'indigenous' people, 'Indian', First Nation, and Native American. Regardless, they will always be the original inhabitants of America.

To find the genesis moment of both subjugation and slavery, we have to travel all the way back to 1452. The kings of Spain and Portugal sought permission and future forgiveness from the Church in Rome—the same people who brought us anti-Semitism. They wanted to absolve themselves of the abominable sins arising from the future crimes they would commit in the conquest of foreign "undiscovered lands" and the subsequent subjugation, enslavement, or elimination of their peoples.

The Church created the 'Doctrine of Discovery' in a series of official edicts that were issued between 1452 and 1493. In his spellbinding 2023 book, 'The Hidden Roots of White Supremacy and the Path of a Shared American Future', Robert P. Jones, the president of the Public Religion Research Institute, shows the authorizing language:

> To invade, search out, capture, vanquish, and subdue all Saracens [Muslims] and pagans whatsoever, and other enemies of Christ wheresoever placed, and the kingdoms, dukedoms, principalities, dominions, possessions, and all movable and immovable goods whatsoever held and possessed by them and to reduce their persons to perpetual slavery.[4]

Mr Jones goes on to describe how these decrees would provide the framework for what happened in America:

> The most relevant papal edict for the American context was the bull Inter Caetera, issued by Pope Alexander VI in May 1493, with the express purpose of validating Spain's ownership rights of lands in the Americas following the voyages of Columbus the year before. It praised Columbus and again affirmed the church's blessing of and interest in political conquest, "that in our times especially the Catholic faith and

the Christian religion be exalted and be everywhere increased and spread, that the health of souls be cared for and that barbarous nations be overthrown and brought to the faith itself.[5]

Once in America, the first Spanish settlers sought to enslave indigenous peoples[6], but they found a problem; unsurprisingly, these folks, whose land it had been, knew it very well and could escape and sustain themselves without a problem.

Sadly, satanic serendipity would intervene on later English and Scottish settlers' behalf, as they found a new people to steal and enslave. But even when African slaves escaped, indigenous people would welcome them in and fight the Europeans who came to demand their 'property' back[7].

The 'Indian Problem' would 'persist' for over two hundred years. Remember, these folks were fighting for their own land, just as Russians were against Germany in 1942 and Ukrainians are against Russians in 2024.

Despite the settlers enacting hundreds of treaties with the indigenous over the years, we will read how money and 'progress' would always triumph over honor and integrity.

Part of that 'progress' was the push out West towards Manifest Destiny. It was driven by the railroads. This is what would move people and goods and link states together, and nothing would stand in its way.

So it would be that, during—and especially after—the Civil War, the settlers turned their full might on the indigenous, with the Plains-Indian Wars of 1861 to 1886. To that point, it was General Sherman, who had distinguished himself with such honor during the Civil War, who wrote to President Grant in 1867, "We are not going to let thieving, ragged Indians check and stop the progress."[8]

This brings us to the thirty million bison that roamed the Western Plains in the post-war years. The indigenous people would use their meat for food and their skins for clothing and shelter. In fact, so industrious were the indigenous that, from snout to tail, they found over one hundred and fifty uses for the dead animal. It's no overestimation to say that the bison were their lifeline.

Not for long. The same rail lines that would carry Manifest Destiny would also allow for a new 'sport': "Hunting by Rail." Easterners would travel west to kill the bison; some for hides, some for tongues, and most just killing for killing's sake. Single hunters would be credited with slaying 6,000 bison[9].

From 1870, over two million bison a year were being slaughtered. By 1875, even representatives in the Texas state legislature grew alarmed and introduced a bill to protect the bison[10]. However, it was nixed, in part, thanks to General Phillip Sheridan, another Civil War hero, quoted as arguing,

> These men have done more in the last two years, and will do more in the next year, to settle the vexed Indian question, than the entire regular army has done in the last forty years. They are destroying the Indians' commissary. And it is a well-known fact that an army losing its base of supplies is placed at a great disadvantage. Send them powder and lead, if you will; but for a lasting peace, let them kill, skin and sell until the buffaloes are exterminated. Then your prairies can be covered with speckled cattle. [11]

The extermination of the bison had the desired effect. The Native Americans were fearsome fighters but had no answer to the unstoppable combination of bullets and money. Thus, without food or skins, the indigenous could not survive. In the Annual Report of the General of the U.S. Army in 1878, General Sheridan wrote,

> We took away their country and their means of support,
> broke up their mode of living, their habits of life, introduced
> disease and decay among them, and it was for this and against
> this they made war. Could anyone expect less? Then, why
> wonder at Indian difficulties?[12]

The wars would continue for another eight years, but the settlers had already won. The bison population had plummeted from over thirty million at the end of the Civil War down to just 325 in 1884[13].

Don't think the settlers were finished with the indigenous people. In 1892, Captain Richard Henry Pratt gave a speech at the National Conference of Charities and Correction in Boston, in which he uttered the line, "Kill the Indian in him, and save the man."[14]

He was speaking of 'educating' indigenous children. In practice, this meant forcibly removing children from their families and taking them far away to boarding schools. In these 'schools', they were forbidden from speaking their native language or acting in any traditional way.

As a demonic tool for assimilation into a patriarchal white society, it was devastatingly effective. Suffice to say physical and sexual abuse was rampant in these institutions. Equally shocking is that these hostels of hell existed all the way into the 1960s[15].

To understand another 'why' for that assimilation, we have to go back in time. When the European settlers first landed in America, long before the United States existed, they had to work with the Native Americans, so they formed treaties. This is how, today, in America, there are three forms of sovereign government; federal, state, and tribal.

It's Article 1, Section 8, Clause 3 of the US Constitution that recognizes the Native American nations as sovereign;

> The Congress shall have power to...regulate commerce with
> foreign nations, among several states, and with the Indian
> tribes...

Subsequent to all the treaties, there are, according to the Department of the Interior, still fifty-six million acres of land (out of the total US land area of 2.4 billion acres) held in trust by the government, for Native American tribes and individuals[16].

To protect the lands further, the Supreme Court ruled in Johnson v. McIntosh (1823) that private citizens cannot purchase land from Native Americans and only the federal government can negotiate for land.

Eight years later, in Cherokee Nation v. Georgia (1831), the Court ruled against the State of Georgia, who were trying to steal Native lands. As we will learn, evil never sleeps. So, undeterred, they came back a year later, in Worcester v. Georgia (1832), but again got struck down by the Court, who ruled that only Congress can negotiate for Native lands[17].

Back then, the greedy settlers wanted Native lands simply because they wanted the land. But, within a few years, there would be a much more pressing need.

It was in 1830, under President Andrew Jackson's 'Indian Removal Act', that the indigenous folks were forced off their fertile agricultural lands in the south and sent up the Trail of Tears[18] to remote, worthless scrubland, like Osage County, Oklahoma. This was made famous in the book and the film 'Killers of the Flower Moon.'

Remember, in 1830, the wealth came from cotton, tobacco, and sugar, and none of them grew on scrub. This was an age before oil, before cars, before highways, and before industry.

It wouldn't be until nearly thirty years later, in 1859, that oil was first discovered in Pennsylvania, and John D. Rockefeller wouldn't incorporate Standard Oil until 1865. However, what happened in the oil industry will serve as one of many examples to remind us of how we must never underestimate the capacity of the contemptible to surpass even their own last atrocious milestone.

The indigenous folks were sitting on scrub land with a fortune in oil underneath it. So it would be that greed and jealousy led to theft and violence. And within a few decades, with the help and connivance of the law, the land and the oil were still there; it's just they had new owners.

So now, with no money and no prospects, it was easy for the powerful to point to the 'Indian problem' and for the ignorant to buy this BS. Come the 1950s, there were few allies to protest when the Urban Relocation Program and the Indian Relocation Act were introduced. Both policies had the effect of 'moving' the Native peoples into the cities, ostensibly for their own furtherance and welfare.

Aside from losing their rightful fortunes, there was another, more pernicious side effect of tearing rural folks from their land and sending them to live in a city. This is from Simon Moya-Smith, Oglala Lakota journalist and the author of 'Your Spirit Animal is a Jackass.'

> Denver's a relocation city, as are Minneapolis, Seattle, and Los Angeles. That's where you get the term City Indian. But as a result of that, there was a culture shock. They weren't around their languages or ceremony, and then all of a sudden, we get substance abuse and homelessness. Before white people came here, we didn't have homelessness, before white people came here, we didn't have hunger and before white people came here, we didn't have all of these things that are plaguing our communities. [19]

This takes us to some more people who really don't care. During the four years that Trump and Republicans held power, they did almost nothing to combat the opioid epidemic that still kills over one hundred and thirty Americans *a day*[20]. It's true that, whilst in office, Trump declared a "Public Health Emergency." However, the fund only contained $57,000 (not a typo) [21].

You will read how this crisis has ravaged many GOP-voting rural communities. If, instead, the Administration had declared a 'National Emergency', this would have allowed the Federal Emergency Management Agency (FEMA), with its $29 billion budget and the logistics to match, to intervene. But then, why would you expect a man who doesn't care about his own family to care about anyone else's?

In complete contrast, we can meet the Wabanaki Nations tribe in Maine. Without any help from the Trump-loving GOP governor and with acutely limited funds, it opened up a culturally sensitive Medication Assisted Treatment (MAT) facility to cope with the onslaught of the opioid epidemic (for which the rich pushers who unleashed it never went to prison). The Wabanaki Nations offered to treat anyone, regardless of color or creed. They used the line, "We're not going to leave you behind." Remember the kindness of strangers as you read the next two stories.

Across red state legislatures, there has been an explicit policy to dehumanize the LGBTQ+ community, and most directly, transgender folks. Since 2016, hundreds of bills have passed in state legislatures to criminalize trans kids and their parents[22]. All from the people who scream about 'freedom.' and 'parental rights', whilst ignoring the rapists and groomers within their own cult.

Later on in the book, you will read about how far back hate against the transgender community goes. For now, though, it's a sour irony that Native American communities, who aren't Christian, more closely follow the teachings of Jesus than the people who scream about their Christianity. To the indigenous, transgender folks are known as Two Spirit. We can hear again from Simon Moya-Smith,

Two Spirit people means that you are blessed with the sight of having an attraction, or having an affection for as many genders, that are in the nations and that tribes. We've had LGBTQ+ people here for 1000s of years, and nobody had a problem. Then they came with this black book. But we have to remember that these Christians have used that black book to demonize everybody at some point. [23]

Staying in red states, it would be two hundred years since settlers last went to the Supreme Court to seek legal permission to steal Native lands before they would try again.

Despite the land-rights cases you read about previously being firmly settled law, in June 2023, the Supreme Court considered a new case. Haaland v. Brackeen was ostensibly about the rights of a white Texas family who had fostered a Native American child. They wanted to end the Indian Child Welfare Act (ICWA) of 1978.

Before that time, apart from the 'Boarding Schools', it was quite normal for state child welfare officers to use the flimsiest of pretexts to remove (kidnap?) children from the tribal lands, taking them away from their families to place them with white, 'Christian' families. Up to one-third of indigenous children may have been 'assimilated' in this way[24]. The ICWA was an attempt to remedy the evils of the past by ensuring that first preference would always be for Native American children to be kept with other Native American families[25].

Coming back to our 2023 case, the plaintiffs, the Brackeen family, who had no connection to Native Americans or anything to do with the tribes, claimed 'reverse discrimination' because they weren't allowed to keep a Native American child.

It's very important to note that Article 1 of the Constitution states that Native affairs are sovereign and political, *not* racial, and as such, Congress treats this as a political rather than a racial matter of law. This should have killed the family's spurious argument of "reverse discrimination" straight away. Indeed, any competent lawyer should have known that it would have been a complete waste of time and money trying to litigate it.

Just for context, before this case even reached the Supreme Court docket, the plaintiffs would have spent hundreds of thousands of dollars to see it pass through a local judge, a federal court and an appellate court.

It's scarcely believable, but the plaintiffs—who couldn't afford to pay for their own lawyer—were joined in their action by the states of Texas, Indiana, Louisiana, and Ohio. Put into perspective, for the Attorney General of Texas to intervene is akin to you stealing some of your neighbor's garden and the State Attorney General siding with you and using all the resources of the state to work against your neighbor. But there's even more.

A partner at the law firm, Gibson Dunn, represented the family. Just to note, these characters are no 'Better Call Saul' strip mall ambulance chasers. This was the law firm that litigated Bush v. Gore in the 2000 election. Their partners, one of whom represented the Brackeen family, bill out at $1800 an hour[26] and the cost of taking a case like this to the Supreme Court is way north of $1 million[27].

So, why would an elite law firm go pro bono to represent a sure-fire loser of a case? Well, here is a clue from the firm's own website;

> Gibson, Dunn & Crutcher's Oil and Gas Practice Group advises the world's leading oil and gas exploration, development and production companies....We also represent financial institutions, private equity firms and government entities active in the oil and gas sector. [28]

That work has helped create the 14th highest grossing law firm in the world, with earnings of $2.7 billion in 2019[29]. Perhaps, uncoincidentally, it is also the firm that litigated the Dakota Access Pipeline that is currently decimating sacred tribal lands[30].

I'm certain Gibson Dunn maintains the highest ethical standards and is saintly in the extreme. However, a more deviant law firm might know if they take children off some or all of the tribal lands, there won't be anyone left to inherit the fifty-six million acres of land held by the government.

In law, where assets have no inheritor, they go to the state. The legal term is "escheated." The more deviant law firm might have also attempted to involve some state legislatures. Then, they can acquire the lands and lease them off to their fossil fuel donors to "drill, baby, drill."

On the subject of fossil fuels, if you're reading this book, then global warming may be one of your concerns. In a 2022 study titled "Up in Smoke," from UCLA and the University of Chicago, it was detailed how five out of California's six largest wildfires occurred in 2020.[31] That year, over four million acres of forest burned.

To put that into perspective, that's the whole of Rhode Island, half of Hawaii, or a quarter of West Virginia gone in just one year. Businesses, homes, and lives were all wiped out. Less tragic, yet more astonishing, was this statistic: in the 2020 fires, one hundred and twenty-seven million tons of carbon dioxide were pumped into the atmosphere.

Don't worry, I hear you say, that should be nothing for 'green' California. Indeed, in 2021, one third of California's energy was generated from renewable sources, like solar and wind. But here's the rub. Between 2002 and 2020, with all that 'green energy,' the state had only made reductions of sixty-five million tons of carbon dioxide.

You don't have to be a Nobel laureate in mathematics to see the problem. All of those eighteen years of hard-earned gains went up in smoke in just one year's fires.[32] Indeed, pollution from wildfires ranks second only to the emissions from the thirty-four million vehicles driving around the state.

You may wonder what this has to do with indigenous people. Allow me a small segue. History may have taught you that, before the Mexican-American War, what is now California had been the home to three hundred indigenous nations. After that war in 1848, the United States took over California[33].

With the push out West and the gold rush, Native Americans had to be 'exterminated.' These aren't my words; they are from an 1894 edition of the Daily Alta California newspaper;

> Whites are becoming impressed with the belief that it will be absolutely necessary to exterminate the savages before they can labor much longer in the mines with security.[34]

Between 1846 and 1873, one hundred and twenty thousand indigenous people would be exterminated. Of the thirty thousand people remaining, most were sent to prison camps (reservations) or enslaved on ranches, with their children being sent to 'Indian assimilation schools.'

The first governor of California, Peter Burnett, at his second State of the State address, was abhorrently honest when he said, "That a war of extermination will continue to be waged between the races until the Indian race becomes extinct must be expected."[35]

Before the settlers came, it was the Native folks who managed the land. The settlers only wanted the gold and had no interest in the forests, except for their timber. Thus, like their Confederate Taliban descendants, they had no understanding nor concern about the conservation and preservation of America for the next generation. In stark contrast, the indigenous peoples understood the land, as you would if your people had been its guardians and stewards for over 100,000 years.

Indeed, they were such astute environmentalists that, to prevent wildfires, they would wait until just before it rained and then start the burn.

The ground tinder would combust, but before the fire got out of control, the rains would come and stop it from spreading. In the words of Margo Robbins of the Indigenous Peoples Burn Network, reported in the National Geographic, "You can too fight fire with fire. There's good fire and bad fire, and the good fire prevents the bad."[36]

This was all so counterintuitive to the European settlers. The US National Forest Service, formed in 1905, had a "10am" policy, which meant that any fire burning from the previous day had to be extinguished by 10am the following day. This resulted in vast amounts of easily combustible tinder being left on the ground.

To get to the heart of why the Anglo-Americans resisted prescribed burning, the National Geographic gave us this gem;

> Many old-time foresters, trained with Bambi-style images of deadly wildfires, resisted this new view. So did many environmentalists. "Emotionally," Sierra Club co-founder David Brower admitted, "I just can't handle blackened trees.

This is what a purity test looks like. These people valued pretty forests over well-managed, thriving habitats. So it would remain until 1978, when California started small amounts of prescribed burns. However, they ran into the problem of the 'pure' environmentalists again, who, this time, didn't like the smoke.

There's more. Preventative burns also open the burner to legal liabilities, whereas if firefighters are just trying to stop a 'natural' fire, they can burn up to a hundred acres without the threat of any penalty.

So, we reach a place of paradox, where today the 'liberal' environmentalists complain about starting small prescribed burns to stop the larger out-of-control fire, yet also wail when that larger out-of-control fire comes. It might not have escaped your attention that, by then, it's the fire that is in control, not the firefighters, and also that the carcinogenic, planet-heating smoke emissions are exponentially greater.

Just to end, there was a line, quite common when I was growing up but not heard much anymore: "All we have to do is leave the world a better place than we found it." This segues into the Seven Generation rule that indigenous people believe, but no one else seems to. Journalist Simon Moya-Smith described it;

> There's the Seven generation rule that you don't make any significant decision, without considering seven generations after you're dead. How will this impact seven generations of my family, of my nation, of my tribe, of humanity, of the animals of the water? Everything, not just me personally. The land doesn't need us, we need the land.[37]

Chapter 3

The Slave Master's MAGA Origin Story

Billions of words have been exhaustively expended examining MAGA and Trump. Much of the talk misses the point, simply by misunderstanding that it's all just the culmination of over four hundred years of radicalization.

I don't use the word MAGA, preferring instead the Confederate Taliban[38]. It paints a far truer historical perspective of who and what they are; their forebears' rebellion against the United States being the actualized epitome of a dreamed reality of a slave nation.

After 1865, they never stopped grieving, they never stopped resenting, and they never stopped fighting for their debased ideology. Theirs would be a generational war in which the battles would have different names, like 'Lost Cause', 'States' rights', 'coastal elites', 'inner cities', 'political correctness', and 'woke', but the fight was towards the same end: domination and control.

In the modern GOP, it's hard to separate Christian fundamentalists—one-third of Republicans (and nearly three-quarters of the Trump primary voting base)—from the modern MAGA QAnon conspiracists (more about them in chapter eight). The two ideas coexist as comfortably as flames dancing in a fire. However, in this chapter, we are dealing with the religious types.

Their guiding force is the Old Testament part of the two-thousand-year-old Bible. Their preachers have sold them a bastardized version of faith, which gives them certainty. That certainty ensures conformity, which is the parent of ignorance, and as ignorance rejects inquiry, so science, which is ever-inquisitive, must be heresy. Thus, we arrive at the intellectual cul-de-sac that allows them to bathe in so many immeasurably indescribable insanities: that God's planet is here for man to plunder, that God will heal them in times of sickness, that God will make them rich, and that God will strike down their enemies.

This sour, satanic succor exists alongside their ultimate dream of a war that will end all wars. In that event, we, the 'unbelievers', will burn in a sea of fire here on Earth, whilst they are raptured to Heaven to meet their God. And so it is we come full circle, for God will save them, so in God they trust.

It's a certainty of the modern age that fake Christians, satanic grifters, avaricious lie providers, and evil politicians will all pour fuel on the fire of malice. However, to unpack, in former Confederate states, the war on women's reproductive rights, the persecution of LGBTQ+ folks, school textbook censorship, and why the teaching of real history is forbidden, we first need to understand that the wealthy elite's original sin was slavery.

Slavery was about domination and the acquisition of free labor to power an agrarian society. Those sitting at the apex of this grotesque experiment would be visited with otherworldly profits. From that money would come the power to Make America Great through the manifest destiny of expansion, which would allow for more slavery and more domination.

Here, we arrive at a paradox. Those fake Christians considered themselves to be righteous. However, in order to vindicate their unspeakable oppression of other human beings, they needed a justification for the institution of their Mephistophelian crime against humanity. For this, the rich demons would work hand in hand with anti-Christian preachers to concoct a horrific bastardization of the teachings of the Bible.

Before we continue with these malignant malfeasants, let's hear from someone who was there. Frederick Douglass was a former slave and a true American hero. Frederick was born in Talbot County, Maryland, in February 1818, the son of an African slave mother and her rapist slave-'master'. He passed through several 'owners' before escaping through the Underground Railroad in 1838.

Out in the free world, through his writings and his advocacy, not just for abolition but also for women's rights and science, he showed what an unshackled, educated, brilliant black man was capable of. Frederick's towering intellect allied with his extraordinary empathy proved that intelligence absent empathy (see most right-wing 'intellectuals') is neither intelligence nor smart. As both a philosopher and the author of several books, including 'Narrative of the Life of Frederick Douglass, An American Slave.' From that, he gave us this impeccable quote about those fake-Christian slave 'owners';

> We have men sold to build churches, women sold to support the gospel, and babes sold to purchase Bibles for the Poor Heathen! All For the Glory Of God And The Good Of Souls! The slave auctioneer's bell and the church-going bell chime in with each other, and the bitter cries of the heart-broken slave are drowned in the religious shouts of his pious maste r.[39]

Remember Frederick's words as we descend back into the den of demons and the bitter lies that would be told in order to make slavery palatable for many ordinary people.

For the Christian settlers, the elimination of the Native Americans, the original owners of this land, afforded no moral quandary. Being non-Christians, they were considered 'heathens' and, as such, fair game to be subjugated and eradicated. The stolen African slave would prove a marginally more perplexing puzzle. As Christians, the Bible said that they should be treated well, but how to enslave them and treat them well? It's a mournful truth, but evil minds are capable of reaching the deepest depths of depravity.

Thus, in the Good Book, there is the story of Noah (of The Ark fame). We are a little time on from God flooding the Earth and killing almost everyone (including every pregnant woman and fetus). Per the story, Noah built a big ark, and along with his family, had two of each animal put in it to repopulate the Earth.

Skip forward to after the flood. Noah is now six hundred years old (really!) with a proclivity for drink. As he lies inebriated and naked in his tent, his son Ham comes in and sees him. A humiliated and furious Noah curses Ham and sends him off to be a slave. So it would be, 1600 years later, the American slave masters, twisted devils as they were, purposefully misread the words and falsely stated that Ham meant dark or black. This would be their biblical foundation for why Africans could be enslaved[40].

This leads us to why the fundamentalists, then and now, are so furious at black people. They knew that their whole unhallowed enterprise of domination, and the 'heritage' they claimed arising out of it, was predicated on a bestial lie that transgressed every teaching of the Gospel. However, they didn't care, because they weren't real Christians.

To give an exact date to the modern MAGA origins, it was 1662. That was when the concept of 'race' was invested into law, and the first time in human history that hereditary slavery had been institutionalized. It came with the innocuous-sounding 1662-ACT XII in Virginia[41]. Within its own old English words, we see the sinful text:

WHEREAS some doubts have arrisen whether children got
    by any Englishman upon a negro woman should be slave

or ffree, Be it therefore enacted and declared by this present grand assembly, that all children borne in this country shalbe held bond or free only according to the condition of the mother.[42]

If the mother was a slave, then it must follow that her children would also be slaves. Note the deviant work-around that absolves the patriarchal rapist slave 'master' from any responsibility, for either the rape, or any children that chanced from it. Then, draw a line to today to see how the Confederate Taliban also absolves rapists from their accountability, yet indubitably criminalizes every pregnant rape survivor who seeks to rid herself of the attacker's progeny.

Going back to the 1600s. This was a time before politicians and before elections. On the elite rungs of society in the South were the fake-Christian patriarchs (landowners), and everything they did was in the service of making a profit. In their agrarian societies, cotton, sugar, and tobacco were wealth, and with no tractors, combines, or electricity, people were the machines, and any wages would mean less profit.

It was they who created the forebears of the Confederate Taliban by performing their early devil's magic of dehumanizing the African slave, while simultaneously elevating the poor white to believe it was in their self-interest to go along with this wicked enterprise. In allowing them the sick satisfaction of looking down on enslaved folks, the landowners purchased enough of those same poor whites' attention to ensure they were always looking in the wrong direction and thus would never pose a challenge to the social hierarchy.

Thinking of that leads me to a survey of Americans imagining a Trump 2024 presidency. When asked what words sum it up, their top picks were "revenge," "power," and "retribution."[43]

Frederick Douglass would describe the seductive lure of power held over another human being as 'The fatal poison of irresponsible power'. Remember that word, 'power,' and you may get some understanding of how they simply cannot allow the truth of history to be taught in former slave states.

In antebellum times, the elites presented themselves as the beneficent masters who needed to look after the 'uneducated savages'. These 'savages' were like a human Schrödinger's cat. They were deemed far too stupid to look after themselves, yet far too dangerous to be allowed into polite society. So would be born the modern myth of white supremacy that would allow, under cover of religion, generations of unspeakable cruelty.

Frederick understood this much better than I ever could and wrote of the madness in the minds of American 'Christians' in 'Narrative of the Life of Frederick Douglass." His words come from 1845, but the sentiments are as true today;

> Between the Christianity of this land and the Christianity of Christ, I recognize the widest possible difference—so wide that to receive the one as good, pure, and holy, is of necessity to reject the other as bad, corrupt, and wicked. To be the friend of the one is of necessity to be the enemy of the other. I love the pure, peaceable, and impartial Christianity of Christ; I therefore hate the corrupt, slave-holding, women-whipping, cradle-plundering, partial and hypocritical Christianity of this land. Indeed, I can see no reason but the most deceitful one for calling the religion of this land Christianity...[44]

Another reason for the fake-Christian fury at black folks is that, over the years, African-American Christianity has preached love and forgiveness to all 'Christians'. This again takes us to the heart of the Confederate

Taliban's fake-Christian dichotomy; it's impossible to be a good person if you let bad things happen to other people.

Now that you know their history, you understand that, for these people, anything was possible. In their surreal upside-down world, they self-justified their benign righteousness. That dissonance allowed them to believe that they did the 'savage' African a favor by bringing him to America and trying to civilize him.

Note that all this was taking place while the 'moderate' northern white gave them the benefit of the doubt, part of which may have been to do with the southerner's genteel mannerisms.

This was by design. Indeed, the Lost Cause was, of itself, a cultural war of mythology; just think of 'Gone with the Wind', and how the segregationist southerners were portrayed as the wronged victims, bearing 'the white man's burden' and the weight of 'Northern Aggression.'

Aiding the deception was the beautiful language of the elite South, with its long, languid sentences and deliberate and measured cadence. This lent a thoughtful and sophisticated veneer to despicable actions that could fool many a clever person. I remember the words of the brilliant broadcaster, Walter Cronkite,

> I never ceased to be surprised when southern whites, at their homes or clubs, told racial jokes and spoke so derogatorily of blacks while longtime servants, for whom they quite clearly had some affection, were well within earshot.[45]

What Mr. Cronkite didn't understand, but what Frederick Douglass did, was that it was about power. That was what could take an ordinary person and turn them into a devil, then and now. Power over another human being and power to do exactly what they wanted with immunity and impunity. Jefferson Cowie, professor of history at Vanderbilt University and the Pulitzer Prize-winning author of 2022's searing 'Freedom's Dominion', wrote,

> For people of European descent, the capacity for violence was their birthright. The final statement of their freedom, white freedom, grew out of the actions of those who had the right to kill with impunity. To understand lynching is to root it in slavery, which fostered the sensibility of freedom for all white people in generations after the Revolutionary War. [46]

This sadistic addiction to cruelty, for a proportion of the population, became something for them to covet and a badge of honor that their descendants would wear with pride. That entitlement to power also gave us the domestic terrorists of the Ku Klux Klan (KKK), and today, it's entitled power that allows vigilante killers and bad cops to murder black men in broad daylight.

Power is why nearly half the fundamentalist Christians 'beliefs' intertwine with the violent, baseless anti-Semitic QAnon conspiracy that Trump is here to save America from a cabal of satanic blood-drinking pedophiles (liberals and Jews, of course). It's power that allows men to abuse children, and it's also power that allows men to force women to give birth against their will. And the point of power is, once vested in evil people, they never want to relinquish it.

Back then, so determined were the slavers to live their abomination of a lie, they were willing to sacrifice the United States for it. The South Carolina Declaration of Secession, dated 24th December 1860, described their grievance as "[A]n increasing hostility on the part of the non-slaveholding States to the institution of slavery......"[47]

Texas was fairly upfront too about their reasons for wanting to succeed. Their Declaration of Causes from February 2nd 1861 stated:

> We hold as undeniable truths that the governments of the various states, and of the confederacy itself, were established exclusively by the white race, for themselves and their posterity; that the African race had no agency in their establishment; that they were rightfully held and regarded as an inferior and dependent race, and in that condition only could their existence in this country be rendered beneficial or tolerable.[48]

Then, for more receipts, we can travel over to Mississippi to read its Declaration of Immediate Causes of January 1861:

> Our position is thoroughly identified with the institution of slavery-- the greatest material interest of the world. Its labor supplies the product which constitutes by far the largest and most important portions of commerce of the earth. These products are peculiar to the climate verging on the tropical regions, and by an imperious law of nature, none but the black race can bear exposure to the tropical sun.[49]

Speaking in Savannah on the 21st March, 1861, the Vice President of the Confederacy, Alexander Stephens, told us in his Cornerstone speech exactly what they stood for;

> Our new government is founded upon exactly the opposite idea; its foundations are laid, its corner-stone rests, upon the great truth that the negro is not equal to the white man; that slavery subordination to the superior race is his natural and normal condition.[50]

Rather than give up slavery and allow the African-Americans to go free, less than one month after Stephens' speech, they would launch a war against America. And, even after their defeat, with their eleven states smashed and in ruins and hundreds of thousands of their own Confederate soldiers and citizens killed, they still wouldn't let their inhuman Luciferian fantasy die. So, when you hear the words "States rights" today, just substitute them for "Confederate rights", and everything is explained.

All this being said, we know that the ability to hold two thoughts in our head and still retain the ability to function is the mark of the intelligent mind. Abraham Lincoln knew, brilliantly, that the Confederacy would kill the United States. Undoubtably, he saw the inhumanity of keeping slaves, but do not imagine that he was pro-black.

Indeed, Lincoln was both the savior of black Americans and a white supremacist. Perhaps part of this was having to deal with the supremacy that had been imbued in America as a whole, and part of it was the sheer conundrum of what to do with four million newly freed black citizens in a nation of just thirty-one million people. At the time, integration wasn't in any politician's mind, as many northern white workers didn't want the competition from black workers[51].

Bearing all that in mind, back in 1854, speaking in Illinois, Lincoln said,

> I should not know what to do as to the existing institution
> [of slavery]. My first impulse would be to free all the slaves,
> and send them to Liberia, to their own native land.[52]

Then, speaking in September 1858 at the fourth presidential debate in Illinois, he said,

> I will say then that I am not, nor ever have been, in favor
> of bringing about in any way the social and political equality

of the white and black races, [applause]-that I am not nor ever have been in favor of making voters or jurors of negroes, nor of qualifying them to hold office, nor to intermarry with white people; and I will say in addition to this that there is a physical difference between the white and black races which I believe will forever forbid the two races living together on terms of social and political equality.[53]

Come the eve of the Civil War, and Honest Abe was still walking the white American tightrope. In his 1860 address at the Cooper Union, New York, he said;

In the language of Mr. Jefferson, uttered many years ago, It is still in our power to direct the process of emancipation, and deportation, peaceably, and in such slow degrees, as that the evil will wear off insensibly; and their places be, pari passu, filled up by free white laborers."[54]

Now allow me to take you back to 1860. Rich, white, Anglo-Saxon Protestant men ruled society. There were no Southern European or Eastern European Catholics, and the newly arrived Irish weren't considered 'white', with many of them being worked as hard as slaves. The difference was that those slaves were, of course, property, as were women. Also, in those times, regardless of wealth, average life expectancy was less than forty years old, and nearly half of all children died before their fifth birthday.[55] Diseases such as smallpox, dysentery, typhoid, malaria, and yellow fever were all rampant in this age, and all with no cure.

I'm not equating any of this to slavery, just pointing out what straight-jacketed times they were. For most citizens, self-survival was at the apex of their priorities, and African-American rights lived nowhere in their thoughts.

All that being said, as most African-Americans were imported as slaves, they would have intentionally had no equal contact with white folks, and this, by consequence, would have shaped white people's prejudices.

From that perspective, without any of the references of the modern world to guide them, it's hardly surprising that Abraham Lincoln, and probably the thirty-nine framers of the Constitution before him, held negative ideas about African-Americans. Those physical chains that held back the African from education, information, and society were the same metaphorical chains that held Lincoln back from seeing the possibility of black brilliance. He probably considered himself very humane for wanting to 'gently' repatriate African-Americans.

At the time, people like Frederick Douglass were very few, because that was one of the points of white supremacy. Real Christians of the Quaker movement and exceptional people like Mark Twain and Eunice Foote (see Chapter nineteen) may have been able to see through it, but without contact, many ordinary white Americans would never have had to think about it.

Looked at a little deeper, it would have been inconceivable for Lincoln to imagine in 1865 that only seventy years later, black athletes would represent America at an Olympic Games hosted by the Confederacy's most evil devotee. Or that less than ten years after those infamous games, southern segregationists and black soldiers would fight (in separate units) to free Europe from the yoke of that maniac's fascist oppression.

And Honest Abe might positively fall out of bed if he had been told that just one hundred years after the Civil War, a great white Texan and a brilliant black Georgian would work together to build on the foundations he laid in 1863 to pass the Civil Rights Act.

But what his 1865 mind, in a thousand lifetimes, could never, ever envisage is the picture of a brilliant black man born of interracial parents being elected the 44th President of the United States of America.

Another point that Lincoln wouldn't have considered, but that Frederick Douglass did, was that of education. As a black, educated, and unafraid American, Frederick was one of the greatest threats to white supremacy and to the patriarchy.

It's a thought that reverberates even today, with the teaching (or not) of history and the banning of books. Frederick knew exactly how important a lack of education was in allowing the monsters to keep slavery going. He quoted from one of his 'Masters';

> A ni**er should know nothing but to obey his master — to do as he is told to do. Learning would spoil the best ni**er in the world. Now," said he, "if you teach that ni**er (speaking of myself) how to read, there would be no keeping him. It would forever unfit him to be a slave. He would at once become unmanageable, and of no value to his master. As to himself, it could do him no good, but a great deal of harm. It would make him discontented and unhappy.[56]

For the 'master' to imagine that anyone needed an education in order to know this was a monstrous way of existing revealed both their depravity and their stupidity. However, where that 'master' was entirely correct was in surmising that no educated person would ever choose the life of a slave.

Back to Lincoln. His sole ambition was to hold America together, and it wasn't until the South forced his hand with their declarations and the attack on Fort Sumter that war was inevitable. After that, the die was cast.

Bearing in mind that black folks had no voice and no vote, we could say that he was playing a masterful game of four-dimensional chess with thirty million American citizens, who ranged from abolitionists to Confederates.

His first seminal move was the Emancipation Proclamation of 1863, which meant that over four million slaves were legally no longer that. Then, two years later, his second was to win the war that saved America.

I'm not a man for the purity test and live by the creed that the perfect is usually the enemy of the good. However, I can see that, for many, it might seem complicated to know that our hero didn't necessarily have heroic ideas. Nonetheless, the only reason that the United States of America exists today is because of Lincoln.

Tragically, the fifty-six-year-old, greatest president of all time, would only have one week from the end of the war to savor saving America. His assassination came at the hands of a Confederate Taliban terrorist, John Wilkes Booth. This man was incensed that, three days earlier, Lincoln had dared to speak of the possibility of a limited extension of voting rights to freed black men, mainly veterans[57]. Once again, the demented rage of white supremacy demanded America lose where it could otherwise win.

For those still perplexed by this very brilliant but very complicated man, I offer you a small part of Frederick Douglass's entrancingly insightful eulogy to Honest Abe, made at the Emancipation Memorial in April 1876;

> Viewed from the genuine abolition ground, Mr. Lincoln
> seemed tardy, cold, dull, and indifferent; but measuring him

by the sentiment of his country, a sentiment he was bound as a statesman to consult, he was swift, zealous, radical, and determined.[58]

In the post-Civil war era, it was the vengeful, embittered fury of the losing Confederate "Christians" that led them to sabotage the nascent, blooming African-American political, economic, and social life of Reconstruction, but not without northern compliance.

The 'moderates' same weak will and lack of ability to join the dots is what we see in most of the news and print media today. It allows many people to be constantly surprised at the deviancy of Republican policies.

We know that supremacy didn't die. Instead, it crafted the 'Lost Cause' lie that infected America. Their South was the victim of "northern aggression," and they had been fighting for their 'heritage' in a 'War Between the States.'

That same one-hundred-and fifty-year-old gaslighting is also the cover Republicans offer for not teaching true American history in former slave-holding states like Texas or Florida. To that point, there's a question worth asking. If the south was so honorable in 1861, then why are Republicans trying so hard today to suppress what was happening in that era?

This reminds me of a line from Imani Perry's poignant and illustrative book, 'South to America', quoting the words of Chris Furr, a young white pastor. He was speaking in 2018 about the removal in North Carolina of the Confederate monument to treason, known as Silent Sam;

> As I looked at Silent Sam, face down in the dirt, all I could think was that it was the end of another battle in a war we just can't quit fighting, because we can't tell the truth about why it started.[59]

The sabotage of Reconstruction had a lot to do with the demented white rage and humiliation of experiencing a black person on a level playing field. Seeing people of color being able to get ahead was too much for many fragile right-wingers. I could just as easily be talking about present times, where we see the manufactured fury from the far-right propaganda machine at the success and talents of Barack Obama, Fani Willis, or Kamala Harris.

One hundred and fifty years ago, the Confederate Taliban could use violence to keep the black folks down. However, post-Reconstruction allowed for a slightly less brutal, yet far more insidious society to form. In that South, the African-American was a citizen, but, by design, so many obstacles were placed in their path in education, employment, housing, and voting that getting ahead was nearly impossible.

Throw in some fake-science 1920s eugenics, and so it was that, not just in the South, African-Americans were set up to fail. Then, in the coming years, by pointing to the crime, desperation, and poverty of broken communities, the far-right had a story to sell.

Thus, by making even the least competent white man feel superior to any black person, the wealthiest white folks could get on with their real work: stealing more of the wealth.

We know that powerful patriarchs don't want people to learn true history. Yet, it is a savage fact that the most eager and most evil student of the Confederacy was a failed Austrian painter, Adolf Schickelgruber, more commonly known as Adolf Hitler. He recognized, in the ostensibly 'free' South, the most sophisticated and effective apartheid police state ever known.

This skinny, rotten-toothed, woman-fearing, genocidal coward truly admired America. Clearly, he applauded the enslavement of Africans, but he was none too keen on Native Americans either. In 1928, he praised America for having, in his words, "gunned down the millions of Redskins to a few hundred thousand."[60]

In his hate-scribe, Mein Kampf, he described America as the "One State" that idealized his vision of a world, so much so that he used it as the blueprint for the creation of his Aryan Wunderland; the Nazi Nuremberg laws were crafted on the Jim Crow South and included the banning of interracial marriage and sex and relegating Jews to second-class citizens.[61]

To see what Americans thought of him, back in 1935, after encoding the Nazi Reich Citizenship Laws, in reward for their 'hard work' at separating the races, forty-five Nazi lawyers sailed to New York to meet with the New York Bar Association to gain "special insight into the workings of American legal and economic life through study and lectures." They received a warm welcome.[62]

Meanwhile, on July 16th of that same year, in Broward County, Florida, a woman called Marion Jones called the police to claim that a black man had come into her house; he had not raped or robbed her, just come into her house. Police started looking for 'suspects' and picked up the first black man they came across: Rubin Stacey. He had been hiding (obviously terrified) in some bushes.

They took him to the station, and, on cue, a mob of cowards turned up. The police set about moving him to a larger jail, and along the way, the mob forced them to stop and kidnapped Rubin. They took him back to Marion Jones's house and shot him before using her washing line to hang him from an old tree by her house. That's terrible, a brutal murder indeed.

However, as great an inhumanity is revealed in the photos of that day. Rubin is hanging from the tree, and there are men, women, and children all dressed up and enjoying the spectacle. Someone had taken pictures for the family photo album, as if this was a perfectly pleasant event.

Never mind these craven weaklings, with not one ounce of humanity, had just taken part in a murder, and never mind, they were standing in a crime scene.

Look at the young girl of about twelve years old on the right of the picture. Any normal child would be buried in her mother's dress, whimpering, doing anything she could to unsee the horror unfurled before her. Instead, she is staring right at Rubin with a sick, smiling, sadistic fascination in her eyes. Of course, that doesn't even begin to question the abomination of a parent who would allow their child to watch this satanically savage spectacle?

As I looked at the other people in the photo, I wondered what sort of unremarkable monsters these must be. Indisputably they were, but they were also the products of an inhumane system. It was a society that seared hate into their hearts and rewarded them with the depraved pleasure that arose from the infliction of violence upon an innocent man[63].

I don't seek to excuse any of Rubin's murderers or the spectators of their individual responsibilities. However, to look deeper into the debauched and diseased depravity that allowed their ancestors to believe that it was normal to enslave and for them to consider that it was acceptable to murder is to find that elite class of even more maniacal monsters who taught the lessons.

Those pastors and landowners, and later on, politicians, knew that for them to stay at the very top, ordinary folks had to embrace the scarcity mindset and the zero-sum game. They knew how fear and hate could band people together and bond people together.

Skipping forward ten years from Rubin's murder to World War II, we meet the very definition of irony, as hundreds of thousands of white southern segregationists and African-Americans went to Europe to liberate it from the yoke of fascism.

For the Europeans, who they were helping to bring freedom to, what must have been headache inducingly paradoxical was that the American soldiers fought in segregated units.

Imagine the monumental lack of self-awareness that had to live inside the segregationists' minds on seeing white Dutch, English, and French citizens welcoming black soldiers with a dignity, kindness, and respect that they adamantly refused to afford them. But then, it was the philosopher Voltaire, nearly two hundred years before that war, who told us that, "It is difficult to free fools from the chains they revere."[64]

You may wonder whether the modern-day Confederate Taliban members' hate consumes them. Clearly, a lot of low-information, fake-Christian members have been so ferociously radicalized by the wash-rinse-repeat cycle of Fox and AM radio propaganda that they can saunter through their own reality on an autopilot of insanity. For others, there is a greater form of delusion.

Where decent people have their worst instincts checked, either by their conscience or the fear of consequence, it is not so for this group. Addicted to cruelty and allergic to kindness, they bask in the certainty that they are in a righteous fight for the freedom to do as they want to do. Ultimately, their victory must involve domination, and with it, a license that affords their actions immunity and impunity.

As to the Christianity of all this, I'm certain that most of them have never properly read the Bible, because everything they believe is anti-Gospel and anti-Jesus. Some of them may have a copy laying by their beds. If so, I have bad news for them. The Old Testament isn't a magic shield against Judgement, and the God they claim to worship sees them and knows exactly who they are. To illustrate the point, from the Bible, we have Jesus' own words;

> When the Son of Man comes in his glory, and all the angels with him, he will sit on his glorious throne..."Then he will say to those on his left, 'Depart from me, you who are cursed, into the eternal fire prepared for the devil and his angels. For I was hungry and you gave me nothing to eat, I was thirsty and you gave me nothing to drink, I was a stranger and you did not invite me in, I needed clothes and you did not clothe me, I was sick and in prison and you did not look after me.'..."Then they will go away to eternal punishment,[65]

For the most fervent, those New Testament words would be 'liberal' or 'woke'. For them, their untreated insanity will always demand to be fed more insanity, so it is they dance through the thunderstorm of hatred, propelled on by the ferociously vengeful sounds of the MAGA rhapsody. It's all to help to stoke the fever that keeps the horror of who they truly are at bay.

But, despite minor victories like 2024, come the day of reckoning, the God they claim as their own will never forgive them and will never save them. Instead, they are to be condemned to an afterlife of eternal damnation in the scorching cauldron of Satan's netherworld.

Chapter 4

The Scared, The Christian, The Angry, The Rich and the Insane. Welcome To The Republican Wunderland.

When candidate Hillary Clinton gave her "basket of deplorables" speech during the 2016 presidential election campaign, the lazy corporate media slammed her for demonizing people. However, history proved her absolutely correct;

> You know, to just be grossly generalistic, you could put half of Trump's supporters into what I call the basket of deplorables. The racist, sexist, homophobic, xenophobic, Islamaphobic — you name it...[66]

It was the ratings-hungry media that ignored the context and gave Trump and his Confederate Taliban both the benefit of the doubt and millions in free advertising. Then, once those deplorables had elected Trump, he set in motion the events that would lead to the restricting of a woman's right to choose, the flooding of America with guns, and the downplaying of a virus that needlessly claimed the lives of hundreds of thousands of Americans. And even after their leader was democratically voted out of office, the deplorables attempted to stage a coup to murder democracy.

The Republican electorate has since Nixon in 1964 been a self-interested coalition, made up of people who hold one or more SCARI traits. I included the Scared first because Republicans aim to make all their voters scared. Next are the (fake) Christian, the Angry, the Rich, and the Insane. Before the end of the book, you will have a forensic understanding of these Americans.

In referring to the most deranged half of Republican voters—what is known as the 'base'—as deplorables, Secretary Clinton was being too kind, which is why I call them and their leaders the Confederate Taliban. Like the ultra-conservative Afghan Taliban, the Confederate Taliban is anti-progress, anti-science, anti-women, anti-children, and anti-LGBTQ+. Where they surpass their Afghan cousins is that they are also anti-black and anti-brown.

I wanted to shine a light on some of these people, and this brings us to Tony Horwitz's epic 2019 book "Spying on the South," which is actually a study of how the New South is still wrapped in so much of the Old South. In it, we travel down to Goliad, South Central Texas, to meet some of what would have been then, Tea Party, and now Trump supporters espousing their grievances;

> By their own accounts, these amiable Texans led fairly comfortable and freewheeling lives. So why did they feel so burdened by bureaucrats in Washington? "Bottom line?" Dave (Fitts, a small business owner) finally exclaimed. "The government won't let us do whatever the hell it is we want to do. That's it.[67]

That fragile man-baby was part of the primary voting base that is Trump's support. These are mostly older, white people who hold anti-immigration, anti-abortion, and anti-government views[68]. Think of them as the most enraged and engaged Grand Old Party (GOP) voters. They are also the ones who choose which Republican politician stands in each election. Nearly two-thirds identify as Evangelical. In short, they are a long way from what today's America really looks like[69].

To win the 2016 GOP primary, Trump took thirteen million votes out of thirty-six million registered eligible primary voting Republicans. His base made up 10% of the eventual 2016 general election voter turnout[70]. These thirteen million SCARI individuals were the first members of his cult.

To them, it didn't matter that Trump lost in 2018, 2020, and 2022. That just reinforced all their biases about how he was being cheated by the 'deep state' and the 'liberals'. Winning in 2024 just confirmed how tough he is. Their beliefs are set in stone, and as they are always right, nothing will convince them he isn't constantly under attack. They are the rubes who pay his $50 million a year in legal bills[71]. All because they believe he is fighting to annihilate their adversaries and restore them to their rightful place at the pinnacle of American society.

For this deranged faction, they don't see the same obese, broken-down, bankrupt criminal that we do. It may sound unbelievable, but no other American political leader has ever had his face superimposed (quite realistically, I will concede) onto the images of Rocky and Superman[72].

The base view Donald Trump as no less than their secular savior, whose sole purpose is to rescue America, and from that insane perspective, the superhero image is quite fitting.

Joe Walsh is a former far-right Tea Party congressional representative and current host of the intelligent and insightful pro-democracy White Flag podcast. He described the base as radicalized;

> What in God's name do I mean by radicalized? Easy What I mean is the Republican Party base no longer believes in truth, they've given up on democracy, they want an authoritarian to rule them and to deliver, 'Their' Pre-1954 America, back to them, and they want to not just defeat their political opponents, they want to destroy their political opponents. This is what I mean by radicalized.[73]

To prove the point, a Republican survey conducted for The Bulwark in January 2023 revealed that 26% of GOP primary voters declared themselves as supporters of Trump rather than the Republican Party. Even more frightening for the GOP is that, if Trump had run as a third-party candidate, a massive 28% would vote for him[74].

This highlights a significant mistake made by the political class, who attribute any rationality to these MAGA members. In reality, their unwavering loyalty lies solely with Donald John Trump. In the 2024 election, had Trump's name been absent from the ballot, some of these supporters would have abstained. However, others would turn up to vote, only to be made even more insane and convinced of conspiracy when they didn't see Donald J Trump's name printed on their ballot paper.

To those who still imagine that a sane Republican with sensible policies could wrestle back the party from Trump, here's a reality check from Rolling Stone reporter Adam Rawnsley;

> Nobody votes for Donald Trump because they've got a checklist of particular policy proposals and they're going

down the list, oh, yeah, okay, and that marginal capital gains tax stuff. Nobody is doing that. He has a charismatic relationship with his audience. He represents more than the sum of his policies to his audience, and the other thing is that his policies aren't fixed.[75]

It's worse than having no policies. The base prioritizes seeing liberals made angry and scared. The phrases are 'owning the libs' or 'liberal tears.' This supersedes even winning. As such, they will vote time after time for terrible primary candidates, like Kari Lake or Blake Masters, simply because they give life to feelings of embitterment and grievance. It was the presenter of the Dirt Road Democrat podcast, Jess Piper (who you will hear more from in later chapters), who spoke of her neighbor in rural Missouri flying a flag that sums up the Confederate Taliban's worldview perfectly[76].

There's more. In order to draw the millions of supporters, resentment isn't enough. A big reason that 2024 GOP presidential candidates Ron DeSantis, Nikki Haley, and Vivek Ramaswamy all fizzled in the primaries, apart from being far too 'ethnic,' was that they were all so boring. For all his failings, Trump offers—much less so in 2024, but still—performance and spectacle. It's one reason the media and many liberals just can't look away. Jason Stanley, the author of "How Fascism Works: The Politics of Us and Them." would describe the 'spectacle' that fascism needs to enrapture the masses;

So, we're looking at someone who is charismatic authoritarian. We also have to really focus on macho authoritarian leader that appeals across many demographics...who see that their interests are going to be furthered by smashing democracy. I think one thing you see in literature on mid- century fascism, for example, the Frankfurt School that the fascist leader transforms politics into spectacle. So, politics becomes a story of good versus bad, and becomes entertainment.[77]

When it comes to Trump, another point that is lost on all but the most acute observers is the distinct lack of his low-information—living proof of the Dunning-Kruger effect[78]—voters at Mar-a-Lago or Trump Tower. This, despite the fact that many of his most ardent followers hold such strong admiration for him that they would willingly face imprisonment or even death.

For the felon, there are two reasons for this. The first is that he is a notorious germophobe. So it is that his part-fascist/part-stand-up rallies serve as a platform for him to witness his followers without actually having to physically engage with them.

The supporters' slavish gullibility brings us to the second explanation why they don't get to visit with him. For this, we have a story from the New York Times about Trump's ability to pump the base for donations. His 2020 campaign trick was the 'recurring donation.' It only works on people who are low information and very trusting;

Contributors had to wade through a fine-print disclaimer and manually uncheck a box to opt out. As the election neared, the Trump team made that disclaimer increasingly opaque. The tactic ensnared scores of unsuspecting Trump loyalists — retirees, military veterans, nurses and even experienced political operatives. Soon, banks and credit card companies were inundated with fraud complaints from the president's own supporters about donations they had not intended to make, sometimes for thousands of dollars.[79]

One supporter, a 78-year-old retiree in California, donated $990 via the payment platform, WinRed. Trump didn't just take it once; he took it eight times, rinsing this gullible rube for $8800. So prevalent was this practice that, in the closing months of 2020, the Trump campaign had issued over half a million refunds totaling over $60 million. His conformable supporters had effectively given interest-free loans to his campaign.

And so we arrive at the final reason that the rubes will never enter Mar-a-Lago; because, to the cult leader, they are, according to a former insider, the 'basement dwellers,'[80] the ignorant suckers and losers who are too stupid to see that Trump's priority was always about staying out of jail and enriching himself and his oligarch donors[81].

All this being said, as members of a cult, the SCARI people will put up with a lot because their dreams are so much bigger than money. It put me in mind of a quote from author James Baldwin. In his spellbinding 1963

book, The Fire Next Time, he described this kind of white person as "the slightly mad victims of their own brainwashing."[82]

So it is, for them, Trump acts as both a mirror and a projector. Through the mirror, they can see their own deeply ingrained grievances and biases reflected. Then his projector offers them the ability to imagine the furious retribution and revenge that they want exacted on modern, secular, tolerant American society.

To this point, there is one thing that links almost every single member of the Confederate Taliban. New Republic writer Timothy Noah characterized it; they always "punch down and kiss up."[83] The irony is that even Trump does it; while punching down at liberals, blacks, and women, he kisses up to Putin, Xi, and Kim Jong-Un.

To get more of a grasp on the Confederate Taliban, we need to travel back in time. Thanks to Lincoln, the enslaved people were free. Then, at the end of the war, General Sherman wanted to cow the South and, as part of Special Field Orders No. 15, ordered reparations to the enslaved population[84]. Had this been allowed, the Confederates would have been forced to confront the diseased demon of white supremacy that had stained previous generations. Instead, a compromise was reached where the slave owners would keep their land. For the newly freed, there were no '40 acres and a mule,' and instead, there would be Reconstruction.

This era lasted for twelve years, between 1865 and 1877. During this period, federal troops were stationed in the Confederacy to ensure the safety of black folks. For the formerly enslaved, it was a roaring success. Unchained, unshackled, and unimpeded, black folks flourished in education, business, and politics[85].

Professor of History at Vanderbilt University, Jefferson Cowie, gave us this insight;

> During reconstruction after the Civil War, after the South
> was subjugated, and there were troops on the ground ensur-
> ing a biracial democracy. And it worked, it was a functioning
> biracial democracy. After the Civil War, the 13th, 14th and
> 15th amendments, emancipation, equal protection and vot-
> ing rights had all been passed.[86]

Unsurprisingly, the Confederates (just like their MAGA descendants) couldn't stand the fact that this blew apart their depraved and demented argument that black folks were like children, too stupid to achieve anything and needing a "master" to provide everything for them. The loss in the rebellion had primed them to be both furious and resentful at seeing progress, and the method by which they made their point was violence and retribution. It's no coincidence that the KKK was founded in 1865 to terrorize mainly black folks.

As northerners lost the stomach for progress, we got the 'Compromise of 1877', with federal troops being withdrawn from the South. In throwing away all the progress of Reconstruction in a foolish, short-sighted dream of reconciliation with that same 'Lost Cause' South, they ignored the fact that the Confederates, imbued with the cancer of hate, never wanted to do anything but destroy the United States.

So it was, post-Reconstruction, the grandfathers of the Confederate Taliban were emboldened, just as any unconfronted bully is, with patriarchal Jim Crow segregation and KKK terrorism still being the norm right into the middle of the twentieth century.

Across the whole of America, up to the 1950s, the patriarchy was in full swing, and straight white men had it all their own way. Hollywood painted a picture of happy families and domestic bliss, but in reality, the patriarch's tradwife was stuck at home, and the smile on their faces was partly an act and partly the result of the ingestion of copious amounts of

Valium. Children were silent because they were terrified of being beaten, gay people had to sneak around in shame, constantly under fear of arrest and public humiliation, and as for black and brown folks, well, no one needed to think about them—unless they needed a maid or a yard boy.

I recall David Corn's fantastic modern history of Republican politics, 'American Psychosis.' The book takes us on a journey into madness. Most importantly, it shows how the Confederate Taliban were always present and also how they were pandered to by every Republican who sought high office.

In the changing 1950s, it was the John Birch Society (more of them later) who showed politicians how to use divide-and-rule tactics to peel away white voter support from the Democratic Party, which, through Franklin D. Roosevelt's "New Deal" policies and support for civil rights, had aligned itself with progress. So it would be that the far-right sought to conflate anything liberal with communism, 'socialism,' and the 'red scare.'[87]

It may sound strange today, but back then, Russia was making solid advances in the fields of science and space travel[88]. And socially, the US had ceded to the Soviet Union the easiest of propaganda victories, allowing them to point to the lack of African-American freedoms in America.

At this point, we need to pull the lens out. In those days, both America and Russia were seeking to spread their competing ideologies throughout Latin America, the Middle East, Asia, and Africa. This was the time of the Domino Theory foreign policy, with the US government terrified that—mainly Latin American—developing world American allies could fall under the spell of communism (or even just social democracy.)[89] For the rich and powerful who owned the multinational corporations that wanted cheap labor and the ability to extract poor nations' resources, this was terrible news.

Back home, civil rights were also about all workers' rights to a decent life—good wages, fair conditions, healthcare, you know, everything the far-right is still fighting against[90].

Today, most people know Dr. Martin Luther King Jr. as a great champion of civil rights. However, in the 1960s, he was one of the first Democratic socialists and someone who actually followed the teachings of Jesus. As the founder of the Poor People's Campaign[91], Dr. King aimed to unite working-class white, black and brown folks in the struggle for a better life. Here's a quote from 1962 that still sounds progressive in 2024.

> As I have said many times, and believe with all my heart, the coalition that can have the greatest impact in the struggle for human dignity here in America is that of the Negro and the forces of labor, because their fortunes are so closely intertwined.[92]

It was this potential multiracial working-class coalition that was the biggest threat to rich patriarchs and white supremacy, who painted the civil rights movement as 'red' and 'un-American.' Ironically, some of Dr. King's staunchest opponents were northern whites whose prejudice demanded they not live or work alongside black folks and also opposed any assistance programs that would help level the economic playing field between blacks and whites[93].

Parenthetically, this segues us into today's poor rural-county Republican voter of the sort you read about at the beginning of the book. To explain, across America, there are just over 3100 counties. While the Democratic Party wins decisively in the densely populated metropolitan areas where over 85% of US gross domestic product is produced[94], outside of the large cities, counties are small and sparsely populated[95]. For citizens in these 2600 small counties, most opportunities for employment are in Republican-donor-aligned industries such as agriculture, coal, fossil fuels (coal, oil, and gas,) meat processing, and prisons, so it's no surprise to see voters opting for the party that's friendly to the business that pays their salary[96].

If we drill down into this a little further, it was the native-born Virginian author, Joe Baegant, who wrote presciently about the corruption endemic in Republican small towns and counties in his beautifully elegiac 2008 book 'Deer Hunting with Jesus.' This system keeps rural working folks—whom Mr Baegant describes as 'American Serfs'—tied to their local area, earning low wages and living a poor life, whilst also keeping them thankful for it:

> "The lives and intellectual cultures of these, the hardest-working people, are not just stunted by the smallness of the society into which they were born. They are purposefully held in bondage by a local network of moneyed families, bankers, developers, lawyers, and businesspeople in whose interests it is to have a cheap, unquestioning, and compliant labor force paying high rents and big medical bills. They invest in developing such a labor force by not investing (how's that for making money out of thin air!) in the education and quality of life for anyone but their own. Places such as Winchester are, as they say, "investment paradise." That means low taxes, few or no local regulations, no unions, and a chamber of commerce tricked out like a gaggle of hookers, welcoming the new non-union, air-poisoning factory. "To hell with pollution! We gonna sell some propity, we gonna move some real 'state today, fellas!" Big contractors, realtors, lawyers, everybody gets a slice, except the poorly educated non-union mooks who will be employed at the local plant at discount rates."[97]

To return to civil rights, back in 1948, Democratic President Harry Truman started integrating the armed forces[98] but never had to follow through in schools or workplaces. Republican President Dwight Eisenhower would, but with the landmark 1954 Brown v. Board of Education ruling that desegregated public schools, the demons were stirring[99].

Mr Corn writes of Nelson Rockefeller, no friend of socialism, who, speaking at the 1954 Republican convention, warned that the Republican party,

> is in real danger of subversion by a radical, well-financed, highly disciplined" minority that was "wholly alien to the sound and honest conservatism.[100]

President Eisenhower had first-hand experience of a spiritual uncle of MAGA, Joseph McCarthy. That last honorable Republican president also alerted people to the right-wing danger in 1954;

> "Whenever, and for whatever alleged reason, people attempt to crush ideas, to mask their convictions, to view every neighbor as a possible enemy, to seek some kind of divining rod by which to test for conformity, a free society is in danger."[101]

As an aside, McCarthy's chief counsel, Roy Cohn, was a closeted gay man, yet a fierce homophobe. He would go on to become Donald Trump's demonic lawyer and mentor. Their noxious relationship lasted from 1973 until Cohn's lonely death in 1986 from AIDS. It may come as little surprise, but once Trump found out about Cohn's sickness, he dropped him like a hot potato[102].

In 1960, John Kennedy's victory over Richard Nixon ushered in the youngest president and also the first Catholic to hold that office. JFK brought a sense of hope and optimism across much of America. We know how that ended, but before that, many on the far right were apoplectic, for to them, an Irish Catholic was a papist and only one step above the black man[103].

In a dress rehearsal for what Trump would unleash in 2020, Nixon dishonestly contested the election results, citing voter fraud. Offering her assistance was a young and determined thirteen-year-old Republican who volunteered to investigate alleged fraud in Chicago.

Four years later, that same woman would become a "Goldwater girl," supporting GOP candidate Barry Goldwater over President Lyndon Johnson. However, Hillary Rodham's views, influenced by the civil rights movement and the Vietnam War, evolved, and a few years later she became a Democrat.

Hillary's early career saw her become a renowned lawyer, serving on the House committee that would investigate Nixon following the Watergate scandal in 1972. Around the same time, she would meet, and a few years later, marry, Bill Clinton, a working-class man from Arkansas. She became the first woman partner at the Rose Law Firm, then the First Lady of Arkansas.

When her husband was elected president, as First Lady of the United States, in 1993, Hillary proposed what would have been a universal healthcare system[104]. In the year 2000, she became a United States Senator, serving two terms, and wasn't done yet, becoming the Secretary of State in 2009 in the Obama Administration.

Despite all this, come the 2016 election, out of over 130 million ballots cast, seventy-seven thousand Democrats in three swing states wouldn't vote for Secretary Clinton and either abstained or went third party. The result of their purity test—ably assisted by FBI Director James Comey, Russian President Vladimir Putin, and Facebook CEO Mark Zuckerberg[105]—was a six-time bankrupt, adulterous, charismatic ignoramus who would later reveal himself to be a fraudster and insurrectionist.

Going back to Richard Milhous Nixon. Until Trump, few politicians embodied such septic immorality. As far back as 1962, he was aware of the dangerous trajectory the Republican Party was on and the extremist views of the far-right patriarchal John Birch Society, which fiercely opposed civil rights and women's rights[106].

Aside from all that, the Birchers wanted to pay no taxes, and limit government spending to defense, police, and the courts. They also bought into every conspiracy theory going. Their buzzwords were "Insiders", "Communists," "Marxists," and "Globalists." Translated, those four words referred to the government, civil rights, public education, and "Jews."[107]

Nixon recognized this infiltration of the GOP and accurately cautioned against it, saying, "Responsible Republicanism abhors demagoguery and totalitarianism, wherever and however it appears."[108] However, just two years later, as part of his presidential election campaign against Lyndon Johnson, he binned his principles by cosseting the Confederate Taliban

This takes us into the heart of why Nixon was so evil. In pandering to the basest instincts of white Americans, he knew exactly what he was doing. Political scientists use the term 'Southern strategy'[109] to describe his campaign to win over conservative white southern Democrats. Former White House Counsel and Domestic Policy Advisor to Nixon, John Ehrlichman, broke it down for us in his memoirs;

> The subliminal appeal to the anti-black voter was always in Nixon's statements and speeches on schools and housing... Nixon said he believed blacks could only marginally benefit from federal programs, because blacks were genetically inferior to whites.[110]

This monstrous eugenics-style thinking was echoed by H.R. Haldeman, Nixon's Chief of Staff. In words taken from his diary in 1969, he wrote;

President emphasized that you have to face the fact that the whole problem is really the blacks. The key is to devise a system that recognizes this while not appearing to.[111]

Nixon saw that by using the 'scarcity mindset'—white fears of black people coming to take what was 'rightly' white—many voters would move towards a protector. Sociologists call this compensatory control[112]. By offering himself as that protector for scared and angry white Americans, he proved his willingness to sacrifice the future of America at the altar of his own ambition.

All this being said, we must hold two opposing thoughts in our heads and acknowledge that post-war America experienced rapid economic growth. Of course, it wasn't by any means equally distributed, yet it still brought benefits to most citizens.

These were times when many men had decent-paying union jobs that provided sufficient income to support a family. Also, for many white Americans, the emergence of affordable suburban houses allowed them to start building generational wealth.

We should never forget that back in those 'good old days', it was the fair taxation of wealthy Americans that played a pivotal role in fostering both that economic growth and the implementation and maintenance of significant programs such as free college education, disability assistance, SNAP, Medicare, Medicaid, and Social Security.

It was also in the 1960s that we met someone who wasn't too keen on those social programs. Ronald Wilson Reagan had been a B-list actor whose principal claim for fame was starring alongside a monkey in 1951's 'Bedtime for Bonzo'.

Reagan was a handsome man, standing six feet one inch and weighing one hundred and eighty-five pounds, with a ruddy, farmer-like complexion that lent him a certain look of trustworthiness. His actors' training and a degree of natural charisma also afforded him the ability to understand tone, pitch, and timing, which was very useful in the new age of television when he had to deliver scripted 'heartfelt' all-American lines.

His spell in politics started with his win in the 1960 Californian gubernatorial election. As a point of interest, Californian politics then were more like Texan politics now; so much so that Section Five of the 1965 Voting Rights Act, requiring Department of Justice preclearance for any change in voting restrictions, names fifteen mostly southern states but also included some counties in California[113].

After the withdrawal from, and lies about, Vietnam, the Arab oil shock of the early 1970s, and the Iranian oil shock of the late 70s, Reagan knew exactly which way the wind was blowing. Americans were distrustful of government and ready for something new. His campaign slogan boldly proclaimed his vision to "LET'S MAKE AMERICA GREAT AGAIN" (yes, really.)[114]

To the detriment of many Americans, in pursuit of this goal, he would slavishly align himself with a powerful demonic coalition consisting of fossil fuel corporations, anti-tax advocates, and Christian nationalists, such as Jerry Falwell and Pat Robertson. The latter styled themselves the "Moral Majority," channeling Nixon's "Silent Majority." This septic cocktail of malignant interests was filtered through organizations like the unironically named Council for National Progress and the Heritage Foundation.

Reagan also bought us deregulation and the lie of "trickle-down" economics. Thus, it was during his presidency that, for the first time in decades, the middle class in America started to contract, as wealth flowed upwards to the richest 1%[115]. Indeed, the number of billionaires soared sixfold during his administration[116]. It's no coincidence that this was also the time that all Republican candidates for federal office were required to sign the 'Taxpayer Protection Pledge.' Set in place by Grover Norquist of the billionaire-funded 'Americans for Tax Reform,' this ensured for the rich segment of the SCARI coalition that no GOP rep would ever vote to raise taxes[117].

This was all eased along with the "get rich quick" individualism of the 1980s, which gave us the slavish fawning over money and rich people in TV shows like Dallas and Dynasty that would replace more progressive shows like The Waltons. Not uncoincidentally, this was also the era when Trump smeared himself into American popular culture. Indeed, since the 1980s, he has appeared in over thirty movies and television shows[118], and been cited in hundreds of rap lyrics[119], many idolizing his swagger, wealth, and power.

The 80s also introduced ordinary people to the rest of America with the fake world of 'reality TV' with shows like Real People and That's Incredible. The Apprentice featuring a then five-times-bankrupt Trump[120], would debut in 2004. These sat alongside daytime talk shows like The Sally Jessy Raphael Show and The Jerry Springer Show, where anyone could become (possibly) famous and (possibly) rich just for behaving like a 'freak.'

Existing alongside all this was social conservatism. This had three main strands. First, a slashing of funding for assistance programs, targeting low-income, mainly black folks. Then there were harsh measures against the LGBTQ+ community (ignoring AIDS for years)[121]. Finally, Republicans were anti-abortion and, in 1988, Reagan sought to introduce a bill that would implement a nationwide ban of federal funding for women's healthcare[122].

It's true that he did speed Russia towards a reduction in nuclear weapons. But it was also under his administration that America continued the Monroe Doctrine ideas of Latin America being the USA's backyard[123]. In doing so, it propped up 'banana republics'[124]—American-corporation-loving, wealth-extracting, ultra-right-wing regimes such as El Salvador, Guatemala, Honduras, Panama, Venezuela, and Nicaragua—home of the Iran-Contra scandal of 1985 that nearly ended Reagan's presidency.

In these nations, citizens endured not just corruption and state-sponsored repression but also the violence of ultra-right-wing death squads and drug cartels[125].

So it is that today, many of the desperate people arriving at the southern border to seek a better life are fleeing poverty and instability directly caused by US foreign policy [126].

A little further afield, the Reagan administration helped the plucky Mujahideen in Afghanistan by giving them the weapons and the training that, once they had dispatched their Russian invaders, would enable them to turn their fury on their former friends.

To that point, the Cold War neo-cons turned a blind eye while Islamic fundamentalism festered and spread from frenemy Saudi Arabia. It was thanks, in part, from American purchases of Saudi oil that these fake Muslims could finance the export of their especially toxic version of Islam (a word that translated means 'peace') worldwide; indeed, without Saudi Arabia, there would be no Osama Bin Laden, no 9/11, and no ISIS[127].

In 1988, Ronald's veep, George H.W. Bush, would triumph in the presidential election, but underneath the surface, the crocodiles were snapping.

Bush had two opponents in the 1988 presidential primary. Jack Kemp was a moderate, Eisenhower-style Republican. Pat Buchanan, however, was a far-right, fire-breathing, former Nixon speechwriter and as instructive of the base of the party of today as anyone could be. Just look at Buchanan's policies nearly thirty years before Trump. Indeed, they are a near-carbon copy of the far-right Heritage Foundation's Project 2025[128], which set out the blueprint for a theocratic takeover of America following a 2024 Republican win.

- Building a border wall of ditches and fences on the Southern border

- A total halt to immigration

- Pull out of all trade agreements and put tariffs on foreign goods.

- Abolish the IRS and institute a flat tax on all Americans. End Inheritance tax and slash Capital gains tax for rich Americans.

- Nationwide abortion ban

- Abolish the Department of Education and promote Christian schools and home-schooling[129]

Traveling forwards to the mid-1990s, we can meet Joseph P. Overton[130]. His legacy is the Overton Window. This is the idea that, over time, fringe ideas can become mainstream. Everything we see today, good and bad, bears this out. To the point of the good, the fight for civil rights and LGBTQ rights all moved public opinion from the right-wing towards the center.

However, for conservatives, using anger and fear, they have shifted from the party of Eisenhower through Nixon and Reagan to the party of fascism.

It has to be stressed that it couldn't have happened without a complicit corporate media and an active far-right disinformation machine. Enter, stage left, Rush Limbaugh and other AM radio shock jocks, Fox and, today, far-right podcasters.

This brings us on to someone who knew how to play that media. Newt Gingrich was the former Speaker of the House. He was actually first elected to the House in 1978 but had to wait fifteen years before right-wing AM Radio could boost him up.

To break the Democrats' forty-four-year hold on the House, he was shameless about how he would get there. Here are his words from 1978;

> "One of the great problems we have in the Republican Party
> is that we don't encourage you to be nasty"[131]

This character was an OG culture warrior who wielded chaos as his weapon, paving the way for the Tea Party and MAGA movements; as such, he occupies a sentinel position in the pantheon of American political demons.

The domestic terrorism in Ruby Ridge, Waco, and Oklahoma City all occurred during Gingrich's tenure as House leader. Instead of condemning them, he would coddle the militia movements, referring to their actions as stemming from "genuine fear."[132] Gingrich used this sympathetic language because he understood his constituency. In this sense, he differed little from Trump, who, twenty-two years later, would describe the murderous 2017 neo-Nazi rally in Charlottesville as having "very good people on both sides."[133]

It's impossible to separate the moral from the political in the modern GOP, as, between their allergy to kindness and addiction to cruelty, they all, shamelessly, claim to be highly moral. Gingrich was no exception to this rule. He frequently spoke about his 'Judeo-Christian values' and the supposed 'liberal' threat to 'western civilization'[134].

However, his unvarnished values shone through while attempting to impeach President Bill Clinton—a 'centrist' Democrat who discarded financial regulations on Wall Street to set the kindling for the 2008 financial crash, oversaw the beginnings of the opioid crisis, and passed the 1994 Crime Bill that would see the mass incarceration of hundreds of thousands of black Americans—for having an affair whilst he, himself, was having an affair. To compound Gingrich's lack of integrity, this was taking place while his wife was recovering in the hospital from cancer treatment. On being outed as an adulterer, being a right-wing hypocrite, he simply sought 'God's forgiveness' for his transgressions[135].

Sadly, it's a truism that, while winning, one can often get away with a lot, and in 1994, Gingrich was winning, having led Republicans to that first House majority since Eisenhower's presidency. To get there, he used the dastardly simple yet effective approach, which is now the GOP's modus operandi; he brought national grievances to local races to enrage and engage the SCARI coalition.

When the 2000 election came about, George W. Bush was pitted against Bill Clinton's veep, Al Gore. It came down to 538 votes in Florida, where Bush's brother, Jeb, was the governor. A less charitable person might suggest this was a thumb on the scale.

One aspect of the 2000 election that people don't recall so much was the insurrection that occurred fifteen days after election day. It took place at the Steven B. Clark Government Center in downtown Miami, where officials had gathered to sort through the disputed votes. A mob of furious, entitled, Brooks Brothers-clad, angry white Republican operatives descended upon the Center, forcing the recount to be shut down[136].

They were more smartly dressed than the January 6th insurrectionists, but their intent was exactly the same: to stop the counting of legal votes that may favor their opponents. As it happened, five unelected Justices on the Supreme Court needed little convincing to throw the election to the Republican candidate, even though he had lost the popular vote.

Just eight months into Bush's first term, America suffered the bloodiest of blows from a soft-spoken, rag-wearing, Muslim cave-dweller—who was actually the son of a billionaire[137]. The nation known around the world for Rambo and Chuck Norris could never tolerate this, and the war machine was duly fired up. Every night for a generation, we saw warriors, cradling M4 machine guns, engaged in sanitized combat.

A certain subset of men saw that gun, and they wanted it. And thanks to the NRA and gun manufacturers, those same American men could buy its near-identical civilian cousin, the AR-15, and become warriors without a war. Or at least that's what we thought until some of them started turning those AR-15s on us.

In the 2008 election, Senator John McCain faced challenges not only from the Bush administration's lies that took us to war in Iraq and Americans' fury at the fallout from the 2007 economic collapse[138], but also his own campaign blunder of selecting as his running mate Sarah Palin, a Tea Party know-nothing.

Fortunately for the world, she'd never get the chance to be one heartbeat away from the presidency. Instead, many Americans craved 'Hope'. So, their decision to elect a skinny brown man with a funny last name (and an even crazier middle one) as president was one of the crowning achievements of the American Experiment.

President Barack Hussein Obama had to sort out the greatest economic collapse since 1929, yet still went out of his way to try to unite all Americans. It didn't matter though, for the indignity of a black man living in the White House was kerosene being poured on the fire of white rage. Indeed, every policy that President Obama attempted to implement would be obstructed by Senate Majority Leader Mitch McConnell, and the GOP.

Just to segue to what people imagine are normal Republicans. In 2023, the political class hailed former Senator Mitt Romney for warning of the dangers of authoritarianism[139]. But back in 2012, even 'moderate' Republicans like him were not immune from throwing red meat to the Confederate Taliban. Speaking in Michigan, as the blink-or-you-will-miss-him GOP presidential nominee in 2012, against Obama, Romney said, "No one's ever asked to see my birth certificate. They know that this was the place..that we were born and raised." [140]

He was feeding the fury of the Trump-stoked 'birther' conspiracy[141]. This BS held that President Obama wasn't actually an American citizen. The lies didn't help Romney, and Obama soundly beat him in the election.

The apex of GOP encumbrance would come in February 2016, after the death of Supreme Court Justice Antonin Scalia. Nearly one year before the 2016 election, McConnell was not even willing to consider a vote on Merrick Garland's nomination for the vacant seat[142].

Despite this, President Obama's signature accomplishments were to right the US economy, endorse same-sex marriage and the 2015 Obergefell v. Hodges Supreme Court decision that legalized it[143], negotiate the Joint

Comprehensive Plan of Action or Iran Nuclear Deal[144] that limited Iran's ability to manufacture a nuclear bomb, and pass the Affordable Care Act that today covers forty million Americans[145].

Come 2016, and voters put into office a six-times bankrupt, fragile craven New York fraudster, who was only ever 'successful' when playing a businessman on reality TV. The satirist H.L. Mencken predicted this scenario way back in 1920;

> "As democracy is perfected, the office of the president represents, more and more closely, the inner soul of the people. We move toward a lofty ideal. On some great and glorious day, the plain folks of the land will reach their heart's desire at last, and the White House will be adorned by a downright moron."[146]

We have to note that Trump's con was to pander to both white grievance about the changing demographics of America with lines targeting Mexicans like "They're bringing drugs, they're bringing crime, they're rapists...," while also spinning a lie about "draining the swamp"[147]. The latter might have resonated with enough Americans who had become very jaded about Washington and corruption, especially as no rich or powerful people went to prison for the lies and lost lives of the opioid crisis, or the lies and lost lives of the Iraq War, or the outright lies and savage economic plunder committed by bankers in 2008.

However, what is also indisputable is that through fifty years of intense programming, the GOP electorate had been coddled sufficiently that they required no further persuasion to support a revival of 'Make America White Again', brought to them by their own downright moron.

Trump's 2016 campaign showed us the art of his deal by being both lazy and shamelessly plagiaristic. It stole Pat Buchanan's whole 1996 campaign and Reagan's 1980 campaign slogan, simply omitting the word "LET'S."

Once in office, what followed was a disastrous four years, marked by enormous tax cuts benefiting the wealthy (his family and donors,) submissive behavior towards Vladimir Putin, and a criminal mishandling of the COVID crisis.

Yet, all this paled alongside his most venomous parting gift to the America he swore an oath to protect. On January 6th, 2021, for the first time in the nation's history, a sitting president refused to allow the peaceful transfer of power and instead, as part of a wider criminal conspiracy, incited a murderous and treasonous insurrection at the Capitol[148].

So it is; since 2016, Trump has, with the help of many 'conservative' idiots, transformed the Grand Old Party into a cult of obedience. Remember the 33% (13 million) of base voters in 2016. Well, according to the New Republic, in 2024, that base is now at least 42% of all Republican primary voters, with another 29% being okay with whatever happens[149].

This was backed up by expert pollster Rachel Bitecofer, who also offered us that 70% of the GOP primary voters were MAGA. She said,

> Look at a basically Republican red district, as red as you can get. They show up to vote, what's the break? 70/30. And so, just make sure that you understand this. When Trump came down the golden escalator and was starting to rise in the Republican primary polls in 2016, it was the exact opposite. It was 30/70. [150]

By 2024, for GOP voters, a fetus has more rights than the mother, Democrats control the weather, white people are being 'replaced', children are being indoctrinated by 'woke' (anti-prejudice) education, Russia is our friend, LGBTQ+ must be 'eradicated,' and guns must be everywhere.

At the intersection of everything Republican is the cult leader and 'strongman,' Trump, a hellion who believes in nothing except self-publicity and self-enrichment. As America's preeminent conman, his 'skill' is to pull off a feat that other Republicans find impossible to match. Trump is not intelligent, but his vacuity affords him the ability to reflect who, and what it is, that the SCARI people want to see.

Trump understands that the fury of the thirty-million-strong base drives the party and that they want control and domination. So it is that he can tell them that immigrants are "poisoning the blood of our country," and liberals are "vermin."[151] Where that isn't enough, he promises to be a "dictator," offering "retribution" and a "unified Reich."[152]

And for the base, so long as he promises them sweet, sadistic salvation from the progress of an America they so emphatically despise, their votes are guaranteed.

As for us poor bastards, super-glued to ringside seats at this carnival of the damned, Trump embodies the living incarnation of the death of freedom, and now elected, is certain to be THE AMERICAN SUICIDE VEST.

Chapter 5

John Wayne: A Plastic Cowboy, But The Ultimate SWIMP Patriarch.

S ome of my best friends are straight white men. Indeed, my godchildren are, and my grandad and uncle were. I'm all in for every good man who wants progress.

This being said, to understand where the Confederate Taliban wants to take us, first, we need to meet an entirely different kind of white man. The Straight White Male Patriarch, a.k.a. The SWIMP.

As we read in the last chapter, until the 1950s, it was the patriarch who went to work and brought home the money. Unless they wanted to, they didn't need to earn respect, be empathetic, or ever apologize. Their obedient wives would stay at home, looking after the—silent until spoken to—children, and self-medicating with wine and antidepressants.

The SWIMPs mindset neatly interposes with fundamentalist religion, which reveres and takes its lead from the Old Testament. As it was then, so it is now. Weak, fragile men with terrible policies always need to force others to submit so they can dominate and control them. The problem for patriarchs is that most people don't want to be dominated by someone else.

It was in the mid-1950s, in both chronology and culture, that the SWIMPs and fundamentalists started to panic. The trigger for their panic would be the Brown v. Board of Education ruling that desegregated public schools. Now, white and black children could go to school together and then learn they weren't so different after all. From there, the SWIMPs knew it would be a small step to them working together, loving together, and living together. If your whole spiel was predicated upon denigrating and dominating black folks, this would have been arrhythmia-inducing.

So the blowback started. Just one year after Brown, William F. Buckley Jr.[153], the father of the modern Republican Party, founded the conservative National Review, and three years after that, in 1958, the John Birch Society[154] of rich, ultra-conservative, fake Christians would be Frankensteined to life to stop progress.

For SWIMPs, compartmentalizing black folks was no problem, but what was much harder to fathom was their own children. White kids were supposed to be controllable, just like the characters in the TV show 'Leave it to Beaver.' Bear in mind the times we are talking about. This was the white-picket-fence America of the new suburbs. In entertainment, it was also the era of the Hays Code[155], a self-censoring age in Hollywood with docile, feminine women, vanishingly few black faces, and no gay ones.

Which brings us to the classic 1955 coming-of-age drama, 'Rebel Without a Cause.' This gave the SWIMPs a window into the future, and they didn't like what they saw[156]. Recall, it was only the year before that the four-year-long manufactured 'moral panic'—caused by Joseph McCarthy and aided by stooges like Ronald Reagan—had ended. This was still a time when any form of collective thinking was seen as 'Red,' dangerous, and subversive to the American way of life.

Even in this stiflingly suffocating environment, Nicholas Ray, the film's director, masterfully imparted fresh new ideas. In 'Rebel Without a Cause,' James Dean's teenage character is both lost and rebellious. His father is an ordinary man who can't control him, either physically or emotionally, and the film conveys a sense of wanting to break out of the stale, pale, humdrum existence of mundane conformity.

Dean's complex character was 1950s youth challenging the patriarchy. He wanted a say, and he wanted to be heard, but he was also willing to stand up for people weaker than him. These were all big no-no's to the patriarchy—what they might call 'woke' today—made worse because the off-screen Dean was equally non-conforming. For the SWIMPs, who required only strong, silent, unemotional masculinity, this was the beginning of a cultural horror show.

Around the same time as Hollywood started offending the SWIMPs sensibilities, so would music. From his first recordings in 1954—when radio DJs assumed he was a 'colored' artist[157]—to his rocket-ship ascendancy to smash-hit fame just two years later, Elvis Presley presented a formidable conundrum for the SWIMPs[158].

Up to this time, music meant handsome, family-friendly crooners like Perry Como and Pat Boone. Elvis came from a different universe. His beautiful looks transcended mere handsome and his pseudo-sexual hip-thrusting performing style, let's just say, got young women very excited.

All that being so, it's got to be remembered that this style of music existed, but only in black communities, which wasn't a problem, as most white folks would never go there, so would never hear it. Elvis was very different. As a white star, he was unchained and untameable. Knowing this, it was hardly surprising that the SWIMPs dreaded the influence this Adonis could have on their youth.

Elvis, James Dean, and other stars like Marlon Brando and Montgomery Clift were all complicated, magnetic young men. They represented a changing male America that would blend both masculinity and sensitivity and were far removed from the swashbuckling, 'injun' taming,' 'war heroes,' and "men's-men" that Hollywood had, up to then, provided as a staple diet to white America.

Professor George Lakoff is a cognitive linguist and philosopher, easily the equal of the GOP's messaging guru, Frank Luntz, yet successive Democratic administrations never listened to him. Nearly thirty years ago, in his 1996 book, Moral Politics, he described the conservative worldview, and if liberals had read it, we may not be teetering on the edge of a fascist theocracy today. He describes a strict father, the patriarch, who holds everything together with the old 'spare the rod, spoil the child' thinking—which all but guarantees that their kids will grow up to hate them and never want to look after them when they're old.

This mind-set is the bastard love-child of Christian fundamentalism and Ayn Rand[159]-selfishness but offers us a throughline to the fragile and scared men who need to project their anxieties onto the rest of us. Professor Lakoff elaborates,

In the strict father family, the father knows best. He knows right from wrong and has the ultimate authority to make sure his children and his spouse do what he says, which is taken to be what is right. Many conservative spouses accept this worldview, uphold the father's authority, and are strict in those realms of family life that they are in charge of. This reasoning shows up in conservative politics in which the poor are seen as lazy and undeserving, and the rich as deserving their wealth. Responsibility is thus taken to be personal responsibility not social responsibility. What you become is only up to you; society has nothing to do with it. You are responsible for yourself, not for others — who are responsible for themselves.[160]

As a minor detour, the 1950s is where we find women imagining that they could, if they wanted, be something other than a housewife. Marilyn Monroe drove right up to the boundaries of what was acceptable. In movies like 'Niagara' (1953) and 'The Seven Year Itch' (1955), she played the very opposite of the sweet, demure housewife, a.k.a. the tradwife. As a sexy seductress, she could have been the patriarchy's nightmare, the sort of woman for whom decent, red-blooded American men would throw everything away, just to have a chance with her.

Fortunately for the SWIMPs, the studio system dulled the sharper edges of her 'feminism.' So it was that in many of Marilyn's films, she was actually either looking to marry a man or needing to be protected by one.

To give you an idea of what the patriarchs had been relying upon as a template until the 1950s, we need to look to someone who affirmed good, manly 'Christian' values and quashed any notions of men being 'weak.' This lodestar was represented by John Wayne, also known as 'the Duke.'

Born Marion Morrison in Iowa in 1907, Wayne was a handsome fellow built for Hollywood, standing six foot four, with broad shoulders and a good square head. In almost every cowboy film he was in, the Duke played a variation of the rugged frontier man who didn't hesitate to mete out violence, often seen saving fragile white women and children from marauding "Red Indians."

So it would be that for at least two generations of Americans who grew up watching westerns, he was iconic. For the far-right, Wayne, like Trump after him, represented both a mirror and a projector. The mirror reflected exactly how a 'real' American man was supposed to behave, look, and think. Then the projector beamed the unquestioning, dominating values of Manifest Destiny and white supremacy.

All this being said, let's go back to September 1940. Men between the ages of twenty-one and forty-five had been called up for the draft. Harry Belafonte, Mel Brooks, Kirk Douglas, Clark Gable, James Garner, Dashiell Hammett, Paul Newman, Robert Mitchum, and James Stewart all signed up and went to fight[161].

It wasn't just men who answered the call. You may remember that this was the time of the tradwife: a delicate, immaculately turned-out, fragile woman whose only purpose was to raise the children, cook, clean, wash, iron, and be silent whilst men spoke.

So marvel at the 'little ladies' who stepped up to do their part. As a fourteen-year-old, future movie icon Audrey Hepburn was dancing to raise money for the Dutch Resistance. Then, there was the actress, dancer and singer Josephine Baker, helping to smash the Nazis by spying for the French Resistance[162]. But what of the Duke? Big John was just thirty-four years old and well within the age limit for combat assignment. So, did he serve?

Well, no, he didn't. His excuse was 'flat feet.' Those flat feet didn't stop him staying in Hollywood, where, fortunately, the bullets were fake, the blood was fake, and the dying was fake. Then, when the filming was over, he could go home, tuck himself up in bed, and thank his lucky stars he had genuine heroes like Audrey and Josephine to protect him.

To see what could be so important as to keep the Duke from service, we need to go back one year to 1939. Wayne was having an affair with the movie star Marlene Dietrich and was on the cusp of a big career, having just made the movie "Stagecoach." It was said that he feared coming back from war and finding out he may have lost his chance at the big time.

So, interposed with his cowardice, there was naked self-interest. It was Bye, Bye Adolf, screw you America, and Hello Hollywood, as Big John Wayne, a 'Republican Patriot,' and the 'man's man' of the Confederate Taliban, would cry off his service. I'd bet good money that there were thousands of brave young men from Illinois, Indiana, and Iowa killing fascists in the European and Pacific theaters who also had 'flat feet.'[163] Indeed, a quick check reveals that 'flat feet' are not any impediment to service today[164]. But back then, it was a good excuse for rich, privileged cowards to escape service.

Still, back in safe, sunny California, Wayne had other priorities. According to Architectural Digest;

> When making a film on location, nothing gives Mr. Wayne more pleasure than spending his free time browsing through whatever antiques shops are available.[165]

Thus, it was that, whilst the Duke was busy hunting for new trinkets, real men and women were fighting for freedom. So, just like his modern disciples, when his country called, he didn't answer.

It should come as little surprise that a man untroubled by fascism abroad would also be equally nonchalant about it at home. In a 1971 Playboy interview, Wayne said,

> I believe in white supremacy until the blacks are educated to a point of responsibility. I don't believe in giving authority and positions of leadership and judgment to irresponsible people.[166]

It's almost possible to taste the irony dripping off this cowardly 'white supremacist', who black and brown service personnel helped to keep safe during WWII.

To that point, we come to the Tuskegee Airmen of Alabama. This mostly black squadron from the 332nd Fighter Group flew fifteen thousand missions, protecting American bombers from German fighter planes. Their one hundred and twelve confirmed kills proved both the courage of the African-American and crushed the myth that black folks weren't as competent as whites[167]. Remember though, back then, the Air Force was segregated, which meant that America was losing where it could otherwise be winning.

Fortunately, the Tuskegee Airmen had an enlightened white squadron leader in Lt. Col. Noel F. Parrish. He saw how black talent could help

America win. Working with Cornelius Coffey of the Coffey School of Aeronautics, the first black-founded and run training school for black pilots, he found exceptional talent for the war effort.

Never let it be said that handsome, heroic Kentucky-born, Lt. Col. Parrish couldn't have just coasted through his military career without ever having to interact with black folks—unless he was giving his drinks order to the serving staff in the officer's mess. However, he chose the harder, more honorable path, and the one that may have cost him 'friends.' But it was that courage, integrity, and love of America that drove him to do what others feared doing. It's just another example of white and black folks working together to actually make America great[168].

Back to Big John. In the post-war years, superstars like Arthur Ashe, Elvis Presley, Gene Hackman, Jimi Hendrix, and Steve McQueen would all serve[169], yet the Duke was still terrified of the prospect. Now, I have no problem with pacifists or conscientious objectors or people who just don't want to die. Indeed, I respect anyone whose choices are genuine. But like so many on the far-right, Wayne was a coward and a hypocrite, and his patriotism was all performative.

Skipping forward a few decades, we have the story of the fraudster, Donald J. Trump. In order to avoid service in Vietnam, he applied for draft deferments FIVE times. Eventually, 'bone spurs' got him out of going to war[170].

This is what privilege looks like, but what was truly sickening was seeing this yellow-bellied, treasonous weakling demean the military service of real men who made a sacrifice for America. Whether it was disrespect of Senator John McCain as a POW in Vietnam or his styling of fallen American soldiers as "losers" and "suckers,"[171] the convicted felon's lack of any form of empathy was absolute.

There are two particular stories that illustrate how unfit Trump should have been for any form of office. The first was a reported conversation with his then chief of staff and father to a fallen soldier, retired Marine Corps General John Kelly.

After seeing the 2017 Bastille Day Parade in France, Trump said to Kelly, of his own planned Military Parade; "Look, I don't want any wounded guys in the Parade." He was referring to the disabled veterans at the front of the parade. Kelly appeared shocked—given his own loss—and replied, "Those are the heroes. In our society, there's only one group of people who are more heroic than they are — and they are buried over in Arlington." The criminal is reported to have dismissed this, saying; "I don't want them; it doesn't look good for me."[172]

Trump's putrefying inhumanity would ooze itself to the surface once again when former Army Captain Luis Avila was invited to sing at the White House in September 2019 at the Joint Chiefs of Staff change of command ceremony.

Captain Avila served his country with distinction through five combat tours in Afghanistan and Iraq. It was during a search and rescue in Afghanistan in December 2011, while on deployment with the 720th Military Police Battalion, that his squad's Humvee was hit by a six-hundred-pound improvised explosive device and split in half. Tragically, three of his buddies were killed in the attack, while Captain Avila survived but lost a leg, suffered two heart attacks, and was left with brain damage from two strokes.

He spent forty days in a coma, and his injuries left him with near-total paralysis. Then, for the first two and a half years of his intensive recovery at Walter Reed Medical Center, Captain Avila had to learn how to eat, see, and speak again[173]. Thanks to the love of his family and his own towering human spirit, over the next four years, he regained forty percent mobility in his body, to a point where, today, he competes in Army ten-miler events and at the Warrior Games[174].

Knowing all of that, Trump's words in 2019 to the nation's highest-ranking military officer, Chairman of the Joint Chiefs of Staff General

Mark Milley, on seeing Captain Avila were, "Why do you bring people like that here? No one wants to see that, the wounded." Like Kelly before him, General Milley had to explain to the craven coward that Captain Avila represented the heroism and courage of the bravest of people: those who joined up to serve, knowing they may have to make the ultimate sacrifice for their country[175].

The toxicity that allows the Confederate Taliban to demean and debase service personnel would have been unthinkable for any Republican candidate before 2016. But today the MAGA base has no problem with Trump and his lackeys constantly disparaging and disrespecting the military[176]. For the SCARI coalition that makes up the Confederate Taliban, it doesn't matter that Trump is a coward, and it doesn't matter that he spits on veterans or knows nothing about the Constitution[177]. All that matters is that he is one of them, and that's better than millions of us.

Trump fits in a long line of modern far-right patriarchs. All weak, vain, insecure zeta males who project their own inadequacies onto their opponents in order to gaslight their supporters into believing them to be 'alphas'. They demand respect while demanding everyone else earns respect. Legendary hard-boiled American crime fiction writer James Ellroy—no fan of liberals—offered this about Trump;

> What gets to me is how everyone in the world has to talk about this dipshit. I have never seen more volcanic, pathetic self-pity in a man. Trump revels in his own grotesque. I know something about men. Real men do not wallow in self-pity[178].

The thing is, a true alpha male never needs to project and never needs to punch down, as their actions speak for themselves. Adam Serwer, in his extraordinary 2021 book "The Cruelty is the Point" would describe Trump's only talent;

> Trump's only true skill is the con; his only fundamental belief is that the United States is the birthright of straight, white, Christian men, and his only real, authentic pleasure is in cruelty…The president's ability to execute that cruelty through word and deed makes them euphoric. It makes them feel good, it makes them feel proud, it makes them feel happy, it makes them feel united. And as long as he makes them feel that way, they will let him get away with anything, no matter what it costs them.[179]

Those words ring in my ears as we come to examine the most rabid of Trump's supporters, a true and open picture of whom we got on January 6th, 2021. Robert Pape, Professor of political science at the University of Chicago, and his team of researchers at the Chicago Project on Security and Threats (CPST) carried out extensive research. Of 700 domestic terrorists arrested following the insurrection, half were,

> "Business owners, CEOs from white-collar occupations, doctors, lawyers, and architects. Their ranks included CEOs, a cardiovascular specialist, lawyers, a design engineer, accountants and the founder and president of a firm that tests satellites"[180]

To those who want to learn about the MAGA base, this is true gold. It also aligns with research from 538 that showed that Trump supporters in 2016 were wealthy non-college-educated voters (earning a median income of $72,000 back then). Many were small-business owners[181].

At a violent event like J6, it was no surprise to see arrests of members of hardcore anti-government groups, like The Oath Keepers, Proud Boys, and Three Percenters. Yet, from their detailed study of the backgrounds and arrest records of the insurrectionists, the CPST revealed that many arrested were wealthy, non-college-educated, older men in their 40s and 50s, with very few having prior criminal records.

Similar to the Obama-era Tea Party, these are middle-and upper-middle class white people furious at the changing America. Astonishingly, over half of them came from counties that *Biden* won in 2020. Indeed, the more rural the area, the less likely they were to send a terrorist. Professor Pape tied it all up for us with this;

"The No. 1 feature of the county sending insurrectionists, aside from simply the size of the population overall, is that these are the counties losing the most white population in the United States. The more counties have lost non-Hispanic white population since 2010—that is, between 2010 and 2020—the significantly more likely is the county to send an insurrectionist."[182]

The overriding reason for them being there was the false 'replacement theory,'[183] that Jewish people were importing brown and black folks to replace white Americans—an insanity that is repeated over and over on Fox, AM radio, and social media. The second most common reason for being at the Capitol was the loony-but-lethal QAnon conspiracy that intertwines with Christian fundamentalism.

This leads us to why the Confederate Taliban and their shrills, like Tucker Carlson, love Russia and Putin so much. For many, it seems so counterintuitive for right-wingers to love our greatest adversary. Journalist Sergio Olmos explained why in his 2022 article for the London Guardian;

As America and the world grow more diverse, critics say, Russia has come to be seen as a beacon of salvation by white nationalists. In 2004, David Duke, a longtime leader of the Ku Klux Klan, described it as "key to white survival". In 2017 Ann Coulter, a right-wing author and commentator, opined: "In 20 years, Russia will be the only country that is recognizably European."............ Devin Burghart, executive director of Institute for Research & Education on Human Rights, said: "There's an attraction to Putin's hard-line authoritarian stand, his aggressive policies, they are attracted to his brand of traditional Christianity and some have liked Putin's attacks on the Russian LGBTQ+ community.[184]

It's possible to link all this to the current war in Ukraine. When Putin invaded Ukraine in February 2022, it was with one purpose: to dominate the Ukrainians and force them to capitulate and become subjects of a new USSR[185].

For Putin, Ukraine represents an example of how life can be better than in Russia. After all, Ukrainians were free—free to say what they want, free to be who they want, and free to do what they want. Bearing all this in mind, how, realistically, could Putin ever allow this nation to flourish? Ukraine is what freedom looks like, and Putin was terrified that Russians might wake up and see him for who he is: a tiny tyrannical troll who has spent nearly twenty-five years, with the help of his oligarchs, stealing Russia's wealth.

In a move that would have Ronald Reagan flipping somersaults in his grave, the American far-right has aligned itself with Putin's Russia over Ukraine and our Western allies. On that point, in February 2024, Trump told NATO allies he may not send American assistance if Russia attacked them[186]. Indeed, since Putin helped sway the 2016 election to Trump, the GOP has repeated every Russian talking point verbatim. There are always receipts. These are the words of Mike Turner, a Republican Congressional Rep from Ohio and the Chair of the House Intelligence Committee, speaking to CNN,

"It is absolutely true we see, directly coming from Russia, attempts to mask communications that are anti-Ukraine and pro-Russia messages, some of which we even hear being uttered on the House floor."[187]

He wasn't alone. Michael McCaul, the Republican chair of the House foreign affairs committee, said,

"Russian propaganda has made its way into the United States, unfortunately, and it's infected a good chunk of my party's base."[188]

To understand this on an even more granular level, Putin is the SWIMP's daddy, The Straight White Male Patriarchs' NorthStar. In terms of influence, he possesses the world's third most powerful army (even though it doesn't appear very competent) and the second largest nuclear arsenal (if the silo doors aren't rusted shut from lack of maintenance). Then, for the Russian leader's enemies, there is exile, prison, or death.

In Russia, husbands can rape their wives, beat their kids, drown their dogs, and never have to worry about recycling. Over there, straight conservative men are in charge, and everyone else does as they are told. That's the world Trump wants, that's the world Musk wants, and that's the world Vance wants. These patriarchs are pissed that, for all of its modern history, men have been in charge, but today, America, in line with the rest of the

WEIRD (Western Educated, Industrialized, Educated, Rich, Developed) world, they are being asked to change in order to make some space at the table for other people.

Patriarchal power leads to entitlement, and entitlement demands to be free from consequences. We can see, in former Hollywood mogul Harvey Weinstein, the entitlement of a prominent man to do anything he wanted—without consequence—to powerless actresses and models. Before the MeToo movement of 2016[189], it was pointless trying to bring a suit against an influential man like him. Besides, anyone who did *"would never work in this town again"*. Weinstein plundered and prospered because he wasn't just one man; he was part of an entire system.

As was Trump, who grew up in a time when rich men could 'grab 'em by the pussy'. In those days, women knew they would never receive the benefit of the doubt from the authorities. So it was that a predator could do anything they pleased in the dressing room of the Bergdorf Goodman department store. Should his 'victim' protest, then a coward like him could smile condescendingly and offer, confidently, a throwaway line like, *'You should be grateful for the attention,'* or *"Stop being so sensitive."* Knowing this, is it so surprising that Trump's pal, the prolific pedophile Jeffrey Epstein, got away with so much for so long?[190]

That was then, and this is now, and there isn't even the pretense of a mask anymore. Here's what the 'thought leaders' of the 2024 far-right think. This from Scott Yenon, a fellow who heads the inimical, billionaire-funded (DeVos, Bradley, Scairfe) Claremont Institute. Speaking at the National Conservatism Conference in 2022, and reported in The Nation;

> He derided career-oriented women as "medicated, meddlesome and quarrelsome."...The culture should return to urging women to pursue "feminine goals"—chief among them,

staying home and having children in the interest of restoring strong families, and through them, a strong nation.[191]

Thinking of mediocre men like Yenon reminds me of a line I heard from the brilliant Missourian, Jess Piper (who you will read more from later). She was speaking about how right-wingers love the 'gotcha' question of 'What is a woman?' I, personally, would always reach for a simple, "someone who isn't a man" answer, but the disingenuous, who always want it to end up with, 'someone with a uterus,' or 'someone who can have a baby,' would never stop asking questions until we ended up there. Jess, being far more astute than I, had this:

> What is a woman? Well, she's the person who crosses the street when she sees you coming. She's the person who puts her keys in between her fingers when she's in a parking garage and you're behind her. She's the person who covers her drink when you come near her at a bar, and she's the person who swipes left on your Tinder profile.[192]

I wish everyone had that answer, as invariably, the person they are talking to will be a dick, looking to punch down, and with that response, they would just shut the hell up.

A real man (and, to be frank, there are many women who I would want in my corner too) helps people. They reach down and offer a hand. It was said that, when Donald Trump thought no one was looking, he cheated on three of his wives, but when Joe Biden thought no one was looking, he helped a homeless man[193].

Just to return to the exact opposite of a real man, we arrive at a creature called Charlie Kirk. This 29-year-old grifting varmint heads a proto-fascist organization called "Turning Point USA," as in turning America back to the 1950s, where mediocre conservative men could do as they pleased. This astroturfed outfit gaslights and indoctrinates its followers with a lot of fake Christianity—the sort that doesn't follow a single teaching of the Gospel. Kirk is a propagandist fashioned in the mold of the classic coward—always punching down at black and brown folks, the LGBTQ+ community, and educated women[194]. Suffice to say, he always kisses up to right-wing power.

Just on the point of indoctrination. At a June 2023 Turning Point rally, a young woman supporter spoke of her confusion about balancing training to become a surgeon *and* having a family. My first reaction was, why does she need advice from this community college dropout turned gaslighting dweeb whose only achievement is to spread hate and disinformation?

Still oblivious to his true station in life, Kirk replies, pushing the right-wing patriarchal narrative, "Go try to spend a couple days with babies, and if it doesn't move you to wanna have some of your own, go do the surgeon thing." He added, "there are a lot of successful, 35-year-old orthopedic surgeons that have cats, and not kids, and they're very miserable."[195]

It would be nice to think that people like Kirk don't matter, yet, between 2016 and 2023, this truly odious zeta male's organization was propped up to the tune of $250 million[196]. This was seed money from right-wing billionaires to promote far-right 'values' and specifically to get them into the mainstream media. By way of proof, all the information you read in the last few paragraphs came from such illustrious sources as Newsweek, USA Today, and the Washington Post. Now you may understand how, seeing their cash buy that level of reach and influence, the billionaires will consider it money well spent.

Indeed, in the 2024 presidential election, "childless cat ladies"[197] became a theme used by Trump, his VP pick, J.D Vance, and many other Republicans to project 'strength' by painting women who would not bow down to the patriarchy (including VP Kamala Harris and pop icon Taylor Swift) as boring, lonely losers in order to win over disaffected men.

Many liberals still don't understand the SWIMP's end game, even though it's quite simple. It starts with the abortion ban. When a pregnant woman is forced to have her baby, she will have to stay home to look after it. This means she can no longer work and thus has no income. That's great news for mediocre, talentless men because a woman without an income can't own a home and won't be independent. So it is that she will require a husband to look after and provide for her.

As far as that provision goes, it was only in 1974, with the Equal Credit Opportunity Act, that women no longer required their husbands' signatures to open a bank account or obtain a credit card[198]. Still, in between bearing lots more babies—fake Christians consider marital rape, which was legal in all fifty states until 1974 and only outlawed by federal law in 1993, an impossibility[199]—'grateful' women will spend their days floating blissfully on a cloud of Xanax and Zoloft, cooking, cleaning, washing, ironing, and minding the children.

Of course, without qualified working women in accounting, journalism, law, management consultancy, or the tech industry, the most second-rate men can take over the jobs that women would otherwise be doing.

You may think that I exaggerate, so I have some receipts. Fake Christian and former Trump administration official William Wolfe is on record as wanting a nationwide abortion ban and the ending of welfare support to single mothers. To top off all that cruelty is his desire for a ban on 'no-fault divorce.'[200]

Then, in 2024, Wolfe interviewed another fake-Christian, Pastor Joel Webbon. This character is the founder of the Texas-based Right-Response Ministries. Just to apprise you of Webbon's ideas about women, he has a YouTube channel anyone can look at. Some of his titles are "The Sin Of

Women[201]and "Christian Nationalism & The Chaos Of Female Leadership."[202]

In the video that I'm interested in, Wolfe asks Webbon whether in a Christian Nationalist nation, women will have the right to vote. Webbon replies,

> No. Because if we had a Christian Nation tomorrow and women had the right to vote, we would not have a Christian Nation in 50 years time...Because the husband has been appointed by God as the head of the household and no fault divorce and women's suffrage have more than anything else ultimately split the household.[203]

This is not a world that I hope ever happens, but I understand the seductive lure of it for a disillusioned man. As a fifty-five-year-old Gen X man, the privilege of the patriarchy made my life 'easier.' The responsibilities and civilities that exist today weren't required. Indeed, it was an age where, if a woman didn't want to sleep with a man, she was either 'frigid,' 'on her period,' or a 'lesbian.' The man's mind would never need to alight upon the thought that it may have been he who was lacking.

Life has many gray areas, and two things can be true at once. Back then, what actually made my life easier was a good job and a house that only cost 4x my salary. For me, solving these two problems will go a long way toward fixing society. In my book 'When Coal Miners Drive Cadillacs', you can read about solutions to do just that and make life better for both men and women.

But for today, don't take advice from weak freaks like Alien Alex Jones, Boring Ben Shapiro, Comrade Carlson, Mad Musk, or Rape Tate. They're all either grifters, liars, or thieves, or a combination of all three.

There are two easy rules to know in order to be a good man; stand by your word and *never* punch *down*. Trans people don't need my help to make their lives any more complicated, nor do gay people. A black man doesn't need me to tell him he should 'work harder,' and a woman doesn't require my 'mansplaining.' Here's the deal; punching down is so easy because the victims have so little power, which explains why it's always the avenue that pathetic bullies take.

Any moderately attuned person can look up and see exactly where the problem lies. Even someone like me can punch up without a problem, whether it's at fascists, supremacists, billionaires, or corporations. Of course, it actually requires some skill to do this. You need a little intelligence, courage, critical thinking, and chutzpah. But over the next four years, if you're willing to stand alongside folks without power and never bully the bullied but always bully the bully, then you're a real superhero and a real tough guy.

And when you live by this code, surprisingly, life becomes a lot easier; people will want to be your friends, and people will want to listen to you, and people will want to work with you.

Chapter 6

Fascism Will Come To America Wrapped In The Flag And Holding A Bible.

I use the phrase 'fake-Christian' in this book because these people are anti-women, anti-gay, anti-black, and anti-progress. But that's too macro. Here, we are talking about at least twenty million voters you will hear described variously as 'Evangelical,' 'Fundamentalist,' and 'Christian Nationalist.'

Those are just different words to describe the same people. These are the 'pro-life' crowd who may well say a prayer before meals and go to church on a Sunday. Yet they have no issues with forced birth, mass shootings, economic collapse, or climate disaster—any or all of which could affect them and their families. Now, armed with the knowledge of how indifferent fake-Christians are to their own, just imagine the vengeance and wrath they'll allow to be reined down upon you.

All that being so, let's get some context. Fake-Christian evangelical fundamentalists represent, according to Pew Research, one-third of Republican voters[204], and nearly three-quarters of the GOP primary base[205]. 84% of evangelical fundamentalists vote for Trump, and there is a strong intersection between fundamentalists and the QAnon conspiracy madness (see chapter eight).

These fundamentalists, who cross the socio-economic spectrum, from plutocrats living in mansions to poor people living in trailers, despise modern society. They believe that evolution never happened and that the Earth is only six thousand years old (not thirteen billion)[206] and can't wait for the End of Times and their—made up in the 1830s and never mentioned in the Bible—rapture to Heaven[207]. Of course, they trust Fox and other far-right propaganda outfits to tell them the 'truth.'

As you read more about them, just know most are irredeemably lost and unrecoverable. However, as they are, metaphorically or not, coming to burn our houses down, we need to understand them.

Fundamentalist Christianity was the backbone of slavery, white supremacy, and the patriarchy. Then, come the 1950s, these were the people incensed at integration, and in the 1960s, apoplectic at women's rights and worker's rights. However, by the 1970s, saying 'ni**er' was frowned upon, and the 'red scare' had died away, so they needed a fresh approach[208]. Whilst they kept their hatred of people of color, 'socialism,' and homosexuality simmering, high-up Protestants alighted upon an insidious new way to enrage, energize, and engage their low-information voters: abortion.

Just note that, until 1975, a whole three years after Roe v. Wade enshrined a woman's right to choose into law, these fake Christians had never uttered a single word about abortion. Yet, by 1976[209], it was on the GOP platform, just in time for Republicans to run against a real Christian who always put America first, President Jimmy Carter[210].

The fake-Christian leaders included such charlatan luminaries as 'Reverend' Jerry Falwell, a segregationist, tax cheat and consummate evil grifter. In 1986, he was called out by President Carter;

> There is nothing any television evangelist can do to shake my faith...'Jerry Falwell can, in a very Christian way, as far as I'm concerned he can go to hell.[211]

Spin forward to today, and the actor, political commentator, and host of the impossible-to-be-dumb-if-you-listen-to-it "Tell Me Everything" show on Sirius XM, John Fugelsang, helps us pull back the curtain on fundamentalists. He described Jesus of Nazareth as a,

> Non-violent revolutionary who hangs out with lepers, hookers, criminals, and who never spoke English. He was a non-American, anti-capitalism, anti-wealth, anti-public prayer (Matthew 6:5), never anti-gay, anti-death penalty never ever anti-abortion, never calls poor people lazy, never fights for tax cuts for the wealthiest Nazarenes, never says torture's okay-under-some-conditions, and he's a long-haired brown skinned (that's in Revelation), homeless Middle Eastern, anti-slut shaming, unarmed, Palestinian, liberal, Jew. And that's if you believe what's actually in the book.[212]

Warnings from the past show us just how prescient some of the Founding Fathers were. The Framers knew the pilgrims fled the old world to avoid religious persecution, and so it was that they went to great lengths to draw up the founding documents to avoid the possibility that America would become a religious theocracy.

James Madison, the chief author of the Bill of Rights and the First Amendment, understood these demons better than many. In his Memorial and Remonstrance of 1785, he urged the Virginia State legislature to reject the state funding of religion. His language may be over two hundred years old, yet his sentiments carry the resounding authority of a heavyweight boxer's punch;

> During almost fifteen centuries has the legal establishment of Christianity been on trial. What have been its fruits? More or less, in all places, pride and indolence in the clergy; ignorance and servility in the laity; in both superstition, bigotry, and persecution.[213]

The Confederate Taliban deny it, but Article 1 of the Constitution is absolutely clear. It states that Congress "shall make no law respecting an establishment of religion, or prohibiting the free exercise thereof." Furthermore, the word 'God' finds no mention anywhere in the Constitution.

If you'd like a receipt. The 1797 Treaty of Tripoli was an attempt to stop pirates in the North African seas from interfering with American trade. It was an international treaty, ratified by the Senate and signed by John Adams. Article 11 of the treaty rather seals the deal on what America is by stating, "As the government of the United States of America is not in any sense founded on the Christian Religion." [214]

Today, on the political right, we have a coalition of fake Christians. It is made up of an unholy diaspora of anti-Gospel fundamentalist patriarchal fire-breathers, hucksters, and con men. Just apprise yourself of these facts. The televangelists, megachurch preachers, and state-funded religious schools want power in order to dominate us. However, power always has a fellow traveler: money. Your receipt comes from the United States Tax Code, specifically Section 501;

> Churches (including integrated auxiliaries and conventions or associations of churches) that meet the requirements of section 501(c)(3) of the Internal Revenue Code are automatically considered tax exempt and are not required to apply for and obtain recognition of exempt status from the IRS.[215]

Churches and religious organizations pay no taxes. No corporation taxes, no income tax, and no capital gains tax. That's it in a nutshell. As a result, every day, these hideous hyenas get to poison American minds and get paid twice for doing it. First, by duping their parishioners out of subscriptions and donations, and then from you, Mr. and Mrs. Taxpayer, who have to pick up the slack in taxes for everything that these self-serving frauds don't pay.

It's quite baffling, as the Bible is clear on this. From Romans 13:6-7,

> This is also why you pay taxes, for the authorities are God's servants, who give their full time to governing. Give to everyone what you owe them: If you owe taxes, pay taxes; if revenue, then revenue; if respect, then respect; if honor, then honor.[216]

One way to get rid of these characters is to tax their businesses that are only thinly disguised as churches. Then, they will all slink off to find alternate employment, although I'm not sure how many carnival barkers the circuses of America actually need.

Until then, working with the Angry and the Rich segment of the Confederate Taliban, the fake Christian flock-fleecers are the driving force behind your rights being ripped away. I recall the words of Republican Utah State Senator Daniel Thatcher in response to attacks in 2023 on the LGBTQ+ community;

> I have had people who claim to be Christian reach out to me and tell me that I can't be a Christian unless I hate certain people. Well, I don't know who your Christ is, but he kind of sucks.[217]

Sadly, all of this is happening whilst the corporate media stands by, possibly in bewildered astonishment, certainly in fear of offending the Confederate Taliban, and definitely giddy with excitement at the ratings and ad revenue that this chaos brings in.

Still, I'm sure that many Americans would like to know the answer to the question: Who are these 'Christians' who believe machine guns are a blessing but abortion is a sin, and who make up over a third of GOP voters?

The corporate media uses the kindly-sounding title 'Evangelicals.' That word paints in my mind a picture of soaring choral singing and happy people having a great time together. Instead, I prefer and will use the term 'fundamentalist,' because if they were brown men in Afghanistan, we would know exactly what to call them; radical Islamic fundamentalists.

Indeed, their leaders make no secret of their fundamentalism. Paul Weyrich, co-founder of the far-right Heritage Foundation (of Project 2025 notoriety) was quoted as saying, "We are talking about Christianizing America. We are talking about the Gospel in a political context."[218]

Rd. Obery Hendricks Jr. is a professor of biblical interpretation and the author of "Christians Against Christianity: How Right-Wing Evangelicals Are Destroying Our Nation and Our Faith." He drew on the point that fundamentalists are less about Christianity and more about 'Churchianity'. This is the moral licensing that you will read about in chapter eleven. This dissonance allows them to ignore all the actual teachings of the Gospel, yet still claim to be pious just because they go to church.

I'm a Christian. At school, I had to go to the chapel twice a day. I was taught moderate liberal Christianity, so I'm cool with Christ and groovy with God. While I never believed that a loaf of bread could feed five thousand people, or that men could part seas or rise from the dead, and I don't go to church these days, I'm down with the basic tenets of the gospel.

One reason I don't go to church is that I could never understand why these places wouldn't open their doors to the poor and the downtrodden.

To this point, in 2024, there was a story about the 'Dad's Place Church' in the City of Bryan, Ohio. It is in Williams County in the northwest of the state. The county went 72% for the GOP in 2020[219].

This small, unassuming storefront church, run by pastor Chris Avell, was allowing homeless people to sleep there overnight. When you know that the nighttime temperature in an Ohio winter can drop to minus twenty, this appears to be a textbook case of a real Christian following the exact teachings of Jesus. It may come as a surprise (or not) that the city council issued a zoning violation to stop Pastor Chris from following the teachings of Jesus[220].

Note, it wasn't the homelessness and suffering of their fellow Americans that upset the city elders and residents of that town and county. Instead, they were incensed that Pastor Chris wanted to do something about it.

Once again, the Bible offers these right-wing hypocrites an unpalatable truth; from Matthew Chapter 25;

> For I was hungry and you gave me something to eat, I was thirsty and you gave me something to drink, I was a stranger and you invited me in, I needed clothes and you clothed me, I was sick and you looked after me, I was in prison and you came to visit me.'... 'Truly I tell you, whatever you did for one of the least of these brothers and sisters of mine, you did for me.[221]

If one of their own preachers does actually try to impart some of the gospel on the Confederate Taliban's members, it's a story that doesn't end well. We can hear from Russell Moore. Formerly one of the top officials in the Southern Baptist Convention. He is currently editor-in-chief of Christianity Today and the author of "Losing Our Religion: An Altar Call for Evangelical America.' One line in his book is "When a church decides Jesus may be going liberal."

Mr. Moore seems like a decent man and stood up for his values by speaking out against both the rampant sexual abuse taking place in the evangelical churches, and the evangelical fundamentalists' embrace of Trump and militant Christian nationalism. For his troubles, he was excommunicated ('cancelled') by the cult in 2016. When asked about his 'liberal Jesus' line in an NPR interview, he replied;

> Well, it was the result of having multiple pastors tell me essentially the same story about quoting the Sermon on the Mount parenthetically in their preaching - turn the other cheek - to have someone come up after and say, where did you get those liberal talking points? And what was alarming to

me is that in most of these scenarios, when the pastor would say, I'm literally quoting Jesus Christ, the response would not be, I apologize. The response would be, yes, but that doesn't work anymore. That's weak. And when we get to the point where the teachings of Jesus himself are seen as subversive to us, then we're in a crisis.[222]

That 'crisis' is all about losing patriarchal power, and this takes us to the rancid sadistic core of the modern-day GOP. Dr. Samuel Perry, co-author of 'The Flag and the Cross: White Christian Nationalism and the Threat to American Democracy,' spoke to the Baptist Joint Committee for Religious Liberty. He described the central tenets of Christian nationalism as Freedom, Order, and Violence;

> The people in power—white Christian men, primarily—get the freedom," he said, noting that everyone else—people of color, people who aren't Christian, women, sexual minorities—gets the order. He said if those other groups violate the order, white Christian men feel they are "justified in perpetrating violence," noting that white Christian nationalism is associated with strong support for "authoritarian violence" that supposedly keeps the peace.[223]

As far as freedom goes, our mistake as liberals was to fight endless battles—battles for education, battles for civil rights, battles for women's rights, and battles for LGBTQ+ rights. We never saw that the fundamentalists are fighting a holy war for their 'Freedoms.'

Their crusade against modern society ends with liberals either being dominated or eliminated; the terrorists who stormed the Capitol on January 6th carried the "Appeal to Heaven" flag. This is a symbol adopted by the far-right (including a Supreme Court Justice) who posit the use of violence may be necessary to overthrow the government[224].

For all these reasons, Christian nationalists stick with the imperfect vessel that is Trump. To them, he represents a trifecta of a rich, 'successful', charismatic preacher, a fearsome warrior for their 'Order', and someone formed in the image of their idealized America: a white, blonde-haired man of northern European ancestry.

For those of you who have gone to church, maybe you recall seeing icons of the slim, regular-looking man nailed to the cross, head fallen to the side. If so, it may surprise you to learn who the fundamentalists see. This is where the far-right's myth of "alternative facts" really kicks in[225]. Their Jesus is a thing to behold. Forget the kindly man who fed the five thousand and healed the sick. If that Jesus came back today, the fundamentalists would call him a 'socialist', and gun him down.

Instead, their Messiah, looking like a hero sent from central casting, is a smolderingly handsome, European-looking, musclebound hunk holding an assault rifle[226].

This Jesus is straight out of the Book of Revelations, and, in their deranged fundamentalist minds, he's not just going to vanquish Satan; he's also their permission structure to smash down on people of color, LGBTQ+ folks, and liberals with all their 'sick and twisted' ideas of diversity, inclusiveness, and tolerance.

This is the patriarchy writ large. For them, domination is everything, and violence is always a solution. It's no coincidence that Trump tells them he will be a "dictator," and they cheer.

Sarah Posner, the author of 'Unholy: How White Christian Nationalists Powered the Trump Presidency, and the Devastating Legacy They Left Behind,' wrote;

> Trump didn't ask evangelicals to change their goal of a government controlled by white conservative Christians. He just tore away the pretense that they wanted to accomplish that by democratic means. In the evangelical world, particularly in the charismatic world where Trump has a firm foothold, people believe they are waging a spiritual war against demonic enemies of Christianity and America.[227]

Now, to move on to the 'order' part. Here's where we get to the shooting of unarmed black men and the murder of peaceful liberal protesters. The Confederate Taliban show a fierce reverence for, and protection of, vigilante killers. In fact, scrub the word 'vigilante' and just replace it with weak and fragile.

There are many examples, but we can look at three of the most egregious. In 2020, there was the case of 17-year-old Kyle Rittenhouse, a doughy, potential mass shooter, who, using an AR-15, murdered two unarmed 'Black Lives Matter' protestors (white, but black allies)[228]. A Wisconsin jury, in 2021, acquitted him of their murders[229].

Then, from Texas in 2020, we have the case of Daniel Perry, a man who had signaled on social media his wish to murder innocent BLM protestors. He followed through, using his car to ram innocent protestors, then shoot dead Air Force veteran Garrett Foster, a white man but a black ally. Perry was tried, convicted, and sentenced to 25 years in 2023[230]. Texas Governor Abbott promised to pardon him and in 2024 did so[231].

In New York in 2023, Daniel Penny, a 24-year-old former Marine sergeant, murdered 30-year-old Jordan Neely, a hungry, homeless, mentally challenged black man. The reason for Neely's death sentence? On a crowded subway, he was behaving erratically, and Penny, twice Neely's size, declared himself scared. Then, employing the deadly skills that were only supposed to be used in combat, he extinguished Neely's life with a six-minute chokehold[232]. In December 2024, a New York jury acquitted Penny of negligent homicide.

The 'Base' adulates these 'men', for they confirm a depraved worldview that is washed, rinsed, and repeated by Fox, AM radio, social media, and GOP politicians: straight white men are under attack, and violence is both an acceptable and necessary response.

Trump understands this, and his use of the words "cast out" and "retribution" are both from the Old Testament and steeped in violence[233].

Once again, we must consult our Bible. Matthew 7:12 tells us to "Do to others whatever you would like them to do to you."

The Confederate Taliban aren't hearing this, which is not surprising. H. L. Mencken described Puritanism, the father of fundamentalism, as, "The haunting fear that someone, somewhere, may be happy."[234]

It's a savage truth, but all these fundamentalists are so furious. They are furious that slavery had to end, furious that working people might collaborate towards a better future, furious that women have escaped the clutches of the kitchen, and furious that LGBTQ+ folks even dare to walk the Earth. What makes them most furious, though, is their deep-down horror that all this progress they so despise is as inevitable as the sun rising in the east and setting in the west.

Pastor Desimber Rose Wattleton, author of the book, "The Church Can Go to Hell," gave us an insight into the fundamentalists;

> It's all about control for me. So, when I hear somebody say Christian nationalists, I'm automatically thinking, this is somebody who wants to scrub the entire country down until everybody looks like them, talks like them, thinks like them, walks like them, lives like them, loves like them, prays like them, worship like them, works like them, until it's just a monolith. And that's what I think about when I talk about Christian nationalism.[235]

An important point to note. When they have got through all the other marginalized groups, these fake-Christians will always find straight white men to come for.

I recall the musician, thinker, and activist Frank Zappa speaking about censorship back in 1986 on CNN's Crossfire talk show. Fundamentalists, calling themselves 'Parental Rights Activists', wanted to cancel and censor (never mind that pesky First Amendment) music they didn't like. Zappa drew a throughline from intolerance and censorship to fascism, saying;

> The biggest threat to America today is not communism. It's moving America toward a fascist theocracy[...] When you have a government that prefers a certain moral code derived from a certain religion and that moral code turns into legislation to suit one certain religious point of view, and that code happens to be very, very right wing, almost toward Attila the Hun.[236]

The show's host dismissed it, but it only took thirty years for Mr. Zappa to be proven right. Ironically, it would be CNN, having gifted Trump millions in free political advertising, that would help to usher us towards the times Mr. Zappa warned about.

There are many brilliant books worth reading about the 'leaders' of the Evangelical and fundamentalist far-right by authors like Kristen Kobe Du Mez and Jeff Sharlet. For our purposes, we just need to know that the 'preachers', many of them in their sporting arena-sized megachurches, are all rich GOP-supporting men and all want to rip away your freedoms.

Just like Trump, these wealthy flock-fleecers are all extremely adroit at persuading low-information and poor people to part with their money on the promise of either power, retribution, wealth, or eternal salvation. Don't just take my word for it. I give you the words of theologian Dillon Cruz;

> It's like Jesus Christ Inc? Like an Olstein-like Mega church
> that have smoke machines, coffee shops, they got all these
> Church-o-tainment kind of things, but they're not living out
> Matthew 25. Are they getting out there in the community?
> Are they opening up their church when it's freezing cold
> outside for people who are experiencing homelessness? Are
> they sharing their wealth, like the Acts 2:42-47? They're not
> Jesus. They're kind of like a social club with a Jesus mascot.
> 237

Mr. Cruz was describing the charismatic Prosperity Gospel. This outfit, founded in the late nineteenth century, came to prominence in the 1980s, with the rise of cable television[238].

Today, half of all Protestant churches are prosperity gospel[239]. The con works something like this. The prosperity gospel preacher tells you to work hard, pray, and donate your money to them. They take your money and tell you that God blesses you and will make you rich. If you're not getting rich, you just need to donate more money to God—through them, of course. You may have spotted the disconnect there.

Where the money goes is to people like Texas-based Kenneth Copeland of the Eagle Mountain International Church in the wealthy exurb of Pecan Acres, near Dallas[240]. Copeland, whose net worth is a barely conceivable $750 million, lives in an 18,000 sq. ft (the size of four pro-basketball courts) mansion, set in twenty-four picturesque acres.

Back in 2015, he relayed to his flock—who would be funding this monument to his own decadence—that 'God' had told him to build it. To those who questioned him, he replied;

> You may think that house is too big. You may think it's too grand. I don't care what you think. I heard from heaven. Glory to God, hallelujah![241]

Copeland, speaking in 2019, gave us another gem while defending flying private rather than commercial;

You can't talk to God while flying commercial. You can't manage that today, in this dope-filled world, get in a long tube with a bunch of demons.

Presumably, the line to Heaven is a little less crackly at 40,000 ft in his $10 million Gulfstream V private jet. This was just one of the three 'P.J's' that he owned.[242]

On that occasion, Copeland was speaking to another televangelist, Jesse Duplantis. This slick, Louisiana-based 'man of God,' with a net worth of *only* $20 million, already owned three private jets but was looking for his congregation to stump up the $54 million to pay for a fourth[243].

Many liberals feign amazement at how many, mostly low-income, GOP-voting white folks fall for such a con. Clearly, a lack of education and minimal critical thinking skills are part of the problem, but it is also by design.

Recall, their sources of information are megachurch pastors (getting rich off them), radio hosts (getting rich off them), TV personalities (getting rich off them), and far-right social media podcasters (getting rich off them).

Now imagine a poor rural white man living in Martin County, Eastern Kentucky—a place of 11,500 residents and also ground zero for where President Lyndon Johnson kicked off his 1964 'War on Poverty'—where even though one third of its citizens still live below the poverty line, 91% of its voters went for the GOP in 2024[244]. Maybe he already holds the Calvinist mindset, which teaches that hard work and self-reliance are a necessary path to self-improvement. Those same Calvinist and patriarchal beliefs would have conditioned people like this man over generations not to take 'welfare.' However, they have no problem taking government 'assistance' like Medicaid, Medicare, disability, or SNAP food stamps. To explain a distinction without a difference, those same programs are only called 'welfare' or 'handouts' when used by black or brown folks[245].

Further hypocrisy lies ahead. Despite enjoying government help, many of these poor religious folks won't vote for other government programs that would help their families. But then, why would they need paid family leave when the wife is a traditional stay-at-home housewife? And why do they need free child care when the mom is always at home? And what need would they have of universal health care when God can heal them?

This way of thinking hasn't worked out very well for millions of poor white folks. But that's no worry because the church pastor can just tell them (from his multi-million-dollar mansion) to keep working harder and donate more to Christ (through him).

Only low information and low education can chauffeur people into this mental cul-de-sac, for it's a place where they admire rich people and vote for Republicans. Then, once in office, those Republicans promptly set about slashing taxes on the rich and offsetting them by gutting any government help, such as investments in rural education, healthcare, jobs, and training.

Eagle-eyed readers may have already spotted the cognitive dissonance here—that by giving their money away to the preachers and voting for the Republicans who cut education and opportunity, those same poor people all but guarantee they will always be poor.

Notwithstanding all that, hustling grifters like Copeland and Duplantis appear almost quaint when set alongside the real pit-viper Southern Baptist fundamentalists.

When these creatures, like Jerry Falwell, Pat Robertson, and Jimmy Swaggart,[246] started appearing on our TV screens in the 1980s, they were christened 'televangelists,' and many people thought that they were comically harmless Bible-bashing loonies catering to the ignorant in the Southern Bible Belt. But we ignored, to our future peril, the darkness in these patriarchal preachers' hearts and their disturbing absence of empathy for anyone who might disagree with them.

Not so the GOP and their billionaire donors, who saw a way to harness these demons into an election-winning coalition that would intertwine Christian nationalism with dog-eat-dog capitalism.

At this point, it may not shock you to learn that Southern Baptists, the largest Protestant 'Christian' group in America, with thirteen million members, were pro-slavery and pro-segregation and are anti-woman, anti-abortion, and pro-gun[247].

Today the Southern Baptists have fully embraced the Seven Mountain Mandate (7M)[248]. This is the true 'Project 2025' dream of Christian nationalists. Evil grifters like Mike Johnson, Mike Flynn, Charlie Kirk, and Ted Cruz are all pushing this. With 7M, the Fake Christians seek to take over every aspect of American life, whether religion, family, government, education, media, entertainment, or business.

These characters take us into Old Testament thinking. In this world, a vengeful God offers only the survival of the strongest, and it's a place where the weak die because they are meek. Seen through this fake-Christian looking glass, one can see how easily it all folds into authoritarian thinking.

Just have a look at the signs that you can buy at your local Hobby Lobby store. This is a chain owned by the Trump-loving, far-right fake-Christian, billionaire Green Family. "IF YOU DON'T SUPPORT OUR TROOPS, GET OUT IN FRONT OF THEM" and "VIOLATORS WILL BE SHOT! SURVIVORS WILL BE SHOT AGAIN!"[249]

I'll never meet the Green family, but if I did, I have this for them from the Bible;

If anyone says, "I love God," and hates his brother, he is a liar; for he who does not love his brother whom he has seen cannot love God whom he has not seen.[250]

In her fantastic book Jesus and John Wayne, Kristen Kobes du Mez analyzed the right-wing Christian movement in minute detail. She noted in one section this fascistic bent;

As religious leaders like (Jack) Hyles championed a militant application of patriarchal authority, other conservatives, too, embraced a nostalgic vision of aggressive, even violent masculinity. In this way, militant masculinity linked religious and secular conservatism. In time, the two would become difficult to distinguish.[251]

Leading on from this, in March 2014, Pastor John Koletas of the Grace Baptist Church in Troy, New York, put on a service honoring;

Hunters and gun owners who have been so viciously attacked by the antichristian socialist media and antichristian socialist politicians the last few years. Our country was built with the King James Bible and the gun.[252]

This outfit lives its true values and holds church raffles, where the prize is an AR-15.

In another church, a year later and eight hundred miles away, violence came calling. It was a balmy June evening in Charleston, South Carolina, when a man who doesn't deserve a name opened fire on the worshiping black parishioners of the Emanuel African Methodist Episcopal Church.

The killer had been sitting in the church for over an hour, attending a Bible studies class and at the closing prayer, he calmly pulled out his Glock .45 caliber pistol and started shooting. His gun was loaded with hollow-point bullets, designed to crush on impact and create catastrophic and unsurvivable injuries.

This worthless coward, who would have, quite possibly, been groomed by stochastic terrorists on Fox, AM radio, and social media, would murder nine beautiful, innocent, kind, real Christians. His violence would impact the lives of all the people who loved and cared about them. The true sickness was that it was all intended to cause a backlash amongst the black community that would spark a 'race war.'

Now, I can't say whether the killer was deranged, evil, or both. What I can say is that the response from white evangelical Christians was astonishing, because there was no response. No evangelicals offered to help. No evangelical vigils were held outside the church. No evangelicals offered their churches to worship in. Indeed, the vapid vipers at the National Rifle Association (which, somehow, styles itself a 'Christian' organization) actually *blamed* the victims for not having concealed carry weapons to defend themselves[253].

Violence from fundamentalists isn't just with guns. We should never overlook the horrible power dynamic between dirty, degenerate, and depraved evangelical fundamentalist men and children. In 2024, Trump's 'spiritual' adviser, Roger Morris, admitted raping a twelve-year-old-girl. He described it as "inappropriate sexual behavior with a young lady."

Morris was the pastor at the Texas-based Gateway Church, a megachurch set on a sixty-four-acre site in Southlake, a wealthy exurb of Dallas. Suffice to say, until the media picked up the story, the tens of thousands of weekly parishioners had no issues with having a rapist preach to them.[254]

It's a little-reported fact that evangelical churches have paid out tens of millions of dollars in compensation to victims of abuse and rape[255]. Of course, cognitive dissonance and copious amounts of Ambien allow the flocks to gloss over that inconvenient truth. This is what the hypocrisy of the "Moral Majority" is all about.

It's not just churches. In 2024, the Department of Education fined Jerry Falwell Jr's., 'Liberty' University, based in Lynchburg, Virginia, $14 million for systemically covering up on-campus rapes[256].

Speaking of Falwell Jr. For someone who preaches purity, this "man of God," loves to watch the pool boy service his wife. Now, I don't care what consenting adults do, as long as they aren't hurting anyone. However, I do care that he is an influential, Trump-supporting, democracy-hating, hollow grifter who is putting on a poisonous performance to earn millions.[257]

Unsurprisingly, Jr. was bred from weak stock. His father, Jerry Falwell Sr., was a heathen beast, quoted as saying of more normal, moderate Christians who believed in a forgiving Jesus; "The liberal churches are not only the enemy of God but the enemy of the nation."[258]

In 1985, when decent people were opposing the apartheid regime in South Africa, Falwell Snr. implored "millions of Christians to buy Krugerrands to prop up the regime."[259]

Just to zoom the lens down to a more human level. A lot of fundamentalist families are furious when their children won't conform. I recall the comedian Lisa Curry explaining that conundrum on the Doomscroll Rewind Podcast;

> I think that a big reason I'm not religious is because I was raised Catholic around a bunch of hypocritical Catholics that were just awful, awful people, and just hid behind the Bible. And they're like, I go to church every Sunday. Well, you go to church every Sunday, but you don't donate money to charity, you don't volunteer your time, you're not kind to people, you

say horrible racial slurs, you bully other people in the family. Okay, so you go to church, you're in a cult, great.[260]

Coming back to politics, we saw an unsolvable puzzle at the beginning of the chapter. If a pastor tries to impart some real teachings of Jesus to the flock, they'll just go to another church, where all their biases can be confirmed.

The pastor's conundrum is also the politician's. GOP hacks know that their policies and statements are all lies. But they also know that to get elected, they need to repeat the lies that the base wants to hear. Which reminds me of the words of Pastor Keith Giles, "There are two types of people you should never trust; a politician who tells you how to pray, and a religious leader who tells you who to vote for."[261]

Chapter 7

The Angry: Why Militia Men Should Be Careful What They Wish For.

In July 2024, Dr. Kevin Roberts, president of the Heritage Foundation, said that "We are in the process of the second American Revolution, which will remain bloodless if the left allows it to be."[262]

Heritage is the influential Washington think tank that created 'Project 2025', a blueprint for a fascist theocratic takeover of America in a second Trump term. Roberts is effectively explaining to liberals that if they bow down, they won't be killed. It's the same language the Taliban use in Afghanistan or ISIS in Syria: comply or die.

We know that for most on the far-right, like Roberts, who wish to reach their Gilead State, winning the 2024 election was their preferred way to murder freedom. However, for millions of GOP voters, violence against a 'tyrannical' government is not just acceptable but may also be necessary[263].

Back in 2020, Trump tried to make it happen by stoking up fear and violence, but he was too heavy-handed and transparent. Then, during the Biden administration, these 'patriots' could have tried to *water the tree of liberty* with some more Timothy McVeighs. However, most of them don't actually want to get their hands 'dirty.' As matters transpired, American amnesia, apathy, and a media that sanewashed Trump ensured that in 2024, they didn't need to.

Still, it's worth seeing what the Confederate Taliban's Aryan Wunderland could look like. Straight white men are in charge. Minorities have no power, women obey men, children obey their fathers, there are only two genders, gays are converted, and traitors are executed.

With the foundations set, we can turn off our wild imaginings and view how their forebears sought to order their societies. To start, let's visit the Antebellum South, where the Confederate States of America lasted only five years. The 'Lost Cause' myth painted their defeat as an honorable loss against overwhelming Northern aggression, but basic examination reveals a much simpler truth.

In their leader, Robert Edward Lee, they were burdened with a weak, highly inexperienced, and hugely indecisive man[264]. Lee's designated rank far exceeded his ability not only to command men but also to wage war. Indeed, on his first outing at the Battle of Cheat Mountain in September 1861, he lost half of Virginia, which is how we got the state of West Virginia[265].

Despite Lee's incompetence, during the war, the Confederacy won most of the smaller skirmishes. However, where it mattered, their smaller army was degraded. Out of the five major battles, it won at Bull Run in 1861, drew at Sharpsburg, but lost at Shiloh, Gettysburg, and Vicksburg[266].

To the point of Lee's terrible command. At Gettysburg, even an enthusiastic paintballer would have recognized that charging men up a hill straight into enemy fire was a recipe for losing a lot of troops[267].

However, this is where the Lost Cause BS kicks in. Few people learned that General Lee—who never rose above the rank of colonel in the United States Army—didn't have the intellectual mettle to strategize[268].

It's instructive to compare Lee with General Ulysses S. Grant. Whilst General Grant was also a man with very limited battle experience, he and his troops were fighting for the greatest cause of all; to save America. That being said, while good for morale, it couldn't guarantee victory.

Thankfully, Grant knew how to fight 'total war'[269]. This meant that the intellectually superior future president recognized not just the importance of the battles, but also that he could break the Confederacy by burning their cities, factories, and fields.

All this being said, and even though Lee and his Confederates were outnumbered, victory was still within their reach[270]. Recall that all they wanted was for the United States to recognize their slaveholding Confederacy. To achieve this, it wasn't necessary to defeat the Union. It would have been enough simply to expel them from their eleven states.

This was perfectly achievable if Lee had allowed his fewer troops to grind the larger Union army down with guerrilla warfare[271].

Should you be skeptical, just cast your mind forward one hundred years to the wars in Vietnam and Afghanistan. Those smaller, weaker enemies couldn't defeat the most powerful fighting force human history has ever known. But their guerrilla warfare changed public sentiment in America, forcing US politicians to end the wars and withdraw from those countries.

The same would have been the case back in the 1860s. Without a doubt, white northern opinion would have got tired. Their newspapers and public sentiment would have all questioned why white men were still dying for black people—before demanding a withdrawal from those eleven states. If you want a receipt, just look at how easily northern whites gave up on post-war Reconstruction.

So, the Confederacy is no good. What about some other characters who imagined an Aryan Nirvana? For this, we must broaden our horizons and teleport ourselves back to *Der Fatherland,* circa 1930, where their idol, a skinny, sissified, woman-fearing, opera-loving, rotten-toothed, drug-addicted[272], genocidal maniac ruled the German nation for all of a thousa,.........sorry, I mean ten years.

But didn't he host the Olympic Games in 1936? And didn't an American win four gold medals in the 100m, 200m, relay, and long jump for the USA? I'm sure that their grandpas were cheering the......oh no, why would he cheer for an African-American? Rather than Jesse Owens, Grandpa would have been rooting for the blue-eyed, blond-haired specimen from the *Meister Race,* who came in....fifth[273].

Then, when the Führer started a world war that killed seventy million people, including the extermination of six million Jews (yes, he really did!), 420,000 brave American troops, fighting with our allies, smashed his Aryan army. But rather than be captured and put on trial by the Allies, being a craven coward, he took the cyanide way out. None of this is to forget that his actions destroyed Germany.

We're on a roll here, so let's not stop. Perhaps Mussolini's 1930s fascist Italy is more their scene. Here, we have a man so pathetic his mighty, advanced Italian army couldn't even win a minor war against some tribesmen in Abyssinia without help from Hitler.

Then at the end of the bigger war, this sweaty swine—whose seduction technique consisted of kidnap and rape—received a fitting tribute for decimating Italy when his own people hanged him from a lamppost. 'Il Duce's' reign lasted only twenty years.

This isn't going so well, so perhaps we need to leave Europe and travel somewhere we can 'civilize' the natives. The fragile fools on the far-right love their "Make Zimbabwe Rhodesia Again"[274] baseball caps, so let's just examine that country

Under white minority rule in what was then Rhodesia, 10% of the population ruled over and controlled the resources of the other 90%. Rhodesia in 1980 was a police state, where the white rulers, headed by Prime Minister Ian Smith, had a well-trained army with helicopters, tanks, and fighter jets. Portugal and South Africa (we'll meet them soon) helped their regime, as did some right-wing Americans[275].

So, what awesome power were they battling? Oh yes, some rebels with AK-47's. Yet, despite all the Rhodesian State's firepower, they still lost. No grand conspiracy. They just lost.

This must be getting a bit demoralizing now, but if I may steal your attention for a little longer, we can travel next door to South Africa. In 1990, this was a country with an even larger economy and a far superior military to Rhodesia. It even had nuclear weapons.

In this ethno-nationalist paradise, 20% of the population controlled all the resources. That included gold, silver, platinum, and diamonds. It was here that Elon Musk's rich father was having a ball; after all, where else in the world could a mediocre man 'acquire' the emerald deposits that would help his silver-spoon-fed son become a self-made man?

South Africa was also a strict fundamentalist patriarchal society, where gays were very unwelcome, so people like billionaire Peter Thiel (see Chapter 11), also a resident, ran away. He came to America, where he was free to be a gay man, working to elect the politicians who smash down on other gay men.

In the end, when it came down to it, the Afrikaners, whose Jim Crow-style apartheid state had run since 1948, understood what happened in Rhodesia would happen to them. I know it goes against all the

'Lost Cause' thinking, but South Africa was actually the world's second apartheid state—after America—to relinquish power.

Following democratic elections in 1994, nearly 8% of the population who are both white and African stayed because they saw a prosperous future, working together with black South Africans to make the land they loved better for all its citizens[276].

I know that the Confederate Taliban doesn't like the sound of all that 'people working together', so perhaps we can expand the idea of Aryan to all 'white' people.

To this end, let's include the Slavs. Which takes us to Russia, where the incompetent, kleptocratic Putin is another shining star for them. That's fine, but just tell me five things Russia has invented that we use today or five ideas Russia has given the world (and please don't say 'Communism') since 1980.

I think we have to visit somewhere entirely different to find their ultimate paradise. The truth is, these characters remind me much more of Saudi Arabia. I know they hate 'ragheads,' but hear me out.

This is a rich, monolithic theocracy, where straight men rule. In Saudi, women do exactly as they are told, gays are unseen, and there is no sex on TV or in the movies[277]. The hits just keep on coming, as over there, public executions are normal[278], and the only immigrants are slaves or servants.

There is one proviso: Saudis don't make anything, don't provide us with any culture, and don't offer any useful ideas. But then, nor did Hitler, Mussolini or Ian Smith.

Coming back to the Confederate Taliban's America, you may remember 'Pastor' Joel Webbon of Right-Response Ministries from chapter five. In late 2024, Webbon proposed public executions for women who made 'false' accusations of rape against men. His words were,

#MeToo would end real fast. False accusing, playing the victim when you're actually not? You know how to end that real fast? All you have you do is publicly execute a few women who have lied.[279]

Maybe those are the thoughts of the men who join 'militias.' These are gangs of untrained, fragile men, with names like the Oath Keepers, Three Percenters, and Proud Boys, who roam the streets of America, armed with weapons of war.

In no other Western Educated Industrialized Rich Democracy (WEIRD), could citizens imagine unregulated private armies, with more firepower than police officers, prowling the streets. Perhaps though, folks in Haiti would understand what they were seeing.

For a proportion of the angry in America, including many in those militias, their dream is to stoke a societal collapse leading to a totalitarian government. To understand more about those who would take us on that path to disaster, we have to meet the poster child for the angry: Timothy McVeigh.

This was a man from a reasonable working family who suffered no childhood abuse or trauma, yet chose the path of hate and bitterness early on. We are talking about someone who was willing to pack a ton of explosives into a truck and, on a Wednesday spring morning in April 1995, calmly drive it into downtown Oklahoma City. There, he would park outside the Alfred P. Murrah Federal Building, knowing that there were hundreds of innocent American men, women, and children inside. As McVeigh lit the truck bomb's fuse, the innocents couldn't have known, but many were living their last two minutes on Earth.

McVeigh was true evil, and he was a coward, and to make his point, 168 of those men, women, and children had to die, and 684 more had to suffer life-changing injuries. Imagine the shattering ripple effects; they were moms and dads, and they had moms and dads, and they were sons and daughters, and they had sons and daughters[280].

It brings to memory a line from Jeffrey Toobin's 2023 forensic study of McVeigh and the Oklahoma City bombing, 'Homegrown.' An FBI agent investigating the bombing condensed it all down to seventeen words when he told one of McVeigh's confederates, "You may be at war with your country, but your country is not at war with you."[281]

I wanted to learn about this character to see if there was a genesis moment or inciting incident. McVeigh was born in 1968, just one year before me. Just like me, he might have grown up watching The Six Million Dollar Man, The Dukes of Hazard, or Magnum P.I. He could have gone to the movies and seen Star Wars or Top Gun or listened to Bruce Springsteen, AC/DC, or Depeche Mode on the radio.

McVeigh was a gifted computer programmer who, back in 1984, owned (as did I) a Commodore 64 personal computer[282]. This was four decades ago at the genesis of computing. Had he applied himself, he could have been anything in tech. If that wasn't in his wheelhouse, he loved guns and could have become a firearms instructor or a deer hunting guide. Or he might have trained to become a teacher, firefighter, or police officer. Regardless of whatever career he chose, he was lucky enough to grow up in a wonderful time for straight, male Gen Xers. For someone like him, 'The American Dream' was attainable if he could be bothered to work for it. Instead, this sadistic shell of a man joined the army for the worst possible rationale: he wanted to learn how to destroy the America that offered him the freedom of limitless opportunities.

The question is still, 'Why so angry?' Like many mass shooters and terrorists, McVeigh seemed incapable of forming meaningful friendships and relationships, especially with women. A psychologist who examined him for his trial noted that he was "extremely self-centred and narcissistic."[283]

His 'friend' and co-conspirator Terry Nichols got married, but his wife couldn't put up with him. He ended up taking a mail-order bride from the Philippines, a small, demure woman who could never answer back and, of course, didn't have any of her own money to be independent.

Which gets us to the heart of the issue: entitled, fragile men who think that they are alphas but are actually terrified of the modern world. They are especially resentful of a modern woman who can work, earn money, and make her own choices—one of which might be to not date them or, if married to them, to seek a divorce.

McVeigh dreamed of a civil war, as do his modern contemporaries, but first, he'd have to go through real Americans, like General Mark Milley, the former head of the Joint Chiefs of Staff. He was quoted in January 2021, at the time of the insurrection, as saying;

> They may try, but they're not going to fu**ing succeed. You can't do this without the military. You can't do this without the CIA and the FBI. We're the guys with guns.[284]

Today, the right-wing propaganda machine doesn't care about that. It was the fraudster, coward, and traitor, Steve Bannon, who took time off from conning his listeners to offer some stochastic terrorism;

> Second term kicks off with firing Wray, firing Fauci ... no, I'd put their heads on pikes, right, I'd put them at the two corners of the White House as a warning to federal bureaucrats, you either get with the programme or you're gone.[285]

It doesn't take much for words like that to turn into actual terrorism. Indeed, that encouragement is the motivation for new deranged pseudo-McVeighs, living in their demented Fox/Facebook/right-wing podcast world, to murder fellow Americans.

To this point, the corporate media always mistakenly refer to 'lone wolf attacks', when disaffected, radicalized white men travel to places like Buffalo, El Paso, Jacksonville, or Lewistown, using their beloved AR-15 rifles to rip holes in the bodies of someone else's sons or daughters, or husbands or wives. Yet the aim of these men is always the same: To make us terrified in the shopping center, make us terrified in the church, and make us terrified in the synagogue. In any other country, they are called terrorists.

The demented dream that supremacy promises never works because this is the modern world, and few people want to live in a country that is a cross between the Antebellum South and the Handmaid's Tale. Besides, if fascism was so great, Apple, Boeing, Coca-Cola, and Nike would all be pushing for it.

In closing, I'll leave you with the patriotic words of a great American immigrant who came here to build his dream: Arnold Schwarzenegger, movie star and real Republican, understands how inclusivity is America's great superpower and also that the fastest way to become one of those failed regimes is to divide people by turning citizen against citizen. His words: "There has never been a successful movement based on hate." "Nazis? Losers. The Confederacy? Losers. The Apartheid movement? Losers. I don't want you to be a loser. I don't want you to be weak."[286]

Chapter 8

The Insanely Stupid Who Love Q And Hate Jews

Insanity and stupidity have an unusual relationship. One can be insane, yet not stupid. However, the stupid appear completely untroubled by their proximity to insanity. Should you consider this to be an overly uncharitable observation, then allow me to illuminate my thoughts.

There is a group of people in America today who think that they can't take a vaccine because Bill Gates has put a chip in it, that climate change isn't real, that Jews control the world, that 9/11 was an inside job, and that there is a cabal of Satan-worshiping liberal pedophiles who drink children's blood and run the world. To top it all off, they believe the 2020 election was stolen, and, until Trump's 2024 win, 'patriots' may have needed to spill blood to take the country back from that cabal of elites in order to install him as the leader[287].

Those 'ideas' come from the 2017 QAnon conspiracy theory. This is a completely batshit crazy manufactured pile of nonsense—that millions of gullible people have bought into. According to Pew Research, four out of ten Republican voters have a very favorable view of QAnon[288].

Before the end of the chapter, we will come back to the insane Q crowd, who helped get Trump back into power in 2024, but first we need to understand conspiracies. However, before we understand conspiracies, we need to understand secrets.

The first rule of secrets is that while most of us can keep our own (whether it's adultery, a criminal record, or indebtedness), no one can keep a secret about someone else. Also, I have to separate what are called 'conspiracies' from 'cover-ups,' of which there are many. With the latter, people, either through fear, shame, embarrassment, or profit, compound a crime with a cover-up (see Richard Nixon and Watergate, George W. Bush and the Iraq War, or ExxonMobil and global warming.) But overarching secret conspiracies—sorry, they don't happen.

Just to illustrate the point, would it surprise me if we found out that the novel virus, COVID-19, *accidentally* leaked from the Wuhan Institute of Virology? Then, through shame and the fear of international humiliation, the authoritarian Chinese Communist Party covered it up? No, it would not. Contrastingly, my head would positively explode were evidence to reveal that the virus was released on the instructions of a cabal of the most powerful people in the world. Presumably, these would be the people sitting around two-hundred-foot-long oak tables in fortified country estates, spending their days deciding who the world leaders will be, what the world leaders will say, and where the world leaders will wage the next wars.

But here's the ultimate reason there are no conspiracies: the bigger the secret, the more people want to reveal it. I don't know about you, but if I hear about someone getting a new car, a new job, or even just tittle-tattle, I have to gossip with someone. So, let me assure you, if I were working at Roswell Air Force Base in New Mexico back in 1945 and an alien spacecraft landed (a favorite conspiracy theory)[289], you can be damn sure I couldn't keep it to myself. Just on that last point about the aliens. Let's imagine that the United States military had even the fragment of a thought that extraterrestrial life may have visited or actually be here. The first thing the military-industrial complex would do is to demand a doubling of the military budget. The industrial side would do it for the money, and the military side, to protect us from a potential alien invasion.

What about the moon landings? The conspiracist will tell us they were faked by Hollywood studios. But, again, how could all the people involved in the 'lie' keep it a secret? Also, if Hollywood had such advanced SFX technology to create this fantastic production, why wouldn't those profit-hungry studios—who, today, are looking to replace their actors with AI—be using it in the 1970s to earn billions?[290]

A lot of conspiracists who tell you that the Moon landings never happened will cite as proof the 'fact' that we haven't been back. They are either ignorant of, or choose to ignore, the fact that we have. Men walked on the Moon five more times. The last footprints left were those of Apollo 17 Commander Eugene Cernan on December 13th, 1972[291]. When confronted with this, the fools usually shut up. For the ones who don't, here's a certain way to silence them. Ask them, how come our greatest rivals, the Russians, never cried foul? How come at the height of the Cold War, the Soviet Union allowed themselves to be repeatedly humiliated in the Space Race, yet just kept quiet about it?

In his fabulous 2012 book about how stories make the human condition, 'The Storytelling Animal: How Stories Make Us Human', author Jonathan Gottschall describes the conspiracy theory as such;

> To the conspiratorial mind, shit never just happens. History
> is not just one damned thing after another, and only dopes
> and sheeple believe in coincidences. For this reason, conspira-

cy theories—no matter how many devils they invoke—are always consoling in their simplicity. Bad things do not happen because of a wildly complex swirl of abstract historical and social variables. They happen because bad men live to stalk our happiness. And you can fight, and possibly even defeat, bad men. If you can read the hidden story.[292]

Humans learned to speak about seventy thousand years ago[293]. Initially, information would save our ancestors' lives from disease, crocodiles, or tigers. Those threats have passed, and today, on average, two-thirds of our conversations are gossip[294]. This means that information/gossip has real social value.

Gossiping leads to social acceptance, which can make our lives easier by allowing us not only to bond with our group, but also to form new connections, jobs, and relationships. So it is that today's conspiracy theories are just toxic gossip and a way for mostly scared, insecure, non-critical-thinking people to gain community and acceptance by sharing misinformation and disinformation.

The inability to think critically is the cornerstone of a conspiracy mindset, which always seeks an answer, even if that answer has to be reached by thinking upside down. Invariably, their information will be spoon-fed by bad actors like Trump, Musk, or Russia. Yet, the insane/stupid people are so desperate to make our random world—that's full of people with free will who make their own, good or bad, choices—completely understandable. Thus, for them, there must always be a simple explanation for everything.

If you still have doubts about the stupidity of the conspiracist, remember, many of the people who tell us about 'the cabal' are also the ones who are terrified about 'chips in vaccines' being used to track them. Yet these are the same inane dupes who spend hours each day on their social media apps. Those would be the same apps that track and record their every search in order to build up a data profile of them to sell to advertisers[295]. But, of course, try explaining to the conspiracist that they are the corporations' most credulous rubes, and they will come back and tell you that you're the one who is being controlled. I recall a line that sums their mindset up perfectly: "Informed people sound like insane people to ignorant people."

Many will laugh and dismiss these people as crackpots and idiots. Indeed, they used to be called the 'tin foil hat brigade'. However, gullible and insane people are dangerous, not just to themselves, but to democracy.

On this note, there is an interesting convergence between the far-right and 'wellness' culture. It isn't too complicated to work out; 'Wellness' is a $1.7 billion unregulated alternative health industry; effectively a big con to separate people from their money.

The wellness brigade also shares common cause with anti-government folks in that they think only they know what's best for their and their kids' bodies and minds. These are the 'my body, my choice' crowd, and they don't need the 'government' telling them what to do. That selfishness also translates neatly into a lack of empathy for others.

As a case in point, during COVID, these deniers ran around infecting anyone they came into contact with, and some even killed themselves with their ignorance[296]. Spring forward to today, and they are the same people who would tell a doctor that vaccines don't work, all whilst their unvaccinated kids are at school running around spreading measles[297].

The end result is that many in the wellness crowd, who love alternative medicines, also question authority and distrust institutions. That distrust aligns perfectly with the far-right mindset. As far as alternative medicines go, let me give you a receipt. This is from Medium;

> Hitler, Hess, Himmler, and many other leading Nazis were into alternative medicine, organic and vegetarian diets, homeopathy, anti-vaxxing, and natural healing. Hess, the

deputy Führer, opened a center for alternative medical practices in Dresden in 1934. Himmler, meanwhile, supported alternative medicine — such as using plant extracts to heal cancer — and authorized experiments on prisoners in concentration camps for this research.[298]

In another lesson from history, from the same nation but from a man who may as well have been from a different planet, we have the German theologian, pastor, and anti-Nazi dissident Dietrich Bonhoeffer. He posited that we should be more scared of the stupid than the evil, as they were the ones who supported and elected Hitler. Bonhoeffer was arrested in 1943 for 'crimes' against the Nazi regime (helping to get Jews out of Germany) and executed in 1945[299]. Whilst in prison, he wrote his book 'Letters and Papers from Prison. In it, there were words that could easily have described a Trump supporter;

> In conversation with him, one virtually feels that one is dealing not at all with a person, but with slogans, catchwords and the like that have taken possession of him. He is under a spell, blinded, misused, and abused in his very being. Having thus become a mindless tool, the stupid person will also be capable of any evil and at the same time incapable of seeing that it is evil.[300]

Bonhoeffer uses the thought that we can usually see the truly evil people and at least make some effort to avoid them, yet we give a pass to the stupid ones. He was describing the Confederate Taliban and QAnon seventy years before we knew who they were;

Against stupidity we have no defense. Neither protests nor force can touch it. Reasoning is of no use. Facts that contradict personal prejudices can simply be disbelieved — indeed, the fool can counter by criticizing them, and if they are undeniable, they can just be pushed aside as trivial exceptions. So the fool, as distinct from the scoundrel, is completely self-satisfied. In fact, they can easily become dangerous, as it does not take much to make them aggressive. For that reason, greater caution is called for than with a malicious one. Never again will we try to persuade the stupid person with reasons, for it is senseless and dangerous.[301]

I wanted to understand more about this brilliant man, so I dug a little deeper. In 1930, he spent a year in New York and had contact with, and became friendly with, the pastor of an African-American church. Perhaps seeing the African American experience in America might have helped him to see the evil of the Nazis before many others did[302].

There's an old quote, "History does not repeat itself, but it rhymes,"[303] and so today, the stupid appear to act willingly as moronic pathfinders for the evil. We only have to look at the events of January 6th, 2021, and the fur-coat-wearing, flag face-painted, horned-hat-wearing wellness guru, Jacob Chansley. He was the so-called "QAnon Shaman," who the idiotic corporate media treated as a comical sideshow[304].

On the surface, Chansley was an unemployed, failed actor who lived with his loving mother and wore that same bizarre headwear around his neighborhood. But let's take a moment to truly examine him.

This domestic terrorist was there on that Wednesday afternoon to stop the peaceful transfer of power and strangle democracy. He and his Confederates smashed their way into the Capitol. They beat and murdered police officers, then rampaged through the hallowed halls of the Capitol, seeking congressional representatives to murder. Whilst all this was happening, outside, his co-conspirators built a gallows to execute the Vice President of the United States. Not so comical anymore, is he?

Released from prison halfway through his sentence, did Chansley repent a single word? No. Indeed, this sinister seditionist was plotting to stand for a congressional seat in Arizona in 2024. How Section Three of the Fourteenth Amendment, barring seditionists from holding office, doesn't apply to him, I can't imagine.

Of course, Trump knew his voter base was composed of people just like Chansley: the scared, paranoid, angry, and unthinking. In Nevada in 2016, he would reveal how he really thought about his 'followers,' with the words, "I love the poorly educated."[305]

A kinder person may balk at me using the terms stupid and insane; yet, having separated them from the 'angry', who salivate at the prospect of an authoritarian leader, how else could you describe many of Trump's voters? Having been educated in the richest nation on earth, they have the freedom to learn anything that they want. If these people chose, they could acquaint themselves with the complete compendium of the GOP's attack on working-and middle-class Americans. Yet, instead, in 2024, they happily tootled off to the ballot box to vote for an insurrectionist felon, who explained that he will be a dictator from day one[306].

It puts me in mind of the words of the writer and philosopher Voltaire, from way back in 1765: "Whoever can make you believe absurdities can make you commit atrocities."[307]

To the modern conspiracist, 94-year-old George Soros is an ultimate Jewish bogeyman. The anti-Semitic far-right speaks of 'Soros-funded politicians', and 'Soros-funded prosecutors.'[308] But why? Well, since 1982, Soros has given away over $32 billion (two-thirds of his wealth) to liberal-leaning and democracy-strengthening causes that help battle climate change, provide voter information, and promote civil rights. For the right wing, his socially progressive ideals make him the 'wrong kind of Jew'.

So it is the SWIMPs have drawn him as a larger-than-life Jewish 'Puppet-Master.' Authoritarians like Trump, Putin, and Hungarian Prime Minister Victor Orban—himself the beneficiary of an education at a Soros-funded university—all smash down on Mr. Soros. However, in order to truly understand the animosity, we need to depart one world of insanity and take a trip back in time to enter another.

If your whole religion was predicated on worshiping a Messiah called Jesus Christ, wouldn't it be an inconvenient truth if it were your people who murdered him? Yet, it was the Romans, furious that Jesus preached of an empire bigger than their own, who killed Christ. It was a Roman governor who gave the order, Roman soldiers who arrested him, Roman prison guards who tortured him, and Roman soldiers who crucified him[309].

That the Romans murdered the 'King of the Jews' and the original Christian simply couldn't stand when, just 300 years later, Christianity would become the religion of the Roman Empire. Then, with the founding of the Roman Catholic Church in about 590 AD, Roman Catholics needed to rewrite history. So it would be that they placed a new bogeyman at the center of the plot, and even though Christ was the King of the Jews and Christianity originated from Judaism, it was the Jews who were chosen as the scapegoat.

Thus, three hundred years before the invention of the printing press and the mass distribution of knowledge, the disease of anti-Semitism was born. This from Oxford University;

From the middle of the twelfth century, there was growing antisemitism in England and across Europe. In part, this was fueled by something called the 'blood libel': fabricated allegations that Jews abducted and murdered Christian children for magical rituals. The official stance of the Church slowly shifted from tolerance of Jews to increasing hostility. This influenced the views of ordinary people. Anti-Jewish feeling was also linked to the crusades, which began in 1096. Christians trying to reclaim the holy land (including famous crusading kings like Richard I) increasingly saw Jews as 'Christ-killers', against whom violence could legitimately be used.[310]

Today, most anti-Semitism is concentrated on the 'people pulling the strings' and 'the puppet masters'. The haters caricature Jewish people as being in control of everything from banks to newspapers to movie studios. It is said that every big lie features one grain of truth, which leads us to the explanation of why Jewish names are so prevalent in merchant and investment banks.

To understand, we need to travel back a thousand years, before there were corporations and before there were banks. In these times, the only wealth was in land, and only kings, lords, and princes had that land[311]. Also, back then, there were only three professions of merit: poet, priest, and warrior[312], and none of these were open to Jews, being as they were the people who 'killed' Christ. For the same reason, Jews were also barred from the most common form of work, subsidence farming[313].

One of the few vocations available to Jewish people was the low-status business of money-lending. Originally, they were forced into this by hypocritical Christians, themselves banned from charging interest on loans[314]. So it would be that right up to the beginnings of the limited liability company in the 1600s, finance and money lending were neither a powerful nor a well-paid nor a high-status profession. However, over the past four hundred years, everything changed. Merchants needed merchant bankers, and kings needed finance to conquer far-off lands, like Turtle Island. This is how the people who had the most expertise and experience became the earliest bankers and also why you probably know the names of financial institutions like Rothschild, Goldman Sachs, Salomon Brothers, and Lehman Brothers.

So to those who still think that 'the Jews' control world finance, well, there's a grain of truth to that, as practice makes perfect. As a thought experiment, imagine if your forebears had been bakers, boat builders, or bricklayers for a thousand years; you'd have an encyclopedic knowledge of those professions. Thus, it was that after a thousand years of forced practice, Jewish folks understood finance very well. Alas, from there, for the demonic and the unthinking, it was easy to blame "the Jews" for every problem in society.

Speaking of demonic, it is notable that long before Hitler, Germany was brewing ferocious anti-Jewish sentiment. From historian Gervase Phillips, we learn that the word "anti-Semitism" can be traced back to German anti-Semitic 'thinker' Wilhelm Marr in his writings from 1879.

In something that would echo both the 'eugenics' BS of white supremacists in America in the 1900s and the 2000s nonsense 'replacement theory', Marr moved away from the superstitious thinking about Jewish people to a more scientific thesis. He posited they were coming to replace 'real' Germans. Mr. Phillips offered,

> Marr suggested that the Jewish threat to Germany was racial.
> He said that it was born of their immutable and destructive
> nature, their "tribal peculiarities" and "alien essence"[315].

Nearly half a century before Hitler, Germans were being primed to resent an 'other.' This would all ease the glide path for the Nazis' ascent to power in 1933. As a lesson to America, even though there were only about eight million Nazi Party members in 1945, or 10% of the population, they had an iron grip of fear and total control over that society[316].

Another place where the 'Jew' is scapegoated is in Russia[317]. There, the Russian oligarchs are predominantly Jewish[318]. These oligarchs acquired state-controlled businesses from President Boris Yeltsin in 1990 at give-away prices and, as a result, became fabulously wealthy.

This brings us to President Vladimir Putin. Every conman, like every magician, needs misdirection; the latter in order to perform their magic, and the former in order to perform their theft. So, for Putin, 'The Jews stealing the money' is a good way to distract, deflect, and disorient the Russian population whilst he loots the state treasury and then blames those same "Jews" for the robbery[319].

Just on an instructive contemporary note, that will help with your critical thinking. In 2023, the despicable Hamas launched a terrorist attack in Israel, killing over 1,200 innocent Israelis and kidnapping another 250. All that is inexcusable. What is also reprehensible is that the far-right government of Israel, who had propped up Hamas for years in order to have a visible Palestinian enemy[320], had been alerted to the coming attack. They even had a name for it: "Operation Jericho Wall." Yet, Israeli Prime Minister Benjamin Netanyahu deliberately ignored the warning[321].

Israel also, as far back as 2018, had learned from the Trump administration about the hundreds of millions of dollars that Hamas had all over the world. This was money that was helping to finance their terror, but again, Netanyahu did nothing[322]. Then, after the attacks, instead of hunting the money or surgically striking the Hamas leadership, the Netanyahu government engaged in the mass slaughter of over 40,000 Palestinians, most of them women and children[323].

Here's where we need to employ our critical thinking skills by holding opposing ideas in our minds simultaneously. The first is that Hamas are ultra-conservative religious theocrats, elected in 2006 but who then never left office or allowed new elections. However, Hamas is not the same as ordinary Palestinians who deserve to live in peace in the land, which, until 1948, was theirs. The second is that despite Israel being a region-destabilizing, settler-colonizing, genocidal, Jewish-supremacist, apartheid state[324], it's dangerous, disingenuous, and anti-Semitic to link the extremist government of Israel with either the Israeli people—who also deserve to live in peace in their own land—or, even worse, 'the Jews.'

At this stage, it's useful to understand how the fake Christians of the American far-right, who have no issues about welcoming neo-Nazis into their fold[325], can be so pro-ultra Zionist[326]. Zionism is a far-right Israeli nationalist political ideology invented in the 19th century that is to the polar opposite of the loving faith of Judaism in the same way that fundamentalist Christianity is anti-ethical to the actual teachings of Christ[327].

To explain, fake Christians live in eager anticipation of the second coming of Jesus Christ[328]. For that to come to pass, all Jews must return to the 'promised land' of Israel—obviously, there's no room in this land for any Palestinians. Then, with all the Jews gathered, Israel becomes the staging point for the battle of Armageddon between the antichrist (Satan) and his followers (Arabs, liberals, the UN, etc.). In that war to end all wars, just as Christians sit at the precipice of defeat, Jesus is to return to vanquish the Antichrist. It may not have escaped your attention that with Israel forming the battleground for Armageddon, there probably won't be many Jews left. Indeed, in the story, half of all Jews will perish in the battle, with the other half forced to convert to Christianity. As for the fake Christians, they are to be raptured to heaven to live with Jesus[329].

If you're wondering why the State of Israel is so intertwined with the Republican Party, it's because they see the American fake Christians as 'useful idiots.'[330] For allowing them to believe their end times fairytale,

Israel receives a blank check, a blanket security guarantee, and the ability to act with unchecked impunity against both Palestinians and its Arab neighbors, confident in the certainty that no matter what, America will bail them out.

As the general election loss in 2024 revealed, the Democratic Party has a more complicated relationship with Israel. It walks the political tightrope of a progressive pro-Palestinian base and the 75% of Jewish Americans—who, while supporting liberal policies in America, still may also back Israel and Zionism[331]. The paradox for liberal Jewish Americans is that both fake Christians and far-right Zionist Israelis despise liberal Jews[332].

Parenthetically, this brings us on to how both Republican and Democratic politicians are so cowed by Israel. To explain, we have to meet the lobbying group, the American Israel Public Affairs Committee (AIPAC). This outfit exists to promote ultra-Zionist views. Their massive spending war chest enables them to fund a primary challenge to any Republican or Democrat who dissents from what is de facto the Israeli government's policy positions. As a case in point, during the 2024 presidential election, they spent over $100 million getting Trump elected[333].

All this being said, the criminal Israeli nationalist leader, Netanyahu, who must keep a brutalized Israeli society in a constant state of war in order to win elections and keep himself out of prison[334], is not the same as the worldwide Jewish diaspora, the vast majority of whom are people who have been, and are, great and valued liberal allies and friends.

And you might need some of those friends because, in order to divide and conquer, hate's always got to be hating. So we get the "Great Replacement theory"[335] insanity propagated by Tucker Carlson and other far-right demons. This posits that blacks and Mexicans are "invading us," and they are going to "replace us." However, that appears to afford an awful lot of credit to communities of color that, previously, the far-right had told us were too stupid and childish to be allowed education or voting.

Yet, here they are, able to challenge white supremacy and domination. How can these two contradictions exist?

Ah, well, not so fast, dear reader, for, obviously, the "darkies" couldn't do this on their own. Of course, they had to have had help. Enter stage left, 'The Jews.' Once again, the most oppressed people in human history have been painted in the role of the "puppet masters," pulling the strings by organizing and financing this 'invasion.'

The far-right is useless at making people's lives better, but in twisted anti-logic, they reign supreme. The sublime, yet chilling depravity of their 'replacement theory' comes in putting all their enemies in one basket. They even stratify them into the level of threat posed, with the blacks at the bottom and the Jews at the top.

Suffice to say, this total bullshit is actually called biology and demographics. If the far-right wanted white women in Oklahoma, Ohio, or Oregon to have more babies, then they could just help to make their lives better. Perhaps give them great education, decent-paying jobs, and fine healthcare. But of course, that costs money, which means the unthinkable: raising taxes on their rich donors.

All this brings us full circle to a place where hate, religion, and conspiracy move in together; QAnon. Remember, nearly half the Republican party buy into this BS because, as you have just read, it fits with their fake-Christian worldview.

Ed Stetzer, an evangelical pastor and executive director of the Wheaton College Billy Graham Center, offered us this;

> People of faith believe there is a divine plan — that there are forces of good and forces of evil at work in the world,". "QAnon is a train that runs on the tracks that religion has already put in place.[336]

I'm not confident that many of these people can ever get out of this dystopia. Samuel Perry, a professor of sociology at the University of Oklahoma, gives us a receipt for this;

> I'm actually not surprised that evangelicals are more likely to believe those kinds of things,"_"Evangelicals are not socially isolated, but they are informationally isolated.[337]

However, to end on a slightly more hopeful note. If someone you love has fallen down the rabbit hole, but you think they can be reached, fortunately, there is a way to cure them. I will not say that it will be a fast process, but you can fight insane ignorance with basic critical thinking.

Say you have a relative who doesn't believe in climate change. Never judge them or shout at them. Instead, just get a piece of paper and ask them to rate, out of 10, their knowledge of the subject. Invariably, confidence will confuse itself with competence, and it will come back as a 7/10 or 8/10, but don't worry.

Next, ask them to write as much as they can about climate change on that piece of paper. They may manage two paragraphs of gibberish. After that, ask them again to note down their knowledge of the topic. You may find that it has fallen to 3/10 or 4/10.

This was the key, for they have done the most important part of de-radicalization for you by admitting their ignorance, all without you judging or humiliating them. Now, they are ready to learn.

This works for anything, whether slavery, 'woke,' CRT, taxation on the rich, gun safety, or elections. I'll offer a small proviso: part of the process is to get them to stop watching the disinformation of the right-wing fake news. After all, if they go back, the cult can entrap them all over again.

Chapter 9

Killer Foxes, Useful Idiots, and Millions of Melted MAGA Minds.

To appeal to many Republican voters, there is a blueprint that long pre-dates Trump and social media. This is from a report detailing the traits of the right-wing messenger;

> His primary rules were: never allow the public to cool off; never admit a fault or wrong; never concede that there may be some good in your enemy; never leave room for alternatives; never accept blame; concentrate on one enemy at a time and blame him for everything that goes wrong; people will believe a big lie sooner than a little one; and if you repeat it frequently enough people will sooner or later believe it.[338]

Far-right devils like Newt Gingrich have used this style of messaging since the early 1990s. However, nothing turbocharged it faster than Fox News. Launched in 1996 by billionaire chaos agent Rupert Murdoch, Fox is a full-time disinformation machine. This is no accident, as it was designed from the ground up to infect viewers' minds with anger and fear[339].

To understand how insidiously toxic Fox has been to America, we need to meet Tucker Carlson. Between 2016 and 2023, he represented the apex of the MAGA messenger and understood everything in that first paragraph. This satanic grifter was paid ten million dollars a year[340] to ply mindless, daily, 'own-the-libs" fear and panic that masqueraded as news and opinion.

Few people symbolize the hate, hypocrisy, and shamelessness of the Confederate Taliban as much as this weak, insincere fool. Lies and disinformation would trip over themselves as they stampeded out of his mouth. This lasted right up to his humiliating termination from Fox in April 2023, after costing his boss, Murdoch, $787.5 million for lies told about Dominion Voting Systems and the 2020 election.

When talking to conservative radio presenter Dave Rubin in 2021, Carlson let the mask slip on his own craven and depraved immorality: "I mean, I lie if I'm really cornered or something."[341]

For anyone with a modicum of critical thinking skills, he is a bullshit artist, but not so for Fox viewers. To them, Carlson acted as a mirror for their own biases and a projector for their fear and anger. Every night, they would hear the music of hate from the Fox choir: *Blacks are getting away with it. Crime is out of control. Teachers are turning kids trans. Democrats are plotting to confiscate your guns, and black and brown people are coming to replace you.*

For his asinine viewers, Carlson claimed to be a *'truth-seeker'*, who was 'just asking questions.' Yet, when sued for his lies, a Trump-appointed Judge credited Fox viewers with more intelligence than they warranted, saying: ".... given Mr. Carlson's reputation, any reasonable viewer 'arrive[s] with an appropriate amount of skepticism' about the statement he makes."[342]

In 2023, internal Fox emails, shared as part of the discovery process in the Dominion lawsuit, showed what Fox hosts really thought. One mail from January 2021, the time of the J6 terrorist attack on the Capitol, revealed that the off-screen Carlson understood Trump's true nature perfectly well:

"Destroying things. He's the undisputed world champion of that. He could easily destroy us if we play it wrong."[343]

Another of Carlson's messages from that same month read, "We are very, very close to being able to ignore Trump most nights. I truly can't wait. I hate him passionately."[344]

All this from the man who had publicly done as much as anyone else since 2016 to enable and grow the Trump brand. However, there's an immutable law of wimpish SWIMPs. Those who punch down will always kiss up. Thus, being a fragile, insecure coward, he would have Trump back on air just a couple of months later, as if nothing had happened.

Carlson represents a silver-spoon-fed third-rate mediocrity. In his younger days, he applied to join the CIA, but as you can see, this spineless fool is wholly incapable of holding one sensible thought in his head and presumably wasn't bright enough to pass the entrance exam[345]. Following that, he tried to make it on mainstream cable TV, however, there he was just one among many bland talking heads. Probably resentful of the 'establishment' that denied his mediocrity a chance to float to the top, he chose instead to burn it down. His opportunity would come when he moved to Fox in 2009[346].

We know that Fox hosts are preaching to a satanic flock, as anti-reality people never want to hear about reality. As regards those viewers, Carlson had the most popular show on cable TV at around four million viewers, but the question for me is, who was in charge? Over the years, the 'base' has been programmed with the lies—that many are very comfortable with—but now, they are so radicalized, all they want to hear about are the 'red meat' cultural issues. Former Republican political strategist Tim Miller would explain this, using the term 'Rage Juice';

> Rage juice is the drug — hate of your perceived enemies and
> people that aren't like you. I think that it is very similar to

drug use, especially in the digital age.. Every time you open your computer on Facebook, you want to get mad at what those other guys are doing to you, you want to be outraged at how they're trying to take something away from you that you want. You want to feel righteous about the fact that your evil fellow countrymen are doing something that goes against your worldview, your moral framework.[347]

One might imagine that it must be exhausting to be so enthused by enragement, but this is the design, and it's straight out of the authoritarian's playbook. That opening paragraph wasn't written about Carlson or even Trump. It was from an OSS (the original CIA) psychological report on Adolf Hitler in 1943.

For years, on Fox, the jelly-spined Carlson vented fury at black people and the LGBTQ+ community. Indeed, after the largest protests in American history, in 2020, he denied they were real, offering to his viewers some nonsense about it being an 'antifa' stunt.[348] Then, more than anyone else, he promoted the quasi-fascist 'Replacement Theory', that Jews are importing black and brown folks to replace white Americans.

As a stochastic terrorist, it could be said, given the reach and influence on the far-right of Fox, there is a lot of blood on his hands. The white-supremacist domestic terrorist attacks that took place in 2018 at the Tree of Life Synagogue in Pittsburgh (eleven killed), in 2019 at the El Paso Walmart (twenty-three killed), and in 2022 at Top Friendly Market in Buffalo (ten killed) can all be traced back, in part, to rhetoric from him and people like him[349].

At this point, I want to take you into the world of indulgent immorality in which the multi-millionaire hosts and billionaire owner of Fox live. For this, we have to go back to 2021, when almost all the hosts, including Carlson, were spreading lie after lie about COVID and the vaccine.

While lies spewed out of their mouths, all the on-air 'talent' were triple vaccinated[350]. Indeed, Fox News, ironically, had an even stricter vaccine mandate than the federal government. This was demanded by Fox's owner, then eighty-nine-year-old Rupert Murdoch—for whom every day is a gift—and who was rightly terrified of contracting COVID.

Indeed, so eager to be safe was this Australian billionaire with an American passport that he traveled to England in December 2020, where he got inoculated just eight days after the release of the first vaccine[351].

Yet, back in America, Carlson and his Fox pals were busily telling their viewers not to get vaccinated[352]. The result was predictable: mass death in red states amongst the Fox News-viewing audience[353].

For those viewers the network didn't kill, throughout most of President Joe Biden's term, they have been conditioned to see "The Biden Crime Family." Somehow, Joe was both a doddering, senile fool but also the Capo dei Capi—'boss of bosses'. Colluding with his son, Hunter, and the 'Deep State', he was systematically stealing *God-given American freedom.*

The right-wing smear was all part of a Russian-sponsored criminal influence campaign[354], parroted by Putin's useful idiots on the American far-right. Its purpose and design were to demean and disparage the reputation of a decent president in order to bring him down to the gutter level of their treasonous fraudster[355].

As hypocrisy is a gift that keeps on giving, we can take ourselves back to 2014, when Joe Biden was Vice President. At the time, Carlson lived in Georgetown, Washington. This is the very beating heart of the liberal elite establishment. He told the Washington Post that, "Hunter Biden was my neighbor. Our wives were friends. I knew him well."

So well, in fact, that he asked Hunter to write a letter of recommendation to help Carlson's nepo-baby son get into Washington's elite Georgetown University. Carlson's wife Susie, would write to Biden, "Tucker and I have the greatest respect and admiration for you. Always!"[356]

I will bet everything I own no Fox viewers knew that Carlson and Hunter were neighbors and pals. There again, as we have seen, people like Carlson knew many of their viewers didn't want the truth. So it was that when Fox tried to tell them the reality that Joe Biden won the 2020 election, they switched channels to Newsmax and OANN.

This was a nightmare for Fox, as fewer viewers meant a lower stock price, which takes us back to that apex predator of chaos, Rupert Murdoch. We get a window into his demented mind when, on seeing viewers desert his network, he had a choice: American democracy or the Fox stock price. I can do no better than give you his words, "It is not red or blue, it is green."[357]

After Murdoch threw him out for costing him nearly a billion dollars in damages, Carlson set up a low-energy show on Mad Musk's Twitter. There, finally, he could slip his mask off and discard any pretense of being a normal human. One of his first tasks was to tootle off to Moscow to interview the war criminal and SWIMP daddy, President Putin.

Just to note, for the Russian government, Carlson and Fox represent terrifically useful idiots, with their anti-American treachery repeated night after night as propaganda on Russian state TV[358].

During his interview, Putin, while not the brightest man on the planet, could still intuit the diminished level of intellect sitting opposite him, but much more importantly, immediately recognized a Zeta male.

Knowing about Carlson's failure to be recruited by the CIA, the Russian leader mocked him with the words, "It is a serious organization. I unders tand."[359]. Putin could be confident that, even if the dimwitted, weak child understood the sarcasm, he'd be terrified to answer his SWIMP Daddy back.

Just to finish up back at Fox. I predict that there is a tsunami of mental illness in their viewers waiting to erupt. In the near term, some will kill themselves, some have killed others, but for many of the rest, the overall effect of being fed a constant stream of misinformation and disinformation will be family estrangement, early-onset dementia, and other mental illnesses.

This gets to the heart of why people like Carlson are so evil. It's precisely because, above all else, he is performing. As such, he sits in the pantheon of cowardly, cancerous chauvinists alongside other right-wing fiends like Alex Jones and Matt Walsh.

To back up my theory, I'd submit that if we cut off their salaries and ended their YouTube and Twitter monetization, then the satanic seditionists would shut up and crawl back to whatever rocks they live under.

On a more biological level, despite the apoplectic rage they have offered daily for over eight years, none of these men appear to have had strokes or heart attacks. If they *really* believed what they were saying, a 'devil's cocktail' of cortisol and adrenaline would surge through their bodies, and their blood pressures would be off the charts. It's not, because these are performers playing a demonic fascist role for money and status.

Absent the political context, these degenerates probably wouldn't matter so much. But as it is, their poisonous hate and lies encapsulate the malignant power to destroy America.

Chapter 10

A Little Bit Of Knowledge Is A Very Dangerous Thing.

Y ou may wonder what education has to do with all this. Well, with fifty-four million children in K-12 and another eighteen million in higher education, that's the entire American youth population, or one in every five Americans, waiting to be made compliant.

To this point, today, for the Confederate Taliban, educated children are a nightmare. After all, these kids may grow up to actually question the dominating patriarchal system, and heavens forbid, dare to vote the GOP out of office. Back in 1970, after anti-war protests on college campuses, Roger Freeman, Ronald Reagan's Education Advisor, knew the score and offered this;

> We are in danger of producing an educated proletariat. ... That's dynamite! We have to be selective on who we allow [to go to college].[360]

To have children taught about evolution, slavery, inequality, and the patriarchal system that keeps it all in place is very vexing. So it is that the far-right push for the "school choice" narrative that parents should be able to homeschool or send their kids to a state-funded church school for the best indoctrination.

By 2023, it wouldn't just be fake-Christian schools that were brainwashing their pupils. Meet PragerU (*not* a university). Founded by right-wing talk-radio host Dennis Prager, their purpose is to brainwash kids with right-wing ideas. If your child lives in Arizona, Florida, Louisiana, Montana, New Hampshire, or Oklahoma[361], this outfit is the approved supplier for school information to help create unquestioning and unthinking citizens. In an alternate universe, some of these titles could be headlines from the satirical Onion website:

Do 97% of Climate Scientist's Really Agree?

Fossil Fuels. Greener Than You Think.

Why You Should Love Fossil Fuel.

The Biggest Bully in school.

Why Public Education is Failing America.

A Short History of Slavery by Candace Owens.

Discipline = Freedom.[362]

The largest donors to PragerU are a pair of fake-Christian billionaire brothers, Dan and Farris Wilks. These two started out as small-town Texas preachers. Then, thanks to the US government-funded fracking revolution, they founded FracTec and got very rich, pocketing $3.5 billion when they sold it in 2012.

They differ from someone like GOP mega-donor Charles Koch of Koch Industries[363]. Charles is focused on ridding himself of government regulation so that his business can pollute more and make more profit. Charles's end is always MONEY.

The Wilks brothers are very different. As the owners of one of the most influential right-wing disinformation sites, The Daily Wire, they prop up shouty sock puppets like Ben Shapiro and Candace Owens, who earn their money by spreading disinformation around the world and poisoning minds[364]. Additionally, through their Thirteen Foundation, the brothers use their vast fortune purely to mainstream far-right Christian theocracy[365].

For these ultra-rich, fake-Christian freaks, 'faith' is their driving force. Faris is on record as having imparted this nugget of wisdom on climate change;

> We didn't create the Earth, so how could we ever save the Earth, or save all the animals even on the Earth, or save the polar caps? [366]

Faris isn't too keen on women choosing what to do with their own bodies either;

> We lament and mourn the great sin of our nation, the many millions of babies murdered, and we pray that you turn these people away from this evil.[367]

The satanic hits just keep on dropping. According to Faris, homosexuality (sorry, Peter Theil), is;

> a perversion tantamount to bestiality, pedophilia and incest...It's a predatorial lifestyle in that they need your children, and straight people having kids, to fulfill their sexual habits.

If I ever met these characters, I would offer just four words of advice: Read the goddamn Bible!!

The next-largest donor to PragerU is the Lynde and Harry Bradley Foundation. Harry Bradley was one of the founding members of the far-right John Birch Society. The Foundation is involved in all the old favorites like climate change denial, voter suppression, election denial, and anti-civil rights actions[368]. They are also big funders of the extraordinarily effective far-right lobbying group, the American Legislative Exchange Council (ALEC)[369] to push all this through state legislatures.

The point of looking at those two (out of many others) was to show that the anti-freedom far-right has money, power, and influence, and they are ready, willing, and able to use it to turn back progress.

To understand the historical context for the war on education, we need to travel back in time to the Reconstruction era after the Civil War. Envisioned by President Lincoln and implemented by his successor, President Andrew Johnson, it aimed to combat the deep-rooted hate that could spread if left unchecked, yet northerners soon grew weary of protecting black southern citizens. They didn't want to, or were incapable of seeing that the traitors never stopped fighting. This is why the vast majority of Confederate monuments to treason were erected long after the war[370].

Their purpose was to remind black people to *know their place*. Even military bases were named after the traitors who rebelled against the United States: Fort Hood, Fort Benning, and Fort Bragg. All are being changed in 2024. However, the fact remains, there isn't one country in the industrialized world with military bases named and monuments erected to honor the *losing* side, especially when that losing side started the war.

It's that 'Lost Cause' thinking that explains why the Florida school curriculum in 2024 sees the 'good' side of slavery[371]. But to find its genesis, we need to travel back to 1894, thirty years after the Civil War, and meet the United Daughters of the Confederacy.

The UDC had five key aims: historical, benevolent, educational—this gives it tax-exempt status, so taxpayers are footing the bill for their propaganda[372]—, memorial, and patriotic. In its heyday, the organization was about 100,000 members strong, but today it's hovers around 25,000. Of course, today they don't need a huge membership because all their ideas are mainstream GOP[373].

From the excellent 'Facing South' website, we get to learn much more about the UDC. Speaking at the turn of the 20th century, the UDC president, Mrs. James A. Rounsaville, defined the true meaning of their deviant agenda;

> It has ever been the cherished purpose of the Daughters of the Confederacy to secure greater educational opportunities for Confederate children, and by thorough training of their powers of mind, heart and hand, render it possible for these representatives of our Southern race to retain for that race its supremacy in its own land.[374]

Indeed, over the years, hundreds of monuments and statues to treason have been erected with UDC money, as well as tens of thousands of flags and Confederate portraits in schools and state legislatures[375], but there's much more.

Post-Reconstruction, the UDC knew that if they could indoctrinate children, those children would grow into compliant and complicit adults. The UDC needed schools to teach children a 'Lost Cause' lie and to discard reality. To achieve this, it would be necessary to make them ignorant of true American history. More of the UDC's unholy plan was revealed in the words of their North Carolina Division President, Mrs. I.W. Faison, speaking in 1909;

> We must see that the correct history is taught our children and train them.... in knowledge of true history of the South in the war between the States and the causes that led up to the war ... There is an expression often used by our people as the "Lost Cause." Let us forget such, for it is not the truth. ...No, our cause was not lost because it was not wrong.[376]

The group's 'historian' between 1911 and 1916 was one Mildred Lewis Rutherford. This OG book banner can enlighten you from her tract, "By A Measuring Rod to Test Text Books, and Reference Books in Schools, Colleges and Libraries";

> Using its considerable political clout, the North Carolina Division also secured Gov. Robert B. Glenn's assurances that he would appoint only Lost Cause loyalists to the new textbook commission. By 1916, the Division itself was reviewing history textbooks and sending their written reviews, approvals, and rejections directly to the state textbook commission.[377]

Propaganda in literature and on film would also be an ally to the ideas of the UDC. "Gone with the Wind" was a novel that paints a romantic picture of slavery and the Civil War period. The word 'ni**er' is mentioned sixty-five times. Margaret Mitchell, the author, described the slaves as being happy to be slaves, and black people, she opined, were too stupid to be free.

As a piece of propaganda for the 'Lost Cause', it matches everything done by the United Daughters of the Confederacy in feeding into Americans' minds the notion that this was not a rebellion but an honorable war of equals: a Union and a Confederacy. With the bar for stupidity set this low, it might not surprise you to learn that Mitchell was ten before she even discovered that the Confederates had lost the war.[378]

To that exact point, between 1889 and 1969, the era of Jim Crow, successive generations of white American school pupils were gaslit to buy into the lies that were the foundation of the 'Lost Cause'. These were the boys and girls who would grow into the fathers and mothers who would keep alive attitudes that should have long been consigned to the dustbin of history.

Thankfully, not all were infected. I'm reminded of some words from one of those pupils; "Books and ideas are the most effective weapons against intolerance and ignorance."[379] That was from Lyndon Johnson, born a poor Texan, but who showed attitudes far ahead of his time and who would enact some of the most significant legislation of the twentieth century. Today LBJ is long gone, but his spirit must be mourning the state of his home state.

Texas is one of the largest purchasers of school textbooks. Indeed, books from Texas are sent to schools across the South. In order to win the lucrative contracts to supply books to the state, publishers will, out of self-interest, self-censor.

Up until 2015, McGraw-Hill published a book called 'World Geography' that described the slave trade as such:

> The Atlantic Slave Trade between the 1500s and 1800s brought millions of workers from Africa to the southern United States to work on agricultural plantations.[380]

Note the subtlety of the word "workers"; not kidnapped and trafficked human slaves. Now imagine being a black pupil in Houston or Savannah who has to learn these lies.

Here's Prentice Hall Classics, 'A History of the United States.' This trash was used across the South, even up to 2019. It whimsically opined on the subject of slaveholders and their slaves: "a few [slaves] never felt the lash," and "many may not have even been terribly unhappy with their lot, for they knew no other."[381]

It would be reassuring to think that the arc of history would bend towards progress, and that these books would be edited to reflect actual history. Unfortunately, in May 2023, Florida, in common with other former Confederate states, sought to sanction teachers for teaching the truth. Indeed, school exams in the Sunshine State featured questions where 'slaves' have a new Orwellian title: 'forced servants.'[382]

If you still think that the Confederates didn't win the peace, just reflect on the fact that it is illegal in Florida for the teacher to deviate from these prescribed words. So it is that for the 2024 curriculum, middle school pupils are being asked to consider whether "slaves developed skills that, in some instances, could be applied for their personal benefit."[383]

The censorship doesn't just happen in the textbooks; it's in the number of books removed from schools. Across America, over 4240 books, including To Kill a Mockingbird and Lord of the Flies, were banned in 2023[384]. Just to note, books are not banned in Australia, Canada, England, or any other functioning democracy. Indeed, you can buy a copy of "Mein Kampf" in Germany.

The false argument for censorship, put forward by many right-wingers, is that it may make children feel 'uncomfortable' to learn about bad things.

For the far-right, here's a newsflash: children *don't* get scared; quite the opposite, they love being scared. As pre-K children, they read books that feature dragons and serpents and trolls. They may even read Jack and the Beanstalk. It's a story about a thief and murderer (Jack). One of the lines is

> Fee-fi-fo-fum, I smell the blood of an Englishman. Be he alive, or be he dead, I'll grind his bones to make my bread! 385

When I went to school, we learned about wars, revolutions, famines, and terror, and I don't know anyone with trauma from that. Hell, the Bible is one of the most violent books of horror stories ever written; incest, rape, murder, and the end of times. Of course, the far-right is not troubled by that, though. Their concern is with kids learning actual factual American history (and science and sex-ed,) then coming home and asking some difficult questions.

History does offer us a warning here. Back in 1821, the German-Jewish poet Heinrich Heine wrote about the burning of books for political or religious reasons; "That was but a prelude; where they burn books, they will ultimately burn people also."[386] His words would prove chillingly prophetic. When the Nazis came a hundred years later, they started burning books first, including Heine's, before moving on to burning people. Come forward to 2024 America and GOP candidates cheerily film campaign videos of them also burning books[387].

The fact is that we don't learn enough history. How many American students are going to learn that, before 1929, the Nazi party had no shot at power in Germany? They couldn't win over enough working-class people, who instead voted socialist and communist. That would all change with the Wall Street rash of October 1929.

After successive Republican presidents' 'laissez-faire' free-market economic policies collapsed the US economy, propelling America and the world into the Great Depression. This was terrible news for most nations, but what made it worse for Germany was the immediate recall of American loans that had helped them make the post-World War One reparations payments[388]. From this pit of economic despair, enough Germans grew disillusioned and moved to support Hitler's party. So it would be that the Nazis grew from twelve of the six hundred seats in the German parliament, the Reichstag, in 1928, to two hundred and thirty seats in 1932[389].

In previous chapters, we saw how Hitler was the greatest admirer of segregation and the methods by which America had used the law to prop up Jim Crow in the South. However, you wouldn't have learned that in school. Nor would anyone have taught you that at the El Paso border crossing, guards used Zyclon B to "de-louse" Mexican immigrants coming into the USA. That same Zyclon B was later used to exterminate Jewish people in the Nazi gas chambers[390].

However, unlike totalitarian regimes like Russia or China, we can learn these facts. One should never lose track of the fact that it's a mark of a great society to recognize and confront the mistakes of the past and make amends. This leads me to think of the phrase that describes the Confederate Taliban's worldview: 'The Future is the Past.' The phenomenon was described by Svetlana Boym in her 2001 book, 'The Future of Nostalgia.'

In essence, remembering can take two forms: restorative and reflective. Authoritarians like Trump revere 'restorative nostalgia': restoring the SWIMPs to their 'rightful place' over everyone else. This is as opposed to the harmless 'reminiscing nostalgia': looking at old photos or recalling happy memories of concerts, parties, pets, or other experiences that make up the tapestry of our lives[391].

It's no coincidence that restorative nostalgia is the norm in China, Hungary, Russia, and other countries whose rulers are terrified of real education and petrified that their people will wake up and want to make choices for their lives that are informed by reason and fact. George Orwell wrote a chillingly prophetic line about this type of control in his masterpiece 1984: "Who controls the past controls the future. Who controls the present controls the past."[392]

To bring things right up to date, nearly sixty years after the Civil Rights Act, the billionaire-funded far-right dragged out a new boogeyman: CRT or Critical Race Theory. With the complicity of their stooges in the unquestioning corporate media, they sold this bill of goods as 'Marxist' indoctrination of little Timmy's and Tabatha's.

Opposing CRT came about in 2020, not surprisingly, as a far-right backlash to the real public anger at George Floyd's murder and the numerous police killings of unarmed black folks.

The creator of the manufactured outrage was a right-wing ghoul, Christopher Rufo. Being a weak, vacant vessel of hate, he freely admitted that 'Critical Race Theory' was 'the perfect villain.'[393] He might have added *to scare white folks and get them to vote Republican.*

CRT is a complicated but true legal theory taught at universities. It posits that America was built from the ground up with race in mind. The theory explains everything from gerrymandering and voter suppression to how black people were excluded from the 1950s suburbs and 'redlined' into the poorest neighborhoods. It also shows how, even up to today, people of color face higher interest rates on loans and receive lower valuations on their properties[394].

These are all empirical and uncomfortable facts. However, if one studies it further, we get to the heart of the issue. In its final distilled essence, CRT postulates that black people can only progress when white people also progress.

Real educational scholars tried to get Rufo into a debate about what CRT actually meant, but they missed the point. Speaking at the far-right Claremont Institute, Rufo felt free to take off his fake-scholarly mask, saying, "I don't give a shit about this stuff." [395] And in doing so, he revealed the truth about every far-right, bullshit, three-letter manufactured 'outrage.'

Chapter 11

Think Upside Down To Understand The Confederate Taliban

Perhaps fifty years in the future, historians may look back and think that we had too much freedom rather than too little. But then, the word 'freedom' means different things to different people.

It was George Lakoff, the visionary linguistics professor at the University of California at Berkeley and author of "Don't Think of an Elephant," who showed twenty years ago how the far-right was co-opting the word. Democrats didn't listen, so today the Confederate Taliban are always banging on about it.

For them, it's freedom to say anything they want without challenge, freedom to control women, freedom to carry a gun anywhere, freedom to intimidate, freedom to be unvaccinated, freedom to pollute, freedom from taxes, freedom to stop people from voting, and freedom to be uneducated. It sounds insane, yet that insanity is their reality.

Now, let's look at some freedoms Democrats want you to have: freedom to control what happens to your own body, freedom to vote, freedom to speak truth to power, freedom to be who you want to be, freedom to be healthy, freedom to breathe clean air, freedom to be educated, and freedom from guns.

Noting all you just read, it is a precondition of being in the Confederate Taliban that you must have no integrity, no sincerity, and no shame. As upside-down thinking is their method of gaslighting people, the solution is to take everything they say or do and turn it around, and then you will arrive at the truth.

So it is that they cut government spending while telling you that government doesn't work. They talk about 'election integrity' whilst making it harder and harder to vote. They talk about 'family values' whilst stealing a woman's freedom to choose. They talk about looking out for Americans whilst they cut social programs. They talk about Marxism whilst banning thousands of books. They talk about groomers while they are grooming children. And they welcome neo-Nazis while they accuse Democrats of anti-Semitism.

The zero-integrity party speaks about freedom, yet, come election time, when we, 'the people,' tried to vote them out of office, their supporters stormed the Capitol to kill our democracy. Yet, all the while, they tell us we are the 'snowflakes' and the 'woke' and the 'sensitive.'

These are the same performative hypocrites who used to talk about 'limited government.' Now they want the government in your bedroom, checking for contraception; in your boardroom, making sure that you're not trying to win a wider audience for your products; and in your kid's classroom, to make sure they aren't getting too knowledgeable about the history of their nation.

For the far-right, alongside 'freedom,' they whine about their 'rights,' but what they never, ever talk about are their responsibilities. In their world of domination, they say, and you do, and if you say, they just invoke their Second Amendment rights, and you won't do anymore.

To the point of whether MAGA is a cult, former governor of Alaska and 2008 vice-presidential candidate Sarah Palin, never the sharpest knife in the drawer, speaking to the far-right Newsmax, argued that it wasn't when she gave this answer;

The definition of a cult, is a group of people who are excessively supporting one another and a cause. [It's] all about conformity and compliance and intolerance of anyone who doesn't agree with what their mission is.[396]

She made the liberal case better than most liberals, but in the Confederate Taliban's upside-down world, this doesn't matter, as they think it is liberals who are in a cult. This despite their donning fake ear bandages at the 2024 GOP convention to mimic the cult leader, who was wearing one after an assassination attempt.

To disabuse readers of the notion that insane stupidity lives only among the followers, we can cast our gaze over the 22nd richest man in the world[397], fossil fuel king and EPA hater, Charles Koch of Koch Industries. Charles (with his late brother David) was the founder of Americans For Prosperity, a far-right organization dedicated to slashing the federal government that has spent billion of dollars funding Republican candidates and lawsuits against the government[398].

In his brilliant 2022 book cataloging the GOP's slow descent into madness, "American Psychosis: A Historical Investigation of How the Republican Party Went Crazy", political journalist David Corn writes about the Koch Brothers-funded Tea Party (pre-MAGA) loonies at a rally hosted by far-right agitator Michelle Bachmann;

Several thousand heeded her call and flocked to a protest outside Congress. (Many attendees had been bused in by Americans for Prosperity, a conservative organization started by the Koch Brothers.) They carried signs depicting Obama as Sambo. One placard said OBAMA TAKES HIS ORDERS FROM THE ROTHSCHILDS—a new take on a persistent antisemitic trope. There were posters referencing birtheris m.[399]

To see how much Mr Koch learned, we can skip forward fourteen years to 2023, with the New York Times reporting that officials in 87-year-old Koch's,

"Network profess optimism that 2024 will not be a repeat of 2016, when Mr. Trump began winning statewide races with roughly a third of the party's Republican base behind him in a fractured, crowded field."[400]

By 2024, Charles' dissonance had become medical emergency-level frightening. Recall, it was he, through his funding of the Tea Party, who helped supercharge the growth of the Confederate Taliban crocodiles. Then he feigned annoyance at these alternate-reality-dwelling, paranoid MAGA monsters not ditching Trump to vote for his chosen presidential nonentity, Nikki 'Nimrata' Haley[401].

David Corn offered us some more gold when he took us inside the mind of another billionaire. This one has a forensic understanding of how to divide people with hate, but is not as smart as he thinks. Not for the first time, Rupert Murdoch of Fox News would reveal his own naïve and childlike myopia about American politics.

Following the congressional failure of the immigration reform of 2012, Murdoch was having dinner with the GOP House Majority leader Eric Cantor. Their conversation was reported as, "What happened to immigration reform? Why not pass the bill?" Cantor, no doubt restraining himself, replied, "Rupert, have you watched your network?"[402]

One of the wonderful things about being a liberal is that one doesn't need to lie. Which means there's also no need for gaslighting. This is a psychological technique employed by narcissists to con people. Groucho Marx summed it up in the 1933 movie, 'Duck Soup,' with the line, "Who you going to believe, me or your own eyes?"[403] So it is that a fiend like Trump wants us to believe his lies rather than our own eyes.

Gaslighting has a very close psychological relative in 'projection.' This is another narcissist's technique, described in Personality Unleashed.

> Narcissistic projection is a defense mechanism that involves attributing one's own unwanted thoughts, feelings, or characteristics to another person.[404]

As an example, this is how the cult can support Russia whilst accusing liberals of hating America.

Moving on to another place for upside-down thinking gets us to the 'diversity' within the Confederate Taliban. To give a few examples, we have Clarence Thomas (Black) Ben Shapiro (Jewish), Nick Fuentes (Latino), Candace Owens (Black), Peter Thiel (Gay), Kash Patel (Asian), Dave Rubin (Gay), Nikki Haley (Asian), and Kanye West (Black.)

For this crowd, acting as 'model minorities[405]'—compliant, unquestioning, self-hating shills for both white supremacy and the patriarchy—affords them a proximity to the world of the straight, white male patriarch they hope will both protect them from white violence and provide them the benefits of better career and life prospects. Their price of entry into this toxic palace of subjugation is to be the patriarchy's mouthpieces by actively disregarding or demeaning the struggles of other people of color.

All this being so, you may have heard about the fake-science eugenics movement of the 1920s. We know what those esteemed 'intellectuals' thought about blacks, Jews, Mexicans, and homosexuality. However, I wonder what some of their modern-day adherents in an Aryan Nation compound in northern Idaho might think when they look at the multi-colored minions of the Confederate Taliban.

Still, it's instructive to examine these ladder-pulling freaks. One of them, Candace Owens, is what passes for a conservative black 'intellectual.' She spends her days lauding Hitler[406] and loving Jim Crow[407].

Owens should thank Lyndon Johnson, Dr. Martin Luther King, and all the millions of folks who fought and, in some cases, died for her right to be a citizen. Indeed, back in those 'good old days' of the 1950s, the GOP would have their brown paper bags ready for her. This is from Medium;

> The test was once a notable example of a once-common form of prejudice. Access to social events, jobs, clubs, and schools was often determined by a person's complexion. According to Georgetown sociology professor Michael Eric Dyson, "New Orleans invented the brown paper bag party — usually at a gathering in a home — where anyone darker than the bag attached to the door was denied entrance.[408].

But there's more. Also, in the 1950s, across half the states of America, interracial marriage was illegal. It was only in 1967 that the case of Loving v. Virginia enshrined it into law[409]. Which is very handy for Mrs Owens, for she is married to a white man.

Here's the grift, though. Back in 2015, she was writing about "social change" and punching up at the Tea Party. One of her posts railing against

Trump was titled: "NEWS UPDATE: THE REPUBLICAN TEA PAR-TY IS LED BY THE MAD HATTER." In it, she lambasted Trump's actions as "racist, bigoted, and downright offensive."[410]In that, she was correct.

We can move on to another zero-integrity 'model minority'. While taking part in a presidential town hall meeting in December 2023 in Berlin, New Hampshire, failed long-shot candidate Nikki 'Nimrata' Haley was asked point-blank, "What was the cause of the United States Civil War?"

Haley, a former governor of South Carolina and no stranger to "States' rights", looked like she had come face-to-face with a tiger. She fumbled an answer of,

> Well, don't come with an easy question....I think the cause of the Civil War was basically how government was going to run, the freedoms, and what people could and couldn't do,.....Government doesn't need to tell you how to live your life.[411]

The media was puzzled why she didn't answer this easy question with the word "slavery." Yet, this was to miss the point. The Confederate Taliban are manifestly unwilling to hear the truth, steeped in lies and hatred as they are. She knew that, had she told the truth and uttered the word "slavery," her campaign would be toast.

Notwithstanding, by May 2024, Nimrata, who had conned one-fifth of anti-Trump GOP primary voters into believing that she was a moderate, folded and bowed down to the cult leader, offering her full support[412].

This brings us to the heart of her evil grift. Haley is clearly intelligent enough to know the pernicious weight her lies carry. That she doesn't care is what makes her so evil. Indeed, to satisfy the bloodlust of the Confederate Taliban and parade her unequivocal immorality before the world, the same month she dropped out of the campaign, she got on a plane to visit Israel.

Yet, instead of going to help people, this heathen beast staged a photo-op, writing on a 105mm artillery shell the words, "Finish them."[413] The 'them' would be some of the 42,000 overwhelmingly innocent Palestinian men, women, and children massacred in what one Holocaust survivor described as a genocide[414].

You may think that the inhumanity of her signing that bomb would disqualify her from the 2028 presidential race. But her political obliteration would come about from just one image.

It is inconceivable to imagine that Trump's Confederate Taliban supporters would ever vote for an 'Indian' woman named 'Nimrata.' Indeed, I'd wager that if a fake story (their favorite kind) circulated about her being a 'terrorist,' then at least ten million MAGA supporters would sit out the election or vote for another candidate.

This leads me on to the 2024 no-hoper, Vivek Ramaswamy. This silly, skinny little brown boy imagined he could, running as a Republican, aspire to the highest office in the land. It's true that it is open to moronic people, but only if they are SWIMPs.

To the point of his color. After pulling out of the 2024 race, Trump supporters posted a spoof image online of poor little Vivek as the manager of a future White House 7-Eleven store. Deep down (or maybe not so deep), that's about all they see him as: a stupid brown clown. In response to this slur, and with the metaphorical spit still dripping down his face, this wannabe president offered no fight or condemnation. Instead, meek and placid Vivek—understanding his place on the lower rung of the ladder of white supremacy—acted as the 'model minority' must and just smiled[415].

I can't leave this creature just yet, as he offers too much gold. After failing in the primaries, little Vivek started his own podcast, unimaginatively called 'Truth.' One of his first guests was a white nationalist, Ann Coulter. She is an idiot, but an influential one—as her ideas can reach Trump—so she's instructive. Ann's none too keen on modern America. Presumably, she dreams of a pre-1954 nation, oblivious to the irony of that era being a woman's patriarchal prison. Anyway, speaking to Vivek, she gave him some neo-fascist 'honesty';

> I agreed with many, many things you said ... when you were running for president, but I still would not have voted for you because you're an Indian.

This time, with her spit dripping down his face, our silly brown boy simply offered; "She had the guts to speak her mind."[416]Still, his willingness to act as the model minority fool was rewarded with a job in a BS government 'department' called DOGE, working with Mad Musk.

To see some more humiliation, let's move on to the thorny topic of sexual orientation within the cult. This takes us to bawling billionaire tech bro Peter Thiel, a former college pal of Musk and also from apartheid South Africa. Today, this character owns Palantir, a $300 billion spy-tech firm[417] gathering vast amounts of data on Americans to use against Americans. Back in 2016, Thiel backed Trump. At that year's GOP Convention, he said, "I am proud to be gay," and "We are told that the great debate is about who gets to use which bathroom. This is a distraction from our real problems. Who cares?"[418]

Ironically, in the 2020 and 2022 election cycles, his money funded ultra-far-right election deniers and authoritarians, who all feigned concern about which bathrooms people used.

I'm very puzzled where Peter thinks he fits into this world of straight white men. Indeed, the demonic cult he supports wants to smash LGBTQ+ folks like *him* straight back to the 1950s. Indeed, at some point in the future, his *friends* may come looking to book him into an Orwellian-sounding "conversion therapy" center so he can "pray the gay away."

You think I exaggerate? Mike Johnson, the Speaker of the House, offered this on being gay. It is "inherently unnatural" and a "dangerous lifestyle."[419] It shouldn't surprise you to learn that Johnson actually worked with a 'conversion therapy' center. While Mini-Mike may be a weak little grifter doing a piss-poor job of posing as a Christian, the fact remains he is just two heartbeats away from the presidency, so Peter should be very worried.

Sticking with Johnson. For a man who has voted against every policy that could help black folks, you may be surprised to learn that he has an adopted black son. Good luck finding a multi-colored Johnson family picture online, though; Mini-Mike knows the Confederate Taliban would never accept that.

All this being so, even demons can occasionally muster the odd ounce of realization. During a 2020 PBS interview, following the murder of George Floyd, in words that Ann Coulter would have a heart attack over—and Candace Owens and her fellow multi-colored GOP minions know but would never dare utter—Johnson admitted what is called "white privilege," saying,

> I've thought often through all these ordeals over the last couple of weeks about the difference in the experiences between my two 14-year-old sons, Michael being a black American

and Jack being white Caucasian. They have different challenges. My son Jack has an easier path. He just does.[420]

To segue, you will have heard the far-right scream the word 'woke'. It's a phrase first used in a political context by African-Americans in the 1940s to describe an awakening to social injustice[421].

One of the GOP's BS claims is that corporations like Disney, Nike, and Anheuser-Busch, the owners of Budweiser, are all failing because they are 'woke'. The far-right trope is 'Go Woke, Go Broke.' It's weird, as all three companies post massive profits every year.

Nike, Disney, and Budweiser, and every other successful corporation, know the fastest and easiest way to get more sales is to broaden their market. That means attracting more young people, more people of color, and more LGBTQ+ people.

It is not that these firms all want to be Democratic super donors. If white supremacists were in the majority, then the corporations would probably market white robes and hoods. Their 'progressive' veneer is performative, and it will last as long as 'progressive' means 'profit.'

While 'woke' as a slur is primarily aimed at black folks, lazy demons will happily project it onto the LGBTQ+ community, too.

In March 2023, Budweiser featured a trans influencer, Dylan Mulvaney, on some of their bottles. The far-right lost its mind and blew up a fake storm, demanding a boycott. The magpie media covered it for a week, then lost interest, but the Confederate Taliban never stopped[422].

In the short term, as in the quarter after the Budweiser furor, sales of Bud Light fell. As a result, Budweiser, being part of the large multinational Anheuser-Busch and principally interested in profit, caved and stopped their campaign.

Here's where matters get instructive: if one side is shouting and screaming at you and no one on the other side is standing up for you, then most companies will give in. Had liberals started a campaign to buy Bud Light, it would have been a smackdown to the bully. Of course, that would require some critical thinking.

As luck would have it, in February 2024, none other than Trump himself told the cult to lay off Budweiser's owners. It transpired that one of his elite UFC pals, Dana White, was negotiating a contract with Anheuser-Busch, and the boycott may hurt his pocket. The felon duly sent out a social media post that said, "Anheuser-Busch is a GREAT American brand that perhaps deserves a Second Chance?"[423] Overnight, the shouting stopped, the threats stopped, and the boycott stopped.

On the matter of trans folks, we can meet the sad case of Caitlyn Jenner. Here is a trans woman who, in 2024, still supported Trump. We will come on to why she is 'allowed' in the GOP later, but first, tragically, we need to hear what the Confederate Taliban actually thinks of her. One Republican opined,

> I'm looking at society today, and it's like I'm watching an X-Men movie. It's like we have mutants living among us on planet Earth.[424]

He's far from alone. Far-right human freak show Michael Knowles used the word *"elimination"* to describe what needs to happen to folks like Caitlyn[425].

Or we could go to Matt Walsh, who a lesser person might suggest was a serial killer in waiting. Speaking on the intelligence-sapping, billionaire-funded Daily Wire, this fragile shell of a man had this to say about trans people like Caitlyn,

> You are weird and artificial, you are manufactured and lifeless, you are unearthly and eerie, you are like some kind of human deepfake.[426]

Still, to absorb that much inhumane vitriol from her 'allies' leads me to believe that Caitlyn is either mentally ill, or one helluva grifter.

To meet someone who is more likely the latter, we can move on to culture war fool Ben Shapiro, also of the Daily Wire. Here is a Jewish man (it's relevant) who appears to have a lot in common with the Jew-hating neo-Nazis with whom he shares passage on the Confederate Taliban's hate train. This black-hating, brown-hating, woman-hating, gay-hating, sissified far-right sock puppet gave us an insight into his hypocritical, grifting mind when he revealed,

> my wife can still look at me.. and she can say, 'I see through all this crap, and none of this makes a bit of difference to me, and the person who you are is not the person who the rest of the world sees."[427]

Shapiro is a 'pal' of another right-wing Jewish 'intellectual,' Dave Rubin. Dave and his husband have two children from a surrogate. As a progressive, I'm all for it. Ben Shapiro, however, is not. When invited to his 'friend' Rubin's anniversary, he declined, citing Rubin's sexuality as the reason.

Of course, as Dave is making money from the grift, he must smile while wiping off the spit of both the anti-Semitism and the homophobia.

Obviously, as an insincere right-wing weirdo, he projects all the shame and humiliation onto liberals—the same liberals who passed the law that allows him to be married to his husband[428].

These two wouldn't be the first far-right Jewish people to work with Confederates. At the time of the Civil War, the Confederacy's Attorney General, and later on, Secretary for War, was one Judah Benjamin. As long as this cowardly slave-owning senator from Louisiana shilled for the Confederacy, Jewish or not, he was welcomed into the fold[429].

Speaking of cowards. You may have heard of the Proud Boys, the street violence arm of the Republican Party[430]. A less charitable person might suggest this 'men-only' group is full of rampant, repressed homosexuals. Nonetheless, they are also proudly white supremacist, or as they like to style themselves, 'Western Chauvinists'. Any man can join, as long as they accept white supremacy—sorry, Western Ch........oh, who am I kidding, neo-fascism!

That Enrique Tarrio, the former 'Chairman' of the Proud Boys, was a dark-skinned Latino man—currently serving 22 years in prison for J6 sedition—is 1984-level brilliant.

Now, my eyes work pretty well, and I know that if this was Alabama in the Jim Crow era, Enrique wouldn't be allowed to break bread with the white Proud Boys forefathers, Peter's "abnormal lifestyle choice"[431] would have landed him in jail, and, along with Ben, Dave and Candance, they'd all the hiding from the KKK.

However, never underestimate the evil in evil genius. A dusting of these self-hating, feeble characters in the Confederate Taliban allows for moral cover. Social scientists call it tokenism[432]. Under the tokenism get-out, the Proud Boys 'can't' be racist because their chairman is a brown man.

So, it goes with black right-wing stooges, like Senator Tim Scott, Kanye West, and Candace Owens. With them as cover, the Confederate Taliban 'can't' be racist. And a grudging semi-acceptance of Peter Thiel (his money comes in handy as well) means that they 'can't' be homophobic against 7.1% of the American population, or twenty-one million people. The same is true of Caitlyn and trans folks, and with Ben and Dave on board, how can they possibly be anti-Semitic?

With this moral cover in place, as we saw in 2024, not only can unthinking black, brown and LGBTQ+ folks be duped into voting Republican, but, much more importantly, policies can be implemented that smash down on the rest of the marginalized folks. This concept is so demonically ingenious, yet so obscure, that they know the corporate media will never question their hate or their motives. Besides, even if they did, the fiends can always point to, or wheel out, one of their 'tokens,' like Ben, Caitlyn, or Candace, to gaslight them.

To understand more about the Confederate Taliban's upside-down thinking, these people on the far-right are endlessly banging on about pornography in schoolbooks. If they really meant that, shouldn't they be a little more concerned about the depraved and violent sexual images and videos that can be summoned instantly on kids' phones? Clearly, they *mean* LGBTQ+, and they want to 'protect' the children from any books or stories that feature anything other than straight men and women.

This brings us to the subject of the far-right's 'family values,' which, for them, appear to be about 'grooming' children. In 2023, a well-connected (as in photographed with Trump and Pence) Republican donor, Tony Lazzaro, was sentenced to twenty-one years in prison. He was engaging in "commercial sex acts" with fifteen-and sixteen-year-old children. Working with his co-defendant, they would recruit "White, small, vulnerable or broken" girls, preferably minors, to have sex with[433].

Then, there was Ali Alexander, a far-right Trump-allied propagandist. This degenerate scurried away from public life in 2023 after being exposed for leveraging his power and influence to demand naked pictures of under-age right-wing boys—perhaps the textbook definition of grooming[434].

Alexander was outed by someone else you probably wouldn't want babysitting your kids. Milo Yiannopoulos appears to be a gay, Jewish, Hitler-loving pedophile (not a typo). As for influence, he was both an intern to Marjorie Taylor Greene and Kanye West's manager. Oh, and he previously suggested that sex between older men and younger boys could be a 'coming of age thing'.[435]

We can move on to Nick Fuentes, 24, a self-confessed Nazi and influential Trump dining partner. This creature described an act that would make him a pedophile in most states when he mused on the bride he'd like;

> If I'm 30 and she's 16, 14-year age difference. When I'm 50, she'll be 36. When I'm 40, she'll be 26. Then now we're talking here, now we're cooking with gas.[436]

We could talk about the puritanical "Moms for Liberty", who should really be called "Moms Against Liberty." From their Philadelphia chapter (sewer?), we find Phillip Fisher Jr., a Republican pastor and convicted child sex abuser. This depraved, disgusting devil pleaded guilty to raping a 14-year-old boy[437].

Separately, in November 2023, out of Florida came a story about the co-founder of 'Moms for Liberty', Bridget Ziegler. In the daytime, she would rail against gay people, but in her spare time, she and her husband would engage in bisexual threesomes. Her husband was Christian Ziegler, the chair of the Florida Republican Party[438]. My only judgement is of their hypocrisy.

Speaking of those who hate freedom, it's a short walk down the road of mendacity to the Southern Baptist Church. Outside of the Catholic Church, the largest amount of sexual abuse and grooming of children was performed by Protestant Evangelicals. In 2022, Guidepost released a 205-page report written for the Southern Baptist Convention detailing over 700 entries of abuse between 2000 and 2019.

Just bear in mind the social stigma of claiming abuse, and it may be the actual number, including those with NDAs, is probably in the thousands. These were vulnerable young people who trusted the powerful church leaders, and those leaders were sinful, slimy Satanists who sexually preyed on them[439]. Yet, you wouldn't have heard one word about this from the same Republican politicians who love talking about "family values" or "groomers." Or if you did, it would probably be to claim the survivors were 'lying.'

Speaking of abuse takes us to Congressional Representative Jim Jordan, a Protestant evangelical fundamentalist who sits in a heavily gerrymandered seat in Ohio. He was the assistant wrestling team coach at Ohio State University from 1986 to 1994. During this period, Dr. Richard Strauss was the wrestling team doctor. Over the twenty years between 1978 and 1994, Strauss may have molested over 2000 young athletes[440].

From the party of 'family values', Jim Jordan is anything but, because he's a shriveled up husk of a human being who was supposed to protect the young athletes, yet did exactly the opposite. As for the cover-up, it's either because Jordan was complicit in the crime, or because he was terrified of people asking how he was so close, yet claimed to know so little[441].

At this point, I sense a question in some people's minds. How could a six-foot-tall, two-hundred-pound wrestler allow this abuse to happen to him? To understand, we have to look at the case of Dr. Larry Nassar, the former USA gymnastics coach found guilty in 2018 of molesting hundreds of teenage female gymnasts[442]. In that case, trust and power allowed Nasser—over eighteen years between 1996 and 2014—to dominate and abuse the young women.

Yet, so it was with Dr Strauss and the university wrestlers. Put yourself in their shoes and imagine the stigma of telling your parents or bringing a complaint. It's not just the 'shame' of having the world know that someone has molested you, but the double humiliation that you were a tough American man from a red state who could have fought back, but didn't.

And then, even this misses the psychological aspect that rocking the boat is goddamn hard. So, the young wrestler keeps quiet about the abuse, not just because of shame and humiliation, but also to avoid being kicked off the team.

Remember, these guys might not be whiz-kids at computers, math or science, but as long as they are still on the team, they've got the hope of a chance of turning professional, and getting a career of fame, money and respect. If they speak up, all that evaporates, and they have to go back home as a 'victim,' feeling like a failure, and take up a job that wasn't their dream.

Before we close out the chapter, I have to ask, how are these powerful Confederate Taliban patriarchs, taking advantage of those without power, any different from a smutty, sweaty studio executive asking a young actress in Hollywood how much she 'really wants the role.'

Aside from the human toll wreaked by the filthy, far-right degenerates, there's something else that's infinitely infuriating. On a political level, all the material you've read about is common public knowledge and could have made dozens of sensational attack ads for Democratic candidates in 2024. Yet, despite living in a country where gossip, sex scandals, and titillation are the simplest way to garner people's and the media's attention, these gift-wrapped stories were considered outside the bounds of decorum by nice Democrats.

Chapter 12

They Want To Crack You And Pack You, So Get Out And Vote. It's Your Superpower.

Way back in 1870, Congress ratified the Fifteenth Amendment[443]. Unlike the Second Amendment, it should have been impossible to misinterpret. It states that,

> The right of citizens of the United States to vote shall not be denied or abridged by the United States or by any state on account of race, color, or previous condition of servitude.

Then, with the end of segregation, we got the Voting Rights Act of 1965, which was supposed to ensure fair voting, especially in former slave-holding states. For Republicans, the VRA represented an abomination. After all, how could white supremacy survive with people of color able to vote?

So it would be that Republicans, also being conscious of the nation's changing demographics[444], came up with a plan to gerrymander—or rig—states' voting maps so they could win where they would otherwise lose.

To see how the GOP pulled off the Great American Voting Heist, we need to hear from one of their most masterfully manipulative mapmakers,

Thomas Hofeller. Speaking honestly about his dishonesty way back in 1991, he said,

> I define redistricting as the only legalized form of vote-stealing left in the United States today.

Hofeller spilled the beans again in 2001 about a topic that the mainstream media was still ignoring, with this quote for the ages;

> Redistricting is like an election in reverse. It's a great event. Usually the voters get to pick the politicians. In redistricting, the politicians get to pick the voters.[445]

Knowing full well the fallacious nature of his endeavors, Hofeller would implore his demonic fellow GOP voter-suppression travelers to delete their data and keep their dealings secret.

Thankfully for us, he didn't feel it was necessary to follow his own counsel. Thus, when Hofeller passed away in 2018, he left behind a veritable treasure trove of 70,000 maps and files on his computer. But for his daughter, Stephanie, this blueprint for gerrymandering would have remained a secret forever.

These maps reveal the Machiavellian mechanics of voter suppression and disenfranchisement that led to GOP supermajorities being established in Arizona, Florida, Maryland, Mississippi, Missouri, North Carolina, Ohio, Tennessee, and Virginia. While we won't focus any more on Mr. Hofeller, it's worth celebrating that Stephanie, despite her father's influence, stood up for justice and progress. She's what the future of America looks like, and that should give us all a glimmer of hope.

The maps were part of a wider far-right strategy to take over America, set in place over the past five decades by people like the Heritage Foundation's

Paul Weyrich, who died in 2008, and the Federalist Society's Executive Vice President Leonard Leo (more of whom in Chapter fifteen). All of this was ably assisted by billionaires and fake Christians. Their plan came meticulously constructed in three distinct phases.

The initial stage involved impeding (mainly black and brown) Democrats from exercising their voting rights, as Weyrich himself stated back in 1980;

> I don't want everybody to vote. Elections are not won by a majority of people. They never have been from the beginning of our country, and they are not now. As a matter of fact, our leverage in the elections quite candidly goes up as the voting populace goes down.[446]

Next, they needed to take over the federal courts and the Supreme Court to swiftly address any challenges to voter suppression. On which topic Weyrich would express;

> Absent scandal, a federal judge can serve for decades on the bench, underscoring the importance of appointing judges who have a proper understanding of their constitutional r ole.[447]

And finally, as you will read, they wish to privatize the public education system in order to promote conformity, compliance, and ignorance, and in the process earn billions.

In this chapter, we will focus on voter suppression and how deviantly it has been implemented.

The relentless determination of the Confederate Taliban to keep on fighting their Lost Cause never waned. The far-right recognized that so much of what happens in America stems from the states. Specifically, they understood how state legislatures and secretaries of state (who organize elections) could determine voting rights. The superbly insightful author of the 2021 book, Laboratories of Autocracy, David Pepper, offered;

> They, the other side knows that the democracy of this country is written in the State houses. In this country, you write the rules of who votes and how they vote, when they vote, when they purge and how you register. And that is the place that determines our districts fair or not. Do you have a fair system? Or do you have a rigged system? Even in Republican areas, they are so much worse than they otherwise would be if they had fair districts.[448]

To that point, the Voting Rights Act was supposed to ensure fair voting, especially in former slave-holding states. Section Two forbade the prohibition of voting based on race, and Section Five forced former segregationist states to seek preclearance from the Department of Justice before enacting any changes in voting laws. Despite long-term quiet segregationist and future Supreme Court Chief Justice John Roberts' vehement opposition, it was to Ronald Reagan's credit that he signed a twenty-five-year reauthorization of the VRA in 1982[449].

It lapsed again in 2007, with the Bush administration choosing not to extend it. Despite this, in 2009, during the first Obama administration, Congressional Democrats held both House and Senate majorities. Even the smallest political will would have allowed for a vote to extend the VRA, but those shortsighted Democrats were too scared and timid to wield power.

So it was that, into that vacuum, the Supreme Court, led by John Roberts, ruled against the Act in the 2013 Shelby County v. Holder case.

This effectively hobbled the VRA by gutting the Section 5 provisions. Since then, the Supreme Court has almost exclusively sided with the Confederate Taliban in voting rights cases to chip away at even more of the Act.

Which brings us back to gerrymandering. As we read at the beginning of the chapter, this is the practice of redrawing district voter maps by the ruling party to concentrate opponents into a limited number of districts. This allows mostly GOP politicians to manipulate voting maps to their advantage.

With voting rights comes the arcane language associated with this process, such as 'cracking' and 'packing.'[450] Legislatures can crack voting districts strategically in order to dilute the influence of their opponents' voters. They can then 'pack' most opposition voters into a single district. The result is the same: to weaken the overall strength of the opposition's votes. Suffice to say, this is unconstitutional[451].

In the pivotal swing state of Wisconsin in 2004, there were eight districts with, as required by the U.S. Constitution, an equal split of population[452]. However, by 2022, still with an equal population split, the state maps had been redrawn to pack half the Democratic voters into only two districts. This left the GOP with six congressional seats and a supermajority in the Wisconsin State Legislature[453].

Cracking and packing take place in twenty-two red states in total[454]. Almost all these states have Republican state houses, state senates, and governors. This trifecta enables the drawing of not just state legislature maps but also those ultra-partisan congressional maps, the direct consequence of which is we get extreme Republicans, such as Marjorie Taylor Green (Georgia), Matt Gaetz (Florida), and Jim Jordan (Ohio), who often run unopposed. The twisted irony is that Democrats don't bother standing candidates in these seats because the gerrymandering ensures they could never win.

On this point, in 2021, Democrats had a chance to pass the Freedom to Vote. John R. Lewis Act[455]. Its implementation would have eradicated voter suppression and gerrymandering. FTV passed the House, but thanks to quisling Democratic Senators Joe Manchin and Kirsten Sinema, it was DOA in the Senate.

For now, in most states, citizens may propose a ballot initiative for the upcoming election by gathering sufficient signatures. Michigan voters successfully approved a ballot initiative in 2018 to establish an Independent Citizen's Redistricting Commission. The ICRC empowered thirteen impartial commissioners to determine the new voting maps.

With the new fair maps drawn, in 2022, voters got to take part in real democracy. To the astonishment of the always-wrong pundits and corporate media, Democrats achieved a blue wave, securing a trifecta of the governor's mansion, state house and state senate.

The GOP knows an incontrovertible truth: that with fair voting, red would become blue. So it is that they do all in their power to stop it. Part of that is voter suppression, which is simply about robbing, mostly people of color, of their enthusiasm, motivation, and indeed, ability to vote. Some of their tricks include removing ballot boxes[456], to make people have to travel further to vote. Then, even when the voters get there, they make them endure a six-hour-long wait in queues to vote[457].

When the Confederate Taliban gets really desperate, they can just do what Republicans in Mississippi did in the 2023 gubernatorial race. Brandon Presley was attempting to unseat the titanically corrupt Tate Reeves. Mr. Presley, a distant cousin of The King, got 46.6% of the vote, losing by about 50,000 votes. On voting day, by pure coincidence, Hinds County, a 90% black district, miraculously ran out of ballots. It had 150,000 voters, and many of them couldn't vote[458].

So, we have gerrymandering and plain-old voter suppression. This was all supercharged following Trump's 'Stop the Steal' lies about how the 2020 election was stolen by Democrats[459]. Then, after the 2022 midterms, which brought with it record young voter turnout—two-thirds of them voted Democratic—the calls on Fox were for the voting age to be raised to twenty-five years old. That requires a constitutional amendment, which means two-thirds of Congress and thirty-eight out of fifty state legislatures, so it's a non-starter[460].

However, the legislatures got busy and started passing laws to tighten up the ID requirements, such as not accepting student IDs and disallowing campus voting booths. Now, to sap their enthusiasm, many students have to travel off campus to vote. This was part of a wider suppression strategy to help steal future elections. It included making postal voting much harder, removing local ballot drop boxes, and also empowering Republican vigilante voter suppressors who, without evidence, could challenge thousands of Democratic votes[461]. Without a peep from Democrats or the Democratic-led DOJ, the result of these blatantly unconstitutional policies was that, in 2024, millions of legitimate Democratic voters had been stripped of their right to vote or had their votes disallowed[462].

To end, if liberals thought voter suppression was bad in 2024, imagine the tricks the GOP will get up to in the 2028 general election. Fortunately, in my book 'When Coal Miners Drive Cadillacs,' I have a solution to dilute the strength of their shenanigans and win big at the next election.

Chapter 13

The Corrupt Evil Grifters And Hollow Fascists Who Would End American Democracy.

To understand most GOP politicians is to know one thing. Most of these bought, paid for, and controlled winged monkeys are on the grift. It starts with the $174,000 salary, gold-plated healthcare, paid sick leave, paid maternity leave, and future pensions that they receive as members of the United States Congress[463]. Lauren Boebert, Marjorie Taylor Green, and Tommy Tuberville all get it. But that's just for openers.

Then, there's the $75,000 a year fee as a 'contributor' to cable news[464].

Throw in the institutions and corporations that will pay for speakers; for someone like Newt Gingrich, it could again be $75,000 plus expenses[465].

Add to all this the fact that, as long as they are not such nakedly criminal fraudsters as 2023's freshman Republican Rep. George Santos, thanks to near non-existent Federal Election Commission enforcement, they can rake in hundreds of thousands of dollars of corrupt-yet-legal Political Action Committee (PAC) donations from corporations or other malign outside interests who want to buy their influence and lavish some of that cash on themselves[466].

And I must never forget the ghostwritten book deal. Ted Cruz received $319,000 from his book deal in 2020. Senator Tom Cotton got $202,000, and Senator Jodie Ernst suckered some publisher for $108,000[467].

All of this is never to ignore the limitless opportunities for insider trading that working in Congress affords. After all, those who sit in the hallowed halls of power have advance information on almost everything, from whether Boeing will be fined to whether Tesla will receive subsidies to whether Pfizer will receive government contracts[468].

It's vital to note that these insidiously perfunctory GOP devils all know their grift depends completely upon their being in office. And to stay in office, they need to stoke the flames of fury and resentment in the base. To ignore that simple rule is to invite a primary challenge from the even-further-right, the result of which will be certain political death.

Out of that comes the trademark of the far-right today. A lack of integrity, wrapped in a steel sheet of hypocrisy, surrounded by an impenetrable wall of shamelessness.

To illustrate how performative it all is, we need to visit the orange dictator, Trump. He was the principal proponent of the lies about Dominion Voting machines that formed the basis for the BS about the 2020 election being 'stolen'. However, after Fox News, which amplified those lies, paid out $787.5 million in damages for defamation, Trump never mentioned either Dominion or voting machines again.

To move on to the second receipt. After he lied about sexually assaulting E. Jean Carroll, he was sued. In 2023, he lost, and a jury awarded $5 million in damages against him. Following that, he couldn't keep his mouth shut and accused her of fabricating the allegation. E. Jean sued again, this time for defamation, and won again. This time, she was awarded $83 million[469]. Because he didn't want to have to pay out another $83 million, the felon shut his mouth after that.

This brings us to the third receipt. In the New York election interference trial, Trump was convicted of paying to suppress a story that could have altered the outcome of the 2016 election. During his trial, he continually committed contempt of court. The $1000 maximum fine for contempt in New York courts proved far too trivial a sum to represent any impediment to his outbursts[470]. However, once the judge suggested he could be incarcerated for contempt, he immediately shut up. From then on, the cult leader scrawled lines for his winged monkeys to parrot outside the court[471].

The point of all these illustrations is to show that Trump is not insane. He is a criminal deviant who knows exactly what he is doing and also when it's in his interests to shut up.

I'm happy to bring more receipts. It was Californian Congressional Rep. Eric Swalwell, speaking to John Fugelsang, who hit the nail on the head with a story about Ted Cruz. Swalwell described MAGA politics as being like wrestling. In that 'entertainment,' there is something called Kayfabe. This from 'Pro Wrestling,'

> Kayfabe is often seen as the suspension of disbelief that is used to create the non-wrestling aspects of promotions, such as feuds, storylines, and gimmicks in a similar manner with other forms of entertainment such as soap opera or movie.

Trump is a huge wrestling fan, and to his supporters, he's the 'good guy,' and Democrats are the 'heels,' or bad guys. This all ties in to the far-right, keeping their voters fed with a constant stream of angertainment.

Mr. Swalwell described a scene in the Senate that took place during Trump's second impeachment. He was standing at a washbasin during a bathroom break when Ted Cruz came in to wash his hands. Cruz held out his fist for a fist bump. Swalwell was taken aback, given the vitriol that the Princeton-and Harvard-educated Cruz threw at Democrats in public. Cruz said, "I want you to know, you guys are doing a really good job." Swalwell couldn't believe what he was hearing. Cruz continued, "I mean it. I really mean it. You guys are doing a good job out there." A dawning truth then crashed down on Swalwell. In his words;

And then I realized, wait, we're not in front of a camera. He's not in front of his colleagues, and he's just being himself. But when he goes back into the Senate chamber or back on Fox News, he's got to put on that MAGA persona, and swing the steel chair around. And you know, just for democracy, another problem is, he thinks the people who are watching us are fans, I think that their constituents, and he also doesn't understand that they think this is all real. And so if they think it's all real, then you have a January 6 because Ted Cruz is saying, we have to not let this happen, and they don't know that he's just a MAGA persona.[472]

To reinforce the point of the grift, we have Jeff Jackson, veteran and freshman congressional representative from North Carolina's 14th District. Jeff uses social media to reach constituents and voters who might otherwise not be interested. In one of his first videos after taking office in April 2023, he said this;

It's really clear from working there for just a few months that most of the really angry voices in Congress are totally fake...The same people who act like maniacs during the open meetings are suddenly calm and rational during the closed ones. Why? Because of cameras in the closed meetings, so their incentives are different...The big thing that modern media and modern politicians have learned is that if they can keep you angry, they'll hold your attention, and they both want your attention. So, if you're a politician, and you show certain media outlets that you can help them keep their audience angry, they'll give you their audience, and because so many politicians are willing to play that game, now they're in competition with each other to see how fake angry they can be.[473]

In my book 'When Coal Miners Drive Cadillacs,' I describe how corporate media are willing partners in this con on the American people. The reasoning is uncomplicated. The multinational corporations like Disney, News Corp., Paramount, Warner Bros., and Viacom that own the television news don't want regulation or higher taxes. But also to attract audiences, they need the most outrageous stories. In turn, higher numbers of viewers mean they can charge other multinational corporations like Ford, Johnson & Johnson, and Procter & Gamble more money to advertise their cars, baby formula, and soap powder. More ad revenue means more profit, which means a higher stock price and more compensation for the CEO and board.

Back to the performance grift. In what seems almost quaintly 'normal' 2016, I read the nonsense that was "Hillbilly Elegy." Its author, now a senator and supremely unqualified vice president, J.D. Vance, was courted by idiotic 'moderate' liberals as having the answer to how to win over low-information rural white voters.

As much as anyone, this pure, hypocritical degenerate is emblematic of the present GOP. Back in 2016, Vance described Trump as 'noxious', reprehensible', and 'an idiot.' Separately, he wrote,

I go back and forth between thinking Trump is a cynical asshole like Nixon who wouldn't be that bad (and might even prove useful) or that he's America's Hitler. How's that for discouraging?"[474]

Remember those words, for we will come back to them. In his book. Vance rails against the federal government and bemoans 'lazy' poor whites who survive on "The Draw"—the federal $1500 a month disability checks used by some citizens in rural America as stand-in unemployment insurance[475]. He paints a picture of the government as promoting a cycle of poverty.

Of course, what his 'story' conveniently ignores is that this man-child only survives because the FEDERAL GOVERNMENT saved his opioid-addicted mom's life,[476] and the FEDERAL GOVERNMENT put food on his table through SNAP—the Supplemental Nutrition Assistance Program (Thanks FDR,) and THE FEDERAL GOVERNMENT sent him to school, and THE FEDERAL GOVERNMENT gave him a chance to be a combat correspondent in the Marines, and then the FEDERAL GOVERNMENT, through the GI bill (Thanks again FDR), paid $160,000 for him to go to the elite Yale Law School[477]. But of course, the government is terrible.

Once inside the Confederate Taliban, Vance retracted his old anti-Trump words and spun 180 degrees, with this quote: "Like a lot of, uh, people, I criticized Trump back in 2016. And I ask folks not to judge me on what I said in 2016."[478]

This weasel-like coward has learned from Trump, the cult leader, to never apologize and always double down on the lies. Which is no problem as for the next four years, his worthless hide is stowed safely aboard the USS Grifter. During that time, he will do his level best to end both democracy and Democrats.

As for the fortunes of the unlucky poor folks he represents in Appalachia. Well, they can drown in the sea of poverty and despair as pampered millionaire baby Vance votes against anything that would have brought assistance, jobs, and investment to their communities[479].

Apart from the money, there are a couple of other reasons that will help to show how weak, unprincipled, yet educated, devils like Vance, along with Ted Cruz, Marco Rubio, and Lindsey Graham, just folded for Trump.

The first is that, for right-wingers, power is addictive. Having news cameras in front of them and journalists asking their opinions flatters their egos. Indeed, it is said the most dangerous place on Capitol Hill is between a GOP politician and a television camera.

Then, there's the possibility of sitting in the White House or flying on Air Force One. This compulsive craving for power and limelight explains why many 'Republicans' debase themselves in front of Trump and put up with his humiliation and degrading insults.

Just on the matter of degrading, we have to return to the human cesspit that is J.D. Vance. Bear in mind that, even though he is married to a dark brown Asian-American woman, he is one of the most rampant white nationalists in Congress.

For receipts, back in his 2022 Ohio senatorial campaign, he offered that Democrats couldn't win "unless they bring a large number of new voters to replace the voters that are already here." This is basically the racist, anti-Semitic 'replacement theory.'[480]

Also in his 2022 campaign, Vance ran an ad in which he asked, "Do you hate Mexicans?". Yet, during a campaign debate, with no sense of irony or self-reflection, the coward cried, "What happens is my own children, my biracial children, get attacked by scumbags online and in person."[481]

Returning to his brown wife. By 2024, as VP pick, Vance had to straddle the complex conundrum of a brown spouse in a party consumed by white grievance and rage. That fury was sufficient for some to call for her 'deportation' (ludicrous, as she is a US citizen). Nonetheless, when interviewed, Vance knew to bow down to the supremacy of the base by preceding his profession of love for her with this: "Obviously, she's not a white person."[482]

Which brings us to the third reason for the GOP grift. We have read about how they stay on message out of fear of inviting that primary challenge from the right after angering the base. But there's even more. Rick Wilson is the founder of the Lincoln Project. As a sane, patriotic, original conservative, he offered that Republicans wouldn't stand up to Trump because they were scared that the "base" would come and kill them[483].

To reinforce this point, McKay Coppins, the author of Mitt Romney's 2023 biography, 'A Reckoning,' gave us a fascinating insight into the relationship of the GOP politician and the base primary voter,

> One Republican congressman confided to Romney that he wanted to vote for Trump's second impeachment, but chose not to out of fear for his family's safety, the congressman reasoned that Trump would be impeached by House Democrats with or without him — why put his wife and children at risk if it wouldn't change the outcome? "Later, during the Senate trial, Romney heard the same calculation while talking with a small group of Republican colleagues. When one senator, a member of leadership, said he was leaning toward voting to convict, the others urged him to reconsider. You can't do that, Romney recalled someone saying. Think of your personal safety, said another. Think of your children. The senator eventually decided they were right.[484]

Romney himself described spending $5000 a day on private security. Knowing the monster he had helped create, he was probably keenly aware of the hell an AR-15-wielding MAGA maniac could visit on him[485].

Speaking of maniacs, the toxic dynamic between Trump, his base, and GOP reps is almost like willing abuse. Senator Lindsey Graham was quoted in 2022 as saying, "You know what I liked about Trump? Everybody was afraid of him, including me."[486]

Graham is, within a voluminous field, one of the hollowest and least sincere politicians. During the insurrection, stark focus was thrown on his line about being afraid. Seeing that the terrorists were trying to break down the doors of the Senate chamber to, presumably, murder congressional representatives, he screamed to the Capitol police, "You've got guns, use them!"[487]

Yet, speaking on Fox News just a few months later, Graham would say that, if Trump was criminally indicted, there would be "riots in the streets." He was wrong again. While some Trump supporters were happy to vote for a fascist and even to stage a coup, risking years in a federal prison for defending the cult leader's fraud was considered a bridge too far[488].

We can move on to fellow GOP senator, cult-happy Ted Cruz. When asked at the Texas Tribune speak-fest in 2022 why so many Republicans would not criticize Trump, he replied,

> "It's a number of things. ... Unlike many people in politics, if someone criticizes him, he turns around and punches them in the face."[489]

There was also 'moderate' GOP Senator Susan Collins, quoted as saying, "I wouldn't be surprised if a senator or House member were killed."

A few months later, a radicalized domestic terrorist went to Nancy Pelosi's home to kidnap her. Instead, he found her husband, whose skull he cracked with a hammer. Obviously, the corporate media never called him a terrorist or described the attack as part of an attempted political assassination[490].

It wasn't just violence aimed at Democrats. In the 2023 race to succeed Kevin McCarthy as House Speaker, Trump backed Jim Jordan. Angry MAGA base supporters fired furious telephone calls and death threats at GOP congressional representatives who would not vote for Jordan.

One of the recipients was Rep. Don Bacon of Nebraska. His failure to comply with the cult marked him for death. Rep. Bacon described his wife's having to sleep with a loaded gun near her bedside. Yet, just two months later, Bacon was back in line, meeting cult conformity standards by voting to cut funding to Ukraine and trying to 'impeach' private citizen Hunter Biden. All in order to appease the MAGA crocodiles[491].

To understand people like Bacon, we can visit Adam Kinzinger. This Air Force veteran and former congressman from Illinois is what a Republican used to look like. As one of only two Republicans to have the guts to stand up to Trump during the January 6th hearings, he spelled something important out:

> Think about your post Congress life, most of these guys will want to go lobby. Well, to lobby, you have to have access to your former members, and to have access to former members, you can't tick them off. And if you go out there and make their life uncomfortable by saying the obvious stuff, we have to defend Ukraine or we have an opportunity for a good border bill, you're not going to have that great access in the post-life.[492]

A representative they wouldn't want to tick off is fake Christian Marjorie Taylor Greene of Georgia. On the surface, this QAnon queen is first among equals in a despicable menagerie of morons and emblematic of the base of the party. Representing a near-impossible-to-lose gerrymandered seat,[493] this maniacal outrage machine jumps aboard every little manufactured wedge issue, whether LGBTQ+, God, guns, CRT, BLM, or Ukraine.

Suffice to say, she doesn't have one useful policy idea and voted against every bill that would help her constituents among them the American Rescue Plan to provide stimulus checks, the Infrastructure Act to provide jobs, and the Inflation Reduction Act that would also provide jobs, and reduce the cost of medications.

Greene's con is to offer herself as a poster girl for "confrontational politics." Her play is to say or tweet the most outrageous things, knowing that, as fear drives through our attention filters, the magpie media won't be able to resist reporting on the performative car crash of shock it causes. Her mad words are legion, but one line from 2020 stands out:

"They destroyed the NFL. They're destroying NASCAR. They're burning our cities and destroying our history.[494]

Those fifteen words of pure lies tell you everything; all roiling resentment, searing hate, and seething anger.

Of course, lazy corporate media journalists wrote long-form stories, trying to dissect the mind of Greene. Fear not, for over the next few paragraphs, you will gain a forensic understanding of her mind.

As for her morality. She was happy to share a stage with Nick Fuentes, a real-life Nazi and a man who opines that the Holocaust was a non-event[495].

To truly meet Marge, though, we need to know that she can instantly turn off the insanity where money is concerned. Her wealth is about $25 million, gifted from her father's construction business[496]. She charges around $15,000 for a speech[497] and was savvy enough, during COVID, to know how to claim a $190,000 Payment Protection check from the same federal government she rails against[498].

And to those who still think that Millionaire Marge isn't a performing evil grifter. As one of Congress's most prolific stock traders with a performance record that would shame many Wall Street hedge fund managers, she has an uncanny knack for increasing her portfolio value by buying or selling just at the right time. As a case in point, with all the inside information that Congress received in 2022 from the DOD about Putin's Ukrainian invasion plans, Greene conveniently purchased stock in Chevron (oil) and Lockheed Martin (defense) two days *before* Russia invaded[499].

There's more. In April 2023, she tweeted,

> "Don't fall for the scam, fossil fuels are natural and amazing. They produce an abundance of energy that we all need to survive along with more products than you can possibly imagine."[500]

That's spoon-fed Koch brothers' propaganda, but let's investigate the facts. Her district in Dalton, Georgia, is home to the largest solar manufacturing plant in the Western Hemisphere. This pre-dated Greene, but the plant expanded with subsidies from the Inflation Reduction Act that she voted against. However, she has never demanded to close this green energy plant.

Then, in 2023, her state commissioned the latest nuclear power station in America. Again, all this non-fossil fuel energy, without a word from Marge about shutting it down[501].

This gets us to the heart of the issue. Greene is addicted to cruelty and allergic to kindness, and she taps into the rage of the same angry white people who would close the newly integrated public swimming pools in the 1960s rather than share them with people of color[502].

However, on its own, that fake outrage isn't enough to win re-election. For that, her district needs to keep prospering. Which means, in part, bringing in the federal government subsidies that help to attract new businesses and expand existing ones. In turn, that brings in the well-paying jobs. So it is that her constituents are happy with all the culture-crazy crap, right up to the point it screws with their jobs and livelihoods. And that is why Millionaire Marge will never call to shutter the government-funded solar panel factories or nuclear power stations, for they are the golden goose that keeps helping her win.

Moving on to another profile in cowardice on intimate terms with hypocrisy and insincerity, we can revisit Ted Cruz. The junior senator from Texas may be a fake Christian, but he's not a fool and, like J.D. Vance, was intelligent enough to pass enough standardized tests to graduate from Yale.

Cruz sums up so much of the modern GOP. On January 6th, he described the attack on the Capitol as a "violent terrorist attack."[503] A few hours later, presumably after receiving a lesson on obedience from the cult, he performed a full U-turn, and in what amounted to a coup, refused to certify the results of the 2020 election.

For him, the Constitution means nothing, democracy means nothing, and fellow Americans mean nothing. But I promise you this: stop paying Cruz and watch how quickly he snaps out of it. Without the money, there is no grift.

While insincerity and shilling for the corrupt corporate and ultra-rich-donor Political Action Committee (PAC) dollar are diseases that infect every GOP lawmaker[504], many Democrats are not immune, and from their ranks, there are two who fascinate me. One is the Maserati-driving, yacht-owning, fossil-fuel-loving senator for West Virginia, Joe Manchin.

The other is Kyrsten Sinema. She is the junior senator from Arizona, made famous for smiling and giving the thumbs-down gesture as she voted against the $15 minimum wage in 2021[505]. Indeed, how little she thought of her constituents was revealed by her many campaign-or corporate-donor-funded trips to Europe, staying in fancy hotels and quaffing down the most expensive wines[506].

These two so-called 'centrists' or 'moderates' will vote to confirm Democratic judges and for some progressive legislation. However, that's only after they've neutered it to render it quite harmless to the interests of their wealthy donor overlords.

To that point, in 2021, the narcissistic publicity hounds both worked merrily with Mitch McConnell and the GOP to scupper the $3 trillion Build Back Better legislation that would have immeasurably improved the average American's life. As a reward, right-wing donors stuffed their pockets with 'campaign donations' (which a less generous person would call bribes.)[507]

Here's the part my brain can't reconcile. By 2024, both Manchin and Sinema announced they wouldn't be standing for re-election. They were despised by the Democratic base for blocking the true nature of Build Back Better and failing to allow for a carve-around the filibuster that would enable voting rights, abortion, and court reform legislation to pass.

Yet, these two Faustian fools were so drunk on the power of being the 49th and 50th Senate votes, they couldn't see the big picture. If they had just allowed for the filibuster reform and those three pieces of legislation to pass, they would be the saviors of the party and liberal American heroes. Manchin could have run for president in 2028 and won, and Sinema could have been vice president and maybe a future president.

Obviously, these grifters needed a reality check. When it came for Manchin, it wasn't from Democrats but via a stab in the back from the GOP. Snubbing Maserati Joe, Mitch McConnell announced he would back the popular Republican Governor of West Virginia, Jim Justice, for the 2024 Senate race[508].

But maybe it won't matter to Manchin as he had already completed his overlord's work by forcing through an oil pipeline deal in the Inflation Reduction Act, for which a suitable financial reward will, no doubt, be forthcoming[509]. As for Sinema, single-digit poll numbers for her Arizona race meant that her campaign was DOA. Still, she will probably get some gig on Wall Street or K Street.

And so, as they bask in the profits of their payoffs, the America that they were supposed to be working for and protecting gets to live out four more years of hell under Trump.

Chapter 14

Never Mind About Choosing Your Voters, Just Send Their Kids To A State-Funded Church School Instead.

As a GOP politician, even though you eked out a victory in 2024, you know that hating women, being a shill for fake Christian fundamentalists, loving neo-fascists, and being owned by billionaire tax cheats is not the most flavorsome recipe for guaranteed future electoral success. You've tried more voter suppression against Democratic voters, but even the six high priests on the Supreme Court blush at your latest batty ideas.

So, what to do? What was that line you heard? "He alone, who owns the youth, gains the future."[510] That they were Adolf Hitler's words is inconsequential, considering you're the people who came up with the mass distribution of guns, banning abortion, and burning the planet.

What you envision are schools where you choose the teachers, you choose the curriculum, and you choose the pupils. These state-funded church schools would never have to worry about pesky constitutional rights or discrimination. But how to persuade skeptical parents to send their kids to these church schools?

Obviously, you can scare them, and for that, you have 'woke,' CRT, and DEI. However, you need a carrot as well. If only you had some cash to tempt parents. Behold, the wonder of the school voucher. You steal from the taxpayer-funded public school budget to subsidize parents who send their kids to state-funded church schools.

Today, the Confederate Taliban is working in plain sight to cower the three million public school teachers and indoctrinate the fifty-four million public school pupils[511]. To do so, they must perform some devil's magic and turn public education into private education.

Bear in mind, today, only one out of ten school pupils attend the 32,000 private schools across America. Of those private fee-paying schools, 84% of them are Christian[512].

The Confederate Taliban's plan to take over public education involves a three-pronged attack. It's not a conspiracy, just multiple converging interests. We see the same stale billionaire devils who fund the drive to ban abortion, kill voting rights, and deny climate change[513]. These folks hate progressive ideas and despise educated people who can oppose them, but as much as that, they resent paying one cent in taxes towards *your* kids' education.

Riding shotgun in Satan's station wagon is the second prong: fake Christianity. Again, billionaire-funded. One demon behind it is Betsy DeVos. This silver-spoon-fed freak was the education secretary in Trump's first term, but her incompetence spared us from catastrophe. She shared the nightmare we avoided in a talk with a 'Christian' Radio station back in 2001,

> To impact our culture in ways that are not with the traditional funding of Christian organization route, but that really may have greater Kingdom gain in the long run, by changing the way we approach things, in this case the system of education in the Country.[514]

As fake Christianity has levels of insanity, we have to welcome back the take-us-back-to-the-1750s billionaire Wilks Brothers (anti-abortion, anti-woman, anti-LGBTQ+, anti-planet). They back the astroturf culture-war right-wingers like 'Moms for Liberty.'

Into this mix, we must never forget the fundamentalist church. They will own and run the church schools that indoctrinate your children.

And so our journey brings us to the third prong. Say hello to the corrupt, hollow, red state legislature politician. These grifting charlatans are ready, willing, and able to sell out their constituents to their donors. To do this, they cut funding to their state's public schools. This means that the schools can't maintain facilities, and also, unsurprisingly, find it harder to attract and keep teachers.

However, when you're the GOP, this is not a problem, as to recruit, they just offer teachers the same pay, but for only four days of work[515]. To anyone in a WEIRD nation, only teaching children for four days a week would seem like madness. Yet across red states, it's normal. As an intelligent reader, it probably wouldn't shock you to learn that the academic results of the four-day school week aren't positive[516].

Once again, though, we must never underestimate the moral bankruptcy of the GOP. So it is, counterfactually, this is actually good news for them. When cash-strapped public schools can only teach for four days a week, they can be branded as part of the 'failing' public school system. This is where the 'carrot' of the school voucher (also known as Education Savings Accounts) comes in. It allows parents the 'choice' to send their kids to a five-day-a-week for-profit church school.

Lily Eskelen Garcia, president of the National Education Association and someone who cares about kids' education, sees the bigger picture and provides us with a receipt.

We know exactly how the plan goes," she said; "You underfund the kids who need the most. You starve the public schools. You take away the funding so they can't deliver quality services, and then when things get so bad that nobody wants to work in the schools, the voucher salesmen, the vultures, swoop in and do this nice little bait and switch. Instead of fixing the schools, they say let's make sure you have the same program as wealthy kids at private schools.[517]

The ideas and mindset of the voucher crowd are not new. It's all about domination and control. This started way back at the end of Reconstruction with the Daughters of the Confederacy, whom we met in chapter ten.

However, to alight on the segregationists' true horror, we have to spin forward seventy years to 1954, when they were required to integrate their schools. This led the fake Christians, like satanic 'pastor' Jerry Falwell, to open 'segregation academies.' Here, white parents, not wanting to send their kids to school with any black kids, could be directly funded by the state government through 'Tuition Grants,' which were vouchers by any other name[518].

Red states could have happily ignored the fact that this blatantly violated the 1875 Blaine Amendment, prohibiting state funding for religious schools. What was impossible to ignore was when their 'Academies' became unviable following the Supreme Court rulings of Colt v. Green (1971), which stripped away their tax-exempt status, and Runyon v. McCrary (1976), which forced them to accept African American students.

But, as the Lost Cause never dies, after a few decades of planning, the demons hit the Supreme Court. In 2002, the Court ruled in Zelman v. Simmons-Harris[519] that states can give the parents vouchers (your taxpayer dollars), and those parents can send their kids to (tax-free) private religious schools. All this, somehow, without violating the Establishment Clause of the First Amendment, which specifically prohibits the government from establishing a religion.

Until 2020, the school voucher idea had shown slow momentum. However, COVID offered an opportunity, just in time for the 2020 election, for the far-right to manufacture a crisis by scaring white parents who were already angry about their kids' schools closing.

Helping the GOP to get the fire roaring were the fragile 'Miss Annes' from 'Moms For Liberty.' These GOP-groomed, billionaire-funded hags aren't intelligent people, but they serve a 'useful-idiot' purpose for their elite overlords, which is to create a feeling that your children aren't safe. So it is that these creatures would scream about 'woke,' CRT, 'trans,' and 'anti-whiteness.'

All this was clickbait for right-wing social media and the Fox Propaganda Network. It would then filter along to the lazy corporate news media, who were so desperate for ratings and advertising that they didn't bother investigating. So it would be that many in the corporate media treated Moms for Liberty as an insurgent Tea Party-style movement. Frustratingly, just one minute of investigation on the internet would show you that the co-founder was the wife of the Florida GOP chair[520].

This was of no concern for the six high priests on the Supreme Court. 2022 gave us a blatant "states rights" ruling, with Justice Roberts rolling out a red carpet for a Confederate Taliban dream, writing;

> A State need not subsidize private education...but once a State decides to do so, it cannot disqualify some private schools solely because they are religious.[521]

It's so important to note that the constitution and the strict regulations that apply to public schools don't apply to private schools. These places don't have to worry about discriminating against black, brown, LGBTQ+, or disabled children. Also, in a private school, there's no requirement for accreditation by the state and no need for the state to assess the curriculum. Thus, books can be freely banned. On top of that, there is no need for the state to certify their teachers. Indeed, they are not even required to carry out criminal background records checks (so much for 'groomers') on private school teachers[522].

So now the private school gets to choose their students rather than the students choosing their school, and if that sounds like what happens to voters in gerrymandering, it's no coincidence. But that's okay because they have a $7,200 voucher to lure parents with[523].

Of course, that isn't enough to buy an entire year's decent education, so it is today that nearly 90% of the folks snapping up the vouchers[524] are just using *your* tax dollars to subsidize *their* kids' private religious education[525].

For example, take hypothetical little Timmy in Arizona. His school fees for a private Christian school are $9,000 per year. With a voucher, the State of Arizona will give his parents a $7,200 discount (no means testing required), paid for by Arizona taxpayers. There's no need to believe me. Here's Joshua Cowen, professor of education policy at Michigan State University and, after two decades of investigations, an expert on vouchers;

> First, vouchers mostly fund children already in private school. Despite supporter rhetoric that voucher schemes are about new opportunities, the reality is 70-80 percent of kids in states like Arizona, Missouri, and Wisconsin were already in private school before taxpayers picked up the tab.[526]

If you're one of my conservative friends, you may imagine that perhaps there are some cost advantages for the local taxpayers; nope, in Arizona, the state's own figures reveal the lie of the efficient market, with per-pupil public education costing less than the value of the voucher[527].

So, maybe the education these kids are getting is superb? Again. No. As a portent for what is going to happen to red state students in places like Florida and Texas, the kids turn out dumber, which, predictably, is what happens when you don't educate them professionally. Here's another receipt from Professor Joshua Cowen, who summed up vouchers for private schools;

> ....new evaluations of vouchers in Washington, D.C., Indiana, Louisiana, and Ohio show some of the largest test score drops ever seen in the research record.[528]

It's a truism that, wherever there is free money, con men will never be far behind. So it is, for grifters, the state-funded church school is a nice little earner, and in many cases, they can win twice; first because as a 'religious school', they pay no taxes. Then they receive up to 10% of the value of the voucher as *administrative expenses*. Jess Piper, former teacher, state house candidate, and host of the invaluable 'Dirt Road Democrats' podcast, described some scenarios;

> A lot of times churches struggle with funding. We see that there is a huge drop in church attendance. What's a great way to fund your church? Start a school, while accepting state paid voucher money. It works out well for the churches.[529]

Jess is right, but as is the liberal's burden, we're always required to provide receipts. So our journey takes us to the door of the $7250-a-year Tabernacle Christian School[530]. This religious outfit has received over $3.6 million between 2014 and 2024 from North Carolina taxpayers through vouchers[531]. We can learn about them from their own website;

Tabernacle Christian School of Monroe, NC began in 1972 under the leadership of Pastor Bobby L. Leonard and the members of Bible Baptist Tabernacle who saw the need for a private, Christian school in Union County, NC to assist parents in the training and educating of their children in a godly environment.[532]

To give you an idea of the sort of 'godly environment' its 251 pupils can expect, Pastor Leonard gave a 'sermon' in August 2023. In it, he criticized women for daring to dress in shorts, saying,

"If you dress like that and you get raped, and I'm on the jury, he's going to go free.... A man's a man."[533]

If 'Pastor' Leonard was a brown man, and this indoctrination camp was in Afghanistan, it would be called a madrasa, and it would be more likely to receive a drone strike than $3.6 million in funding.

Still, none of what you have read has dampened the enthusiasm of the GOP state legislature in North Carolina, which has allocated nearly $200 million per year of taxpayers' money to fund private Christian schools like Tabernacle[534].

To see how many of these shams end up, we can visit another GOP supermajority state, Wisconsin. Between 1990 and 2013, 41% of these 'private Christian schools' went bankrupt. It helps that, unlike taxpayer-funded public schools, the state never audits taxpayer-funded private schools, which means fraud and waste go undetected[535].

Still, perhaps, before going bust, these 'schools' might have had to take on a child who needs extra attention. No worries, they have a workaround. Jess Piper suggested what can happen;

He might have some sort of disability. He goes to the school with the voucher, and takes his money with him. They don't give him services. He goes back to the public school every single day, and uses the services from that defunded public school. That's the scam.[536]

So now the struggling public school is legally required to take that pupil back and educate him without any extra funding. And the child's parents don't know that anything is amiss, because he is still getting looked after. Of course, the strain this puts on the public school system means that it collapses even sooner. As for the owners of the tax-free voucher school, without doing any work, they still get to pocket that $7250. That's what legalized theft looks like.

Despite all this, there are fight-backs. When voters are offered the choice, they always reject vouchers because they actually know what their public schools do for their kids[537]. Paradoxically, this is especially the case in rural areas of red states. Rural residents know their school, and they know the teachers. Then factor in that it might be the only school for miles and also the largest employer in a small town.

This puts the local GOP rep in quite a pickle, as the last thing they want is for it to close. However, no such quandaries trouble the dogmatic dominators in the state capitols. With their GOP supermajority state legislatures, they can just smash these unpopular measures through. So it is that nineteen states are running these programs today[538].

Real Christians also accept the insanity of the state-funded church schools. Lori Walke, a senior minister of the Mayflower Congregational United Church of Christ involved in a lawsuit against the State of Oklahoma, had these words;

As a pastor, I care deeply about religious freedom. But creating a religious public charter school is not religious freedom. Forcing taxpayers to fund a religious school that will be a 'place of evangelization' for one specific religion is not religious freedom.[539]

She wasn't alone. Bruce Prescott, formerly of Mainstream Oklahoma Baptists, said,

> Religious schools–like houses of worship–should be funded through voluntary contributions from their own membership, not money extracted involuntarily with state taxes from members of a religiously diverse community.[540]

Obviously, fake Christians don't care what real Christians say. Indeed, ultimately, we know the far-right wants the public school system to collapse. Jack Schneider, education historian and co-author of "A Wolf at the Schoolhouse Door" offers,

> In the long-term, the challenge is that you weaken the system so badly that it never really recovers. That's a feature of voucher plans, not a bug, and many voucher advocates will talk quite openly about this aim.[541]

So it is that the state government, having gutted the education budget, can blame 'woke' teachers and 'socialism' for ruining the public education system. Then, once there's no more public school, they can contend that there is no more voucher money and move on to the real prize.

That would be the privatization of schooling and the requirement of those who want education for their kids to take out loans to pay for it. In doing so, they create a potential $200 billion loans-for-school industry for their pals on Wall Street and in big business. Don't take my word for it. Once again, we have receipts.

Charles Siler was a former lobbyist for the right-wing Goldwater Institute. This outfit was at the spearhead of the voucher idea. Speaking to Jennifer Berkshire, co-author of the 'Wolf at the Schoolhouse Door,' he laid out a conservative vision for education and explained how the far-right see it as a choice for consumers, but most of all, see themselves as not having to pay for education out of their taxes;

> They want to see is all the tax money returned to taxpayers. And then, if education is important to you, then you decide for yourself that it's important. And you place a value on how important it is, and how much you're willing to spend on it. And I think they would be happy to see a student loan market pop up for K 12 education. I think that would be like an ideal vision to them because then you're making money on loans, you're making money at the private schools, you're making money in taxes that aren't being paid. And I think they would even appreciate corporate sponsorships of public education."[542]

Our horror story has a foundation. Let's meet libertarian economist Milton Friedman. This buffoon was the godfather of the lies that are "supply-side" and 'trickle-down' economics. His worthless Ayn Rand-style ideas probably seemed avant-garde in the mid-1970s with the economic hardship caused by OPEC-induced inflation. Back in those desperate times, he fooled people into believing that corporation don't need to pay any tax and businesses must have no regulation[543]. Indeed, 1976 must have been a really quiet year in economics, because he won a Nobel Prize for this BS.

Perhaps it's best to hear Milton's demented, childlike, right-wing view of the world in his own words. This is from a research paper by Nancy MacLean, Professor of History and Public Policy at Duke University, quoting Milton's own words:

> "In my ideal world, government would not be responsible for providing education any more than it is for providing food and clothing," Friedman repeated in 2004 what he had long maintained. "Private charity would be more than ample to assure that there were schools available for every child." He was as frank in addressing a meeting of the American Legislative Exchange Council (ALEC) four months before his death in 2006. Said Friedman: "the ideal way [to give parents control of their children's education] would be to abolish the public school system and eliminate all the taxes that pay for it."[544]

This would be a bounty for private equity predators and their backers, the mistresses of Wall Street. Just assume that half of all parents take out loans; that's twenty-five million kids at $8k a year, creating a $200 billion a year industry.

Obviously, to sweeten the pie, the state will gift the private equity vultures all the (currently taxpayer-owned) public school buildings and land. And we haven't even factored in all the other juicy for-profit industries, whether school consultants, fees for the 26 million bus trips every day, school meal fees, after-school activities fees, or school book fees.

You may wonder how they think their middle-class Republican voters are going to enjoy having to pony up for Timmy's and Tabatha's education.

But then, this is the GOP. They just want to dominate and control, and if their own voters try to challenge them, they can always just stop them from voting.

Chapter 15

The Supreme Legislature's High Priests Who Rule Over All Of Us.

While most liberals look to Congress at the Capitol to see what legislation is passing, an extraordinarily effective quiet coup has been taking place just a five-minute walk away at the Supreme Court.

To get some idea of the level of threat, this is the satanic mill where six Republican high priests first forced women to bear their rapists' babies and then legalized the machine guns that can then murder those babies. I wish I was making this up, yet the first scenario arose out of the 2022 Dobbs ruling and the second from the 2024 Garland ruling[545].

From your high school civics classes, you may have learned a little about the Supreme Court of the United States (SCOTUS). Perhaps you imagine it is as old as America. Actually, the court building at 1 First Street NE, Washington D.C. was only built in 1935. It is younger than President Jimmy Carter, younger than sitting Senator Chuck Grassley, and younger than the actor Clint Eastwood. The corporations IBM, Coca-Cola and Ford, are all older. To throw some real shade, the first McDonald's restaurant was built just five years after the court.

The point I'm making is, there is nothing historic and nothing cast in stone or unchangeable about the Supreme Court or any of its procedures. Yet for elite liberals, despite the horribly partisan and downright cruel nature of many of the court's decisions, stasis appears their default state.

To drill down into how the court entranced, seduced, and promoted obsequience amongst liberals, we need to visit a veritable spider's web of self-interest. Many liberal journalists, lawyers, professors, and intellectuals look up to and back with nostalgia at the civil rights era Warren Court[546]. And from that was born a deference and servility that they afford no other body of government.

These people see the Supreme Court as the high-water mark of a career. Arguing before the court is a mark of honor. Reporting about the court makes the journalist feel they are engaged in important work. And parents dream of their children clerking for a Supreme Court justice. I'm reminded of Upton Sinclair's words;

> It is difficult to get a man to understand something when his salary depends upon his not understanding it.[547]

All this being said, we need to work with the facts that we have. To understand why the Supreme Court justices vote the way they do, just know that there are two ideas of how the Constitution should be interpreted: Originalism and the Living Constitution.

The first one posits that the Constitution is a fixed document written in 1787 and is sacrosanct. The second is more pragmatic, more in line with what the Framers intended; that times change and so should the way we interpret the Constitution.

As the latter is self-explanatory, we will focus on the former: 'Originalism'. When you learn that the word hadn't been used before 1981, the year the Space Shuttle first blasted off to the stars, you might see where we are going[548].

Originalism lives in the same world as Old Testament fundamentalism. Originalists claim to believe that we cannot imagine interpreting what was in the founders' minds when they wrote the Constitution and that we must view it rigidly. This being the case, let's examine the positions at the time of the long-dead framers.

In 1787, wealthy white landowning men were in charge of everything. Women could not vote and had no autonomy over their own bodies, and people of color were not free and could not vote.

Remember, dear reader, the founders were living in an age where Amy Coney Barrett would be the property of her husband, and Clarence Thomas would just be property. Back then, Catholicism was heresy, which nixes six of the current justices, and there were no corporations or industry, or cities or suburbs. It would be another seventy-two years before oil was discovered, the electric light bulb was ninety-three years away, and the first automobile wouldn't turn its wheels for another hundred years. These really were the dark ages.

Despite all that, the Founders were very clear about the Constitution, thinking that it should be looked at every twenty years to make sure that it was up to date. In letters to James Madison in 1789, Thomas Jefferson wrote that "......no society can make a perpetual constitution, or even a perpetual law." And "Every constitution then, and every law, naturally expires at the end of 19 years." [549]

It was Jefferson who also gave us, "The dead shall not rule the living", which rather gives a lie to the whole spurious concept of originalism.

They knew that the world was changing and the Constitution would have to adapt, and that adaptation is not a radical notion. Theirs was that concept of the 'Living Constitution'; that the Constitution is a living document that must be interpreted according to the times we live in.

For the Originalists, the Constitution is whatever they want it to be. That's what unadulterated hypocrisy looks like. It should come as no surprise that the Originalists are all Republican appointees.

The real tragedy is that the elites in society, especially those elite liberal lawyers, journalists, and politicians, allowed the spurious concept of originalism to pass into modern discourse without challenge or pushback.

If you tried to explain originalism to anyone else in a WEIRD nation, they would think that you were insane. Perhaps people in Afghanistan, Iran, or Saudi Arabia would understand your point of view, but someone in Canada, England or Germany? You wouldn't be locked up in an asylum, but if you were already there, you probably wouldn't get out!

The theocratic nature of originalism and the Confederate Taliban would come together on two particular issues. First, to fight against integration and the Voting Rights Act, and then to work to outlaw abortion. With these two issues, the far-right could gin up SCARI voters again and again[550].

I sometimes think of the six conservative justices as high priests and the Supreme Court as the Supreme Legislature. Whilst it's true they will have to defer to an autocratic Trump, absentia the fraudster, they have done whatever they want, and what they want is to rule over us.

To see how far the justices have fallen in integrity and honor, just go back to 1980, when Robert Bork was the first Supreme Court nominee to fail to get seated. That he was a stooge for big business was no particular obstacle; however, senators drew the line at him being a segregationist and a sex pest. In opposing his confirmation, Senator Edward Kennedy prophetically spoke of Bork's vision of America;

> ..is a land in which women would be forced into back-alley abortions, blacks would sit at segregated lunch counters, rogue police could break down citizens' doors in midnight raids, [and] schoolchildren could not be taught about evolution...[551]

None of this would be an impediment to being seated in 2024, but back in 1980, there was no Rush Limbaugh or Fox News, and decorum still existed. So it was that Ronald Reagan was forced to withdraw Bork's name from nomination.

How times change. All three of the Trump-appointed justices lied shamelessly during their confirmation hearings, describing Roe v. Wade as 'settled law.' Yet, once they were sitting pretty on the bench, they couldn't wait to strike it down.

It's impossible to understand the modern court without knowing how the right wing played the game of politics so well. For this, we need to take a couple of paragraphs to acquaint ourselves with the far-right Federalist Society (FedSoc) and its Executive Vice President, Leonard Leo. Harvard Professor Dr. Christopher Rhodes gives us an idea of who the Federalist Society (FedSoc) is:

> Beginning with Ronald Reagan, the Federalist Society has developed extensive connections with every Republican administration. The organization and the GOP have created a pipeline to the judiciary, making Federalist Society membership almost a prerequisite to gaining a judicial appointment during periods of Republican control. All six of the Repub-

lican-appointed justices currently on the Supreme Court are affiliated with the society, as were nearly all of the federal judges appointed by Trump.[552]

A small proviso. By 2024, the Heritage Foundation of Project 2025 notoriety may have exceeded FedSoc in the insanity stakes, but it's Leo's work that has borne such toxic fruit, and as such, represents a cautionary tale. Tom Carter, Leo's former media relations director, gave us some more insight into Leo;

"He figured out twenty years ago that conservatives had lost the culture war. Abortion, gay rights, contraception—conservatives didn't have a chance if public opinion prevailed. So, they needed to stack the courts."[553]

Leo, working with Harlan Crow and Ginny Thomas, was behind the Supreme Court ruling for Citizens United v. FEC in 2010. Of course, none of it could have happened without the bought-and-paid-for Clarence rigging the case for them. From that, we get unlimited First Amendment 'free speech' for corporations, meaning unlimited donations to GOP politicians to buy elections.

It wasn't always this way. Back in 1907, the Tillman Act banned corporations from spending on campaigns. This remained so until two cases in 1976 and 1978, when the Supreme Court ruled corporations could use their First Amendment rights to spend on elections with some financial limits[554].

Spin forward thirty-two years to Citizens United with Big Oil, Big Food, Big Tech, Big Ag, Defense, Pharmaceuticals, Insurance, Wall Street, and far-right activists free to spend unlimited funds on local, state, or federal elections to buy influence. The only restriction was that they couldn't give directly or coordinate directly with the candidate. Think of that as nothing more than a distinction without a difference.

So it is today that we have Exxon Mobil, which is a 'person' for First Amendment rights but not a 'person' when we want to sue it for setting fire to the planet. Thus, they become a corporate Schrödinger cat. On the one hand, they can pump unlimited contributions to the GOP, and on the other, claim that all their climate-change denial is protected speech.

To this point, in 2019, Exxon was hit with a multi-billion dollar lawsuit by Massachusetts Attorney General Maura Healey. She bought it on behalf of the state for the decades of fraud and crimes that Exxon has perpetrated on the American people. They counter-sued, claiming that they were being discriminated against for exercising their First Amendment rights. Speaking following their counter-suit, Attorney General Healey had these words;

> Americans need to be concerned about the acts of a big corporation seeking to stamp out the efforts of one little Attorney General from asking questions. It's as simple as that. Exxon itself has taken the rather extraordinary step of filing and action against me to say that I don't have the authority to ask questions. The day that happens in this country, that's a serious problem. Exxon is using the First Amendment that I am interfering with Exxon's First Amendment rights. I don't know how they get there, but that's what they've articulated, and they're coming at us.[555]

Attorney General Healey was bewildered because she was an honest person playing by the rules, but the far-right never was. It was the former president of Peru, Oscar R. Benavides, who said, "For my friends everything, for my enemies the law."[556]

The Confederate Taliban understood this quote very well and spent fifty years making it a reality, and for 'good' reason. They know, once they have the judges on their side, they are untouchable.

Today, liberals wonder how the corruption of at least three of the high priests isn't an issue, especially when every judge in America, from a magistrate, where you go if you have a traffic offense, all the way to the Federal Court of Appeals, is subject to the Code of Conduct for United States Judges. It states,

> An appearance of impropriety occurs when reasonable minds, with knowledge of all the relevant circumstances disclosed by a reasonable inquiry, would conclude that the judge's honesty, integrity, impartiality, temperament, or fitness to serve as a judge is impaired.[557]

Astonishingly, the Code doesn't apply to those nine Supreme Court Justices. They are expected to police themselves, and the only redress Congress has is impeachment, which entails the inconceivable scenario of a majority in the House and ten Senate Republicans voting to impeach a Republican Justice.

So, with no worries about impeachment, partisanship and corruption barely need to cover its face. In 2003, John Roberts was seated on the bench. At the time, his wife was a run-of-the-mill lawyer. Yet, just two years after John took his seat, Mrs. Roberts became a 'legal recruiter,' earning ten million dollars over eight years. Don't be surprised to learn that she was very popular with people and firms who had business before her husband's court[558].

Moving on to the exceptionally angry Samuel Alito. He is also not just extremely corrupt, but totemically partisan. That upside-down flag, also shown on the cover of this book, according to the US Flag Code, was originally a sign of a fort or ship in extreme distress[559].

Today, it has been adopted by the far-right and neo-Nazis to symbolize 'America in distress.' Alito flies this outside his home. At another of his homes, he flies the Appeal to Heaven flag. That would be the same flag carried by the fake-Christian terrorists at the J6 insurrection. It invokes 'God's anger' and represents the call for a violent overthrow of modern secular America.

To expunge any doubt of what he thinks of modern America, he is on record as explaining his Christian nationalism and how "there are differences on fundamental things that really can't be compromised."[560]

Then, we come to Clarence Thomas. He is perhaps the most egregious example of SCOTUS corruption, having been bought and paid for by a billionaire property developer, Harlan Crow. For background, Mr. Crow is a man with a penchant for Nazi memorabilia.

He has purchased Thomas's unsalable properties, paid for Thomas's adopted child to go to a $6000-a-month private school, and lavished numerous $500,000 'holidays' on him[561]. During these 'holidays', with no hint of irony, dozens of rich 'rent-seeking' devils, who all have business with the Supreme Court, just happen to meet Clarence[562].

To see how the corruption works. Back in 2012, Leonard Leo used Kellyanne "Alternative Facts" Conway (Trump's former adviser) as a 'bagman' to funnel a 'payment' to Thomas, via his wife, Ginny[563]. Then, without any connection at all, in November 2012, a brief was sent to the

Supreme Legislature to hear the Shelby County case that would, one year later, gut one of the far-right's greatest nightmares, the Voting Rights Act. That ruling was ground zero for why gerrymandering and voter suppression are worse than ever.

We will come back to the Supreme Court, but before a case reaches One First Street, Washington D.C, it has to pass through the 94 federal and 13 appellate courts[564].

During the Trump administration, Leo guided over 200 FedSoc judges into the federal judiciary[565]. Bear in mind there are only 870 federal judges in total, and all the FedSoc appointees were in their thirties or forties. So it is that, with their lifetime appointments, they will be on the bench for decades, blocking abortion and voting rights, eliminating LGBTQ+ rights, boosting fossil fuels, and allowing guns everywhere.

To understand what pain those two hundred Trump judges can inflict, just below the Supreme Court sit those thirteen appellate courts, staffed by 179 federal judges. If your game is insanity or domination, then just have your appeal heard in the Fifth Circuit Court of Appeals down in New Orleans. Covering the whole of Louisiana, Mississippi, and Texas, this is the funnel for many of the most despicable cases that reach the Supreme Court. Here sit seventeen judges; twelve of them are Republicans, of whom the six maddest are all Trump appointees[566].

It's the Fifth Circuit that sent the Dobbs case that resulted in the abortion ban up to the Supreme Court. The Fifth Circuit was also where Exxon filed its countersuit against Massachusetts. And the Fifth Circuit is where corporations brought the cases to gut the Environmental Protection Agency, Consumer Finance Protection Bureau, and other regulatory agencies.

So it is today that all those issues that liberals cherish—the environment, women's healthcare, safety regulation, gun control, and voting rights—eventually end up in the Supreme Court before the nine Justices who represent the third branch of government, the 'Supreme Legislature'.

Thus, even if the legislative (Congress) and the executive (the President) enact laws, all the Citizens United crowd have to do is appeal up to the 'Supreme Legislature.' Once there, with their friends leveraging a 6-3 majority, the six high priests hold a veto power over every other branch of government, and it will almost always be 'Goodnight Vienna' to liberal policies.

To illustrate that point. In June 2024, the six GOP activists barred the Alcohol, Tobacco, and Firearms Agency from enforcing a Trump-era ban that made semi-automatic rifle bump stocks illegal[567]. Just to note, the $99 bump stock fits on the trigger of a $500 AR-15-style semi-automatic rifle, transforming it into a fully automatic machine gun (four seconds to empty a thirty-round magazine).

These would be the same bump stocks that were banned in 2017 after being used in the worst mass shooting in modern history. At a country music festival in Las Vegas, bump stocks allowed the shooter to fire over a thousand rounds in under eleven minutes, killing sixty and wounding eight hundred concertgoers.

As we have read, your safety means nothing to the six high priests, but for their safety, absolutely no guns are allowed in the Supreme Legislature. That's their hateful hypocrisy. However, remember their guiding principle is power. So it was again in June 2024 that they made every fan of Project 2025 ecstatic by overturning the 40-year-old 'Chevron Doctrine.'

Before that time, it had been accepted by US courts that the federal government passed laws that would always be imperfect. It was then up to the experts (exactly who 'Project 2025' seeks to get rid of) in federal agencies like the EPA, FDA, or ATF to provide a reasonable interpretation of the law to allow the courts to decide what to do. In turn, that allowed those government agencies to protect you and your family.

In effect, what this now means is that the six justices are now the self-appointed experts on everything. In practice, it will look a lot like Justice Neil Gorsuch, who ruled in the 2024 case of Ohio v. EPA, against the

EPA stopping polluters from giving you cancer. Mr. Gorsuch didn't listen to experts, and in his ruling, wrote no less than five times about how the government was trying to limit "nitrous oxide emissions."

This silver-spoon-fed, incompetent imbecile couldn't distinguish the difference between 'nitrous oxide' and 'nitrogen oxide'. The former is the 'laughing gas' anesthetic you may get when you go to a dentist. The latter, the cancer-causing, planet-heating greenhouse gas the EPA was seeking to limit[568].

This is precisely why we have experts working in federal government agencies to advise the courts before they rule. But for Gorsuch and the other five high priests, evidence doesn't matter, facts don't matter, and science doesn't matter. All that matters is that we must obey them. For proof, I have a receipt from the dissent in the Ohio case of liberal and sane Justice Elena Kagan;

> In one fell swoop, the majority today gives itself exclusive power over every open issue — no matter how expertise-driven or policy-laden — involving the meaning of regulatory law.[569]

Equally despicable news came on the first day of July 2024. The six high priests dropped a bombshell by ruling that a president is a king above the law and has immunity from actions taken in office so long as they believed they were part of their official duties. Don't believe me. This is from liberal Justice Sonya Sotomayor's dissent;

> The President of the United States is the most powerful person in the country, and possibly the world,".....“When he uses his official powers in any way, under the majority's reasoning, he now will be insulated from criminal prosecution.

Orders the Navy's Seal Team 6 to assassinate a political rival? Immune. Organizes a military coup to hold onto power? Immune. Takes a bribe in exchange for a pardon? Immune. Immune, immune, immune.[570]

A lot of liberal tears were spilt after this, but that's the past. Looking four years into the future, after a possible Democratic victory, if we are talking about workable solutions, the simplest first step would be to apply the 'Code of Conduct for United States Judges' to the Supreme Court, as it is for all other judges. To do that, we need fifty-one senators to bypass the filibuster.

After that, there is not another country in the high-income world where a Supreme Court holds this much power and is this unaccountable to their citizens. There are suggestions for enacting age and term limits. In Germany and Switzerland, the maximum age for a judge is 68 years old. In Australia, Brazil, England, Israel, Japan, New Zealand, and on the European Court of Human Rights, the maximum age is 70 years old.

However, America does things differently, with Article III of the Constitution bestowing lifetime appointments on justices. This is how we have 76-year-old Clarence Thomas, sitting for thirty-three years on the bench, and 74-year-old Samuel Alito, with eighteen years on the bench.

In July 2024, President Biden proposed eighteen-year term limits, but as they wouldn't have been retrospective, Clarence, Sam, and John could all still have served another eighteen years[571].

There is a much simpler and much smarter path that Democrats don't bother talking about. Clearly, it will have to wait until 2029, but as the ultimate solution to extremism is always moderation, we get to court expansion. The Judiciary Act of 1869 gave us the nine justices for nine courts of appeal.

However, today as there are thirteen appellate courts, simple logic dictates that there should be thirteen justices on the Supreme Court[572]. To effect that change, Article III of the Constitution gives Congress sole discretion over the number of justices.

Chapter 16

The Confederate Taliban Are Coming To Check That You're Still Pregnant.

For women, pregnancy must rank as one of the most meaningful human experiences. For nine months, a mother nurtures inside her a life that will bring a lifetime of hopes and happiness and headaches and heartaches. But before that, it's only normal to imagine the mother should be afforded every health advantage to ensure the safe delivery of her baby.

So it might be astonishing to learn that, across one-third of America, just being pregnant can be a death sentence. To illustrate the point, let's talk about the planned birth of 25-year-old Jaci Statton from Oklahoma. Her pregnancy turned cancerous and became a threat to her health. She went to the hospital, where the staff told her,

> The best we can tell you to do is sit in the parking lot, and if anything else happens, we will be ready to help you. But we cannot touch you unless you are crashing in front of us or your blood pressure goes so high that you are fixing to have a heart attack.

In Oklahoma, medical staff facilitating an abortion (medical care) risk up to five years in prison and the loss of their medical license[573]. Oklahoma is no outlier. That's a woman's lot should she live in Alabama, Arkansas,

Idaho, Indiana, Kentucky, Louisiana, Mississippi, Missouri, North Dakota, Oklahoma, South Dakota, Tennessee, Texas, and West Virginia. Here, abortion is completely illegal, with no exceptions for rape, incest (which is also rape) or fetal disability.

As far as preserving the life of the mother goes, those fourteen Confederate Taliban states offer mealy-mouthed exceptions. But the laws are written opaquely so as to terrify doctors and medical staff into erring on the side of caution. Thus, by design, the exceptions put the mother at as much risk as possible, up to and including her death[574].

The cognitive mechanism the Confederate Taliban employs to make their "argument" is something to behold. To them, abortion is immoral and an affront to God. Therefore, women who get abortions are sinful. From this deranged standpoint, abortion is worse than rape. That is the strict father patriarchal worldview for you. It was the radio show host, Howard Stern, who said,

> You know, if guys got raped and pregnant, there'd be abortions available on every corner. Every street corner you'd have a different clinic that would take care of the problem.[575]

I'm reminded of the words of one of our smart, funny, and superbly intelligent friends, John Fugelsang. As the son of a Catholic nun and a Franciscan brother (like a priest), he knows the Bible back to front. On his 'Tell Me Everything' radio show, he spoke about abortion the way I wish politicians would;

> Just so you know, the Bible never bans abortion. Judaism, Jesus's religion, never bans abortion. Abortions are free and legal in Israel right now. God makes it very clear that life begins with first breath in Genesis. He gives abortion tips

for unfaithful pregnant wives in Numbers chapter Five, and God makes it very clear in Exodus 21 that he regards a fetus as property, and a woman's life has more value in his eye. You can be against abortion, you can fight to criminalize abortion, but don't claim Jesus is the reason.

Before we continue, let's get a bit of medical science. This is from the National Institute of Health:

Today, the prospect of survival is only about 1 in 10 at 23 weeks, and if the child lives, it is more likely to be handicapped than not. At 24 weeks, the chance of a normal survivor is about 50%, and after this, the odds are in favor of a normal survivor.[576]

From this, we can see that a fetus is not a viable independent life (i.e. a baby) until about 24 weeks. Even then, it is still entirely dependent on the mother. After all, the umbilical cord carries food and oxygen to the fetus from the mother. Thus, for the fetus to live, so must the mother, but if the fetus dies, the mother can still live.

It might not surprise you to learn the Confederate Taliban wasn't listening and come 2023, gave us a true American horror story. Texan Kate Cox was a 31-year-old pregnant mother of two. Her twenty-week-old fetus had Trisomy 18, a fatal chromosomal condition that all but guaranteed her baby would die in the womb or shortly after being born. For Mrs. Cox, the condition, left unaddressed, could lead to infection and infertility and even death.

During her pregnancy, she had been rushed to the ER four times with severe cramping and fluid loss. However, doctors advised her that there was nothing they could do without breaking state laws. These laws mean up to ninety-nine years in prison and up to a $100,000 fine for anyone assisting an abortion[577]. There's more. Even if a mother suffers the tragedy of a miscarriage in Texas, she can be charged with murder for "causing the death of an individual by self-induced abortion."[578]

So, in 2023 America, Mrs. Cox had to hire a lawyer to petition a Texas court to seek 'permission' to get an abortion (medical care). The case ended up before the nine Republicans on the Texas Supreme Court (zero medical qualifications). They ruled in the states' favor, stating that it wasn't a sufficiently serious case to justify an abortion. With her life, literally, hanging in the balance, Mrs. Cox had no choice but to flee her home state to seek medical care.

Let's just go back and imagine if Mrs. Cox was forced to give birth to a child with severe physical or mental conditions. Raising any child is expensive, but that cost increases exponentially where disabilities are concerned. In practice, would she need to modify her home? What if she rents a property that she can't modify? Then, would she have to quit her job to look after the child? Looking deeper, with all the time she needs to devote to this child, what time would she have for her other children? Then, what about the strain this could put on a marital relationship?

If she lived in 'socialist' Europe, Australia, or Canada, the government would assist her, providing the care the child needed. Sadly, she's in the Confederate Taliban's Texas, where women are sacrificed but guns are sacrosanct.

For the Confederate Taliban, dreaming up new inhumane and insidious ways to make people's lives more miserable appears to be just another day at the office. Take Ohio Republican Rep. Jean Schmidt. In 2022, she imagined the hypothetical situation where a thirteen-year-old child victim of rape became pregnant as "an opportunity for that woman" to have a baby and that she should just give her rapist's baby to a member of her family to raise[579].

Schmidt's demented fever dream became a sad and sick reality that same year. A nine-year-old Ohioan girl was raped and made pregnant. Just stop and think about that: a child—whose only concerns should have been how quickly she can get her homework done, what ice cream to have after dinner, and when she can meet up with her friends—was raped. That's horrific.

But then, just for the cruelty, GOP politicians forced her to travel to Indiana to get an abortion (medical care), because Ohio had instituted a six-week ban with no exceptions for rape or incest[580].

One of the many hypocrisies of men on the right is that they are the 'alphas.' I'm, of course, thinking of states just like Ohio and Texas, where weak men claim they need to protect 'little ladies'—who run corporations, fly fighter jets, and sit on the Supreme Court.

We simply need to look at their cult leader to understand why they appear to help one of the weakest forms of men, rapists. If the GOP really were the party of law and order, solving rapes would be a top priority. Instead, a rapist has only a 1% chance of being convicted[581].

To understand why, just know that no investigation can take place without the attacker first being reported to the police. Then bear in mind, in eight out of ten cases, it will have been a partner, former partner, family member, or acquaintance who has assaulted the woman[582]. So, the survivor will probably have to deal day to day with her assailant.

And, even if she can summon the courage to report it, society gaslights the survivor into asking whether her actions contributed to the attack. We know the lines; *"What was she dressed like?", or "What was she doing there?"*

In January 2024, using FBI, Bureau of Justice, and CDC data, a study was released detailing rapes in those fourteen states that banned abortion with no exceptions. In the eighteen months since July 2022, when Roe was overturned, there were 519,981 rape victims. Those women weren't just statistics; they were wives and daughters and mothers and sisters. For

64,565, or 12%, of them, they didn't just get attacked; they were forced to give birth to their rapists' baby[583].

As a man, it's impossible for me to fathom the violation and trauma of rape. But then, I have some empathy, which places me in direct contrast to the Confederate Taliban.

Just when one thinks they can't sink any lower, they plumb even deeper, more demonic depths of immorality. Which brings us to a candidate running for the Michigan state legislature in 2022. Robert Regan, a father of three daughters, said, "I tell my daughters if rape is inevitable, lie back and enjoy it."[584]

Lie back and enjoy it. What's going on? I doubt that Karl Jung could unpack this creature, even with an assist from Dr. Freud. You may not be surprised to learn that he lost, with his own daughter's imploring voters *not* to vote for him.

Returning to the study, the vast majority, 88%, of those women survived their violent assault without getting pregnant.

While thinking about that, I recalled a section from war reporter and author, Sebastian Junger's sublime 2016 book on belonging, 'Tribe.' In it, he compared the trauma visited on rape survivors with that of PTSD in soldiers;

> Rape is one of the most psychologically devastating things that can happen to a person, for example—far more traumatizing than most military deployments—and according to a 1992 study, close to one hundred percent of rape survivors exhibited extreme trauma immediately afterward. And yet almost half of rape survivors experienced a significant decline in their trauma symptoms within weeks or months of their assault.[585]

In the book, he quoted Dr. Rachel Yehuda. She is the director of traumatic stress studies at Mount Sinai Hospital in New York. As an authority in studying PTSD and intergenerational trauma, she offered this insight into treatment;

> Treating combat veterans is different from treating rape victims, because rape victims don't have this idea that some aspects of their experience are worth retaining.[586]

Dr. Yehuda is entirely correct for those women who were attacked but *didn't* get pregnant. They were attacked and survived, and society tells them to get on with their lives.

We could talk about what trauma this might instill in the survivor, whether from a fear of men or a fear of trusting men. Indeed, nothing can ever diminish their unremittingly horrific experience, and the courage and strength it takes to deal with it must be greater than most men will ever possess. This being said, as bad as it undoubtedly was, it could have been even worse.

To see what that 'even worse' looks like, we only need to look to the 64,565 women in the study who didn't just suffer the violence of rape with all those after-effects. For them, the crime lived on, as they were forced to give birth to their unwanted and unplanned rapists' baby. This caused me to think a little deeper.

There's a reason, in a free society, that women choose when they have children and who the father will be. In the father, they are looking for the best qualities that can be passed on to their child, whether attractiveness, humor, intelligence, kindness, or success, all to allow the child to have the best chance in life. Being raped eviscerates that freedom.

It's also an incontrovertible truth that decent, kind men don't rape women. Psychology Today described some traits of the rapist: "aggressive behavior and a lack of empathy: psychopathy, narcissism, Machiavellianism, and sadism."

These are the polar opposite of the characteristics that a mom dreams their child will grow up to possess. As an adopted child, I know better than many how much of me is nature and how much is nurture, and I'm fully cognizant that my bad traits never came from the good people who adopted me.

None of this even gets us on to thinking about the suffering that this inflicts on the mother, not just from the violent event itself, but from having to see her rapist's image reflected in her child. Or having to wrestle with the truth that, in spite of the imperfectly violent union that led to their creation, half of that child is her; they will look like her, have her characteristics, and she will love them.

But the corollary is that, no matter how well she raises them, she will see those undesirable characteristics that aren't hers and know that they were *his* but be powerless to do anything about it. And we haven't even gotten to how the mother explains to her child who and what their father was and how that knowledge will cascade through the child's life in terms of intergenerational trauma.

To that point, sadly, the Confederate Taliban will never stop wanting to punish women. So it is that in many red states, rapists are afforded custody rights to see 'their' child[587]. In the words of Darcy Benoit, a mom forced for eight years to co-parent with her rapist,

> It's just been hell—I've been stalked, harassed, tormented, and so has my son,"_"I've had protective orders on him, but they expire every year, and he violates them often.[588]

As far as mental health treatment goes, the fact the mom couldn't travel to another state to receive an abortion is a fair indication that they are not privileged or wealthy. So they probably also couldn't afford the years of $100-an-hour mental healthcare that could help to guide them through this complicated trauma. This in itself is a guarantee of future bad health outcomes.

But, even if they could obtain treatment, to see how challenging that would be, allow me to take you on a small segue. The military has a term: "Unit cohesion[589]." In a modern professional army, the aim of training is to reach the Herculean goal of building a fraternal bond where soldiers are prepared to die for their buddies. It's partly love and partly self-interest, as, on the battlefield, it's the person next to you who will probably save your life.

Once suitably trained and in their 'band of brothers' (I know there are many sisters as well) with a bond as strong as any family, they are ready to be sent into hell.

There, intoxicated by feelings of brotherhood and the euphoria of engaging in and surviving combat, they are rewarded with an 'angel's cocktail' of the brain's natural feel-good drugs—dopamine, oxytocin, and endorphins—the secret of every happy person. Then imagine one day out on patrol, their Humvee is struck by an IED, and two of their buddies are killed. It's important to note one doesn't need to be either physically injured or physically present to experience post-traumatic stress disorder (PTSD.)

That being so, they are now left trying to hold two diametrically opposed thoughts in tension. There are exceptional memories of soaring friendships and the exhilaration of participating in and surviving combat that they won't want to forget. But intertwined with that is the horror and pain of the loss of friends and comrades that haunt their days and dreams[590]. This is from Dr. Rachel Yehuda;

> For most people in combat, their experiences range from the best of times to the worst of times.

Here's the substantial difference between the veteran and the rape survivor. Society, rightly, lionizes the former. The VA, money no object, will offer the best treatments and counselors. Today, PTSD treatments using MDMA and psilocybin have shown the ability to reach a holy grail in treatment: suppressing the traumatic memories while leaving the positive ones intact[591].

In contrast, look at how society treats the rape survivor, especially one raising her attacker's baby. No one is interested in her trauma. No one is offering her counseling. No one is offering her experimental treatment to assuage the 'devil's cocktail' of cortisol and adrenaline surging through her body. And if her kid grows up with behavioral problems, then he's a 'freak' or a 'loser,' and the mom is a 'crap mother' or a 'failed parent.'

Knowing all that, if we return to the study, it pointed out the most dangerous place to be a woman in America; it was Texas. That's where 26,313 women were forced by the state to give birth to their rapist's baby.

To segue, this is the lived reality of the Trump Abortion Ban. Just try to imagine the unmitigated cruelty that must fester within the minds of the judges, politicians, and voters to inflict such suffering on their fellow Americans. Coming back to Texas, as with all the most repressive societies, the state empowers private citizens to spy on each other. Indeed, Texans can file lawsuits against anyone who 'aids and abets' in facilitating an abortion[592].

Just to further illustrate the sanctimoniousness of the far-right, the Bible they use as a prop is very clear on this subject. You might know the phrase "An eye for an eye", but not where it came from. It's from Exodus 21:25:

> If men strive, and hurt a woman with child, so that her fruit depart from her, and yet no mischief follow: he shall be surely punished, according as the woman's husband will lay upon him; and he shall pay as the judges determine. And if any mischief follow, then thou shalt give life for life, Eye for eye, tooth for tooth, hand for hand, foot for foot.

Read literally, "life for life" translates as a death sentence for any fake-Christians who harm pregnant women. I don't wish it, but it is straight from the Old Testament part of the book they profess to follow. Of course, no Democrat or journalist would ever dare to point this out.

Some may still wonder about the hypocrisy of the 'small government' crowd, now wanting government interference in people's bedrooms, bathrooms, and consulting rooms. However, it's easy to unpack when we understand that the 'freedom' the far-right loves shouting about is *their* freedom to tell *you* what to do.

Extreme right-wing fundamentalism is the same everywhere. Whether they are brown men in Saudi Arabia, black men in Nigeria, or white men in America. This being said, in the autocratic theocracy that is Saudi Arabia, abortion is legal where there is a risk to the mother's life, or to preserve the mother's physical health. Indeed, across the Islamic world, fewer restrictions are put on women than in half of America. Even in Afghanistan, women are treated marginally more humanely, with abortion allowed where it is to save the life of the mother[593]. And in Israel, the home of Christianity, women have complete freedom to choose what happens with their own bodies.

Back in America, the Confederate Taliban not only want their lunch, they want to eat ours as well. For them, the fetus is a lovely get-out, as it costs them nothing. All the responsibility is on the woman, and as soon as the child is born, they are...well, marvelous George Carlin tells it to us perfectly in his 1996 HBO special, "Back in Town";

> Conservatives are obsessed with a fetus from conception to nine months after that they don't want to know about you. They don't want to hear from you, no neonatal care, no day-care, no Head Start, no school lunch, no food stamps, no welfare. If you're preborn, you're fine. If you're preschool, you're fucked. Conservatives don't give a fuck about you until you reach military age. Then they think you are just fine, just what they've been looking for. Conservatives want live babies so they can raise them to be dead soldiers. Pro-life, they're not pro life. You know what they are? They're anti-woman. Simple as it gets, anti-woman.[594]

For the patriarchal far-right, MAN + WOMAN + SEX = CREATION, and creation is good, so everything that stops creation must be bad.

In their deranged, unscientific minds, each sperm or egg is a potential life. To follow that ignorant, twisted logic, of course abortion 'kills' the fetus. But condoms stop sperm, and IUTs, the morning-after pill, and IVF all prevent fertilization of the eggs; thus, they must all also be banned.

We know that these despotic demons aren't concerned about what happens after creation, just that the fornication by virile men, including rapists, leads to procreation and lots of babies. This is the fake-Christian and patriarchal dream, and it's also why not just birth control but gays, lesbians, and transgender people must also all disappear.

For the exceedingly fragile right-wing men who want to end abortion, forced birth is actually deviantly ingenious. The pregnant woman will have to look after the child, so she won't be able to work. As raising a child is very expensive, and with the government offering no paid family leave, pre-K, or paid child care, just to survive, she must get married. Now her patriarch can trap her in the home, and, whilst looking after the child, she can serve the husband by cooking, cleaning, washing, and ironing. Thus, the patriarch gets himself a baby and a servile wife, who can provide more babies.

But, we haven't finished with advantages for the far-right. Come election time, because the wife depends completely upon her husband, she will judge it in her own economic self-interest to vote Republican[595].

As far as the law is concerned, I will give those six corrupt hacks on the Supreme Court a lesson in constitutional law that liberals are too scared to give them. The Fourteenth Amendment is transparently clear, even if you read it in its "Originalist" form, with no modern interpretation:

> All persons born or naturalized in the United States, and subject to the jurisdiction thereof, are citizens of the United States and of the state wherein they reside. No state shall make or enforce any law which shall abridge the privileges or immunities of citizens of the United States.[596]

Here's where the logic comes in. A mother is a citizen of the USA, born or naturalized. But a fetus is *not* born and *cannot* thus be a citizen. As a result, it's offered no privileges anywhere in the Constitution. Indeed, it has no more rights than a pineapple.

Also, according to the Fourteenth Amendment, no states may "deprive any person of life, *liberty*, or property, without due process of law." Liberty is the magic word. That is synonymous with freedom, autonomy, and choice.

But don't think that the Confederate Taliban doesn't have a plan for that. Fetal Personhood means that from the moment of conception, the fetus will have rights[597]. Given what you've just read, one would imagine even a first-year law student should be able to argue against this madness.

To that point, even the post-lobotomy simpletons on 'Fox and Friends' realize the elephantine weight around the GOP's neck that these anti-woman policies represent. However, the insane base requires complete domination and so will keep electing far-right demons who smile as they make women's lives hell.

Which brings us to the fake-Christians on the Alabama Supreme Court. In February 2024, they ruled that frozen embryos are children—the Fetal personhood argument. This effectively banned IVF in the state, despite IVF actually helping to start families (1 to 2% of births per year in the US.)[598]

Initially GOP politicians, like Nikki 'Nimrata' Haley, cheered this. That only lasted for a couple of days. Presumably wealthy—one course of IVF costs over $12,000—educated Republicans got on the phone and demanded they backtrack[599].

The business of exposing duplicity can get rather monotonous, but you should know that, to help start their families, IVF was used by Nikki Haley (yes!), Mike Pence's wife, and Justice John Robert's wife[600].

Still, as insanity's only dietary requirement is to be fed more insanity, in 2024, Trump offered that, should he win, states could monitor women's menstrual cycles to check whether they were pregnant[601].

By 2024, sadly, many millions of women of all ages, but, most astonishingly, young ones, couldn't be bothered to vote or voted Republican[602]. By doing so, they ensured women get to experience an America where rapists run free, forced birth is the norm, and a pregnancy might mean a death sentence. But, before that, neo-Nazi and Trump dining partner Nick Fuentes offered all women a reality check with the words "Your Body. My Choice. Forever."[603]

Chapter 17

Sisters Who Hate Other Sisters

Back in 2022, brave and dynamic Michigan State Senator Mallory McMorrow offered the nation a masterclass in how to take down the Confederate Taliban. After being falsely accused by her toxic Republican rival of 'grooming," simply because she spoke up for LGBTQ+ kids, this young suburban mom fired back with words many Democrats are terrified to say, even in their dreams;

> People who are different are not the reason that our roads are in bad shape after decades of disinvestment or that health-care costs are too high or that teachers are leaving the profession. I want every child in this state to feel seen, heard, and supported, not marginalized and targeted because they are not straight, white, and Christian. We cannot let hateful people tell you otherwise, to scapegoat and deflect from the fact that they are not doing anything to fix the real issues that impact people's lives. And I know that hate will only win if people like me stand by and let it happen.[604]

Senator McMorrow is a true patriot who's got grit and is willing to fight to make America the best it can be. Some elite Democrats acted surprised at the positive response to her comments, but they shouldn't have[605]. After all, the courage to stand up and fight for what's right is one of the most admirable qualities anyone can have.

We have seen how many Democrats are terrified of upsetting 'our friends on the other side,' so they never fight, which makes them look weak. Senator McMorrow stood up to the right-wing trolls and bullies and said what many are thinking. This is what 'fight' looks like, and it's what 'authentic' looks like. The only confusing part was imagining how anyone couldn't find this popular. Indeed, had Democrats stood more candidates like her, they might have won in 2024. Still, remember Senator McMorrow's words as we read on.

In 2024, liberals pull their hair out in amazement and frustration at the fact that so many white women—the largest recipients of affirmative action and Diversity, Equity and Inclusion programs[606]—vote Republican. According to Pew Research, it was 47% in 2016 and increased to 53% in 2020, where it stayed in 2024[607].

Part of the explanation lies in the unyielding fragility of fake Christian men, petrified at the thought of a self-reliant woman. Thus, through poisonous, patriarchal, 'purity culture,' young girls are indoctrinated in fundamentalist churches to grow up 'pure' (virgins) by being suspicious of sex before marriage and of their own bodies[608]. The result of all this brainwashing are women who become tradwives, requiring patriarchal father-figure-style men to 'look after' them. This leads us on to a conversation about why red states don't need sex education and why teenage pregnancies are higher in those states. Clearly, young women exposed to this form of child abuse can experience deep trauma in adulthood.

Returning to white women voters, we find ourselves in the paradox of political disconnection, as we know from the last chapter that today, across red-state America, abortion is outlawed, putting women's lives at risk. So, while it's easy to understand why conservative men need compliant wives, why would any woman vote against her self-interest or that of her daughters? As ever, nothing is simple, and in 2023 in red states like Kansas, Kentucky, and Ohio, where there were amendments on the ballot to enshrine women's choice in the state constitutions, Republican-voting women helped ensure that they passed[609].

Yet, here's where we get to the conundrum, wrapped in an enigma and surrounded by a puzzle. When it's time to vote for their state and congressional representatives, many of those same Republican-voting women stay loyal to the GOP. This, despite it being as sure as the sun rising in the east and setting in the west, the GOP rep they put in office will always be everything that any sane woman should despise—anti-children, anti-healthcare, anti-education, anti-science, and of course, anti-abortion.

That last part never had to be. An Equal Rights Amendment would enshrine sex equality in law and ensure safe access to medical care for all women. This was ready to be enacted in 1972. Clearly it wasn't, which is why today, we see ten-year-olds forced to bear their rapist's babies. To meet the person who, as much as anyone, we can curse for this, let's visit with Phyllis Schlafly.

Like all self-hating, sadistic women, she was, above all else, a moronic shill for the patriarchy, too asinine to acknowledge that it was the tireless struggles of the 19th century suffragists that allowed her to speak in public. Schlafly would cheer on Joseph McCarthy's witch-hunts in the 50s and was also an early member of the John Birch Society.

But her tour de force was that she was the driving force behind the derailment of the Equal Rights Amendment in 1972. That was the pivot point that would turn the GOP into an anti-woman party. This, however, was no concern for Schlafly, who was quoted as saying, "A woman should have the right to be in the home as a wife and mother." She should have just deleted "*have the right to,*" and we would arrive back at the tradwife.

Phyllis railed against the standard fake-Christian fundamentalist bete noirs of abortion on demand, same-sex marriage, integrated schools—she was a fan of 'school vouchers' and home-schooling—and women in the military[610].

Doubtless, disappointingly, she became a mother to a gay son. That poor lamb seems to have grown up mightily confused, shilling for the same Confederate Taliban who would send him to 'gay conversion therapy.'[611]

Obviously, Phyllis was none too keen on black folks. Back in 1971, her hate tract, 'The Phyllis Schlafly Newsletter', offered on its front page,

> Everybody is against busing — but how do we stop it...... and other Federal court decisions which pave the way for busing from suburbs to inner cities?[612]

The purest distillation of the hypocrisy of this demented ladder-pulling freak lived within the fact that she was the kept wife of an equally unhinged wealthy lawyer.

For a receipt to illustrate her derangement, in 2016, at the time of the MeToo movement, her fathomless cruelty allowed her to mock "aggressive females on television talk shows yapping about how mistreated American women are." All while backing a self-confessed sex criminal for president[613].

As we know, Schlafly wasn't alone. It's a sad and simple reality that a lot of working and middle-class women who voted Republican in 2016, 2020, and 2024 will be very comfortable with their choice. To understand, we need to widen the camera lens. In times of slavery, these women would have been the 'Miss Annes'; both handmaids and enthusiastic supporters of slavery. Then, during segregation and since, they have profited from what author W.E.B. Du Bois called, back in 1935, a "public and psychological wage" just from being born white[614].

From the opening chapter of the book, you may recall how the elite class designed America to ensure lower-class whites never rose to the top. Instead, they sold these Americans the notion of the 'scarcity mindset,'[615] conditioning them to believe black and brown people are coming to take their place on the social ladder. To survive, they must 'fight' to protect their higher status. This self-sabotaging paradox explains why, despite these people perhaps also wanting good healthcare, excellent schools, paid family leave, and paid sick pay, or being the recipients of government assistance programs like disability, Medicaid, SNAP, or Social Security, they vote again and again for GOP politicians. Those same Republican devils manage a politically incredible bait and switch by offering their voters the sick salvation of seeing people of color smashed down on while simultaneously doing all in their power to cut funding or even eliminate those wonderful ideas and programs thus ensuring that their own voters' lives never meaningfully improve.

As far as the GOP-voting women's roles go, some may lack the chutzpah or skills to get a job or may just like being kept. Indeed, many may enjoy the life of the tradwife. For them, preparing the husband's dinner, looking after the children, and tidying the house is a job in itself, as it was for the 1950s American housewife.

However, be under no illusion, the 1950s were a time when women 'knew their place.' Back then, when friends came round for dinner, the men spoke of business, politics, or sports, whilst the women were relegated to listening demurely and absolutely never voicing an opinion on anything other than cooking, children, or clothes. Of course, if women choose this life, that's fine. The problem arrives when the Confederate Taliban wants to impose it on the women who don't choose it.

At this point, allow me to introduce another fragile, Miss Anne-like, ladder-pulling hypocrite, Megyn Kelly. Between 2004 and 2017, Kelly worked at Fox under one rapist, Roger Ailes, and then in 2016, she hosted a Republican debate with another. There, she made the unforgivable mistake of forgetting she was part of a cult and asked Trump about his calling women "fat pigs" and "disgusting animals."

In the spirit of the weak little sister he is, Trump lashed out. Speaking to CNN, he said,

> She gets out there and she starts asking me all sorts of ridiculous questions, and you could see there was blood coming out of her eyes, blood coming out of her ... wherever.[616]

For her 'insubordination', Kelly was booted out of Fox but landed a $69 million two-year contract with NBC. There, she whined about not being allowed to wear 'blackface' anymore (slavery, ripped apart families, lynchings, Jim Crow apartheid state, but hey, don't hurt delicate Megyn's feelings). She got fired, but not before collecting the full $69 million on the way out. That's what failing up looks like.

To understand Kelly is to know that she's a cancerous, evil grifter who's in it for the money. It wouldn't startle me to learn that her medicine cabinet was full of anti-anxiety drugs, just to cope with the malignant monstrosity the mirror throws back at her every morning. As the $69 million showed, she could have been a normal opinion host at NBC, but she's so hollow that even after being abused by Trump, her love of the grift overpowered any inkling of self respect and led her back, like a beaten dog, to her master.

Yet, even though she never stopped furiously peddling lie after lie about vaccines, COVID, and the 2020 election, it wasn't enough for the cult leader. After all, a petulant SWIMP never forgets and never forgives. Thus, eight years later, in March 2024, Trump spoke of her in appropriate terms, saying, "Megyn Kelly. May she rest in peace," adding, "She's sort of making a career by pretending she likes me."[617]

Today, this wretched, empty shell of a woman is fully on board with the dawn of fascism and the end of freedom. This being said, of course, she lives her truest values. You might imagine that taking place somewhere deep red, like 'anti-woke' Florida or 'gun-em-down' Texas.

Alas, my dear reader, when dealing with the Confederate Taliban, one must never underestimate their Mariana Trench-like levels of hypocrisy. It is this piousness that allows Kelly, a mother to a teenage daughter, to split her time between homes in two states. They are both places where women are free, guns are locked up, and gay people are unafraid: solid-blue Connecticut and solid-blue New Jersey.

Chapter 18

Dead for Under A Dollar.

Fifty-nine cents won't buy you anything at McDonald's, won't buy you anything at Starbucks, and won't buy you anything at Walmart. What it will buy you is an American life, for it's the cost of a perfectly legal-to-buy and legal-to-own M885 green-tipped bullet that will slot into the magazine of an AR-15-style semi-automatic rifle[618].

If it's ammo for a 9mm semi-automatic pistol you're after, then life gets even cheaper, as these are just twenty-seven cents each[619]. Whoever you are and wherever you live, 'DEAD FOR UNDER A DOLLAR' is the reality of American life today. Bear this in mind as we take an odyssey through insanity.

If you grew up watching Westerns, you may be familiar with the scene. Two gunslingers face each other in a dusty street outside the saloon, eyes narrowed, hands hovering over their holsters, ready to draw. In those places, seemingly, every man had a gun or two. But then, it was the Wild West. Or was it?

As ever with Hollywood, it was a myth. Take Dodge City in Kansas. This was the home of the fictional Marshal Matt Dillon in the hit TV show 'Gunsmoke.' This series ran from 1955 through 1975. Every week, millions of Americans saw the gunslinging marshal on the frontier of violent justice, protecting the townsfolk from the lethal outside world.

The truth is much more mundane. According to the book "Gunfight: The Battle over the Right to Bear Arms in America" by Adam Winkler; " Frontier towns—places like Tombstone, Deadwood, and Dodge—actually had the most restrictive gun control laws in the nation." He describes a sign from 1879 in Dodge City stating, "THE CARRYING OF FIREARMS STRICTLY PROHIBITED."

Indeed, the first law that Dodge City passed when it became a municipality was a gun law that stated:

> any person or persons found carrying concealed weapons in
> the city of Dodge or violating the laws of the State shall be
> dealt with according to law.

Similarly, in Tombstone, Arizona, open carry was banned, and in Wichita, Kansas, visitors to the town would drop their guns off with the sheriff and get a token in exchange[620].

As we know, there was violence in the West, but it was the Union Army and 'hunters,' wiping out the remains of the indigenous people and their buffalo. Then, on the site of their native lands, came those western towns.

As those places were all new, they needed to attract citizens and businesses to come and settle.

To put it into perspective, think of a modern city. Gunshots are not a welcoming advertisement for either new homeowners or businesses. As it is now, so it was then. Regular folk would never settle in a town where their welcome was armed bandits trying to rob them or drunks taking potshots at them. So it was that the town's elders simply banned the carrying of firearms within the town limits.

To see how far backwards we have come, in Missouri, the State House of Representatives voted in 2023 to override a law that stopped "14-year-olds walking down the middle of the street in the city of St. Louis carrying AR-15s."[621]

In this chapter, you will read about the AR-15, a semi-automatic rifle, colloquially known as an 'assault rifle'.

While this style of gun 'only' represents about twenty million of all the four hundred million guns in America[622], understanding the visceral 'political' appeal of the AR-15 rifle among a subset of scared, weak, and angry men is central to learning a deeper truth: how and why poisonous GOP politicians, right-wing media, the National Rifle Association (NRA), and the high priests on the Supreme Court have enshrined insanity as legality.

Our journey will take us along a path to illuminate why Americans are being gunned down in schools, churches, and on the street. By the end of the chapter, I will show you that, while gun safety reform might seem hopeless and intractable, when viewed from a different angle, there are solutions.

Before we continue, here are a couple of paragraphs on guns to put matters into context. One in every three Americans owns those 400 million guns[623]. Then, across the nation, there are 78,000 gun stores; nearly twice as many as there are supermarkets[624].

Guns are used in eight out of ten murders[625]. According to the FBI, most of those homicides are committed using handguns[626], as they are easy to conceal, which means the assailant can get close to their victim, and the closer they get, the more likely the gunshot wound is to kill them.

Sadly, just having a weapon at home can put the owner and their family at risk. Of the 48,000 gun deaths in 2022, over half were people who killed themselves by suicide[627]. However, there's more. This from Cathy Shuko writing in Hopkins Bloomberg Public Health;

> "In reality, having access to a gun triples a person's risk of suicide, and nearly doubles the risk of being a homicide victim. For a woman living with an abusive partner, the risk of being murdered increases five-fold, if the partner has a gun."

Returning to the AR-15-style rifle. They are only used in three in every hundred deaths, but, because of their lethality and association with their military cousin, the near identical M4 rifle, the violence they visit is so much more emotive, guaranteeing media coverage[628].

With that grounding, we can acquaint ourselves with the AR-15. For that, we have to travel back to 1957. Ike Eisenhower was president, Alaska became the 49th state and Gunfight at the OK Corral was playing in movie theaters. This was also the year that the Armalite Rifle 15 was designed[629].

To better understand the gun, we need to skip forward to 2023. There's a video you can see on YouTube. We are in San Antonio, Texas, a state where anyone over twenty-one can legally carry a gun. In the footage, taken from a police officer's Body Worn Camera (BWC), we see at least four cop cars lined up on a street outside a suspect's house.

An officer tries to reason with the suspect, who has been reported for discharging his weapon in public. The cop's BWC shows him, almost pleading with the guy, saying multiple times, "Don't reach for it....DO N'T DO IT." The man ignores the commands and opens fire. Instead of returning fire, the cop starts running for his life. He sprints past two other police cruisers before entangling himself with another terrified, fleeing fellow officer. Once extracted, he continues his sprint, desperate to reach the solid cover of a brick building. As he runs, he's screaming, breathlessly, "He's got an AR... He's got an AR...... He's got an AR......." The fear and panic in his voice is blood curdling. Remember, this isn't some civilian caught up in a school or mall shooting; this is an armed cop, fully trained, wearing a bullet-proof vest, and backed up by at least four other cops[630].

Bear that in mind as we now head to Louisville, Kentucky, in 2023. A bank robbery is in progress. We see two AR-15-wielding cops cautiously climbing the steps to the bank's main entrance. As they are at the doors, gunshots ring out. One cop spins around so fast he falls over before gathering himself to race down the steps and take cover behind a large concrete flowerpot. The point again here is that this was a strong, well-trained, heavily armed cop who had backup. They must have known something that we don't[631].

I need you to forget the nonsense that you have seen in Hollywood action movies. On screen, when someone is shot, we may see a spurt of blood, and they fall to the ground. But, dear reader, prepare yourself for the reality. It was revealed in a 1962 Defense Department analysis on field use of the AR-15 rifle;

> "On 13 April, 62, a Special Forces team made a raid on a small
> village. In the raid, seven VC were killed. Two were killed by

AR-15 fire. Range was 50 meters. One man was hit in the head; it looked like it exploded. A second man was hit in the chest; his back was one big hole." [632]

Here's another report of a Ranger Company firefight with Vietcong in 1962;

"At a distance of approximately 15 meters, one Ranger fired an AR-15 full-automatic hitting one VC with 3 rounds with the first burst. One round in the head-took it completely off. Another in the right arm, took it completely off, too. One round hit him in the right side, causing a hole about five inches in diameter."[633]

Today, anyone using a $750 AR-15 can empty a thirty-round magazine as fast as they can pull the trigger, which is about six seconds. That's less time than it took you to read that last sentence. The bullet explodes out of the muzzle, traveling at 3300 feet per second[634]. In that second, it can cross nine football fields.

For more of a picture, the F-22 Raptor is currently the fastest fighter jet that the US military can put up into the sky. It can fly at 1534 mph[635]. The Sidewinder missile that can shoot that jet down streaks through the sky at 1918 mph[636], but a bullet from an AR-15 will overtake them both at 2056 mph.

Now that you know what the gun can do, can you blame those cops for running for their lives? I don't, because while it's true they were trained to protect us, they know that one bullet could punch straight through their Level IIIA ballistic vest, and from there, the story has only one ending: a flag-draped coffin, a six-gun salute, their wives as widows, and their kids as orphans.

Before we go on. If you have never held a gun, or used one, it's impossible to convey the feeling of immense power they bestow. Millions of gun owners understand the awesome responsibility that comes with ownership—but not all.

If you have little status, a handgun or shotgun will elevate you to the position of someone who can't be messed with. However, the semi-automatic rifle, such as an AR-15, multiplies that feeling 10x. Now, imagine that tremendous power in the hands of an untrained, immature, mentally ill, or furious person.

So it is that we come to Uvalde, Texas, in 2022, and a mentally damaged young man with violent behavioral issues and lethal fantasies that he had shared for months before on Instagram.

Just to segue, this is a company owned by billionaire oligarch Mark Zuckerberg. On Instagram, as on most social media, if you use a copyrighted U2 song on your holiday video, your account will be immediately censored. However, in line with their enragement/engagement business model, and because they are treated as platforms rather than publishers, the radicalization of young men, fetishization of guns, and discussion of future murder are all perfectly acceptable[637].

Back in Uvalde, minutes after he turned eighteen, still too young to rent a car or drink a beer, he went to the Daniel Defense website to purchase two DDM4V7, AR-15-style semi-automatic rifles, and 375 rounds of ammunition[638]. A couple of the advertising slogans for that AR-15 the boy might have seen were "LIGHTER, STRONGER, AND EVEN MORE BADASS" and "USE WHAT THEY USE."

Once he received the weapons, the boy would wait a further eight days before announcing his murderous rage to the world.

At 11am on Tuesday, the 24th, May 2022, having first shot his sixty-six-year-old grandma in the head, the eighteen-year-old set off for his former school, Robb Elementary, where pupils range from seven to ten years old. He'd start shooting at 11.28 am.

Over the next terrifying hour and twenty-two minutes, the killer would turn that school into a slaughterhouse, massacring nineteen children and two teachers.

In total, 376 law enforcement officers would attend the scene, many of them scared[639]. Despite parents and relatives begging for someone to go in and save their children, it wouldn't be until 12.50pm that a Border Patrol tactical team shot the killer dead[640].

To grasp how we reached a place in time where an American boy could walk into an elementary school with a battlefield rifle and murder nineteen children, we have to take a trip back in time.

On the 2nd of January 1964, just over a month after President Kennedy's assassination, with the war in Vietnam heating up, Colt, who had bought the rights to the AR-15, started selling the AR-15 SP1 Sporter Rifle. It retailed for $189.50. In today's money, that's close to $1800. It was a sales flop. Colt's patent ran out in 1977, and it wasn't until 1989 that the AR-15 started being produced again[641].

Now, a small intermission to understand the mindset of folks back then. Let's hear some words on the subject of guns from a friend of the book, Ronald Reagan;

> I would think that some of the bills that have been suggested, such as not carrying a loaded weapon, on a city street, or in town this might certainly be a good one. There is absolutely no reason out on the street today a civilian should be carrying a loaded weapon.[642]

He was speaking just before the signing of the 1967 Mulford Act, which banned the open carrying of loaded firearms in California.

Reagan was reacting to some Black Panthers turning up at the state legislature with rifles in a show of armed self-defense. Their argument was that citizens be allowed to carry guns, pursuant to the Second Amendment. In the Panthers' case, it was to protect themselves from white violence.

If we strip out the part about black people, theirs was a mirror of the argument that the NRA and right-wingers would push through the Supreme Court forty years later.

Speaking of the NRA, two Union soldiers, bemoaning the military's lack of marksmanship skills, had formed it after the Civil War. Over the years, it promoted sporting and hunting. As to its responsibilities, during the gangster era of the 1920s and 30s, it worked with Congress to pass legislation to register short-barreled rifles and fully automatic machine guns. Their leader, Karl Frederick, said;

> I have never believed in the general practice of carrying weapons. I think it should be sharply restricted and only under licenses.[643]

In 1957, when the NRA moved to a new headquarters. At the entrance was their motto, 'FIREARMS SAFETY EDUCATION, MARKSMAN-SHIP TRAINING, SHOOTING FOR RECREATION.' So far, so normal.

Despite men with guns killing John Kennedy, Robert Kennedy, Dr Martin Luther King, and Malcolm X, in the 1960s, demand for the AR-15 was near nonexistent. To find an inflection point, we need to travel all the way forward to 1977. Here we have new hardline right-wing culture warriors in the NRA, flexing their political muscle. Their motto changed to become: "THE RIGHT OF THE PEOPLE TO KEEP AND BEAR ARMS SHALL NOT BE INFRINGED." This was when the NRA and the fake-Christian's, found common racial and patriarchal cause. But it was still too early to have the courts allow their dream of guns everywhere.

Moving forward in time to 1989, the assassination survivor, Ronald Reagan, spoke following the deaths of five children in the 1989 Stockton School shooting, saying;

> I do not believe in taking away the right of the citizen for sporting, for hunting and so forth, or for home defense. But

> I do believe that an AK-47, a machine gun, is not a sporting weapon or needed for defense of a home.[644]

Substitute the word 'AK-47' for 'AR-15,' and imagine what Fox, the NRA, or the Republican Party would say if one of their own tried to proclaim that today.

It was the 1990s that brought us the rise of the angry, disconnected white man. What these men couldn't or wouldn't see was that it was mostly rich Republicans screwing them over. They were the factory bosses using automation to cut workers' jobs or 'offshoring' those jobs by setting up factories in cheap, low wage, low-regulation countries like China or Mexico.

Then, stir in the inability of these men to find the emotional language to deal with the socially changing America; at the same time as they were falling down economically, they were watching the advance of college-educated women and people of color. This would lay the tinder of fury in the fireplace of the American body politic. All that was needed was a match. Enter stage left the GOP, Fox, AM hate-radio and the NRA to sell disaffected white men a narrative and start the rage fire.

Concurrently, the 1990s were also the time that ordinary non-gun-owning Americans saw, but wouldn't understand, the patriarchal violence of the militia movement. Incidents like Waco and Ruby Ridge were both caused by deranged, mediocre men wanting to stockpile as many guns and as much ammo as possible, and those same men never wanting to be told how to behave or how to be responsible. They would be the precursors to the modern white-supremacist patriarchal gangs, like the Proud Boys, Oath Keepers, and the Three Percenters.

We haven't spoken about the Second Amendment. Later we will come to the words, but to begin with, let's examine the meaning. Back in 1991, speaking to PBS, conservative Nixon Supreme Court appointee, Justice Warren Burger had this to say;

> The Gun Lobby's interpretation of the Second Amendment is one of the greatest pieces of fraud, I repeat the word fraud, on the American People by special interest groups that I have ever seen in my lifetime. The real purpose of the Second Amendment was to ensure that state armies–the militia–would be maintained for the defense of the state. The very language of the Second Amendment refutes any argument that it was intended to guarantee every citizen an unfettered right to any kind of weapon he or she desires.[645]

Justice Burger served on the Court from 1969 to 1996 and was present for the Clinton administration enacting both the 1993 Brady Bill, mandating background checks and a waiting period before a handgun purchase, and the 1994 Assault Weapons ban[646]. That ban—supported by Ronald Reagan and Gerald Ford—was in place from 1994 through to 2004, at which point Republicans refused to renew it. If it had been, men would have just continued along with their hunting rifles, shotguns, and pistols.

Returning to the NRA. This five-million-member organization's principal purpose is to help gun manufacturers sell more guns. So it would be, after fifteen children were murdered at Columbine High School in 1999, the organization had a choice to make. It could pivot towards gun reform or double down on fear.

They chose the latter, promulgating the lie of the "good guy with a gun" and linked any gun control with the taking away of all guns and all freedom. Of course, primarily, they chose power and profits over people. Just remember that this was still a time when just a quarter of gun owners offered 'personal safety' as their reason for ownership[647]. The majority still cited target practice and hunting.

In his spellbinding, 2021 book 'Gunfight: My Battle Against The Industry That Radicalized America' Ryan Busse, a former gun industry executive, wrote about how the NRA would transform itself. In this time before the Tea Party and before Trump, Mr. Busse describes how the NRA made its "believers" disconnect from the reality of humanity by linking everything to the gun.

> The NRA rightly sensed that this kind of extreme dedication could be juiced and then harnessed to change basic laws of US politics. It was coming to know that even political authoritarianism is more acceptable than the mere threat—real or perceived—of guns being taken away.[648]

Moving into the 2000s, the NRA was all in on the politics of fear and grievance. They linked all fear of crime to "inner cities," God was co-opted, and the gun was even touted as being able to protect owners from a totalitarian (Democratic-led, of course) federal government.

It wouldn't be the government that Americans needed to be protected from in 2001, after the son of a Saudi billionaire, Osama Bin Laden, smashed into the homeland, giving President George W. Bush a baptism of fire. Then, when Bush responded exactly as his theocratic enemy wished, insecure men got to see brave US forces deployed overseas.

These troops were carrying M4 carbines—a successor to the M-16 and a near-straight cousin of the AR-15, except the fire selector switch can go to fully automatic. Back home, fragile men saw that gun and wanted it. And the NRA and GOP were there to make sure that they got it.

In the 43rd President, the NRA found a perfect bumbling fool to pass, in 2005, the innocuous-sounding 'PROTECTION OF LAWFUL COMMERCE IN ARMS ACT.' Few could have imagined how wide the floodgates of hell would open.

Just picture you're in the business of selling guns. Suddenly Congress passes a law that says that you can make as many of your lethal weapons as you want and you can advertise them to (mostly) men in the most jaw-droppingly provocative fashion. The "CONSIDER YOUR MAN CARD RE-ISSUED" from the top of the chapter was one ad strapline for an AR-15 semi-automatic rifle made by Bushmaster Firearms Internation-al[649].

In any other business, except social media, this is unimaginable. If your car is defective, the car manufacturer can be sued. If your boiler blows up, you can sue the boiler manufacturer, and if you get injured on a roller coaster, you can sue the roller coaster maker.

However, if you are Bushmaster Firearms International of Carson City, Nevada, and one of your customers uses one of your products to slaughter their fellow citizens, nothing happens[650]. All this despite you advertising it with the slogan, "FORCES OF OPPOSITION BOW DOWN: YOU ARE SINGLE-HANDEDLY OUTNUMBERED."

There is an immutable and irrefutable law of nature that tells us when actions have no consequences, bad things are sure to follow. So it would be that from the year 2000, gun manufacturers amped up their political donations to the NRA and GOP politicians to promote fear and watched their sales soar.

Then, four months before Barack Obama took office, the Supreme Court handed down the Heller v. District of Columbia decision that has led to thousands of Americans being needlessly killed[651]. It was cheer-led by, now deceased, Judge Antonin Scalia (together with some of 2024's favorites, Roberts, Alito, and Thomas).

For the first time in American history, a private citizen's gun ownership was seen as independent of a 'well-regulated militia.' Until then, gun owners required a permit to carry on the street, and open carry was more or less non-existent[652].

In the Heller ruling, five Justices conveniently gaslit America by disregarding the first thirteen words of the Second Amendment;

A well-regulated Militia, being necessary to the security of a free State, the right of the people to keep and bear Arms, shall not be infringed.

Justice Burger knew what we know. The 'well-regulated Militia' of then is the National Guard of now. In contemporary life, I can't offer a better example than the brave National Guards troops protecting our democracy from "enemies foreign and domestic" after the J6 terrorist attack.

Yet, for the high priests, apparently stopping guns from being able to be carried everywhere violated a citizen's Fourteenth Amendment rights."[653] To illustrate their naked disingenuity, the Fourteenth Amendment is very clear:

> No State shall make or enforce any law which shall abridge the privileges or immunities of citizens of the United States . . . [654]

It might not have escaped your attention that the same freaks who, as we read about in chapter fifteen, would later deny that the Fourteenth Amendment protected a woman's right to choose what happens to her own body also rejected the Fourteenth Amendment rights of the 70% of non-gun-owning citizens to be safe in the streets. Of course, we owe a big thank you to all the meek liberals who deferred to the 'almighty' Supreme Court and just let this pass into law.

Just on the subject of guns everywhere, we can hear from former Marine Corps Lieutenant Colonel and veteran of tours of Iraq and Afghanistan, Joseph Plenzer, speaking to Dr. Celine Gounder on her epic 'American Diagnosis' podcast;

> True freedom is not being able to walk around everywhere you go with a loaded weapon. True freedom is being able to walk around everywhere in public without needing one. Both Kyleanne (Hunter)... and I had been to places and countries that literally are coming apart at the seams where you did need to carry loaded weapons with you everywhere you went for your own physical safety. ... I'll tell you, it's a real unpleasant experience to live for a prolonged period of time in a place like that. It's a joy to come back to the United States where, in most places, you don't feel compelled to carry a gun with you when you go out in public. [655]

Today, when the gun lobby needs more business, they just go to their six pals on the Supreme Court to get rulings like the Bruen case of 2023, which held that New York's near nine million citizens should be permitted to conceal carry[656].

As these Justices claim to be 'originalists,' we must go back in time to 1787 to see what the framers intended. New York's population in 1787 was under 30,000 people. There were no stadiums, subways, or skyscrapers. The NYPD wouldn't even be formed until fifty years later. Oh, and the only guns were single-shot muskets that took over a minute to load.

Just to illustrate once more how dangerous a gun in an urban environment can be. When the domestic terrorists stormed the Capitol on January 6th, 2021, most did not have their guns, as it's a criminal offense to carry a weapon in the District of Columbia. But just imagine if they did. The Second Amendment would have killed the First. After all, the right to free speech doesn't amount to much when someone else has a loaded gun pointed at your head.

Speaking of loaded guns, today, we have reached a point where every GOP politician is terrified of sullying his A+ NRA voting record. To see this in practice, let's meet Republican congressional representative Steve Scalise of Louisiana, a self-described "David Duke without the baggage."

In 2017, whilst practicing for a congressional charity baseball game in Virginia, a shooter walked onto the field and opened fire with his legally purchased rifle, wounding several lawmakers, Scalise included. The shooter was chased and shot by two brave Capitol police officers, who were both wounded during the encounter. One of the officers to save Scalise's life was Crystal Griner (we will return to her later.)[657]

Democrats were horrified at violence being directed against members of Congress and wanted, as they do after every mass shooting, to pass legislation. Scalise took matters more nonchalantly, shrugging off the bullet to the head. In fact, he said that the event "fortified" his support for gun rights[658].

So it is that, up to 2024, he had an A+ rating from the NRA[659]. That means that he has blocked, or tried to block, every meaningful piece of legislation that would make gun owners more responsible and prevent guns from getting into the hands of damaged people, like his own would-be executioner.

To this point, following the Uvalde massacre, Congress passed the first piece of limited gun legislation since 1994. Scalise whipped GOP congressional delegates in the House to vote against the bill. 193 Republicans voted against keeping Americans safe. It only passed because fourteen sane Republicans voted for it, but it leads us to an interesting point on both guns and Republicans[660].

One might imagine that Scalise has his pockets stuffed full of Benjamin Franklin's from a chest in the NRA basement marked, "POLITICAL PAYOFF FUND", but it's not so. In 2020, the NRA was only the 33rd highest donor to his campaign, lower down than real estate and accounting.

As we have seen, much of the base of the Republican party has been so terrified and radicalized by Fox, right-wing radio, and the NRA that they want no gun control, for the gun is as much a part of their identity as their own faces. Indeed, they may actually think the NRA is too soft. It is not without coincidence that these characters are also the anti-mask, anti-government, MAGA mentalists. The problem for Republicans is, as we know, they built this beast, and now they can't control it.

Thus, for Scalise to win re-election, he needs to win over GOP base primary voters. That means no surrender to gun control, and should he displease the monster, he gets a primary challenge from the even more looney right. Then he loses his $174,000-a-year prestige job and all the cash from campaign donations, speaking engagements, and stock trading 'opportunities.' Never to forget that post-congress life as a lucratively remunerated cable news pundit or political lobbyist. Thus, the man who got shot has to pretend to love the gun that shot him. It's pure unenlightened self-interest that drives Scalise, and it is why meaningful gun control with Republicans is nearly impossible.

To drill down a little further into Scalise's immorality, there's an acidic footnote to the story. In 2022, he voted against the Respect for Marriage Act, which ensured that LGBTQ people could enjoy the same freedom to marry that heterosexual couples do. That law would have helped people like Officer Griner, the person who saved his life in 2012 and who identifies as lesbian[661].

Still, despite the doom and gloom, there are still places in America where people can be confident no one will be carrying a loaded gun. Certainly, 'woke,' caring, lovey-dovey liberal cities, like New York and Los Angeles, won't let you. But what if I told you that there are no guns allowed at a Trump Rally, or a GOP Convention, or at the place where they hand down all the deranged rulings: the Supreme Court? Outrageous, isn't it?

Just as drug dealers don't get high on their own supply, so it is with all the fiends who push these 'guns everywhere' policies. The judges and politicians know that if they let angry, armed, and insane people near them, those people will probably start shooting.

You want a receipt? On July 13th, 2024, at a Trump rally in Butler, Pennsylvania, a man chose a path that would have made him known to your grandchildren's grandchildren. This isolated, far-right, white, twenty-year-old sought to brand himself into future history books by changing the course of history.

Unlike past presidential assassins like John Wilkes Booth and Lee Harvey Oswald, notoriety eluded this assassin when his 450-foot shot from his legally owned AR-15 rifle missed Trump by inches. This allowed Secret Service snipers time to shoot him dead. Just to add, a local police officer spotted the gunman in time to stop him. However, the cop backed off when he saw the AR-15; he knew what death foretold looked like[662].

A point missed by the media was that, without open carry, the assassin could never have gotten close to Trump. This reminds me of the prophetic words of Republican Don Mulford, sponsor of that 1967 Mulford Act, who said, "openly carrying a gun is an act of violence or near violence."[663]

We know he was talking about the Black Panthers, but the principal stands. We only have to look to 2021 to see open-carrying, unregulated militia men walking into the Michigan State Capitol building, their loaded weapons representing a show of force, domination, and 'near-violence,' designed to cower the state's politicians into lifting COVID restrictions.

Today, Don Mulford's pal, Ronald Reagan, would be called a RINO (Republican in Name Only) for his stand on gun control. He, by contrast, would probably think that a proportion of America's gun owners had lost their minds. Could Reagan believe it was normal for kids to be murdered in their classrooms? So normal that in 2022, 'murder' was the leading cause of death for children under 19 years old[664].

To this point, in 2024, Texas schools were required to have "Bleeding Control Stations" stocked with, amongst other items, "tourniquets approved for use in battlefield trauma care by the armed forces of the United States." [665]

Imagine the trauma of being one of the fifty million American schoolchildren, not knowing whether today is the day that a fellow pupil comes to school with a gun in his hand and murder on his mind. How is this mental torment any different from what a soldier in a war zone faces? But, again, as with the survivors of rape, no one is interested in schoolkids. So it is, many students must live with the devil's cocktail surging through their bodies and with undiagnosed PTSD. None of this is helped by kids having to take part in 'active shooter drills' to prepare them for the day when death walks through the door[666].

Just going back to the ghost of Ronald Reagan. Try explaining that, rather than infuriate the Confederate Taliban by legislating, hollow GOP politicians want active shooter drills or to have parents buy bulletproof backpacks for their kids—about $200 and completely useless against an AR-15 round—or to arm school teachers. He may have the same question about the armed teacher that smart folks do. If fully trained and equipped cops are terrified of entering schools whilst the shooting is underway, what chance does an untrained teacher stand?

Following the 2018 Parkland School massacre in Florida that killed 17 people and injured 17 more, Trump suggested that had the school football coach been armed, he could have stopped the shooter. Former Marine Corps sniper and the author of 'Jarhead', Anthony Swofford, wrote on the subject;

> He would not have been able to draw his weapon (a side arm, presumably) quickly enough to stop the shooter, who, with an AR-15, would have had the coach outgunned— any shots he managed to fire would have risked being errant, possibly injuring or killing additional students. As some studies have shown, even police officers have missed their targets more than 50 per cent of the time. In firing a weapon, Feis would have only added to the carnage and confusion.[667]

Today, we know that the NRA and the gun manufacturers need ordinary people who feel safe now to feel scared. This way, they have to go out and buy a gun just to feel safe again. This fear messaging works. While gun owners make up less than one-third of the population today, two-thirds of those gun owners cite 'personal safety' rather than sporting or hunting as their reason for ownership[668].

Combine all that fear rhetoric from the NRA and Fox with GOP politicians who refuse to act on even the most basic gun safety, and by 2023, we arrived at some truly abominable cases.

In Daytona Beach, Florida, a three-year-old boy, the son of a Florida corrections officer, died after shooting himself with a gun he took from his father's nightstand[669]. In Harris County, Texas, a four-year-old girl was shot and killed by her three-year-old sister[670]. Then, in Newport, Virginia, a six-year-old shot his teacher in their first-grade classroom[671].

If these shootings happened in Britain, Canada, or Germany, they would be headline news for a week. However, it's America, so many people might reconcile these events by telling themselves that toddlers don't know what they are doing. But adults do, and it would have been an adult who allowed their loaded, chambered, safety-off gun to be easily accessible.

As for those legal gun-owning adults, in North Carolina, a 24-year-old man, using his legally owned gun, shot a six-year-old boy. The boys' crime? Accidentally letting his basketball fall into the man's yard[672].

In Texas, a twenty-five-year-old man got out of his car and, using his legally owned gun, shot at and seriously wounded two high school cheerleaders. The girl's crimes? After practice, they accidentally mistook his car for theirs and pulled on the door handle[673].

In upstate rural New York, a sixty-five-year-old fired his legally owned twenty-gauge pump-action shotgun at a car in which a twenty-year-old woman was traveling as a passenger. She died. The young woman's crime? Being in a car that had accidentally turned into the man's driveway to perform a u-turn[674].

In Kansas City, an 84-year-old man shot his legally owned gun through his door and critically wounded a 16-year-old boy. The boy's crime? Whilst going to pick up his siblings, he rang the wrong doorbell[675].

Sadly, cruelty is a state of mind whose appetite is never satisfied. Which brings us to a Christian retreat in Cleveland, Texas, in April 2023.

At around 11.30 pm, Wilson Garcia, the host and a father of five, had to go next door to ask his thirty-eight-year-old neighbor to please not shoot his AR-15, as there were children trying to sleep. This indignity caused the neighbor to stop shooting outside his own home and come round to Wilson's.

There, with his legally owned gun, he wrought carnage, murdering Wilson's wife, his son, and a family friend. The other two victims were Diana Velázquez Alvarado and Julisa Molina Rivera. These two real Christians sacrificed themselves by using their bodies as human ballistic shields to absorb the supersonic rounds that would have certainly slaughtered the other children[676].

Speaking of children. So many times, we hear about the number of victims and perhaps their names, but we never know who these people were. I was thinking about the twenty-year-old woman we read about four paragraphs back, who was shot just for being in a car that turned into a man's driveway. Truthfully, the only reason this came into my mind was because the shooter was found guilty of second-degree murder in January 2024 and sentenced to 25 years to life in prison[677].

His young victim was one of 15,149 gun homicides in 2023. Her name was Kaylin Gillis. I looked up her obituary, which must have been written by the people who loved her the most. Kaylin lived in the picturesque small town of Saratoga Springs, NY, thirty-five miles from the Vermont border. She loved artistry and dreamed of becoming either a veterinarian or a marine biologist.

Then I saw all the people that she had left behind; apart from her loving parents and boyfriend, there were her sisters, grandparents, aunts, uncles, and cousins, as well as many extended family and friends."[678]

There's an important fact to remember about the Confederate Taliban. They don't care about your kids, they don't care about people killed in the crossfire, and they don't care about all the people left behind in the wake of their violence. The shotgun shell that killed Kaylin cost sixty-eight cents, and it was fired from a gun used by a weak man, steeped in a Fox News, right-wing, child-like view of the world. It's a place where no one is important but them, and they don't need you telling them what they can or cannot do.

This brings us to the most common type of gun violence reported in the news: mass shootings. These are usually defined as four or more casualties in the same event.

Many mass shooters choose the AR-style semi-automatic because a rifle allows the scared man to maintain distance from their victims, and the thirty-or even one-hundred-round magazine affords his shaky hands multiple shots at targets without having to stop to reload—the point at which the shooter is most vulnerable to being tackled.

Whilst mass shootings make up only 1% of shootings, because they can happen anywhere and to anyone, they sit atop our minds. They are also almost exclusively perpetrated by young white men.

Sadly, there are too many examples to choose from: whether the Virginia Tech shooting of 2007 that killed thirty people, or the Sandy Hook Elementary massacre of 2012 that ended the lives of 26 people, including twenty children, or the Las Vegas Strip shooting of 2017 that claimed the lives of fifty-eight people[679]. However, another hideous event comes to mind. It didn't involve an AR-style rifle, but as the shooter survived, we get an insight into his mind.

At 12.51pm on Monday, the 30th of November 2021, fifteen-year-old student Ethan Crumbley walked into Oxford High School in Oxford,

Michigan. He was carrying a 9mm Sig Sauer SP 2022 handgun that he had asked for and his parents had bought him just four days *before* the shooting.

In a killing spree that lasted five minutes, he murdered four students and injured seven others. The cost of each bullet that struck his victims would have been about twenty-seven cents[680].

To the boy's state of mind, The Detroit News detailed how, two weeks before the shooting, Crumbley was reported to the principal for,

> A math homework sheet is overwritten with a drawing. There is a gun, a bullet and a bleeding shooting victim. At different points, hand-written additions to the page read "My life is useless," "Blood everywhere" and "The thoughts won't stop, help me.[681]

On the morning of the killings, his parents were called to the school, where the counselor showed them more violent drawings.

If anyone needed more indication of his instability before the killings, this fifteen-year-old shared images of his gun on Mark Zuckerberg's Instagram.

So, this kid has all these demons in his head, yet his parents wouldn't take him to a psychologist. Instead of the help the child was pleading for, they bought him a gun, which they then stored in their underwear drawer, where it was easily accessible.

For his crimes, Crumbley was sentenced to life without parole. His parents were sentenced to fifteen to twenty years in prison for involuntary manslaughter, not just for buying their son the gun, but also for not warning the school about the gun, even after the school warned them about his demonic thoughts[682].

But, once more, we have to think about those four stolen lives lost at the hands of an insane, fragile little boy who couldn't legally drink a beer nor drive a car. Their names were Tate Myre, Madisyn Baldwin, Justin Shilling, and Hana St. Juliana[683]. These were young people who could have helped to make America's future better. Instead, before they even graduated, their mothers and fathers had to live out every parent's worst nightmare: burying their own children.

Theirs would be a life sentence to be lived out in the wreckage that the boy and the gun left behind. Then, there were all the other people who cared about these four young Americans: their brothers, sisters, aunts, uncles, grandmas, grandpas, friends and lovers.

For the consolation of their memories, they can know we did nothing. Sadly, it's an absurdity within the American mind that allows this to happen again and again.

As to that wellspring of that delusion? Is it the deranged fifteen-year-old boy with the gun, or maybe the Supreme Court Justices who allowed that gun on the street? Perhaps it's the craven politicians who won't legislate to stop that boy from wielding the gun in the first place? Or is it the millions of our fellow Americans who keep voting those politicians into office?

You might imagine that this is an intractable problem that we just have to live with, but it isn't. In their 2021 book, "The Violence Project: How to Stop a Mass Shooting Epidemic", Professors Jillian Peterson and James Densley, drawing on DOJ-funded research of every mass shooting since 1966 and every school shooting since 1999, identified almost guaranteed traits of school shooters. In their research, they not only studied the shootings but spoke to family members of both victims and shooters and even some shooters. Professor Peterson described the personality type;

There's this really consistent pathway. Early childhood trauma seems to be the foundation, whether violence in the home, sexual assault, parental suicides, extreme bullying. Then you see the build toward hopelessness, despair, isolation, self-loathing, oftentimes rejection from peers. That turns into a really identifiable crisis point where they're acting differently. Sometimes they have previous suicide attempts. What's different from traditional suicide is that the self-hate turns against a group. They start asking themselves, "Whose fault is this?" Is it a racial group or women or a religious group, or is it my classmates? The hate turns outward. There's also this quest for fame and notoriety.[684]

Professors Peterson and Densley's recommended solutions were to put 500,000 psychologists in schools to allow children to talk through their problems before they get to the stage of becoming a shooter.

Bear in mind, there are 90,000 schools in America. With five psychologists in each school, these professionals could not just stop school shooters but also help with promoting positive mental health for children at the most vulnerable times of their lives. It would cost about $30 billion, which would be repaid by all these young folks growing up with control over their minds and emotions. Sadly, no one is paying for this, and it probably won't happen.

A comfortable explanation for gun violence might be that it is America; a frontier society, born out of the violence to take the nation from the Native Americans who were already here. Then a 250-year-old slave society, a revolutionary war, a civil war, segregation, two world wars, a war in Korea, a war in Vietnam, and most recently two simultaneous wars in Afghanistan and Iraq.

War is not an unusual part of the history of any other WEIRD nation. What those other nations didn't experience was slavery and segregation. To that exact point, we can't disconnect what has happened since the year 2000 with guns from what has happened in politics.

Most of it is the Confederate Taliban's stoking of a perceived loss of white male patriarchal status and fear arising out of that. More specifical-ly, right-wing politicians and right-wing media have conditioned scared, low-information, mainly men, to believe the gun is a problem solver.

From this, it's hardly surprising that if you look at a graph of, specifically, mass shootings with AR-15 style rifles from the year 2000, they skyrocket. Always note that people aren't going to shopping centers with shotguns, and they aren't terrorizing schools with hunting rifles. It's this particular semi-automatic rifle that makes a weak man feel strong.

This takes us on to the "concealed carry" owner. These people imagine they are the 'good guys' with the gun that can stop the 'bad guy'. Just a quick aside: even in the most pro-gun states, until 2008, concealed carry required a permit. Since then, it has become permitless, which means guns for everyone.

To get into the mind of the concealed carry gun owner, Sean Illing spoke to firearms journalist Stephen Gutowski, founder of TheReload.com, on the podcast, "The Conversation About Guns We're Not Having." I want-ed to give Mr Gutowski the benefit of the doubt, as he appeared to be a lucid and intelligent man but I was struck by his reasons for carrying a gun, as they all seemed to be about the imaginary and perceived dangers of a world we don't live in. Tellingly, it all boiled down to him being afraid of single combat and using the gun or pepper spray as a leveler.

> I think guns are an equalizer personally. Obviously, there are terrible things that people can do with guns. What happens with a gun depends on who's using the gun. But guns are the great equalizer. This is a reality. If you don't want a world where just the physically dominant can lord over people weaker than them, then I think on the whole guns are a good, a net positive...because even though I'm six foot, 1, 250 pounds, like I might run into someone bigger than me, or in better shape or better able to handle me in a physical fight. And I don't want to get into a physical fight with anyone.[685]

To ensure that he wasn't an outlier, I found another gun rights activist using the same narrative. This from Rory Miller, speaking on the outstanding American Diagnosis podcast;

> I like strong people way better than I like weak people. When everybody's strong, there's a mutual respect. If you're strong, and you're willing to use your power, there's no consequence-free way to abuse you, to exploit you, or to hurt you. In that sense, self-defense is about not letting anyone exploit you against your will. For me personally, they extend my sphere of influence. If I see someone killing a child twenty meters away, without a handgun, I can't do anything except to watch, and that would hurt... The other incredibly valuable thing about firearms is... humans are tool-using creatures, and if you would remove those tools then we revert

very quickly to might makes right, to the biggest and the strongest just takes what they want. Tools allow the smaller and weaker to have their own say in that equation. They're a huge equalizer.[686]

From the way they spoke, these were two very fragile, very terrified men. Yet, I would bet dollars to donuts that they both live in some lovely, quiet suburb or exurb, where the closest they come to crime is watching the TV news. Remember, nearly three quarters of Americans feel confident enough to face the world without a gun and pepper spray.

As for the nonsense about humans without guns resorting to other tools to kill each other, it's total BS. There are no guns in the hands of civilians on the streets of Australia, Canada, England, France, or Japan, and those folks aren't beating each other to death with tire irons or hammers, or even their fists.

If you don't believe me about the lack of the cave dweller in us, look at almost every mass shooting in America. Once the shooter runs out of ammunition, he either surrenders, runs away, shoots himself, or opts for suicide-by-cop. What he never, ever does is take his AR-15, spin it barrel first, and start clubbing people over the head with it. That's only in the movies.

Just allow me to indulge you with a fact. According to Pew Research, only one in four police officers have ever fired their service weapon on the job[687]. That's three quarters who have never fired their guns. Cops! So, what Walter Mitty life must a normal American be leading to imagine that they are going to get into worse scrapes than a cop? The answer is simple; a Fox 'news'-watching, AM radio-listening, irrationally scared life.

All this leads us on to the open carry crowd, which is composed of two distinct groups. The first is the invariably white male, probably of low status, but my oh my, a semi-automatic long gun makes them feel tough.

Then there's the second subset. These are more than likely just plain old bullies who again haven't been able to make it in the real world, but their long gun can intimidate anyone they don't want to hear from.

And the truth of the matter is that no one is going to mess with them, with their AR-15 slung across their tactical vest and a Glock 17 pistol strapped to their thigh.

Skip to Arizona in the 2022 midterms, where armed, right-wing "poll watchers", who had no authority vested by federal or state government, were stationed at drop boxes to intimidate lone voters. Imagine what could have happened if voters had also turned up with semi-automatic weapons. Just having two angry people with guns in proximity means any misjudgement could blow up into violence. It never needed to be but was always going to be once the gun could leave the home.

In Texas, you need a license to go fishing and a license to go hunting[688]. However, since 2021, you don't need a license to carry a handgun. Unsurprisingly, since 2021, police have reported an upsurge in gun shootings following disputes.

In one case, a man, Tony Earls, claimed to have been robbed of twenty dollars and his car keys at an ATM. So, in a densely populated area of Houston, this angry, untrained civilian furiously fired off nine shots at what he thought was the robber.

In the path of his bullets was the happy, loving Alvarez family, driving to a Valentine's Day dinner. Sitting in the rear passenger seat was their nine-year-old daughter, Arlene. We'll never know how great she could have made America, because one of Earl's twenty-seven-cent bullets struck and killed her[689].

A horrific certainty must be that Arlene's parents could never imagine burying their daughter just nine years into her life. They probably envisioned the wonder of seeing her go on her first date, graduate, get her first job, and get married. Instead, what GOP politicians and Tony Earls visited upon them was a life sentence of shattered dreams and of imagining what could have been.

A Texas grand jury refused to indict Earls, using the line, "everything about that situation, we believe and contend, was justified under Texas law."[690]To cement the upside-down thinking in Republican America, the prosecutors are looking for the ATM robber to indict them for felony murder. All the while, Arlene's actual killer, Earls, walks free to do it all over again[691].

We hear so much from the GOP and the gun crowd about the rights of gun ownership, but they never talk about the responsibilities. From the American Diagnosis series, we can hear again from retired Marine Corps Lieutenant Colonel Joseph Plenzler. He described the responsibility of having a rifle in the Corps;

> First thing that you hear "Safety is paramount". We go through a full week of training before we allow our Marine to put ammunition in the rifle. Set protocol; weapons are unloaded until you get to the range. You don't load them up until you get to the firing line. Once you complete that round of fire, you unload and show clear. Before you leave the range, you will be checked through to make sure that you don't have a hot weapon, or you don't have any ammunition. Once you get back to the barracks, you clear them, and clean them, and then store them in a locked armory.[692]

Another veteran of Afghanistan, former Black Hawk helicopter pilot Chris Marvin, described how many of the two million veterans who rotated through the twenty-year wars in Iraq and Afghanistan may be gun owners. He pointed out that the difference between them and a civilian was that they were all vetted, i.e., a background check. Then, they were trained in safe use and safe storage. After that, soldiers have weeks of training before qualification and have to re-qualify every year.

For a lot of veterans who are gun owners, it's normal to assume that just because they had to go through all this and know something, then other people must have too[693]. Sociologists call this 'the Curse of Knowledge', and it's a bias that we all have[694]. You must have heard it said or said to someone, "Oh, I thought everyone knew how to do that!". Veterans know their weapon, because it was what would keep them and their buddies alive. Chris Marvin adds,

> It doesn't take long, though, to explain to them that while they may have purchased the firearm from an authorized gun dealer, they may store it safely, they may use it exclusively at the range, or they may have other weapons that they use for hunting... and they go about their gun ownership in a very methodical, safe way... their next-door neighbor doesn't have to do any of that. And they'll say, "Yes, yes, yeah, sure he does. He has to do exactly what I did. Training and safety and accountability — all the things that I did to get a firearm." No, he can go a gun show and without a background check, make a person-to-person purchase, and bring his gun home — a gun that he never used before, he's never been to the range with, doesn't know the parts of, doesn't know how to take it apart or clean it or whatever... and all of a sudden, the veteran says, "Well, that's stupid. Why shouldn't he have to go through all the things that I went through?[695]

We don't even have to look far to see a real-world example of sensible gun laws. Up north in Canada, there are approximately twelve million registered guns in a country the size of America, but with a population of just thirty-eight million people. That represents about one gun for every three people, which, proportionately, is about the same as America.

To own a firearm, Canadians have to be over eighteen and pass the Canadian Firearms Safety Test. There are exceptions. As the hunting of bears, geese, moose, and deer is a very popular pastime across Canada, children as young as twelve years old can get a Minors Firearms License that allows them to borrow rifles and shotguns and purchase ammunition.

Assault rifles like the AR-15 were banned in 2020 after a mass shooter killed thirteen people in Nova Scotia. The Canadian Prime Minister, Justin Trudeau, said then,

> Other than using firearms for sport shooting and hunting, there is no reason anyone in Canada should need guns in their everyday lives.[696]

Background checks cover the lifetime of a gun owner, and 'harassment' is one reason a gun license can be taken away. Both open carry and concealed carry are illegal in Canada.

From all this, it will not surprise the smart reader to learn that gun violence, adjusted for population, is only 13% of what it is in America[697]. As for mass shootings, they are nearly unheard of, with just three happening in the past ten years.

A lot of this common-sense approach to guns also reflects a culture where men don't feel the need to walk the streets with a gun, pretending to be tough when they are actually very scared. For Canadian men, the gun does its job, then goes back in the gun cabinet.

Back in America, never think that you're alone in wanting sensible gun reform. In April 2023, a Fox News poll showed vast majorities of respondents wanting gun control. Over 80% of people supported criminal background checks for all guns, mental health checks on prospective gun owners, and raising the age to buy a gun to 21 years old. Over 60% supported banning assault rifles and semi-automatic rifles. Remember, this was a Fox News poll, not some Dudley-do-right liberal think tank[698].

As far as restrictions on the second amendment crowd's 'right to bear arms' go, no American can own a claymore mine or a Stinger surface-to-air missile. However, if someone wants to buy a pre-1986, fully automatic M-16 rifle today, in 37 states, it's still possible.

The only issue is, to transfer a National Firearms Act (NFA) firearm—machine guns and short-barrel shotguns—you will need to complete ATF Application Form 4. Then add in a $200 check for your application, submit your fingerprints, two passport-style photographs, and detailed information about you and the firearm. After that, you sit tight for nearly a year while the ATF background checks you and, if approved, returns your paperwork. Then, you can collect your machine gun[699].

There is one other small impediment to ownership of a fully automatic rifle. The cost: They sell for over $20,000, or forty times as much as an AR-15. Suffice to say, there have been no recorded mass shootings with genuine machine guns. In fact, since the NFA was enacted back in 1934 to stop gangsters from getting hold of guns, no legal machine gun has been used in any crime.

Criminally, in June 2024, the high priests on the Supreme Legislature ruled to legalize bump stocks, which, effectively, turn a semi-automatic rifle into a fully automatic one.

Whilst this chapter has revealed a lot of madness, it doesn't mean that there aren't solutions. Clearly, nothing will happen until after 2029, but it doesn't mean that we shouldn't find new allies and frame the argument differently. $700 assault rifles with 100-round magazines are 'cop killers.'

Message that the AR-15, when loaded with legal fifty-nine-cent, M885 green-tipped bullets, is powerful enough to punch straight through their Level IIIA kevlar vest.

This is real life and death, so what are their police unions doing about that? Part of the answer to gun reform is also part of the answer to police reform. We appeal to that most basic part of a cop's self-interest: making it through the day alive to go home to their family.

Then another strand of messaging. One of the biggest lies is enabled by what we citizens never see: the carnage. Yet, when soldiers are on the battlefield, they can't look away, nor can the cops and medics who have to respond to the shootings.

I always thought that if people saw the gory devastation that real bullets cause, they may be woken from the slumber of watching Hollywood's family-friendly sanitized violence. On that point, Hollywood isn't stupid. They know if their movies showed heads exploding and arms being ripped off, people wouldn't want to watch them.

To this point, it sounds gruesome, but perhaps some parents would release an image of their child's injuries to show us what they have to live with. Then, addicted as they are to spectacle, every news network would cover it, and it would smash the GOP and NRA's lie that guns should be with anyone, anywhere, anytime.

As far as legislation goes, if Democrats win in 2028 and can get fifty-one senators to vote to bypass the filibuster, they could repeal the 'Protection of Lawful Commerce in Arms Act'. Then gun manufacturers would have to take responsibility for the irresponsible way they advertise their products.

In conjunction with this, I would recommend enacting a law requiring gun insurance. Just like car insurance, in the event of an incident, the insurers will compensate the injured party.

The insurance industry also means political muscle. Up to now, it's just been a few congressional representatives trying to battle the gun lobby and they always lose. Now it would be a battle between the tiny $20 billion gun lobby and the massively powerful $1 trillion insurance industry. To know their power, insurance is the third largest lobbying group in America, and that money buys a lot of congressional representatives' time.

I know that insurers have no interest in helping Americans, and they would only work because they were earning premiums, but, regardless, this is what real-world interest convergence actually looks like.

If you are dubious about the power of insurers, then we have real-world examples. In Iowa, maniacal GOP legislators tried to pass a law, to allow some districts to arm teachers. EMC Insurance of Des Moines refused to cover the state against the liability of a teacher accidentally shooting an innocent pupil. Obviously, no other insurer would cover this risk either, and the idiotic idea sits in the legislature, spinning its wheels[700].

Bear in mind that once insurance is in place, good things would probably just happen because of insurance companies' lobbying. After all, these guys don't want to be paying out for multi-million-dollar lawsuits, so they would press for the reforms.

Because all gun manufacturers would need liability insurance to stay in business, they may decide to tone down the advertising of AR-15's to avoid the possibility of lawsuits.

We know that, for most Americans, the problem with guns is when they come onto the street. So, insurers would charge much higher premiums for owners who took their guns out of the home. With exceptions for hunting and gun ranges, this would, more or less, ban guns from public areas. Suddenly, the number of school shootings and other mass shootings would drop right off.

Clearly, insurers would demand 'violent offender checks,' and mental health checks to ensure that the gun wasn't being bought by a criminal or the insane.

Regarding the gun in the home, insurers would require their policyholders to undergo safety training to avoid shooting an innocent bystander.

Also, we would see insurance companies mandating that their gun-owning policyholders practice safe storage to avoid their premium rising or losing cover. That safe storage might mean a lockbox.

This would stop their kids from getting hold of them and shooting themselves or someone else.

Further fear of jacked up premiums would lead people to keep a record of who they sold their gun to in order to avoid selling it to criminals.

And can you imagine insurers being happy with the gun show loophole, where anyone can buy a gun with no background check and no waiting period? Those shows would either comply or lose their own insurance liability cover.

As we all find out with insurance, when there is a cost attached to our behavior, we are a bit more careful. With car insurance, your bad driving jacks up your premium or makes it impossible to get insurance. So, it would be with guns. Just think back to almost all the shootings you've read about in this chapter and try to imagine whether many would have happened if those men had needed gun insurance.

Chapter 20

The Great Unregulated Exxon Mobil Scientific Experiment (Sorry Kids, It's Going To Get A Little Hot In Here)

Exxon Mobil Oil Corporation knew nearly fifty years ago how they were murdering the human race. My receipt is from one of their 1977 reports;

> In the first place, there is general scientific agreement that the most likely manner in which mankind is influencing the global climate is through carbon dioxide release from the burning of fossil fuels. present thinking holds that man has a time window of five to 10 years before the need for hard decisions regarding changes in energy strategies might become critical.[701]

Even more astonishing was that way back before the Civil War, in 1856 in New York, Eunice Newton Foote was the first scientist to discover the link between carbon dioxide and increased planetary warming. From her paper, "Circumstances Affecting the Heat of Sun's Rays," she noted;

> An atmosphere of [carbon dioxide] would give to our earth a high temperature; and if as some suppose, at one period of

its history the air had mixed with it a larger proportion than at present, an increased temperature...must have necessarily resulted.[702]

Apart from being an outstanding scientist, she was also a great progressive. As an abolitionist, she helped the Underground Railroad, and, as a staunch women's rights campaigner, she helped pave the way for every working woman today. Sadly, it was because she was a woman in a patriarchal society that she was forced to credit her discovery to an undeserving man[703].

Then, the only way she could get her paper published was to work with another man. Fortunately, he was a progressive. We've met him before; his name was Frederick Douglass, and he owned a printing press in Rochester. It might not have escaped your attention that when progressives work together, progress is always the result. Bear this in mind, as later on, you will read about the antithesis of these brilliant people.

I know that my MAGA readers love pre-1954 America, so let's go back and visit a bastion of mid-twentieth-century American innovation, Bell Laboratories. This institution was owned by AT&T, a government-allowed monopoly telephone supplier, operating at a time of 50% corporation taxes. It was at Bell where the foundations for the internet were laid[704]. Then in 1954, its scientists discovered how, when exposed to sunlight, electricity flowed freely through silicon wafers, and from that invented the solar panel. Four years later, instead of batteries, solar panels were bolted to the Vanguard 1 satellite, allowing it to transmit information from space for decades, rather than days[705].

During this age of extraordinary American optimism, TV viewers would tune in to see the 'Bell Laboratory Science Series, which ran between 1956 and 1964. In one episode, from 1958, titled 'The Unchained Goddess,' a scientist lays out the problem of global warming;

> Well, it's been calculated a few degrees rise in the Earth's temperature would melt the polar ice caps. And if this happens, an inland sea would fill a good portion of the Mississippi valley. Tourists in glass bottom boats would be viewing the drowned towers of Miami through 150 feet of tropical water. For in weather, we're not only dealing with forces of a far greater variety than even the atomic physicist encounters, but with life itself.[706]

That horror story may yet come true. However, in the post-war period, American scientists led the world and worked in all the big corporations like AT&T, 3M, and Exxon.

It was back in 1982 that Exxon scientists predicted the future of atmospheric CO_2 with near-perfect accuracy and the global warming and consequent climate change that would accompany it[707].

In that same year, Exxon Manager Roger Cohen, Director of the Theoretical and Mathematical Sciences Laboratory at Exxon Research, wrote;

> There is unanimous agreement in the scientific community that a temperature increase of this magnitude would bring about significant changes in the earth's climate.[708]

We have to distinguish between Exxon's honest, forward-thinking scientists and its gluttonous, profit-hungry executives. To do so, let's return to the charismatic clown, Ronald Reagan. Back in 1980, he sold Americans on the power of the 'individual'—who is completely helpless against powerful special interests. His election was won by climbing into bed with two symbiotically related satanic forces. First, those fossil fuel interests, who were terrified of Jimmy Carter's talk of one-fifth of US energy being renewable by the year 2000[709].

Then there was the 'Moral Majority' of fake-Christians, who sped the nation on the path to Christian fundamentalism. Part of their despotic beliefs is a faith that tells them man has dominion over nature and the Earth is man's to plunder.

All this would have been unknown to Exxon scientists, who still had noble plans for their company. To them, Exxon was not just an oil company but an energy company, and if they had their way, it could have worked with the government to help decouple America from oil and gas by pivoting to solar, wind, and other renewables.

It wasn't to be, and an inflection point would come in June 1988, when NASA scientist James Hansen testified before Congress that,

> Global warming is affecting our planet now. It is time to stop waffling so much and say that the evidence is pretty strong that the greenhouse effect is here. [710]

The following days' New York Times headline was, "Global Warming has Begun, Expert tells Senate."[711]

One year later, in 1989, Exxon founded the 'Global Climate Coalition.' This unholy diaspora included Shell, Chevron, and many other planet-heating corporations[712]. To understand their purpose, we need to go back a couple of years.

In 1987, Reagan revoked the Fairness Doctrine, ending the need for 'fair and balanced' fact-based news coverage. This single act would allow for evil grifters to dismiss, distort, and deny facts, leading to the poisoning of the minds of millions of Americans.

So it is that we arrive in 1988 at far-right darling and AM radio hate-monger Rush Limbaugh's three-hours-a-day rants, blaming, in his words, climate change "hysteria" on "liberal hoaxers," "environmental wackos," and "commie libs."[713]

He would be joined less than a decade later by Rupert Murdoch's purpose-built disinformation machine, Fox News.

Just to go back to the marriage of fossil fuel and fake-Christianity, here is Fred Palmer, former lobbyist for Peabody Coal, one of the largest coal companies in America, speaking in the late 1990s;

> You're doing God's work every time you turn your car on and you burn fossil fuels and you put CO_2 in the air. You're doing the work of the Lord. Absolutely. That's the system that's the ecological system we live in.[714]

It may be cold consolation, but, as bad as Rush Limbaugh and Fox are, imagine how much worse off we'd be had the tech bros' social media doomsday machines existed in the 1990s?

Still, to keep on profiting, the pestilential fossil-fuel reprobates deployed the same playbook as Big Tobacco had in the 1950s. They muddied the waters with highly paid quack 'scientists' and concerned-sounding foundations like that aforementioned 'Global Climate Coalition.'

That diaspora of the despicable would provide fodder for non-critical thinkers, especially in the corporate media, with talking points like these: "There's no consensus among scientists that climate change is real", and "Climate change is natural and normal—it's happened at other points in history" and, "This is the coldest winter we've had in years! So much for global warming."[715]

With those lines, instead of outright denial, the devils cloaked their language in the cover of plausible deniability[716]. This is much harder to argue with in a one-minute segment on cable news or when it's thrown at a climate scientist in a senate hearing by disingenuous hacks like Ted Cruz or Marco Rubio[717]. Which, of course, is exactly what the fossil fuel devils needed in order to keep on digging, pumping, polluting, and profiting.

To reach normal Americans, devious Republican communicators like Frank Luntz toned down the urgent language. It was he who advised George H.W. Bush to stop using the apocalyptic-sounding, 'global warming', and start employing the much friendlier 'climate change', as in, 'Climates change, but it's normal and nothing to worry about.'[718]

This brings us to our friends in the US auto industry. As we have read, their most profitable products are the cheap-to-build and highly popular light-duty pickup trucks.

As a relevant aside, I was always struck by the irony of seeing a giant Ford F-150 truck with a bumper sticker reading, "SUPPORT OUR TROOPS." The driver probably didn't realize the paradox of his fourteen miles per gallon gas-guzzler being the reason for both American troops dying in the Middle East and for making the planet uninhabitable for his own grandkids. There again, knowing what we know today, it's just as likely he wouldn't give a damn. Still, he was a great friend to the oil companies.

Now, I'm not completely naïve. If I were the CEO of Exxon, I'd want people driving around in 14 mpg V8-powered trucks simply because they have to buy my product four times as often as a Toyota Prius hybrid driver, whose car does 52 mpg (and only emits one-fifth of that trucks' CO_2 emissions.)[719]

However, today, progress has overtaken the Prius and brought us the oil industry's perfect nightmare; the Electric Vehicle. After all, no EV driver will ever need their product.

So it is that to really 'support our troops' and help save the human race, the most patriotic thing an American could do is drive an American electric car or truck.

Still, that's the future. Today, thanks to the fossil fuel industry, we have had twenty-five years of lies, misinformation, and obfuscation that have hurtled us towards the climate crisis, yet nothing will stop these people in their pursuit of profit.

To illustrate how determined they are, at the Conference of Policies (COP) 27 Climate Summit held in Glasgow in 2022, there were 636 oil and gas lobbyists[720]. This was more than the delegations of any one country, all with the sole purpose of muddying the waters to keep on hawking their planet-heating, cancer-generating products.

By 2023, any pretense the event wasn't just a business meeting for interested fossil-fuel sellers was blown away with COP 28 being held in the oil kingdom of Abu Dhabi[721].

To the matter of those planet-heating products. According to an exhaustive study by the Carbon Majors Database, in the eight years since 2016, just fifty-seven oil, gas, coal, and cement producers were responsible for emitting 80% of all greenhouse gases.

To give you an idea of who they are, one-third of the pollution came from private businesses; their names may be familiar: Exxon, Shell, BP, Chevron, and TotalEnergie.

Another third are state businesses, such as Saudi's Aramco, Russia's Gazprom, the National Iranian Oil Company, and Coal India.

The final one-third are state industries, like the Chinese coal industry, who alone pumps out one-fifth of worldwide pollution[722].

If you thought that story was wild, there's more. Few people know how heavily subsidized the fossil fuel industry is. Our friends at the International Monetary Fund inform us that $7 trillion out of the $109 trillion world economy is subsidies on fossil fuels[723].

In high-income nations like America, this means cheap land for drilling, lax regulations for polluting, and favorable tax credits[724], but how do subsidies work in low- to middle-income countries? Their politicians know that fuel, whether electricity or gasoline for cars, has to be heavily subsidized; otherwise their citizens couldn't afford it and would riot in the streets[725]. Which would be terrible news for those politicians when seeking re-election.

Also, these nations need to industrialize, and it takes energy to do so. For politicians stuck in the old mindset, unsustainable energy subsidies on coal and gas power stations are the fastest way to provide grid-scale electricity (even though many of these nations' grids are very unreliable and power cuts are frequent) to the population. And to get more energy, they just build more power stations and burn more fossils.

Ironically, part of our salvation may come from countries like China and India, where renewables account for over a fifth of their energy mix, and are increasing rapidly year on year[726]. Then there's Pakistan, where a solar revolution has taken place, born from consumers' fury at the unreliable power grid and ever-increasing electricity prices, and assisted by the low cost of Chinese solar panels. In 2024, Pakistanis added one-third of their total grid capacity from solar power alone[727].

Whilst the adoption of renewables is helping to slow down the annual growth in carbon emissions, every year they still hit record highs, causing fires, floods, and storms[728]. This is bad news for the planet but much worse news for us humans.

Coming back to America. To buy land to put a solar or wind farm on would cost you at least $2000 an acre. Yet, to give you an idea of how subsidized fossil fuels are, in 2020, the Trump administration auctioned off millions of acres of land to the oil and gas industry, with bidding starting at just $2 per acre[729]. Doubtless, after the 2024 election win, this will continue. Yet, despite this huge government assistance to the fossil fuel industry, even in Texas, solar and wind are more profitable than fossil fuels and great for rural jobs[730].

However, there's another stumbling block. GOP politicians have so maximally misinformed their voters that to endorse those job-creating and profitable renewables over fossil fuels is to invite a primary challenge from the even more deranged MAGA right[731]. So, for our GOP hack, if it comes down to earning another term in office or ruining the planet, well...

However, at least the far right's subversively sinister motives are understandable. For me, it's liberals and green activists whom I paint with a lot of my disdain. Many just moan about the 'climate crisis' or 'climate emergency,'[732] whilst offering no workable solutions that won't hurt working people.

In my book 'When Coal Miners Drive Cadillacs', you can read about solutions that don't just help to solve global warming but can also heal the political divisions in America.

Chapter 21

Welcome To Florida. Authoritarian Paradise And America's First Underwater State.

"MAKE FLORIDA A SWAMP AGAIN." Doesn't sound too hopeful, does it? Yet, if the state continues traveling backwards under Republican leadership, by 2050, it may be so.

In this chapter, I wanted to write a cautionary tale about the entirely avoidable situation that may force Florida's citizens to make the unenviable choice of staying and losing everything or leaving with nothing, as the Sunshine State becomes America's first failed state.

An indisputable truth is that the world is getting hotter. In the near term, to counter that, Floridians can turn down the temperature on their air conditioners. However, the weather, influenced by man's unregulated, unscientific climate-altering experiment, poses a much more dire threat. More heat means hotter seas, which will mean stronger hurricanes and more devastating floods. Very soon, the state simply won't be able to afford the costs[733].

Then, all that fancy beachfront real estate on America's longest coastline will be unsaleable, and the coastal communities will have to migrate inland.

At what cost, though? When your $600,000 home becomes unlivable, who will pay to relocate you? And what if Disney, who provides a good portion of the state's income through Disney World and its resultant tourists, moves to a more welcoming home? Over the next thirty years, Florida is going to have to make some tough decisions.

Unfortunately, today's Governor DeSantis will not make them, as when he's not failing outside Florida, he's only interested in stoking up white cultural rage inside. He is true evil, but in this chapter, you will also learn how liberals were complicit in throwing Florida's thirty electoral college votes away and in allowing Floridian democracy to be stolen.

This never had to be. Back in 2018, Andrew Gilum, the Democratic nominee for governor, lost to DeSantis by less than 32,000 votes out of 8.2 million ballots cast in a $106 million race[734]. Just to add, in that election, over four million eligible voters didn't bother voting.

DeSantis is not a smart man; however, he passed enough standardized tests to graduate from Harvard and Yale. Like the ghouls working on the Heritage Foundation's Project 2025, he appears to have studied how to implement a neo-fascist government.

His model appears to be tiny Victor Orbán, (see chapter twenty-two), the authoritarian Prime Minister of Hungary. Like DeSantis, he's another pathetic, perpetually angry little man engaged in a systematic dismantling of all things 'liberal.'

So it is that anything in the far-right's Florida that doesn't align with the image of the SWIMP is labeled, 'woke.'

In 2023, DeSantis tried to go presidential, however, he didn't read the memo properly. Every demagogue knows fascism feeds off cruelty. However, it also needs carnival and spectacle, yet all this creature offered was sadism. His campaign was self-sabotaged by him being a terrible retail politician who neither smiled nor bothered to remember the names of his own voters.

It's astonishing how few people saw through this flaccid Trump-without-the-charisma. This goes especially for his moronic donors, who coughed up the $160 million to parachute him into the 2024 GOP presidential primary; all for the damp squib to give up and pull out after the first race in Iowa[735].

However, even though just one third of Florida's voters chose him, he was in control there and could wreak merry havoc. Like Orban, DeSantis knew he had to rig the voting system.

Without irony, he employed the phrase "Election Integrity' to do it[736]. Thus, with not a word from the Justice Department or most liberals, within one cycle, insane gerrymandering resulted in whole black voting districts being cracked and packed. So it is today that, in a near 50-50 state, the GOP has twenty out of twenty-eight Congressional seats and a supermajority in the state legislature[737].

None of this would be possible without a second strand of authoritarianism: having judges who were beholden to him. Indeed, DeSantis appointed five Federalist Society members (recall Leonard Leo) out of the seven Florida Supreme Court judges. These are the people who hear the liberal challenges to the acidic abortion ban, bonkers book bans, gung-ho gun laws, and villainous voter suppression laws and, unsurprisingly, leave them all in place[738].

Just to note, whilst DeSantis's carnival of cruelty was taking place, our intrepid sentinels of inquiry in the national corporate media were giddily boosting him up as that—however laughable today—potential president. Their moronic disingenuity is to be expected. What's harder to excuse are those liberals who failed to join two dots and allowed DeSantis to win.

To this point, we need to go back in time to the early hours of Sunday, 12th June 2016. Inside Orlando's Pulse nightclub, a haven for the LGBTQ+ community, around three hundred vibrant weekend revelers were living their happiest lives, dancing and singing. These gleeful, harmless people would have been completely unaware of the gruesome abomination that was minutes away from befalling them.

A man with a legally purchased AR-15 rifle approached the club and started shooting. Even though the door was staffed by an off-duty policeman, he was outgunned by the rifle. Having breached the entrance, the deranged gunman transformed what should have been a refuge from the outside world into a scene from a battlefield. The repellent results of his satanic endeavors were the ripped and torn bodies of forty-nine of those innocent weekend partygoers.[739]

Dot two came on Wednesday, February 14th, 2018, at the Marjory Stoneman Douglas High School in Parkland. At 2.21 pm, as most pupils would have been looking forward to going home, a nineteen-year-old former student walked into the school, again with an AR-15 rifle, and over the next thirty minutes, stalking from room to room, used his weapon of war to turn classrooms into killing fields. He murdered fifteen students and two teachers that day. Just to note, again there was a police officer on site, but he was too terrified to do anything because he knew what the AR-15 could do.[740]

When we join those dots, these events both took place *before* DeSantis was elected. Yet, he was part of the same far-right who wanted no restrictions on guns and who made no secret of wanting to ban abortion and of despising both LGBTQ+ folks and black folks.

Once elected, DeSantis brought a version of Project 2025 to Florida. In June 2022, four months before the mid-terms, the six high priests of the Supreme Court made abortion illegal in half of America. For Florida's voters, this triggered a fifteen-week ban. Just to note, DeSantis never made any secret of wanting an even stricter six-week ban.

Then, in July 2022, with most liberals still sitting on their hands, Florida passed the anti-LGBTQ+ "Parental Rights in Education' bill (known much more appropriately as the "Don't Say Gay" bill). This censored any classroom discussion of LGBTQ+ issues; teachers could be fired for dissent, and right-wing parents could sue 'offending' school districts for any infractions. The bill was a step along the path to the elimination of LGBTQ folks and especially the 'T'—transgender[741].

Just a quick segue; it's difficult to explain the sheer volume of hate and rage that festers inside of freaks like DeSantis, and not just him. We know that the reprobate-like MAGA hags, 'Moms for Liberty,' were spawned and are based in Florida.

If ever there was a time for Democrats to run a dynamic progressive woman who could show Floridians that she would fight for them, this was probably it. The only sitting Democrat to win a statewide race—serving Secretary of State for Agriculture, Nicky Fried—stood, but the party establishment thought they knew better. So, instead of fighting, they put up a man from a different era who didn't realize his opponents wanted to set him on fire and eat him. While former Republican Governor Charlie Crist was a decent enough fellow, he had no fight and enthused no one.

As it was, Hurricane Ian blew in to decimate the state but boost DeSantis, with President Biden coming down to the most corrupt state in America and offering unlimited, no-strings-attached Federal Emergency Management Agency (FEMA) money.

DeSantis snatched the cash and sneered at Biden, which—when filtered through the funhouse mirror lens of the idiotic corporate media—made him look 'tough' and 'decisive.' Despite all this, Crist still took 40% of the vote.

Come his second term, with no worries of re-election, DeSantis took the gloves off. In January 2023, still with nary an ounce of liberal pushback, he (with Christopher Rufo from chapter ten) 'took over' the well-respected liberal New College in order to turn it into an indoctrination academy for junior SWIMP's[742].

Nice liberals weren't too concerned either when, in February 2023, to feed white cultural rage, he showed his supporters the 'irrelevance' of black folks by banning Advanced Placement African-American history studies[743].

Of course, all this brainwashing needed censorship, so there were the book bans. In April 2023, Florida became the censorship capital of America with 1400 titles banned since 2021[744]. As it was mostly LGBTQ+ and black folks' stuff, again, liberals didn't see it as being too important[745].

It is an unimpeachable truth that the unchallenged bully will always demand more. So it would also be in April 2023 that Florida's citizens were thrown to the lions. Despite it being opposed by over three-quarters of Floridians—many of whom weren't paying attention during the previous five years—the state legislature passed a bill expanding permitless concealed carry across the state, opening it up to anyone of legal gun-owning age[746].

That same month, the legislature also instituted a six-week abortion ban[747]. Oh dear, liberals probably should have learned the meaning of the word 'solidarity' five years ago.

Anyhow, now people started screaming, but now it was too late. I'm reminded of the old quote, "The only thing necessary for the triumph of evil is for good men to do nothing."[748]

Thus, thanks to the people back in 2018 and 2022 who didn't care about LGBTQ+ folks, black folks, or dead school kids, today, the GOP wins ever bigger margins in the elections, women are second-class citizens, and the gun is almighty.

Still, if many Floridians weren't concerned about their fellow citizens, perhaps one might imagine they would want to protect their 'property values' by building in some climate resilience. Seemingly not. There's an instructive quote from one of the richest people in America, Thomas Peterffy. Just so we know who we are dealing with, this is from Forbes Magazine;

> He owns about 75% of Interactive Brokers, which has a market capitalization of over $33 billion, making Peterffy one of the 25 wealthiest Americans with an estimated $26.2 billion fortune. He also holds an estimated $3 billion in investments and cash, as well as over 560,000 acres of land, primarily in Florida, where he moved in 2014. He is a major backer of Republican politicians and free market causes.[749]

In words that should be carved into Mount Rushmore, he gave the most chillingly honest summation of why and how we may sleepwalk into an extinction-level, planet-wide climate disaster: "I don't have a care about it at all. If something needs to be done to save it....it's not going to be my problem."[750]

Mr. Peterffy owns a $52 million mansion on some of the lowest-lying land in Florida. It's guaranteed to be uninhabitable, uninsurable, and possibly underwater within a few decades.

Never say Floridians weren't offered help. The bright folks at the US Army Corps of Engineers proposed a six-mile-wide, 20ft tall seawall, to protect South Florida from storm surges. A Miami City commissioner nixed that idea;

> The $40 billion in assets you're trying to protect will be diminished if you build a wall around downtown because you're going to affect market values and quality of life.[751]

This isn't surprising. Republicans have controlled Florida for the past twenty years and deny climate change, even while the state experiences worse and worse catastrophes every few years.

Just going back to Hurricane Ian. It was the worst natural disaster in the state's history, killing over one hundred and fifty people and causing over $112 billion in damage to thousands of homes and businesses[752].

Bear in mind, in 2023, Florida's state budget was only $110 billion, and 80% of its government revenue comes from a 6% sales tax on goods and services. It doesn't take a genius to see that, with one of these hurricanes every few years, the state will become economically unviable.

This dystopian future is being ushered on even faster given that Ivy League-educated Governor DeSantis is also a climate change denier. He calls it "politicization of the weather."[753]

We can't make logic out of madness, but as is ever the case, Republicans have no problem losing themselves in a sea of their own hypocrisy. After the floods and the hurricanes smashed his own state, DeSantis demanded Washington provide FEMA disaster assistance. Yet in 2012, as a Tea Party congressional rep, he voted against federal aid to help the citizens of New York and New Jersey after Hurricane Sandy. He's not alone, as this is a trend common to almost all Republicans[754].

There's a question worth pondering; at what point will other Americans who have to foot the $100 billion hurricane bills decide that enough is enough? The fact is, without the federal government, Florida is finished;

the state would be bankrupt, and it would become, once again, a home for alligators and algae.

To envision how a failed state scenario might come about, cast aside images of a dystopian future where terrified regular citizens queue for food and gas rations while secessionist militiamen engage federal troops in urban combat. Instead, think more of a slim, slightly balding, glasses-wearing actuary from a Midwestern insurance company carefully assessing risk.

If there was a category marked "HIGHEST RISK: DO NOT QUOTE," that's where I'd put property in Florida. Don't scoff, as we may get there faster than you imagine. In 2024, the average cost of home insurance in Florida was $6000, a figure that had doubled in just three years[755].

Very intelligent people will also soon figure something else out: when a bank writes a thirty-year mortgage, its only security in case of borrower default is the home itself. Here again, Florida poses a big problem. What if the bank's asset is underwater, or the roof has blown off and the home-owner didn't have insurance?[756]

This issue isn't just for homeowners—businesses in Florida must also consider their long-term viability as what lender will loan money for a business when the business may not be there in fifteen years? Then, prescient of all that is coming, what insurance company is going to cover that business?

What about the largest business in the state? Imagine if you were the CEO of Disney, under attack from the ungrateful imbeciles in the Tallahassee State Capitol. Bear in mind that in 2022, Disney brought in half of the fifty-eight million visitors to Florida[757].

Yet, instead of lauding its praises, DeSantis spent millions of taxpayers' dollars trying to bully the Mouse. Their crime? Disney wouldn't bully the bullied and smash down on LGBTQ+ folks.

Don't fool yourselves that it isn't just self-interest. They need profits, and that means visitors, and discrimination is bad for business, as it means fewer visitors.

Disney doesn't care whether you're white, black or brown, man or woman, gay or straight: All the Walt Disney Company wants is for you to watch their movies and buy their merchandise. And then, if your parents can afford it, maybe you will be lucky enough to go to Disney World, where a seven-day Magic Ticket costs $519 per person[758].

On the matter of profits, as Orlando is probably going to be uninhabitable within thirty years, how does Disney survive when it's too hot for visitors to walk around the park?

If I were in the Disney boardroom, listening to Governor Snowflake, I'd be planning to find a new home for Disney World and those millions of visitors. Just consider all that employment in the theme park, hotels, shopping malls, rental cars, gas stations, and everything else that fifty-eight million people need. What state wouldn't bend over backwards for them?

I'd wager that before 2050, Disney is gone, and with them, their visitors, jobs, and tax revenue. But long before all this happens, the insurance companies will stop writing home and business cover, and the banks will stop lending on those homes and businesses.

I feel so sorry to think of all the millions of decent people in Florida, but, on its current trajectory, the future is as inevitable as the sun rising in the east and setting in the west.

One thing you can be absolutely sure of is that the Florida branch of MAGA will not assume even one scintilla of blame for transforming the Sunshine State back into a swamp. In fact, even as their state sinks, they will be right there demanding federal assistance, right up to where the gators and the snakes come to Make Florida Theirs Again.

Chapter 22

A Lesson For America From The Confederate Taliban's Afghan Cousins.

Historians find it hard to explain how, after twenty-one years of war in Afghanistan, we came full circle, with everything old becoming new again. Back in 2001, the Taliban, an extreme right-wing religious group, were in charge, and today, those same Taliban are in charge. Back then, they dominated and controlled women, LGBTQ+ folks, and any dissenting voices, and so they do today. And back then, other terrorists used the country as a training ground, and so they do today[759].

America's longest war cost over two trillion dollars. More tragic was the human toll of 2461 fallen and 20,744 injured service personnel[760]. This doesn't even consider the hundreds of thousands with PTSD or other war-related mental issues. But how many people know why it happened and why it is so important a lesson for 2024 America to understand?

To know a country, first, one needs to know its people. The Taliban are from the Pashtun sect, which makes up half of all Afghans. These are Sunni Muslims closely linked to Pakistan and Saudi Arabia. Of the rest of the population, Tajiks comprise a quarter, and Hazaras make up just over a fifth. Both these groups are Persian.

Afghanistan was founded in 1747 by Pashtuns, and for centuries the majority of wealth was held by a small minority of rich Pashtuns, who resented having to give up any of their money and power[761].

The Taliban were part of the US-backed Mujahideen of the 1980s, who were battling the invading Soviet Union. It's hard for me to think of what happened in 2001 without being reminded of Ronald Reagan's ominously prescient words from 1983;

> Afghanistan's freedom fighters—the resistance or mujahidin—represent an indigenous movement that swept through their mountainous land to challenge a foreign military power threatening their religion and their very way of life.[762]

It's absolutely true that Afghans were fighting for their freedom against the Soviet Union. However, in 1990, after defeating the Russian bear, there was nothing to keep the various sects intact.

At this point, following centuries of Pashtun rule, Tajiks had risen in society. Many Pashtuns resented this, and none more so than the Taliban, whose base was made up of the scared, the angry, fake-Muslims, and the insane. Their aim was to Make Afghanistan Great Again by uniting all Pashtuns, from the far-right religious crazies to the more secular and moderate pro-Western folks.

As it turned out, the majority of Pashtuns were not too keen on living in an extreme conservative religious theocracy. This wasn't what the Taliban wanted to hear, so, in 1996, they just took over the country and dominated those who opposed them so they could control them. Any of this sounding familiar to you?

The Taliban, as with their Confederate Taliban cousins, deceived scared people, and gave vent to the furies of angry people. However, what they never did was make anyone's lives better. Indeed, all their regime promoted was religious intolerance and economic stagnation.

Still, no one would have paid any heed to this non-strategic, landlocked country but for the Taliban's fateful decision to host Osama Bin Laden and his Al Qaeda terrorists. That ruinous choice would set them on a collision course with the most powerful nation humanity has ever known and would consign the Taliban's toxic legacy to the trash can of history. Or so America thought.

After 9/11, the United States sent 130,000 brave troops seven thousand miles to Afghanistan. Their mission was clear; to destroy Al Qaeda and the Taliban and avenge the fallen innocents. The Taliban had no army, navy, or air force. Despite this, their primitive, AK-47 wielding fighters fought fiercely, and whilst there was much close combat, US troops had the advantage of being able to call on air support, whether by drone, missile, or fighter jet.

This being so, back in Washington, the powers-that-be probably assumed a similar outcome to the hundred-hour 'Desert Storm' war that expelled Saddam Hussein from Kuwait in 1991[763]. Then, once their speedy victory was complete, they could start "Nation Building."[764] This idea comes from the rebuilding of Germany and Japan post-1945.

However, there was a fatal flaw in the establishment's thinking. Before World War II, both Axis powers had some semblance of societal order and governance. It was from those foundations that Germany and Japan were quickly rebuilt after the war.

Still, for the right-wing neo-cons, all Afghans needed was to rid themselves of the Taliban and enjoy some democracy and free markets. From there, they would be well on their way to being able to buy Barbies, Boeings, and Big Macs. The problem was, nobody told poor, corrupt, no-civil-society Afghanistan that it was supposed to become Australia overnight.

It was bad enough not to learn the post-war lessons from Germany and Japan, but they hadn't even taken any pointers from what happened in Russia just ten years earlier. There, Mikhail Gorbachev—ironically, the man who withdrew Soviet troops from Afghanistan in 1988—ruled between 1985 and 1991. He brought in 'Glasnost,' meaning openness of speech, and 'Perestroika,' defined as the restructuring of the economy[765].

Unfortunately, the Russian people used their 'glasnost' to scream about how there was no bread or milk on the shelves, and from this, there was little chance of 'perestroika.' Soon, Mr. Gorbachev was gone, and with him, any chance of working with Russia.

Just a quick note to elites. If you are in the business of nation building, remember this: every solution must start with some candy in order to entice the people; thus, bread before ballot boxes and electricity before elections. And as far as good old democracy goes, recall that the USA has had a form of democratic government since 1789. That's over two hundred and thirty-five years to respond to people's problems, and it still isn't right.

But then, as they showed in 2016 and 2024, the elites running the war didn't recognize their own Taliban either. This being said, to understand why America lost its longest ever war and what lessons it holds, we need to go much more granular. For that, allow me to take you on a trip back to 2010.

I was working with my business partner on a project to bring English language teaching to girls' schools in Afghanistan. If the chatterers in the media, politics, and international aid circles were to be believed, this was the holy grail of Western assistance. We will learn a little more about these people as the chapter goes on.

For us, though, we knew educated girls would grow up to be empowered women and considerate mothers. In turn, their kids would be much more likely to become teachers rather than terrorists and scientists rather than suicide bombers.

On our project, we were working in Mazar-e-Sharif, the second largest city in Afghanistan. It is set within Balkh Province (a province is like a state), about one hundred and sixty miles from the capital city, Kabul. Balkh borders two other countries, Tajikistan and Uzbekistan. A warlord ruled the province, as many were. He was a Tajik named Atta Noor.

As a corrupt patriarch, he took a cut off the goods coming across the border. This ensured that the weak central government didn't receive the import taxes that would help make life better for all Afghans and make the country more stable. That being said, self-interest was at his heart, so he spent some of the monies to ensure his province was safe from the Taliban. You may see a disconnect there.

Still, we started our project at the Fatima Balkhi School for Girls before rolling it out into twenty other schools, setting up what we called Language Labs. For under $10,000 each, they comprised twenty laptops using English language learning software. We trained a female teacher and left the Labs as a demonstration of intent for anyone to see.

From the outset, we knew that, for our project to succeed, it had to involve local people. There's an old proverb: "Give a man a fish and you feed him for a day. Teach him how to fish, and you feed him for a lifetime."[766] So it was that the laptops came from a local Afghan computer manufacturer (yes, they had a computer industry.) The workstations came from local factories. Then, we needed a sustainable electricity supply, so we used local solar panels.

Every step of the way, we tried to use local contractors and local suppliers; after all, these were the people who would be sending their children to the schools, and it was seen as a badge of honor to be included in building something so important.

We saw the Language Labs as a model for how aid should be distributed. By telling local people what was coming and how it would benefit their lives, we won hearts and minds.

Having completed these labs, we needed funding for more. As we wanted to help people in Governor Noor's province, we assumed he'd want to help us. Sadly, his alacrity didn't extend as far as his wallet. However, he bestowed upon us his patriarchal blessing, which was enough to get us to the central government.

On visiting the Ministry of Education in Kabul, the minister was very receptive. He just wanted a $250,000 bribe. Upfront. If we paid, he would give us $750,000 of government funding for 75 labs in 75 schools. The stickler was that, by paying the bribe, there wouldn't be enough money to complete the project.

This is the true insidiousness of corruption. First, useless but well-connected people, like that gentleman, pay to become powerful ministers. Then, once in office, they get to stay powerful through more corruption. So it would be that, after stripping $250,000 from the $750,000 contract, our project would have to be cut down in the number of language labs, the quality of labs, or the amount of equipment. So, we said, 'thank you, but no thank you.'

I'm reminded of a line from Canadian Deputy Prime Minister Chrystia Freeland's magnificent 2012 book, 'Plutocrats: The Rise of the Super-Rich and the Fall of Everyone Else.' Mrs. Freeland was speaking to Naguib Sawiris, an Egyptian telecom billionaire, who opined on the subject of corruption,

> I've never understood in my life why all these dictators, when they stole, why didn't they just steal a billion and spend the rest on the people.[767]

Mr. Sawris is obviously a clever man, but he might have missed a simple point about the people who covet power; they are always greedy dominators.

Let's perform a thought experiment that will show the true cancer of corruption. It takes place in Afghanistan but could apply to any of the other war-torn, low-income countries of the world that rely upon overseas development aid.

Imagine that international donors provided $10 million to build 1,000 Language Labs. Very few leaders would steal all the funds. More likely, they would allocate $7 million to the project and then steal the rest. But this is just the start of the problems.

With only $7 million to pay for a $10 million contract, belts need to be tightened. But recall the society we live in. All the way down the line, bribes must be paid, which strips even more money out of the project.

Maybe the new schools needed to be earthquake proof, but bribes had to be paid, so they weren't built to earthquake proof standards. Perhaps they were supposed to get off-grid solar power, but bribes need to be paid, so they need to rely on an unreliable electrical grid. Then, money was supposed to be set aside to pay 1,000 teachers, but bribes ate into that too, so there aren't enough teachers. What if top-spec laptops were supposed to be ordered, but with the cuts, those computers get downgraded to a lower spec that may not work for very long before breaking?

So, by the end of the project, normal citizens see a $10 million white elephant, because that was what it cost. However, the actual value parents, pupils, and taxpayers received may only be $4 million. Thus, what they really get are some substandard schools, with substandard computers, and some well-meaning but poorly paid and poorly trained teachers.

Then consider that this is a spider's web running through society. Everything seems to cost a lot: the schools, the roads, the bridges, and the hospitals. But the projects either never happen, or if they do, the quality is terrible. And from that, resentment seeps in...at the government.

Ironically, the people who recognized how malignant corruption was—albeit in a different arena—were the people you might least have expected to recognize it: the Taliban are a hundred percent maniacal demons, but I cannot deny they understood the importance of paying their fighters good wages and paying them on time.

Contrast this with the Afghan police. Whether it was because they were so poorly paid (if at all) or it was a power play, some police looked for ways to supplement their income.

One of those ways was at roadside checkpoints. To travel from town to town, citizens had to pass through three or four security checkpoints. It wasn't uncommon for the police to charge them a toll at each checkpoint. The Taliban also levied tolls, but only once. Neither was fair, but it was the police who were supposed to be protecting the people, not shaking them down, and citizens knew it, which led to resentment[768].

It wasn't just in the police where there were problems. Poor morale and corruption were given as reasons the Afghan army collapsed so quickly in the wake of the withdrawal. But what if many Afghan soldiers didn't actually exist in the first place?

Don't take my word for it. Since 2012, SIGAR, the Special Inspector General for Afghanistan Reconstruction, has been responsible for accounting for funds and spending. Over the years, the Inspector General wrote sixty-two quarterly reports to Congress, some running to 150 pages, and many warning of the fraud, corruption, and waste.

It was our friends at the BBC who reported on the SIGAR concerns over 'ghost' soldiers; these were real names on a real roster that received a real salary but didn't belong to a real body able to pick up an M4 carbine and fight. The BBC said;

> A 2016 report by the US (SIGAR) claimed that "neither the United States nor its Afghan allies know how many Afghan soldiers and police actually exist, how many are in fact available for duty, or, by extension, the true nature of their operational capabilities.

In a more recent report, SIGAR euphemistically expressed "serious concerns about the corrosive effects of corruption... and the questionable accuracy of data on the actual strength of the force."[769]

Going back to our language labs, every Western aid organization that saw them loved them, then they walked away, and we never heard from them again. It was the same story, trying to solicit help from embassies and their diplomats. For us, it was obvious that many diplomats just enjoyed the parties, and the aid organizations, while well-meaning, were just plain ineffective. The fact was, these were all clique bodies who had a network, and if you weren't in it, they weren't interested.

In their defense, they faced the paradox of the aid worker in a war zone that aid workers in regular low-income countries don't face; both groups were terrified of being kidnapped by the Taliban. But they wouldn't delegate projects to honest and trusted locals to make the country better off and dilute the power of the Taliban. Instead, they used powerful, corrupt 'rent-seeking' businessmen, who, without oversight or interest in their community, either stole the money or stole part of it and did a substandard job with the rest.

So it was; during our time there, we knew of schools that were half-finished, and other schools where laptops sat in cupboards because there were no teachers trained to use them[770].

To explain some of why that was, we need to zoom the lens out. In 2014, while the possibility of peace in Afghanistan still existed, another free but not fair presidential election took place.

Ashraf Ghani, a Pashtun, won it. This technocratic bookworm, educated at Columbia University, became a professor at Johns Hopkins University before going to work for the World Bank. He probably should have stayed there for whilst there is a place for technocrats, where it isn't is as the leader of one of the most violent, war-torn countries on the planet. However, Ghani spoke great English and understood elite mannerisms, so America backed him. Then, once in office, he seldom left his palace and, over the seven years of his administration, made few genuine efforts to unify the country.

Moving on, whilst America was fighting the War on Terror in Afghanistan, it wasn't too interested in the War on Drugs in Afghanistan.

Thus, with breathtaking incongruity, the US sat back and allowed the cultivation of record amounts of opium year after year[771]. I know it was all out of a misplaced notion of self-interest; the war planners were scared of eradicating the opium crops and turning farmers into fighters[772].

However, they should have pulled the camera back a little and seen the big picture. It was the Taliban acting as middlemen who earned millions of dollars from those drugs. That money then paid for the bullets that went into the guns that were used by Taliban fighters to wound and kill American soldiers.

As for the farmers. They could have grown other crops, but the government had no taxes from which to offer any subsidies (try telling that to a taxpayer-funded American farmer in Iowa) to grow alternatives. So instead of growing barley, maize, or wheat, out of self-interest and survival, they grew opium.

This takes us to another big reason for the loss in Afghanistan: the feelings of people in the rural areas. There was no investment, and there was no protection, as most of the government's funds went into protecting and boosting the cities. So, with many rural Afghans having no faith that tomorrow would be better than today, when the Taliban came to town, it was a combination of fear and apathy that allowed them to take over.

An undeniable fact was that mostly American development aid made up 80% of the government's budget[773]. By controlling the purse strings, America controlled the behavior of the politicians. But we ignored the huge corruption that poisoned citizens' faith in their government. Indeed, the best use of those 130,000 American troops would have been to protect local communities from not just the Taliban but also corruption, allowing them to function and go about their daily lives. If this had happened, there would have been the possibility of creating a content, prosperous middle class. Then, with something to lose, the people would have fought a lot harder against the Taliban.

But as it was from 2001, the years passed and the billions were wasted, but citizens never saw their lives get better. In fact, so bad was life that one in ten Afghans numbed themselves from the hell of their existence with heroin[774].

When, just before he left office, Trump declared that he was pulling out, that was the signal to the Taliban that they could take over. The felon didn't care what happened to US personnel in the withdrawal. Driven by spite and revenge, the purpose of his terrible capitulation of a deal was to hand a poisoned chalice to his successor, Joe Biden.

Suffice to say, Trump didn't give a damn about the macabre fate awaiting the Afghan citizens he was selling down the river of death. So, come 2021, the Taliban swept through the country with a level of speed and intensity that shocked Western observers—who, seemingly, hadn't been paying attention for the past twenty years.

As they took Kabul with next to no resistance, President Ghani was helicoptered away to safety in neighboring Uzbekistan, leaving the people he swore to serve to be hunted, beaten, hanged, and shot[775].

He wasn't the only one to flee the fight. Instead of facing the Taliban, many poorly paid, low-morale soldiers gave up or ran away. This was also the case with the powerful warlords who ran the provinces. Our friend, Mr. Noor, the governor of Balkh Province, made sure to spirit himself away to Turkey.

If it was that hard for soldiers and warlords to face the Taliban, imagine what it must have been like for the civilians ranged against these devils. Within days of taking power, the Taliban brought forth 'revenge' and 'retribution.' It helped that they'd been left with some nice toys; M4 carbines, Humvees, and helicopters[776]. However, there was a much more useful tool: The HIIDE-Handheld Inter Agency Identification Device. This is from its manufacturer, L-1 Identity Solutions: "The HIIDE is the most powerful tool ever developed for biometric identification. Users can enrol and match or verify with the three primary biometrics; iris, finger and face."[777]

Many civilian Afghan personnel working with coalition forces had enrolled in this system for ease of identification. For them, it was unimaginable it would fall into the wrong hands, yet that's exactly what happened. My business partner was one of those being hunted by the HI-IDE-equipped Taliban. By design, it's impossible to fool, and had they identified him, he probably wouldn't be alive today.

You may remember the Fatima Balkhi School for Girls, the home of our first Language Lab. In 2021, the Taliban let the girls return, but with a cruel Kafkaesque sting in the tail. This is from the Associated Press;

> Dozens of girls, many of them formal students for the first time in their young lives, fidgeted on cracked wooden bench-es during an assembly in the shattered remains of the Fatima Balkhi school, which serves students of all ages. There were no chairs, no desks, no notebooks, no pens. But the students must come every day _ no excuses.[778]

Today, Afghanistan is a failed state, in much worse condition than when America went in. Paradoxically, though, for all the American blood and treasure expended over those twenty years, it is China who is profiting[779].

As the Taliban's new and unquestioning friend, Mr. Xi and his pals are using Afghanistan as a southern resource area for the low-cost extraction of the rare earth minerals used in the batteries and motors of Chinese electric vehicle brands such as BYD, Xpeng, and Zeekr, which will compete for market share with US companies like Ford, General Motors, and Tesla.

And whatever happened to all that opium? As ever, with authoritarian dominators, it's 'do as I say and not as I do.' With the Taliban frittering away the future generation's mineral inheritance, they didn't need drug money, so they instituted a national ban on opium. This led to a 95% reduction in the crop. The West cheered. As ever, they misunderstood.

The ban was absolute, and with no help for the farmers to transition to other crops, they and their families had no income, which led to starvation in the rural areas[780]. I can hear some saying, "But think of all the heroin we've kept off the streets." I'd reply with, "Money never sleeps."

So it is that as Afghan production dried up, opium growers in Myanmar (part of the Burmese Triangle of opium production that was supplying US troops in Vietnam) were happy to pick up the slack. Today it is they who grow, refine, and export thousands of tons of heroin to sedate the minds of desperate people with desperate lives all over the world[781].

To end, I would love to ask a few questions of some of the Ivy League 'educated idiots'—mostly Republican, but many 'moderate' Democrats too—who were so eager to send young men and women to war.

What was it all for? Why waste two trillion dollars on a misadventure only to end up in a worse place than we started? What about the thousands of new graves at Arlington and the tens of thousands of wounded veterans, and all the shattered lives and broken dreams? I haven't even gotten onto the 120,000 dead Afghans or the nation that was supposed to be built but is now, once again, a failed state.

Afghanistan offers America an exemplification of a gruesome future. It was a place where the 'rent-seeking' powerful gorged themselves on the riches, whilst ordinary people didn't feel like they had a say and didn't see their lives improve meaningfully. Afghanistan's society corroded before collapsing, and when it did, it was apathy and anger that finished it: the apathy of normal people who couldn't get ahead and the anger of the dominators who wanted to divide the population to use that as a path to power.

Chapter 23

How To Steal America.

In 2023, Ohio voters used true direct democracy to pass two ballot initiatives. The first was to enshrine abortion in the state constitution, and the second was to legalize marijuana. Former GOP senator Rick Santorum went on cable television to project;

> Thank goodness that most of the states in this country don't allow you to put everything on the ballot, because pure democracies are not the way to run a country.[782]

Rick's no friend of freedom, and he keeps it no secret. Indeed, freedom is something the Ohio GOP state legislature isn't very keen on either. On seeing that the abortion ballot was coming, they tried to raise the threshold for a ballot initiative to pass to a near-impossible-to-hurdle 60%.

You have read of the fifty-year campaign to pack the courts with right-wing judges to ensure the law bends the Republican way. However, in June 2023, the Heritage Foundation, a far-right 'think-tank,' that all Republicans since Reagan have used to staff their administrations, gave us a new plan that involves even more cruel and unusual ways to screw over their fellow Americans. With links to dozens of other ultra-conservative organizations, their Project 2025 detailed exactly how they intend to take over and gut the federal government.

With the help of billionaire Trump supporter and Oracle founder Larry Ellison, Heritage compiled a database of 20,000 far-right apparatchiks who will staff the 4,000 top-level political appointments in the civil service. Below them are the two million other civil servants, of whom at least 50,000 may be replaced by a law brought in by Trump late in 2020 (but rescinded by President Biden) called Schedule F. According to the Heritage Foundation president, Dr. Kevin Roberts,

> In 2016, the conservative movement was not prepared to flood the zone with conservative personnel," "On Jan. 20, 2025, things will be very different. This database will prepare an army of vetted, trained staff to begin dismantling the administrative state from Day 1.[783]

Just to ensure that these weren't rogue operators, we can hear from the Governor of Florida, Ron DeSantis. Being that he has implemented his own version of Project 2025 in his state of twenty million people, his words are instructive. Whilst being interviewed by Fox News in 2023, he spoke of eliminating whole branches of the federal government, "We would do Education, we would do Commerce, we'd do Energy, and we would do IRS."[784]

Also in 2023, Russell T. Vought, who ran the Trump administration's Office for Management and Budget, explained to those who hadn't been paying attention that, "What we're trying to do is identify the pockets of independence and seize them,"[785]

All this was calmly reported on the inside pages of the moronic New York Times under the banal, benign, and boring heading "Trump and Allies Forge Plans to Increase Presidential Power in 2025", instead of "HOW REPUBLICANS PLAN TO IMPLEMENT A DICTATORSHIP IN 2025."

For anyone who is interested, none of the Confederate Taliban's plans are secret. With breathtaking audacity, their www.project2025.org lays out a 920-page blueprint for an authoritarian takeover of America[786].

Skip forward to 2024, and we have far-right 'influencer' Jack Posobiec speaking alongside Steve Bannon, Trump's former White House chief strategist, at CPAC, the Conservative Political Action Conference. With words that should have disabused journalists of any illusions about the GOP, he hit us over the head with a metaphorical hammer: "Welcome to the end of democracy. We are here to overthrow it completely." [787] Whilst Posobiec is a fragile freak, he is also a creature who has the ear of Steve Bannon.

Just to illustrate how mainstream Republican this event was, let's look at the CPAC guests. We have Trump, Bannon, Ramaswamy, Vance, and Megyn Kelly. Then, to bring some international stench to the proceedings, there were the current presidents of Argentina and El Salvador, as well as the former prime minister of the United Kingdom[788].

All this was taking place whilst many moderate journalists and voters still thought that politicians like Mitch McConnell could take back the Republican Party to make it look more Bush-like, but they were so wrong. McConnell represents the country club conservatives. They are happy with big business, small regulation, tax cuts, loose gun laws, and veiled racism. But Mitch was a short-term fool who, to get his three justices on the Supreme Court, coddled the Confederate Taliban.

Think of Mitch as their useful idiot, presenting a veneer of 'decorum' that allowed them to get in the door. From here, it would only take one election victory, and the Confederate Taliban's unholy alliance of Scared, Rich, Christian, Angry and Insane could usher in an America many have warned about, but the media would not alert you to.

Stealing a democracy doesn't come cheap. To meet the Confederate Taliban's financiers is to meet a despicable directory of demons who want to stop marginalized people from voting, chain women to the kitchen, eliminate LGBTQ people, flood the zone with machine guns, and suffocate us with pollution.

Many of these donors are fragile, friendless freaks, some of whom we have met through the course of the book. For the rest, who they are and what they do is inconsequential, although I'm thinking of one in particular. Coming in hot at number one in the evil charts is GOP mega-donor and former industrialist Barre Seid, a ninety-year-old Chicagoan. He 'donated' his company, which amounted to a gargantuan $1.6 billion gift, to freedom thief Leonard Leo of the Federalist Society. Oh, and in doing so, Barry gave a big F.U. to America by dodging $400 million in taxes[789].

In the run-up to the 2024 election, we arrived at a point where, for the Confederate Taliban, there were no enemies to the right. What is pure madness is also a convergence of interests. Elon Musk floods Twitter with far-right voices. Steve Bannon's 'War Room' podcast broadcasts hate and disinformation for three hours a day. Billionaires back neo-fascist candidates for office, and Fox 'News' aired segments that are rebroadcast on Russian state television.

We have the far-right fake-Christians who ban books and indoctrinate children. Then there are the hideous hyenas in Congress like Greene, Gaetz, and Gosar, whose purpose is to gaslight ordinary folks into thinking that Washington is broken. Throw in the white nationalists dreaming of an Aryan Wunderland and the six high priests perched atop the Supreme Court—ripping up rights that were settled years ago—and you may think we've arrived at Dante's Gates of Hell.

"The Republican Party, as it exists today, is dangerous to the country." If Bernie Sanders or Alexandria Ocasio-Cortez said that, it may pass over your head. Actually, they were the words of Liz Cheney, the pro-big business, pro-fossil fuels, pro-gun, anti-voting rights, and anti-abortion former GOP congressional representative for Wyoming and daughter of former VP Dick Cheney, speaking to NPR in December 2023[790].

If American democracy dies, there will be no civil war, no tanks in the streets, and no mobs with guns moving house to house. Indeed, it might not even look like it's dead. Later on, it may resemble a hybrid of the USA and Russia, but to get there we may have to travel, figuratively, via Hungary. You may wonder what a tiny Eastern European country with a population of under ten million people[791] and an economy 1/130th the size of America has to do with this.

Perhaps not, though, when you learn that, in 2022, CPAC was being held in Budapest, the capital of Hungary. Then, in 2023, Hungarian Prime Minister Victor Orbán came to attend the US CPAC. Orban has met Trump three times, once in 2019 in the White House and then twice in 2024 at Mar-a-Lago. Tucker Carlson also hosted several of his shows from Hungary.

For the Confederate Taliban, Hungary represents a fever dream. It's a place where there are vanishing few people of color, abortion is illegal, and LGBTQ+ folks are invisible. In Hungary, the courts do as Orbán wants; the media sings Orbán's praises, and Orbán and his oligarch pals control all the major businesses. To top it all off, the patriarchal fake-Christians in the Hungarian Catholic Church give all this hate and grift a veneer of 'respectability' by giddily welcoming his anti-gospel policies.

Not one bullet was ever fired to get this far, and, unlike Russia, no secret police are required to enforce compliance. Indeed, since 2010, Orbán and his ruling Fidesz Party have set up a system to ensure it is incredibly difficult for the opposition to win another election. Anna Grzymala-Busse, the director of the Europe Centre at Stanford, described it;

> Since 2010, most of Hungary's civic institutions—the courts, the universities, the systems for administering elections—have come to occupy a gray area. They haven't been

eradicated; instead, they've been patiently debilitated, dele-gitimatized, hollowed out[792]

Hungary represents by far the easiest blueprint for a right-wing takeover of America. Orbán terms his government an 'illiberal Democracy,' and Transparancy International describes elections there as "free, but not fair."[793]

To any normal person, Hungary looks like a regular European country. The stunningly attractive capital, Budapest, is a magnet for tourists, and there is even a Formula One Grand Prix held there every year. What the tourists don't see is the extreme Christian nationalism, the demonization of the stated enemy—brown people, intellectuals, and LGBTQ+ folks—and the massive corruption.

In Hungary, everything is upside down, and this makes it infuriating to argue against. Political scientist Paul Kreko, author of "The Hungarian Far Right," calls it an 'information autocracy';

> Information autocracies use information as the main tool for manufacturing legitimacy for the regime and changing the behavior of citizens and voters. Information autocracies are special, in that they define themselves usually as some kind of democracy, even if the democracy is mostly not liberal and not based on the rule of law[794]

This all happened and was enabled in plain sight. Hungary is part of the European Union. That's the same EU that cries about democracy and freedom in Ukraine and is terrified of Russian tanks rolling into Poland. Yet, for fourteen years, they have, ostensibly to raise Hungarian living standards, sent EU Structural Funds amounting to 3.3% of Hungarian GDP each year to Orbán[795]. Over that time huge West European corporations like Thyssen-Krupp, Bosch, Mercedes-Benz, Audi, Opel, and Daimler—for whom profit, not democracy, is their concern—have used Hungary as a useful source of cheap labor and an assembly plant to make their own companies ever more profitable.

For readers, it's so important to note that Hungary, unlike Russia, was a democracy. Orbán came to power in 2010 through a legal, democratic victory. It was only after winning the 2010 election that he engaged in a "lightning speed assault" on the civic institutions—the courts, education, and the media.

To the point of how few people know that modern fascism lives and breathes in Hungary, we have to start to tie some of those strands together.

The ability to control the information space means that Orbán controls the ideas, and if anyone dares lodge a challenge to his ideas, then the courts are there to stop them[796]. This is why the modern autocrat doesn't need a Stasi-style secret police. Speaking about the media, Gabor Miklósi, an editor at 444, one of the last remaining independent journals in Hungary, said;

> He controls most of the national papers, most of the radio and TV stations, all the local papers in the countryside. He doesn't do it in obvious ways—he does it slowly, by putting his cronies in charge, or by subtly making life difficult for his critics. .... Orbán has managed to preserve the appearance of formal democracy, as long as you don't look too closely.

The evil genius works like this. Back in 2010, if you were a TV or newspaper owner, your lifeblood was advertising. So it was the Fidesz Government would only place adverts with their oligarch pal-owned far-right media and withhold adverts from the moderate news sources.

But there was a second, chilling punch. Any companies that placed advertisements in the moderate media were cut out of bidding for government contracts. Thus, within a year, no one was advertising in the moderate media, and those newspapers and TV stations went bankrupt. And guess who was there to buy them up? Yes, Orbán's oligarchs[797]. For receipts, we can hear again from DemDigest,

> More than 500 media outlets were put in a huge foundation called KESMA. In a country of 10 million people, this organization dominates about 80% of the media. Also, the overwhelming majority of the state advertisement goes to pro-governmental media. ...[798]

So now almost all the media is owned by the ruling parties' cronies. Just consider how you get your information, then imagine if ABC, CBS, NBC, The Washington Post, and every independent news outlet were suddenly owned by Rupert Murdoch. So it is that today in Hungary, it's nearly impossible to get a non-government opinion in the press. This is real "1984" stuff.

There's more. Professor Timothy Snyder used the phrase 'anticipatory obedience' in his seminal 2017 book 'On Tyranny' when describing how the modern autocracy functions[799]. Thus, in Hungary, what law firm would criticize Orbán or take up the opposition's cause for fear of being put out of business? And what university would allow students to think critically to challenge and protest the government? Ditto businesses that want to promote diversity and book publishers that want to show any other view of the world than that of SWIMPs[800].

You may wonder how Orban gets away with all this. Politico shed some light on that for us;

But at home, his power rests on a far more basic concept: patronage. Want a contract to build a road? A project for your village? A license for a radio station? A job for your struggling grand kid? For many Hungarians, the answer to these questions leads, directly or indirectly, to the ruling Fidesz party. Orbán has won loyalty from a host of business people, small-town politicians, television personalities and even musicians on the simple reasoning that supporting him is a good career move. Keeping such a system running, however, requires vast resources. And for years, those EU funds played a key role in sustaining it.[801]

Suffice to say, voter districts are heavily gerrymandered to ensure the opposition is 'cracked' and 'packed'. In 2022, the ruling Fidesz Party won just 54% of the vote, yet controls 66% of the seats in parliament, giving them a supermajority[802].

To cement in a voting advantage, the 5% of the population who are unemployed or on social welfare are classified as government employees. Then, with them and their families completely dependent upon the government, guess who they vote for come election time.

However, even this isn't enough to guarantee re-election. For this, Orbán cunningly uses more of the free EU Structural Funds money for voter giveaways. From the Journal of Democracy,

At election time, Orbán's government typically rolls out massive benefits to potential supporters, and 2022 was no exception. This year, he paid a "thirteenth-month" pension to seniors, exempted people under 25 years of age from income tax, and buffered Hungarians from inflation by freezing fuel and food prices. In prior election years, such handouts have won many people over.[803]

For those who fear the Hungarian far-right may have cracked the code of modern fascism, not so fast, for it is completely dependent upon those EU structural funds, and if that tap gets turned off, so does the voter bribery machine. But there's worse news for Hungary. Despite offering €30,000 payouts to families having three children[804], it has one of the lowest birth rates in Europe. Combine this with its anti-immigration policies, which ensure there won't be the workers to pay the taxes that fund the care of its rapidly aging population, and one can see a future of dramatic problems lying in store for Hungary.

To leave Hungary and come back to America. The guardrails just about held during Trump's first term. However, the Confederate Taliban has plans for that. Trump's VP pick J.D. Vance is a pathetic man-baby, however his words are instructive. He let slip back in a 2022 interview with James Pogue for Vanity Fair, something strikingly similar to the Heritage Foundation's Project 2025;

> I think that what Trump should do, if I was giving him one piece of advice: Fire every single mid-level bureaucrat, every civil servant in the administrative state, replace them with our people.

He would go on to describe standing up to the courts if they tried to stop Trump. However, realistically, when the Confederate Taliban has the military, CIA, FBI, DOJ, Homeland, and all the media, who is going to be able to stand up to them? Mr. Pogue ends up completing our thoughts for us with, "This is a description, essentially, of a coup."[805]

In case we weren't listening, Vance would write the foreword for Heritage president Dr. Kevin Roberts' new 2024 book on how to steal America. In the giddily gushing prose of a middling tenth-grader, Vance wrote about how the far-right needs to "circle the wagons and load the musket s."[806]

In August 2024, the stochastic terrorist went further. To capitalize on the aftermath of the failed far-right assassination attempt on Trump, Vance treasonously attempted to stoke up political violence against Democrats by stating that, "They even tried to kill him."[807]

We know domination is, of course, a reason for the Confederate Taliban stealing America. However, never underestimate its fellow dark traveler: greed. Over in Hungary, Mr. Orban has a pot of gold worth $181 billion, but the American prize is nearly 160 times larger at $29 trillion.

Also, don't go harboring any foolish notions of American corporations saving you. In a country of 340 million citizens with the largest economy on earth, do people really imagine all the mega-corporations would up sticks and leave just because a new regime took over? They didn't leave Hitler's Germany in the 1930s[808], they didn't leave Russia in the 2000s, and they didn't leave Hungary in the 2010s.

Business, for all its faux 'woke' credentials, is all about staying in business. Thus, out of pure self-interest, if it became profitable to smash down on women, people of color, and LGBTQ folks, what do you think corporations would do? I have a receipt. In July 2024, the billionaire boss of Warner Bros., David Zaslav, who also owns CNN, was reported as saying that it "mattered less to him which party wins, as long as the next president was friendly to business."[809]

To win power, Trump and his fake populist shills forged a coalition of 80% white SCARI people. They offered tax cuts for the rich and protectionist tariffs against our allies. These all sat alongside the GOP's cruel sugar of ethnic nationalism, anti-woman, and anti-LGBTQ 'policies.'

Logic dictated that no American with even the slightest amount of common sense would vote for a tariff war with Europe or China in which they would have to pay more for everyday goods and a subsequent recession in which they may even lose their jobs. Yet they did, and they also chose to live in the same world as fake-Christian abortion-banners, and gun nuts wanting to open-carry AR-15s everywhere. None of this is to forget who they put into office: GOP politicians who want to privatize schools, eliminate Medicaid, and raise the retirement age—all to fund massive tax cuts for their ultra-rich donors.

Trump and his confederates gambled correctly that many voters were extraordinarily low-information and completely devoid of any critical thinking skills. Some of them were the 46% of Latinos who gave the GOP their votes and cost Democrats the election[810]. Many of them held the sort of patriarchal values that would align neatly with any Bush-era Republican—pro-business, limited government, anti-immigration, anti-abortion, anti-LGBTQ+, and the tradwife. Before the election, they may have turned a blind eye to the "Mass Deportation Now"[811] signs at the 2024 GOP convention. However, after the election, they found out that in the Confederate Taliban's world, the only 'real Americans' were those with northern European ancestry.

Republicans also knew that they had the corporate media part-cowed, part-owned, and part-giddy-at-the-ratings. So it would be that profit-hungry 'both sides do it' outfits like CNN 'sanewashed' Trump and the GOP by acting as stenographers rather than journalists and simply parroted all their lies about Democrats, immigrants, the economy, transgender folks, Joe Biden, and Kamala Harris as if they were truth.

From this, many GOP voters were made mad about hardworking Haitian immigrants or the cost of a dozen eggs. Of course, that misdirection ensured that those same easy-to-fool voters would never think about who was really screwing them over.

Chapter 24

Hope.

First they came for the socialists, and I did not speak out—because I was not a socialist.

Then they came for the trade unionists, and I did not speak out—because I was not a trade unionist.

Then they came for the Jews, and I did not speak out—because I was not a Jew.

Then they came for me—and there was no one left to speak for me.

—Martin Niemöller[812]

Chapter 25

An Americans Best Friend Will Always Be Another American.

There's an innate human quality that can't be faked, purchased, or stolen. It's a superpower synonymous with character, honesty, and trustworthiness. Abraham Lincoln had it. Marilyn Monroe had it. Frederick Douglass had it. So did Albert Einstein, Harriet Tubman, Mark Twain, Dr. Martin Luther King Jr., and John F. Kennedy. Through the course of this book, you will read about many others who also possess it.

It's integrity, and it's what allowed these extraordinary individuals to be so without ever having to punch down or disrespect anyone less fortunate.

We know the true purpose of the heinous abomination that is racism and white supremacy was to separate working white, black and brown people so the greedy could keep on stealing from the needy. The devils knew if people got together, they would actually see they were more similar than they were different.

This led me to think of the Hollywood actors who, just ten years on from the McCarthy 'witch-hunts', bravely supported the civil rights struggle. Heroic World War II veterans like Paul Newman, Burt Lancaster, and James Garner were all straight, white, handsome, talented men who could have ambled comfortably through their careers without a care. Instead, they chose the harder, more challenging path by standing up for their values and standing alongside the marginalized, just because it was the right thing to do.

James Garner spoke about how Hoover-era FBI agents tried to intimidate him and the other famous participants in the 1963 March on Washington[813]. The agents warned they wouldn't receive any protection against the white terror that may meet them. Hoover, a bitter and twisted little man who, having avoided the draft, misunderstood the character of the men he was dealing with: heroes uncowed by European fascists and ready to stand valiantly against American fascists[814].

I can hear people murmuring the words, 'white saviors,' and I'll be the first to say it would have been great if Harry Belafonte, Sidney Poitier, and Martin Luther King Jr., could have changed attitudes all on their own. But in that imperfect world, that was asking the impossible.

I will also absolutely concede the point that no one was sending Burt Lancaster to the back of the bus, no one was burning Klan crosses on James Garner's front lawn, and no one was spitting on Paul Newman for trying to go to school.

But here's the thing. Had they chosen to be as abominable as John Wayne, their careers wouldn't have suffered one iota. So, how was it anything other than beneficial for those powerful men to want to be friends and allies?

White America knew and trusted famous stars like these, and they could smash through their attention filters in a way that no person of color ever could to 'wake' them up. Just these folks standing alongside their fellow black and brown Americans would be 'social proof', showing that it was perfectly acceptable for whites, blacks, and browns to work together and be friends together.

For those who are still dubious, bear this in mind: they were doing the polar opposite of what the John Birch Society, the KKK, and far-right segregationists wanted them to be doing.

This brings me to another son of America, who was a better person than the times required him to be. If the name Anthony Dominick Benedetto isn't familiar to you, then Tony Bennett may be. Tony was the maestro behind hits like 'Rags to Riches' and 'I left my heart in San Francisco'.

Born in Queens, New York, in 1926 to Italian immigrant parents, Tony faced the harsh challenges of growing up during the Great Depression. However, when World War II broke out, he bravely joined up to fight for freedom. Serving in the 63rd Infantry Division, he fought in the Battle of the Bulge and shared firsthand experiences of war that Hollywood will never show us;

> On the front line, we'd see dead soldiers, dead horses and big craters in the ground where bombs had exploded. To me, it's a joke that they make 'horror' movies about things like Dracula and Godzilla, and they make 'adventure' movies about war. War is far more horrifying than anything anyone could dream up.[815]

His last official mission was battling to liberate a concentration camp located thirty miles south of the infamous Dachau death camp in Germany, which was still under the control of German soldiers. In his 1988 autobiography, "The Good Life", he wrote;

> The main thing I got out of my military experience was the realization that I am completely opposed to war...Although

> I understand why this war was fought, it was a terrifying, demoralizing experience for me... life can never be the same once you've been through combat.

Before coming home, a senior officer demoted Corporal Bennett to private. His crime was to have a drink with a fellow soldier who was a buddy from high school. His buddy happened to be black, and the officer—with no sense of irony for what he was fighting against—was apoplectic that black and white were mixing.

Back home in the 1950s, Tony witnessed his friends Nat King Cole and Duke Ellington being denied entry into the same hotels and concert halls he had access to, and it infuriated him. He said,

> I'd never been politically inclined, but these things went beyond politics. Nate and Duke were geniuses, brilliant human beings who gave the world some of the most beautiful music it's ever heard, and yet they were treated like second-class citizens. The whole situation enraged me.[816]

Not only did Tony sing and perform exquisitely, but his integrity led him to stand alongside friends like Harry Belafonte and Martin Luther King Jr. at the March on Selma. So it would be that he didn't just fight for freedom in Europe; he fought for freedom in America too.

Just two years after the March on Selma, in the neighboring state of Georgia, Julia Roberts was born. Today, we know her as a Hollywood icon. However, what made this moment even more extraordinary was the fact that none other than Martin Luther King Jr. and Coretta Scott King paid for Julia's hospital delivery bill[817].

To understand, we need to go back to 1963. Julia's parents, Walter and Betty Lou Roberts, made a choice that would make their lives much harder. They co-founded the Actors and Writers Workshop, the only integrated performance school in Georgia. Just think about the courage and compassion it must have taken to stand up to the hate of the segregationist politicians, the White Citizens Council, and KKK terrorists.

Despite the absolute danger this put them in, the Roberts kept running their theater school. Then, one serendipitous day, the Kings, parents of two children who loved acting and performance, stumbled upon this welcoming haven of creativity and inclusivity, and a deep, enduring friendship blossomed between the two families.

As part of that friendship, the Kings offered their support by helping to pay for Julia's hospital bill. That gesture and the connection between those two southern families sum up, as well as any, the spirit of Dr. King's iconic "I have a dream" speech.

Fighting the good fight is exhausting but necessary, for domination never tires of ways to create division in order to maintain control. One of their methods is to single out a specific group as the scapegoat or an 'other.' Invariably, this will be a marginalized group because they are easily identifiable and few powerful allies.

This brings us on to the Confederate Taliban's sinister agenda against the transgender community. Their aim is to 'eradicate' trans folks, not necessarily through violence, although they are capable of that, but through oppressive laws and demonization.

Their campaign of hatred is enabled by the far-right media, fundamentalist churches, and even the New York Times[818]. This avalanche of intolerance puts immense stress on already vulnerable individuals, leading to mental health struggles and, tragically, suicide. To the inhuman Confederate Taliban, this systematic approach actually solves the 'problem,' one transgender person at a time.

To this point, you may be surprised to learn where the first gender reassignment clinic was located? You might guess a liberal city like San Francisco or Portland, but it was actually in Germany in 1919.

It was founded by Magnus Hirschfeld, a Jewish-German doctor. He believed in caring for individuals who identified as homosexual, bisexual, and transgender. Hirschfeld's Institute for Sexual Research was a testament to the progressiveness of German society over one hundred years ago.

Unfortunately, within a decade, the nation would fall under the spell of a skinny, rotten-toothed, woman-fearing, cowardly, genocidal maniac. As regards his treatment of trans folks, in 2021, Scientific American gave us this;

> Adolf Hitler was named chancellor on January 30, 1933, and enacted policies to rid Germany of Lebensunwertes Leben, or "lives unworthy of living." What began as a sterilization program ultimately led to the extermination of millions of Jews, Roma, Soviet and Polish citizens—and homosexuals and transgender people. When the Nazis came for the institute on May 6, 1933...Troops swarmed the building, carrying off a bronze bust of Hirschfeld and all his precious books, which they piled in the street. Soon a tower-like bonfire engulfed more than 20,000 books, some of them rare copies that had helped provide a historiography for nonconforming people.[819]

Spin forward to Oklahoma in 2024. This is a 'red' state. Notwithstanding, Democrats still got one-third of the votes in the 2024 election[820]. With good policies, in the future it is quite possible to flip it. However, until then, it's a place where just being yourself is enough to get you murdered.

Nex Benedict was a 16-year-old non-binary student at the Owasso High School in Oklahoma. In pictures, they look like a cherub, and as a straight-A student, they probably would have grown up to help make America great.

Whilst attending school, just for being themselves, this decent, harmless, and kind child was set upon and savagely beaten by three worthless, cowardly thugs. The school called neither for an ambulance nor the police. Instead, his mother was forced to take him to a hospital, where Nex was checked over and discharged, but the next day at home, they collapsed and died. A coroner's report ruled Nex's death as a suicide, but failed to detail how their devastating final decision was a reaction to relentless abuse, bullying, and beatings [821].

Whilst nothing can absolve Nex's attackers from their culpability, children have to learn to hate. So it is that someone had to teach them how to see an American like Nex and treat him as something less than human.

Much of that hate comes from places like the Fox Propaganda network or far right podcasters. Many of their 'sources' are found on the far-right billionaire-run social media doomsday machines, where stochastic terrorists like Matt Walsh and 'Libs of Tik Tok[822],' a.k.a. Chaya Raichik (a Jewish woman who smashes down on the marginalized, is loved by fascists, and has three million followers on Twitter), spread their poison. Just a point to note: most of these rancid weirdos only exist because the doomsday machines pay them in advertising revenue.

Then there are the people in power. In the same month as the attack, Oklahoma State Senator Tom Woods offered this about Americans like Nex;

> We are a religious state and we are going to fight it to keep that
> filth out of the state of Oklahoma because we are a Christian
> state — we are a moral state.[823]

These are the words of a fragile, fake-Christian freak who wants to dominate and control people. The Bible is very clear on how to treat not just Nex, but all people. Matthew 25:7 offers Jesus' own words: "So in everything, do to others what you would have them do to you."

Fake-Christians like Woods are what evil looks like in 2024. It is actually the banality of evil because the stochastic terrorism is spoken in measured terms by a lawmaker in a position of power and influence.

Thinking of that reminds me of the words of Jackie Goldberg, the president of the Los Angeles Unified School Board. She was speaking in 2023 about a mob of ignorant, billionaire-funded, far-right hags, along the lines of 'Moms for Liberty.' They had gathered outside a North Hollywood elementary school to 'protest' against any book that mentioned LGBTQ+ people. Ms. Goldberg said,

> I want to be very, very, very clear. Nobody has to accept me.
> I'm not looking for your acceptance. But you better treat me
> the same way you treat everybody else. That's how we live in
> this country. You don't have to love me. You don't have to
> like me. You can think I'm the devil incarnate. But you better
> treat me like a decent human being because that's how I treat
> you even though you don't believe that I have the right to
> exist.[824]

I'll say this to those who talk about 'trans' having gone too far. That's what people said about civil rights in the 1960s, about gay folks in the 1980s, and about women's rights after 'Me Too.'

The truth of trans folks, especially trans kids, is that it's none of my business. It's between the child, their parents, and their doctors. One of the most important aspects to understand is that being transgender is not a lifestyle choice; it's at the very core of someone's being.

But here's the real issue. The problem isn't with transgender folks: it's with the people who won't accept them being who they want to be.

This brings me on to one of the disingenuous 'arguments' used by the far-right and parroted by a few liberal 'useful idiots': that men will transition so they can enter women's restrooms and refuges to assault them.

Allow me to offer some small insight. I grew up in the 1980s. At school, girls being sexually assaulted was terrible, but not uncommon. Then at college, I recall a character literally grabbing women 'by the pussy.' And, in adulthood, I've known weak men who beat and controlled their partners. Suffice to say, in all those instances, the abuse took place without the visitation of a single form of consequence on any of the offenders.

Here's a newsflash for anti-trans liberals. Men who beat, control, rape, and murder women are fucking proud of being men. Even though none of them will have ever seen combat, wrestled a tiger, or rescued a child from a burning building, each one of them will revel in their false machismo and toxic masculinity.

Only the most simple-minded dotard could imagine that a controlling, violent man would ever voluntarily surrender the undiluted privilege of looking like, dressing like, and acting like a man. For receipts, men commit nearly nine out of ten female homicides[825].

Now we are orientated: for those who transition, imagine all the questions. Would their friends and family stand by them? Or want to be seen with them? Or still want to talk to them? Through a combination of embarrassment, ignorance, or 'shame', the honest answer, certainly for many older men, is quite possibly not.

Not unrelatedly, all empirical studies show that trans folks are at a much higher risk of murder than other communities and also are much more likely to commit suicide[826]. But then, given everything you have read in this chapter, is that surprising? Which takes us right back to the point about having the courage to stand alongside the marginalized.

Of course, nothing I write can ever bring back Nex, or any of the other Americans who are beaten or murdered just for being themselves. Nor can I imagine the enduring pain and sadness that burns inside all the people who loved and cared about them.

Fortunately, as a liberal, it's possible to inoculate yourself against ignorance. Indeed, as far as understanding the trans community goes, much of the steam could be taken out of the right-wing BS and lies if we actually heard from the community. Instead, every cable news head-to-head only features two straight people. And a straight man writes almost every moronic newspaper opinion piece on trans folks.

Hopefully, in ten years' time, historians will look back and write about how this just fits into a long line of fake 'moral panics' cooked up by the failing far-right to keep their decrepit hate machine rolling forward.

Thankfully, today does offer us some shining beacons of hope. I'm thinking about Taylor Swift, a white woman from rural Pennsylvania, who also happens to be the most famous pop star in the world. In October 2018, she wrote on Instagram;

> In the past I've been reluctant to publicly voice my political opinions, but due to several events in my life and in the world in the past two years, I feel very differently about that now. I always have and always will cast my vote based on which candidate will protect and fight for the human rights I believe we all deserve in this country. I believe in the fight for LGBTQ rights, and that any form of discrimination based on sexual orientation or gender is WRONG. I believe that the systemic

racism we still see in this country towards people of color is terrifying, sickening and prevalent.......[827]

Liberals shouldn't deceive themselves. For Taylor to speak out for progressive causes in the Obama era would have probably been the kiss of death for her young career. Even as a famous star in 2018, it led to her management becoming terrified of losing fans and having to get extra security.

At this point, I must emphasize, I will never diminish the incredible bedrock contributions of women of color who make up the most crucial and undervalued Democratic voting bloc. Indeed, at least 93% of black women vote blue at every election[828].

However, it's important to acknowledge the vast impact of an influential white woman like Taylor Swift. Imagine if she was a MAGA and QAnon fanatic. Or think how easy it would be for her to just remain apolitical and silent and avoid the hate mail and threats that come with standing alongside the marginalized.

In the 2020 biographical Netflix documentary "Miss Americana," we see her grappling with that 2018 decision to speak out. She understood the potential backlash and the pressure from her management, including her father, to keep quiet. In the father's defense, he was probably struggling with two concerns that weren't necessarily in tension. Whilst clearly troubled about losing revenue from right-wing supporters, he was probably infinitely more terrified at having to buy bulletproof cars to protect his daughter[829].

For the Confederate Taliban, just to have Taylor, a blonde-haired, blue-eyed, influential white superstar speaking out about issues, is a veritable nightmare. The demented freaks can attempt to 'dismiss' brilliant women of color like Stacey Abrams, Letitia James, or Kamala Harris as "activists" or 'DEI', or some other BS. But Taylor Swift poses a real conundrum for them.

To illustrate the point, in the 2024 presidential election campaign, Taylor endorsed VP Kamala Harris. For this, Trump raged on his social media platform' Truth Central,' "I HATE TAYLOR SWIFT."[830] Fortunately, as an American icon, she was impossible for the MAGA mob to cancel. However, at their core, the Confederate Taliban know the true 'threat' she represented. Being a trusted messenger who embraced diversity and inclusiveness, she not only provided social proof of empathy but may also have caused—sadly, not in 2024—her millions of young fans to wake up and consider political issues.

As far as winning people over goes, there is still a window to get through to a small percentage of GOP voters, maybe around 10%. However, there's no need to make life so hard for ourselves. For as long as I can remember, some liberals have made fun of rural folks. There are many examples, but one came to mind. It was videos online of young folk mocking the southern restaurant chain, 'Cracker Barrel,' and calling their food disgusting[831].

We're supposed to be the people who welcome inclusivity and consider others' feelings. So, just for a moment, let's consider the feelings of those who actually enjoy eating at 'Cracker Barrel.' Remember, it's only the cult of the Confederate Taliban that forbids people from enjoying different things. For progressive folks, the whole point of "diversity" is that a Cracker Barrel can exist in the same town as a food truck selling Vietnamese street food.

Still, sometimes it's best to keep your mouth shut, for what happens next may surprise you. So it was that, in 2023, Cracker Barrel posted on their social media page a photo of one of their restaurants with a rainbow-colored chair to celebrate Pride Month.

Here's my question. If this restaurant chain chooses to foster inclusivity, how is that bad? We know that the purpose of a business is to make profits, and to do that, they must expand their customer base. Showcasing a 'Pride' chair serves as both a virtue signal and a marketing strategy to attract new customers.

Then, think a little deeper. Many of the existing patrons of the chain, possibly rural Republican voters, live in areas where they never see a Democrat or hear their messaging. Now they might see this 'Pride' chair in a beloved and trusted establishment, and it may spark some curiosity about different people and different messages.

Pulling the lens out, for liberals, it's so reductive and self-defeating to demean or disparage our fellow Americans' accents, clothes, or interests, whether hunting, NASCAR, rodeo, or wrestling. Smart people don't have to like or agree with everything others choose to do or watch, but they know to show enough respect to not embarrass, humiliate, or push away potential friends.

If you're still not sold, making fun of rural culture is a surefire way to guarantee they won't vote for Democrats. Joe Walsh, the former Tea Party culture war Republican and current champion of democracy, pointed out a hard truth that holds Democrats back but helps the GOP: "Republicans are assholes, but Democrats are elite snobs who look down on me." [832]

Should you remain skeptical, bear this in mind. Texas, the home of progressive fighters like Beto O'Rourke, James Talarico, and Jasmine Crockett, has 38 electoral college votes out of the 270 needed to win the White House. In 2024, Kamala Harris wasn't able to seal the deal; however, in 2020, out of 11.3 million ballots cast, Joe Biden came within 630,000 votes of victory[833]. With a few more Texan friends, in 2028, we could turn the Lone Star State blue. Think about that.

Chapter 26

Everyone Sees Color. It's Just A Question Of What You Do With It.

When I was six months old, the luckiest thing that would ever happen to me happened. Along with my twin brother, Ed, we were adopted. My father, Sankary, was originally from Sri Lanka, and my mother, Ruth, is a white English lady. We grew up in England. My grandfather, Jack Crook, was English, and my grandmother, Kathleen Kelly, had Irish roots. It's worth mentioning that until 1976, England had no laws banning racial discrimination[834], which meant that signs reading, "NO IRISH. NO BLACKS. NO DOGS." were not uncommon in shops and boarding houses[835].

Irish people in Protestant England had historically faced discrimination because of their Catholic religion and their perceived "otherness." Therefore, it was quite a big deal for my English Protestant grandfather to marry my Catholic grandmother. This being said, when my parents got married in 1963, my grandparents refused to attend the wedding.

Now, some may leap to conclusions and label them as racists. But let me try to explain their perspective. You see, my mom was a slim, attractive, white lady living in England during the 1960s. She could have easily married a white man and lived a comfortable life in which race and 'discrimination' were other people's problems. As ever, I bring a receipt. Her sister, my aunt, whom I love very much, did just that by marrying my uncle, whom I also loved very much.

However, by marrying my dad, who was a man of color, my mom made her life 'harder.' Doors that were once open to her would now, literally, be closed. I recall a story about her going to rent an apartment with one of her fellow white English friends. That friend could barely believe that a landlord would refuse to rent to a mixed-race couple—until she was woken up by seeing it with her own eyes.

But it's not just about the challenges my mother might have faced. My grandparents also would have felt an irrational, yet understandable, sense of shame or 'humiliation.' Doubtless, they would have been afraid of being judged by the harsh standards of the time. And honestly, it's a natural human response.

Being the first to do something marks us out as 'different,' and different can mean alone, and alone was what once got our ancestors eaten by tigers. But more likely in the modern world, it means fewer social connections, and fewer social connections mean poorer life outcomes. Certainly, back then, it would have been hard to fight that evolutionary 'stay in the cave' thinking, but there is a way. It's called 'contact theory,' and we'll come to it later.

Going back to my grandparents. To their great credit, they came around, in part thanks to contact theory and positive associations, and we had one of those families actually pleased to see each other on holidays and at celebrations.

This being said, being around older folks with older ideas can mean making some accommodations. I remember sitting down watching the TV news in the early 1980s in their apartment. There were some Iranians protesting and burning British flags outside an embassy. My grandmother shouted at the TV, "send 'em back," as if to say, *these ungrateful, disruptive foreigners come to our country and don't appreciate how lucky they are.*

Now, those characters on television looked more like me than I looked like my grandma. However, even my twelve-year-old mind could process what was happening. Remember that this was taking place nearly forty-five years ago in unsophisticated, monocultural times. During my grandma's lifetime, the British Empire ruled over one-third of the world, and she had lived through a world war where Britain was the only nation in Europe that Hitler didn't conquer. As a conservative woman, her patriotism meant loving England, and anyone that didn't must be bad.

Despite all that, I knew how much my grandparents loved me and my brother. After all, it was their apartment we were staying in, and it was their ice-cream we were eating, and it was them who'd take us to the movies.

The larger point here is that winning people over means letting the little things slide. The only elephant-sized proviso is this: as with my grandparents, their *intentions* must be good.

This leads me on to the term 'colorblind.' It's always been a con. Right-wingers use it so they never have to address structural problems, and elite liberals use it because they are terrified of talking about 'race' and 'upsetting' the mythical swing voter instead of trying to win over some of the eighty million folks who don't vote[836].

Here's the truth. When I'm out, I don't just see color; I see everything: men, women, disabled folks, old people, young people, people with pink hair, tall people, people with glasses, people with tattoos, and every shade of color from Mad Musk's weird translucent cream to Corrupt Clarence Thomas' dark brown, and I'm not alone.

Color doesn't have to be scary or be a problem. It's just melanin that's responsible for lighter or darker skin, nothing more, nothing less, and it's why even neo-Nazis go brown in the summer.

Just to get a better handle on all this, we need to go back in time. It's only been over the past ten thousand years that similar-looking people started living side by side in agricultural societies[837].

However, realistically, seeing different people only came about in the past four hundred years. That coincided with the exact moment deviant patriarchs and preachers invented the concept of 'race' and, with it, the satanic story of superiority. From there, things didn't work out too well for many black and brown folks. Not much was helped by the fact our brains are superb pattern recognition machines[838].

Everything about how we think has to do with patterns. It's how, just by the pattern of their silhouette, we can make out our loved ones in a crowded shopping mall, and how, just by their shape and gait, we can recognize our dog amongst thirty other dogs in the park.

The pattern recognition machine served a very useful purpose in our forebears, as it was that ability to see differences that may have alerted them to the snake, tiger, or crocodile.

Indeed, evolution considered fear of the unknown to be so vital to our survival that it tasked one of the oldest parts of our brain, the amygdala, to deal with it. It is there that, when encountering a threat, the brain decides whether you should run, hide, or fight[839]. That's one of the main reasons your ancestors survived for thousands of generations in order to produce you.

The problem is, our brains have evolved very little over the past hundred thousand years. So it is that when we see people different from us, either from different races or from different places, the uncertainty and surprise can trigger our amygdala. Immediately, we ask: *Are they a threat? Am I safe?* It's most apparent with people of different colors, simply because it's so obvious, but this biological science doesn't have to be negative[840].

Which leads me to recall a story about one of America's greatest sons, Mark Twain, written by his biographer, Ron Powers;

> Race was always a factor in his consciousness partly because black people and black voices were the norm for him before he understood there were differences. They were the first voices of his youth and the most powerful, the most metaphorical, the most vivid storytelling voices of his childhood.[841]

Also, there is a little-known anecdote about the movie icon Marilyn Monroe, which further illustrates the smoothing influence of contact. She spent her youth in foster care in California, which shaped some of her values. This is from Time magazine, referencing historian Lois Banner's 2012 biography, 'Marilyn: The Passion and the Paradox';

> Though some of the caretaker families were terrible to her, Banner says that she did find one family—the Bolanders—whom Monroe particularly liked. There, her foster father worked delivering mail in Watts, a largely African-American neighborhood. As a result of her own poverty and her close contact with people of other races, Monroe grew up with progressive views on race and what Banner calls a "populist vision of equality for all classes.[842]

Having been kept apart by law in the South and fear in the North, it has only really been since the 1950s, with integration in the Army and trade unions, that black, brown and white folks have mixed.

As many stories in the book have shown, positive associations break down prejudice. This is from Rutger Bregman's brilliant 2020 book, Humankind: A Hopeful History, describing the work of the psychologist Gordon Allport;

"The American scholar suspected that prejudice, hatred, and racism stem from a lack of contact. We generalize wildly about strangers because we don't know them. So, the remedy seemed obvious: more contact.....Even more remarkable were the data gathered by the US military during the Second World War. Officially, black and white soldiers were not supposed to fight side by side, but in the heat of battle, it sometimes happened. The army's research office discovered that in companies with both black and white platoons, the number of white servicemen who disliked blacks was far lower. To be precise, nine times lower........Perhaps the most powerful proof for Allport's contact hypothesis came from the sea. When African Americans were first admitted to the largest seamen's union in 1938, there was initially widespread resistance. But once black and white seamen actually began working together, the protests ceased.[843]

As ever, two things can be true at once. So it is that white people have inherited an unfair system, but a system they didn't create. This being said, it's an undeniable fact, witnessed by the seventy-seven million votes for Trump in 2024, that many white people have entrenched themselves in a hate-driven movement that is completely devoid of positive ideas for America.

However, for me, hope can beat hate, but only when hope fights. In my book, 'When Coal Miners Drive Cadillacs,' I offer hopeful, workable solutions that can win friends and build bridges to create a better future for all Americans.

Chapter 27

No One Wakes Up In The Morning Wanting To Be A Neo-Nazi

In 2010, one of my best friends, whom I have known since we were ten years old, fell upon hard times and had nowhere to live. Now, despite being a man of many flaws, I know enough to hold out my hand to help a friend when their life is falling apart.

So, I took my buddy in, and after six months, he was ready to go back into the world. After he left, I was clearing out some of his things when a notebook caught my eye. As there was no cover, I saw it was filled with scrawl about 'the white race is under attack' and 'white pride.'

Bear in mind, I'm a brown man, and my friend was a white man, so I can't say it didn't cause me both anger and pain. However, I never spoke to him about it, as it would have been a conversation without a destination, for nobody wants to be reminded of bad times.

It was only years later, when researching this book, that I reflected on it again. Thinking back, he met the grooming standard for neo-Nazis. As a down-on-his-luck, alienated, low-information white man, despotic fiends could steer him into believing that someone, whether Jews, blacks or browns, was to blame for his misfortune.

We will return to my friend later. But for now, we need to understand a little about neo-fascists. For that, there's a pyramid of bad. At the peak (of evil) are the leaders, invariably fragile men who want power and domination. Truthfully, whether we call them neo-fascists, neo-Nazis, white supremacists, or Christian nationalists, they are all the same, and if you're black, brown, a woman, or a white liberal, they are going to fuck you up.

In the middle of the pyramid are the—mostly online-fascists: people like white nationalist Nick Fuentes, a so-called Groyper[844] who raves about Hitler, Holocaust denial, race war, and a 'pure' Aryan Nation. Many of these influencers, podcasters, and keyboard warriors seek to place an intellectual spin on eugenics, race-mixing, and wanting to deport all black and brown people (to where, I'm not sure!). However, without exception, they are all jelly-spined men who need a fascist state to do their dirty work for them. But there are cowardly, violent exceptions in the form of the domestic terrorists who target places like churches, offices, schools, or shopping malls.

As we reach the bottom of the pyramid, we find the vast majority of the neo-fascists, like my friend, who are there because they are lost, indoctrinated, or need brotherhood. These people are reachable.

To this point, there was a video out of Nashville in 2024 of some neo-Nazis with their swastika flags and Sieg Heil salutes. They weren't from Nashville and were chased out of town by patriotic locals. I wouldn't have said a word about this, except one of the balaclava-hooded Nazis is spouting indoctrinated nonsense propaganda with the words "immigrants poop in the street."[845]

It was the word 'poop' that got me. Only the most polite people would use this term. A truly angry man, ready and willing to beat a black or brown man, wouldn't ever have used that phrase. Instead, they would have said, 'crap' or 'shit.' Thus, straight away, I realized that the person speaking was a disconnected little boy who had been groomed and radicalized and given a sense of belonging by much more sinister people.

As to the sort of person who may have groomed him, I'm reminded of Stuart Rhodes. He is the founder of the neo-fascist, anti-government Oath Keepers movement. For attempting to murder American democracy, Rhodes is currently serving an eighteen-year sentence in a federal correctional facility in Maryland. To understand him, we need some background. He was born to regular working parents, joined the Army as a paratrooper, never saw combat, and when discharged, went to Yale Law School.

Rhodes is quite recognizable by his eye patch. There is a fascinating story behind that. Somehow, with all that training and education, he managed to shoot himself in the face while cleaning a gun. For those not familiar with firearms, that idiocy would have required him pointing a loaded gun at his face, with the safety off, while pulling the trigger.

Apart from nearly blowing his head off, there was also the paradox of him being fiercely anti-government whilst greedily gobbling down the benefits of the government-funded GI Bill that subsidized his $150,000 Ivy League college education[846].

The hypocritical hits keep on coming. Later on in life, as a strict patriarchal father of six children, Rhodes lived in the woods of Montana. Despite his own expensive government education, he didn't feel it was necessary for his kids to attend school.

Then, come 2009, in furious response to the indignity of a black man in the White House, he founded the Oath Keepers. This unregulated private army was dedicated to 'resisting' what they saw as the 'New World Order.' Their platform was basically to demand no gun control, spout crap about white 'genocide,' and prepare for a civil war against the (Democratic) totalitarian federal government[847].

The unbending irony of these entitled, eggshell men is unending. They always whine and complain about their "rights" but never talk about their responsibilities. I have no problem with them living in the woods. My problem comes when they ruin other people's lives with their indoctrination or attempt to use their guns to murder our democracy.

Notwithstanding that, I'm pretty sure that the government allowing them to live their anti-government militia lifestyle is a textbook definition of what freedom actually looks like. There again, as we know, their 'freedom' is not our freedom. Don't believe me; this is from his eldest son, Dakota

> We lived in extreme isolation in increasingly paranoid and militant right-wing political spheres everywhere we moved in the country.[848]

For me, one golden rule of being a good father is teaching a son how to be a good man. Part of that is offering a balance of love and non-violent discipline. Another part is educating them never to punch down and to look out for people less fortunate than themselves.

This was not Rhodes' way. Indeed, the reason that Dakota was living in the woods, subsisting on a diet of his father's hate-filled rhetoric, was that he was being groomed to follow in Rhodes' neo-fascist footsteps.

In his late teens, Dakota had little education and few friends. Still, everyone needs a little luck. Dakota's came when returning one evening from an Oath Keeper's meeting. He had a conversation with a gas station clerk, who mentioned that the local fire department was recruiting. The BBC reported that,

> Joining the fire department exposed Dakota to a new set of values that initially seemed to mirror what he had heard at home: lessons about civic responsibility and preparedness. But at the fire station, people weren't talking about ancient battles, stockpiling guns and food, and raging against the government. They were getting out and helping people.[849]

In 2018, Dakota, his mom, and his sister escaped from Rhodes' clutches and found a new life far away from him. It was then that Dakota, a man who had lived inside the belly of the beast, gave us some truths that corporate media will not tell us, describing his father as a "self-interested shapeshifter with no true belief."

He would expand on that by giving us his description of the Confederate Taliban;

> I saw that the inner circle of Oath Keepers were bullshit, and that expanded into realizing that the militia movement was bullshit, to realizing that the entire Republican Party was bullshit.[850]

I wanted to know how Dakota resisted the satanic lure of fascism. Whilst his work at the fire department explains a lot, there also was a nugget of gold hiding in plain sight in his BBC interview. Far back in his youth, he spent a small period growing up in urban Washington and in the suburbs of Connecticut. In his words;

> Having a set of neighbors that was so diverse that my street looked like the set of Sesame Street_ I thought that was just how the entire world was.[851]

Perhaps for Dakota, that initial inoculation of inclusiveness, together with the pride of working in the fire department, was enough to protect him from the disease of prejudice that could have seen him sharing a cell next to his father. Indeed, in 2024, Dakota stood as a Democratic candidate for the Montana State House. For me, on its own, that should be something to celebrate.

There was another story of salvation from hate. This time by former neo-Nazi Christian Picciolini. He gave a TED Talk in 2018 entitled "My Descent into America's Neo-Nazi Movement & How I Got Out." Christian now works to deradicalize extremists, and has helped over one hundred white supremacists and jihadists to leave the life. He revealed his secret to bringing these people back from hell;

> I never argue or debate or tell them that they are wrong. Instead, I don't push them away, I draw them in closer, and I listen very closely for their potholes and I help to fill them in. I try to make people more resilient, more self-confident, more able to have skills to compete in the marketplace so that they don't have to blame the other. People become extremists, because they want to belong, not because of ideology of dogma. What bought them out was receiving compassion, from the people they least deserved it from, when they least deserved it.[852]

So it is, every day, neo-fascist and white supremacist unregulated private armies, like the Oath Keepers and Three Percenters, are out there 'befriending' and grooming young men. They have a particular focus on recruiting military veterans. If you are thinking that this won't impact your life, just know the FBI had to vet the National Guardsmen protecting the Capitol after January 6th for fear of an insider attack[853].

Tragically, there is a semi-symbiotic relationship between fascists and some veterans. For the fascists, they can recruit people with knowledge of tactics and weapons. Also, the kudos of having some of the most respected people in America in their groups is a great recruiting tool.

For the disillusioned veteran, these groups offer not just a sense of bonding, belonging, and brotherhood, but also the respect that comes from employing the skills that the United States military would have taught them.

It reminds me of a non-related, but instructive, post from Duane France, a combat veteran of Iraq and Afghanistan;

When veterans leave the service, many of them feel as though they have lost their sense of purpose. They were once counted on, depended on, they were good at what they did and they loved it. They were important...and losing that sense of accomplishment, that sense of importance, is very difficult.[854]

What these stories show us is that it isn't the ideology of hate that wins over many recruits to neo-fascist groups; it's their disconnection from purpose, autonomy, and community. This is something I tackle in my book, 'When Coal Miners Drive Cadillacs.'

Going back to my friend from the beginning of the chapter, all he needed was someone to give him a chance to breathe and to take some of the stress out of his life. In his case, this meant letting him stay for a few months, which was enough time for him to get back on his feet. Since then, he's met and married a lovely woman, started a family, and runs a successful business.

And so it is that if we show people empathy and help them attain a decent life, then like an ice cube on a hot summer's day, the destructive lure of hate groups melts away.

Chapter 28

The Benefit Of The Doubt And The Magical Ability To Fail Up

To see how the Benefit of the Doubt affects different people, we have to travel back to 1989. In a case that made worldwide headlines, a twenty-eight-year-old investment banker was brutally raped and beaten in New York's Central Park. Democratic Mayor Ed Koch—who may as well have been a Republican—called it the "Crime of the Century." Just to inform you, this was an era when New York City had a million fewer citizens than in 2023[855], but a murder rate of four times higher than that of 2023[856].

The media of the time referred to "wolfpacks" of teenagers roaming wild and feral in the city. An article from the Rupert Murdoch-owned New York Post stated;

> They were coming downtown from a world of crack, welfare, guns, knives, indifference and ignorance. They were coming from a land with no fathers. ... They were coming from the anarchic province of the poor.[857]

The cops duly arrested five black and Latino boys, all aged between fourteen and sixteen. Then, without parents or lawyers present and with no DNA or eyewitness evidence, confessions were coerced from them.

In the month after the attack, one Donald J. Trump took time out from his daily grind of fraud and theft to promote this wedge issue. The traitor published full-page ads in all the New York papers, calling to "Bring back the death penalty."

In this fevered climate, with the chances of a fair trial sitting at exactly zero, the young men were convicted of attempted murder, rape, robbery, assault and riot and sentenced to between six and thirteen years.

It would not be until twelve years later, in 2002, that an incarcerated serial rapist would confess to the crime, with DNA evidence found at the scene, backing up his confession. Only then were the Five vindicated, but not before being robbed of some of their most productive years.

You may wonder what happened to the corrupt cops, the incompetent prosecutors, and the ineffective DA who ignored all the evidence, or the stenographer-like journalists who printed all the lies. Well, nothing. None of them suffered any fallout. There were no firings, no lost pensions, and no need for apologies. Quite the opposite; as they walked between the raindrops, they all received the benefit of the doubt. The only ones to lose were the five young men.

Well, not quite. The prosecution's criminal ineptitude also hit New York City taxpayers, as it was they who paid out the $41 million damages settlement to the Five for their wrongful imprisonment[858]. That was money that could have paid to fix up the city's schools, hospitals, and roads.

Someone else to suffer no consequences was the ever failing-up Trump. With his lies, he had played the news media like a fiddle to garner even more publicity and celebrity. All this would help him con Americans into thinking that he was a 'doer' and a 'tough guy.' He would wash, rinse, and repeat this bullshit impression many more times and have it down to a fine art by the 2016 election.

Outside of Robert Edward Lee, no one in American history has received such a large helping of the benefit of the doubt: insurrection, rape, fraud, theft, and treason. Yet to the corporate media, Trump is just being Trump.

On a sidebar, just to note, in 2023, whilst the felon was promoting fascism and attempting to turn American against American, one of the Central Park Five, Dr. Yousef Salaam, was elected to serve the people of New York on the City Council. That's what being a 'real American' looks like.

We can see the benefit of the doubt at work again if we go back to January 6th, 2021. The traitors were handled with kid gloves and given polite warning after polite warning. They really were treated like visitors, right up to where one murderous domestic terrorist was shot. Bear in mind, this was only after she had assumed the form of a rabid animal and attempted to smash her way through a glass door in order to slay members of Congress.

Yet, even after all that, the terrorists all got to leave and fly back to whatever rocks they lived under, until eventually, the FBI came calling.

Dear reader, allow me to paint an image of what that day might have looked like had those blood-baying Confederates been black. Imagine if it was black people scaling the walls of the Capitol. Imagine if it was black people building a gallows to hang the vice president. Imagine if it was black people beating cops with BLM placards.

I *know* there would be a brigade of five thousand troops rolling down the mall. Once at the Capitol, the order would have been handed down to the brigade colonel: '*weapons free*'. Cue, the frenetic roar of a thousand fully automatic Colt M4/A1 carbines. Pretty soon there would be piles of eviscerated black bodies, and a media that would stroke its chin and say, '*Well, what did they expect.... Terrorism......Law and Order.....It's the Seat of Democracy.....*'

The ability to walk through the raindrops isn't something that is just denied to people of color. It's also out of bounds for many low-income white folks, even brilliant ones.

Tonya Harding was born in 1977 in rural Clackamas County, near Portland, Oregon. If this was the 1980s or even the 1990s, it would not have been uncommon to have heard her described as "white trash." That phrase comes from the way elite whites thought of and described, low-income, and non-property-owning white people in the 1800s[859].

Tonya grew up in a dysfunctional, abusive home. Her father was her mother's fifth husband, and her mother was a volatile alcoholic. Tonya had three older half-brothers. Of them, one died from crib death, and another molested her from the age of five[860].

You may have heard the phrase "Adverse Childhood Experiences." This relates to the ten types of childhood trauma measured in the CDC-Kaiser Permanente Adverse Childhood Experiences Study[861].

Half of the ACEs are personal, like physical abuse, verbal abuse, sexual abuse, physical neglect, and emotional neglect. The other half relate to family members, such as having an alcoholic parent, a mother who's a victim of domestic violence, a family member in jail, a family member diagnosed with a mental illness, or parents getting divorced.

Each experience counts as one, on a scale of one to ten. The more you have, the more likely it is that your life is going to go off the rails. Some people will experience none, and possibly half of children may experience one (divorce), but Tonya's young life was buffeted by at least five.

With that start, life was never going to be plain sailing, but everyone needs a little luck, and Tonya's was that her mother had a thwarted ambition to ice skate.

So, from the age of four, without being pushed, Tonya took to the ice. Her mother would take her to the skating rink at 4:30 am, where Tonya would practice for three hours, then go to school, and, after school, come back to practice some more. As she got older, she started entering competitions.

A small segue. Traditionally, ice skating is a sport of slim, pretty girls, usually from nice middle-class backgrounds. The competitions featured lots of *nice* music, *nice* performances, and *nice* judging. It's a place to be *nice,* and the *nice* establishment didn't want the boat rocked.

So it was that if one didn't fit the look, the United States Figure Skating Association (USFSA) would not help them along. To illustrate the point, Tonya had small teeth, widely spaced apart. As skaters are expected to perform to world-class standards and smile a lot whilst they are doing it, this was holding her scores down. As luck would have it, a fan offered to donate $6000 towards the orthodontist's work to 'fix' her teeth.

Tonya found a little luck once again when someone else not only saw potential in her, but encouraged it. Diane Rawlinson, a former figure skater, would become her coach for nearly twenty years. Unfortunately, she was about the only positive, stable influence in Tonya's life.

As a skater, Tonya had grit and guts. She may not have looked like other competitors or been educated like them, but, my goodness, did she know how to skate. The high-water mark of skating is the triple axel jump, at she excelled. Put into perspective, as of 2021, only nineteen women had ever landed this jump in competition.

Sadly, even being great isn't good enough to avoid bad luck. In Tonya's case, it found its form in the shape of an abusive partner, whom she turned into her husband. In spite of him, and despite all the countless dramas in her life, she still reached two Olympics with little help from the USFSA.

It was precisely because of the way she looked, the way she spoke, and where she came from that they wouldn't give her the benefit of the doubt. They were the elite ice-skating gatekeepers, looking down on the 'poor' girl. It didn't matter that she was the best person for the job. Her kind didn't *belong there.*

This rags-to-riches tale of a young woman from rural America, who overcame misfortune and, through grit, determination, and hard work, triumphed in a sport where women like her weren't *supposed* to be, should have made her a poster child for the American Dream.

Tragically, misfortune would find her again when her husband and one of his sociopathic friends decided to 'scare' her skating rival, Nancy Kerrigan, with death threats that then escalated to trying to break her knees.

Tonya's career never really recovered from that incident, but that being said, what if she had received the benefit of the doubt way back when she was ten years old?

What if the USFSA had taken this prodigious talent under their wings and helped her become an even better version of her professional self? How many gold medals would she have won for America? Tonya was just another example of wasted brilliance. Don't blame her. It was America that chose to lose where it could otherwise have won.

This puts me in mind of the story of Serena and Venus Williams. The system would have happily failed them. However, it was thanks to their father, the awesome and inspiring Richard Williams, who drove his daughters to be the best they could be. It was he who took them to practice, playing on the cracked and litter-strewn courts of Tragniew Park, Compton, California. The sisters would practice in the dark and in the rain, all while avoiding the gangs of East L.A.

Despite endless adversities, Richard and his daughters never gave up, and even if they hadn't become professional tennis players, they would have been something special; Venus was a straight-A student who spoke French, German, Italian, and Chinese.

Back in the 90s, many white "experts" thought Richard Williams was a fool (translated: a no-nothing, uppity black man) for pulling his daughters off the junior tennis circuit to avoid burnout.

The truth was that he was a genius who gave his daughters just the right amount of love and discipline. He also managed the insanely rare feat of knowing his own children sufficiently well to see they were tough enough, both mentally and physically, to go straight into the pros[862].

Yet, despite all their hard work, talent, and determination, nothing was certain for the Williams sisters. Even Richard Williams, with his irrepressible determination, reached the limits of what a black man, training two black girls in the lily-white 1990s tennis scene, could achieve on his own.

A lucky break came in 1991. An enlightened white coach of champions, Rick Macci, gave Richard the benefit of the doubt[863]. He agreed to train the sisters at his camp in Boca Raton, Florida. With that stability, combined with their talent and determination, they soared to indelibly stamp themselves into the sporting history books, with Venus winning seven grand slams and Serena twenty-three.

So, while, today, they're known as two of the greatest women athletes of all time, it might never have happened were it not for black and white working together[864].

Chapter 29

Black Canaries, Exotic Dancers and a Lesson in Sociology.

To most Americans, the 2008 financial crisis was a housing crisis. Much lesser known is that the predatory lending Wall Street vultures had performed a dry run ten years earlier. It happened during the Clinton administration. This is from a 2012 University of Pennsylvania study;

> The growth of subprime lending has been disproportionately concentrated among African Americans and in African American neighborhoods. In 1993, subprime refinancing loans accounted for just eight percent of home loans in African American neighborhoods and one percent in white neighborhoods. By 1998, the number of subprime refinancing loans had dramatically increased to fifty-one percent of the total loans in African American neighborhoods compared to only nine percent in white neighborhoods.[865]

A truly wicked feature, reported by the Wall Street Journal, was that two-thirds of those subprime loans went to people with credit scores *high enough* to qualify for conventional loans[866].

These folks can thank Bill Clinton for repealing the Glass-Steagall Act[867]. Without the pesky oversight of government regulators, the predatory lenders could con regular people into signing up for what looked like good rates. The sting in the tail was hidden away in the small print and would only bite a year or two into the future.

When that rubber hit the road, it passed unreported in the media because it didn't affect any middle-class white people. Even if it had been commented on, we know the narrative; that people of color were complicit in their predicament; probably the agents of their own misfortune for overstretching themselves or buying too big a house or not working hard enough to make the payments.

All of this would allow the predatory lenders more time to move on to their real prize: lending to white people, and in doing so, they dug a hole that America nearly didn't get out of.

To see the true origins of the black canary, we need to travel back in time. We know that in order to create slavery, there needed to be a story, and it was predicated on the notion that black people were inferior, but also that they were dangerous to both white prospects and to pure white women.

Post Civil War, to get Jim Crow segregation off the ground, there was the imagination of the fear of race-mixing[868]. The myths were further propagated by so-called 'scientists' in the 1920s with eugenics[869], where the weak-minded morons conjured up 'theories' that black people (but also disabled and poor) were genetically inferior to white people.

Sociologists have a phrase: attribution bias[870]. To people we like, we attribute good intentions and give them the benefit of the doubt. However, towards people different from ourselves, we assign bad motives and are suspicious of what they are doing and what they may want to do to us.

In the picture, you can see two fictional criminals. On the right is Stringer Bell, from the sublime HBO show, 'The Wire.' He's a money launderer for a street-level drug gang. On the left is Marty Byrd, from the outstanding Netflix show 'Ozark.' Aside from being a money launderer for a Mexican drug cartel, he is variously involved in theft, murder, and domestic terrorism.

Even whilst you read that, I'll bet your brain was performing mental somersaults while it tied itself in knots, trying to explain, excuse, or rationalize Marty's crimes. Stringer wasn't so lucky. You took one look at his picture and probably didn't even need to finish his bio before you made up your mind—GUILTY!

Let's follow that line of thought. Where does your brain go when you hear about the 'broken black family'? Actress and activist Kerry Washington gave us a throughline to history;

> The breaking down of the black community, in order to maintain slavery, began with the breakdown of the black family. Men and women were not legally allowed to get married because you couldn't have that kind of love. It might get in the way of the economics of slavery. Your children could be taken from you and literally sold down the river.[871]

If you still harbor doubts that your black brothers didn't do more to deserve their Dickensian fate, let's hear from Emmanuel Acho's brilliant "Uncomfortable Conversations with a Black Man";

Before I go any further, a few words on the worst of all arguments: that this is just how black families are. As if black people are genetically disposed to this brokenness. If broken families were in the nature of black people....How to explain why black people didn't have broken families when they were back in Africa? As an African and first-generation American, I can confidently say that in Nigeria, family ties are every bit as strong, if not stronger, than they are here.[872]

What Mr. Acho has hit on is this. Nigerian-American families are strong. Just as Somali-American families and Jamaican-American families are. Because it was never to do with color.

Still, to show the bias in action, we just have to travel to Flint, Michigan. There, for four years between 2014 and 2018, residents, unwittingly, drank lead-polluted water that was being deliberately piped by the Republican-led state into their majority-black city[873]. Or there was Jackson, Mississippi, another majority-black city, where in 2022 the groundwater was so polluted that residents were being told not to shower. For those who partook in the decadent luxury of a wash, the advice was not to open their mouths[874].

These are major cities in the most advanced, powerful, and wealthy nation human history has ever known, yet residents, *black residents*, couldn't even get access to clean water. If this were Sacramento or Tallahassee, it would be wall-to-wall news, with politicians calling it a disaster and demanding that FEMA act.

Yet, inside the blinkered minds of many white Americans, it must be that these black and brown people have done something to deserve their fate; besides, if they hadn't, they'd be living out in the lovely suburbs.

However, attribution bias always ignores the fact that the suburbs were built exclusively for white people in the 1950s. Indeed, black folks were deliberately excluded from the cheap Federal Housing Authority home loans, as their very presence may have upset the *comfort* of white residents[875]. The great Lyndon Johnson understood that madness and, speaking in 1965, summed up the problem perfectly;

> Until people, whether they're purple, brown, black, yellow, red, green, or whatever live together, they'll never know they have the same hopes for their children, the same fears, troubles, woes, ambitions. I want a bill that makes it possible for anybody to buy a house anywhere they can afford to. Now, can you do that? Can you do all these things?[876]

Sadly, he never truly got his way on housing. "Redlining" meant that banks would only lend money to black folks to buy in black areas. So, while black people were still fighting for equality, immigrants from white backgrounds realized the American Dream by purchasing one of those 1950s Levittown-style ranch homes for only $11,000, which today may be worth $400,000[877].

On a small segue, if you ever get a chance, listen to the great Randy Newman's sublime song 'Rednecks' from his 1974 album, Good Old Boys. It's a three-minute masterclass that might as well be a three-year degree in political science, so well does it explain fragile white resentment, Jim Crow, low-information voters, redlining, and color-blind liberals[878].

Coming forward to the modern age, we have seen many more black men portrayed as criminals rather than heroes on the screen. In real life, as we know, the news media relies on spectacle to attract viewers. So, it assailed us with stories of 'gangs' who would shoot you as soon as look at you, and negative image after negative image about black folks.

A whole language existed, and still exists, to dehumanize black men: 'animals,' 'gangsters', 'hoodlums,' 'predators,' and 'thugs.'[879] We know that once a group has been dehumanized, it's harder to care about them, so it is that people literally stop seeing young inner city men as human beings.

From that, so-called 'moderates' voted to cut funding to cities for assistance programs, using as moral license the BS of the 'Welfare Queen.'[880] Then, paradoxically, the 'savings' from those social programs were pumped into militaristic policing to combat the resulting spike in crime from disillusioned and desperate young people. All of this was giddily reported on the 'news' to make white folks even more scared and angry.

Rising out of that, we saw the specter of the dead segregationists that lives inside white America's willingness to see 'blackness' as a weapon. To understand the perniciousness of this cancer, we only have to look at the police reports of officer-involved shootings. In them, there are descriptions of superhuman strength and physical intimidation, with black men described as "berzerk," "demons," or as "strong as Hulk Hogan." [881]

In the 1990s, the term "super predator"[882] was coined to describe any black man who was involved in violent crime. It's important to note that this moniker was never applied to child-raping, fake-Christian pastors, Hell's Angels, or neo-Nazi militiamen. Then, as anything with the word "super" in front of it denotes extraordinary powers, extraordinary levels of force must be used to combat it. From this dehumanization, it was easy to 'justify' both higher levels of police violence against black men, and also much longer prison sentences than a white criminal might receive[883].

On the matter of sentencing and incarceration, think back to the inner-city crack epidemic of the 1980s. Then, low-income folks, perhaps in an East Harlem tenement in New York, used this crystallized cocaine to numb themselves against the pain of despair, despondency, and destitution. Meanwhile, just nine miles away on Wall Street, after a hard day of insider trading and pumping fraudulent stock, bankers would adjourn to some upscale midtown club to snort cocaine off the semi-naked bodies of exotic dancers.

Back then, both crack and powdered cocaine were listed by the Drug Enforcement Administration as Schedule II narcotics[884]. In the nigh-on impossible eventuality that the NYPD vice squad raided the club, our Wall Street banker would need to be holding half a kilo of cocaine before any judge even thought about handing down the same ten-year sentence that a crack user would receive for holding just five grams.

So, instead of treatment, our inner-city brothers got prison, and instead of empathy, they got hostility, so thank you again to the corporate media for your terrifying coverage-without-context-of crack, and thank you to Bill Clinton for your 1994 Crime bill.

The system wasn't finished screwing our inner-city friends over. With fathers carted off to prison for the smallest of offenses—for the far-right, this was a feature of the system rather than a bug—families were left without a breadwinner. So, a son has to step up and become a man from a young age just to help pay the bills. Then the kid gets jammed up for a crime that wouldn't be a crime if you or I did it and goes to prison to join the father.

This is the cycle of crime and punishment, mostly from the profitable 'war on drugs.' Don't take my word for it. A sitting United States senator had these prescient words on the subject;

> If you look at the war on drugs, 3 out of 4 people in prison are black or brown. White kids are doing it too, in fact, if you look at all the surveys, white kids do it just as much as black and brown kids. But the prisons are full of black and brown kids because they don't get a good attorney, they live in poverty, it's easier to arrest them than to go to the suburbs.[885]

Perhaps the words of a nice liberal like Bernie Sanders or Elizabeth Warren? Actually, they were from libertarian Senator Rand Paul. He is a current member of the far-right 'Freedom Caucus,' and back in 2010, he spoke about ending the Civil Rights Act[886]. Yet, here he was, just four years later, speaking to an overwhelmingly white audience at the Iowa Republican convention.

As far as Paul's motivations go, one thing is for certain. This three-term senator didn't need to court any black voters to win. However, as a libertarian, he hated government spending and would have despised the $45,000 it costs to keep an inmate locked up. Still, if there's one thing you take away from this book, it's taking your allies where you can find them, even if they are Rand Paul[887].

This spins us forward to 2016, where Bill Clinton's harsh crime bill was still helping to lock up many inner-city men. Ironically, this may have been part of the reason for Hillary's loss. Just looking at Pennsylvania, Michigan, and Wisconsin, the three states that decided the election, she received 245,000 fewer votes than Barack Obama in 2012, mostly in urban areas. Bear in mind, she only needed 78,000 votes to win.

Directly resultant from her loss, the six high priests on the Supreme Court brought in the Trump Abortion Ban. To liberals, this was a bolt out of the blue. However, not for low-income, mainly black and brown women. Over forty years ago, way back in 1977, the Hyde Amendment blocked any federal funding for abortion care[888]. For years, that meant no Medicaid or Affordable Care Act assistance for these women.

As it is, communities of color represent a crystal ball. Everything that will happen to a working-or middle-class white person will have already happened to them. And it's precisely because they have less representation, less wealth and less empathy that they can be used as a testing laboratory for all the despicable things that the right-wing elites have planned for the rest of us.

Chapter 30

Frankly, My Dear...Why Mad Musk Would Be Bankrupt Without DEI.

This chapter will not be some pity piece on how downtrodden black people are, as all the evidence shows they are one of the strongest, most dynamic, and vital pieces of the rich tapestry that make up the American quilt. Indeed, over the course of the chapter, you will learn how a lot of the exciting and vibrant 'soul' of modern America that is projected out onto the world came from African-Americans.

While I will never diminish the impact of Native American, Asian, and Latino cultures in brightening the nation, the purpose of this chapter is to show how one of the most overlooked legacies of white supremacy was to render invisible just how integral to America black folks were.

We can start with country music. The country and western scene that we know today wasn't always so. Until the 1920s, integrated sessions between what was then called hillbilly music and blues artists were common[889].

Then, as music became more commercial, out of the self-interest of pandering to despicable politicians, patriarchs, and pastors, profit-seeking record companies started separating "hillbilly" records from "race" records. One was deemed authentic country, and the other was 'colored' music. And so black folks were erased from the country music scene. Despite this, Andrew Chow, reporting for Time, revealed who the tutors of the country music scene royalty were;

This marketing ploy meant that many black artists were pushed to the margins of country music, even if they remained influential behind the scenes. Lesley Riddle, a black guitar player, helped A.P. Carter of the Carter Family hone his repertoire of mountain songs and greatly influenced the fingerpicking guitar style of Maybelle Carter, who is considered one of the most influential guitarists of all time. Rufus "Tee Tot" Payne mentored a young Hank Williams; Gus Cannon taught a young Johnny Cash. Bill Monroe, called "The Father of Bluegrass," talked of his indebtedness to the guitarist Arnold Schultz. But all of those black artists would be vastly eclipsed by their mentees.[890]

I need to give you an even better receipt, so let's take a trip back to 1939. The proto-fascist 'American Bund' was using the slogan "America First"[891] (nothing Trump does is original). Meanwhile, industrialists like Elon Mus....sorry, Charles Lindbergh and Henry Ford were swooning over and actively assisting Hitler[892]. Thank goodness there were some brilliant folks helping to add fun to American life.

Sister Rosetta Tharpe was born in Cotton Plant, Arkansas, in 1915. Raised by her mother, she moved around and ended up in New York. She was a prodigious talent who would be dubbed "The Godmother of Rock and Roll." Playing a combination of gospel music married to what would become rock, Rosetta was a pathfinder and trailblazer. To see how much all anyone needs to do is listen to thirty-three-year-old Sister Rosetta singing 'Up Above My Head,' first recorded in 1939 and re-recorded in 1947[893].

Listening to that song, Elvis, Little Richard, and Johnny Cash are right there in the music. Never to detract from these brilliant people, but, just for context, at the time Sister Rosetta re-recorded the song, Eric Clapton was three years old, Keith Richards was four, Jeff Beck was five, Jimi

Hendrix was eight, Elvis was twelve, and Little Richard and Johnny Cash were both sixteen[894].

Sister Rosetta was playing music like no one before her. She was the earliest adopter of the electric guitar and of the guitar distortion effect that would come to define the sound of rock and roll, and rock music after that.

You want some receipts? Jimi Hendrix cited her as a great influence. Chuck Berry said that his entire career was "one long Sister Rosetta Tharpe impersonation", and both Johnny Cash and Ringo Starr would acknowledge her as a huge inspiration[895].

Gayle Ward, music historian and author of Sister Rosetta's biography, "Shout Sister Shout!: The Untold Story of Rock and Roll Trailblazer Sister Rosetta Tharpe", offered a big one; Rosetta's influence on the King:

> Not only did he dig her guitar picking—that's really what he dug—but he dug her singing, too."_"When you see Elvis Presley singing early in his career ... imagine he is channeling Sister Rosetta Tharpe...It's not an image I think we're used to thinking about when we think of rock & roll history – we don't think about the black woman behind the young white man.[896]

It wasn't just Elvis. Rolling Stone magazine described Bob Dylan, saying of her,

Sister Rosetta Tharpe was anything but ordinary and plain. She was a big, good-looking woman, and divine, not to mention sublime and splendid. She was a powerful force of nature. A guitar-playin', singin' evangelist.[897]

In 1964, when Rosetta went to England to play impromptu at Manchester Railway Station, Jeff Beck, Brian May, and Keith Richards all came to see her and hear the electric guitar sound that would influence their amazing music.

The wicked thing of all this is, even though we've just heard acolytes from a veritable who's who of rock 'n roll royalty, until 2022, I was completely oblivious to Sister Rosetta. I had to be woken up by Michael Harriot of the Drapetomaniax: Unshackled History Podcast[898]. That's what being invisible looks like.

It wasn't just the influence of black music that was invisible to me. My history books didn't record any black innovation either. Some of this was ignorance, but much was by design. However, in our everyday lives, even the Confederate Taliban has a lot to thank black innovators for.

Our homes (and their churches) are nice and warm because Alice H. Parker invented the gas heating furnace.

Then, look at the plastic cable insulation on the lead of every electrical device. Without it, Mad Musk's Tesla cars would be useless. For helping him become a billionaire, the silver-spoon-fed nepo-baby can thank Walter Lincoln Hawkins.

All that food in our fridges wouldn't have gotten to your supermarket without the thermostat that's used on long-haul trucks and trains; WWI veteran Frederick McKinley Jones invented it. Also, red-state voters in places like Wyoming and Montana can thank Frederick for their snowmobiles.

Oh, and he wasn't finished. During WWII, while John Wayne was hiding in Hollywood, Frederick helped save American lives by inventing a field hospital refrigeration unit to store blood[899].

From the look of them, many Trump supporters enjoy fried potato chips. So, they can all tip their red caps to George Crum for inventing them. Not unrelatedly, after eating all those chips, a lot of those cult members may need to use a computerized blood pressure monitor. Michael Croslin conceived this.

Out in the garden, John Purdy invented the folding chair that even MAGA's use. Oh, and when they buy Super-Soakers for their grandkids, they can thank Lonnie G. Johnson for his innovation.

Then, we have the supreme irony of MAGA followers' homes being protected by a black woman. It was Mary Van Brittan Brown who conceived the first home security system[900].

Moving out into the world, in order to mail in multiple election ballots and bomb threats, they have to use an outdoor four-legged mailbox. They can thank Phillip Downing for that.

The three-light traffic signal that Mad Musk's self-driving cars may or may not stop for was thanks to Garrett Morgan. He also came up with the gas mask, a version of which police officers needed as the terrorists attacked the Capitol on J6.

Richard Spikes pioneered the automatic gear shifter, without which MAGA supporters' three-tonne-gas-guzzling pickup trucks couldn't drive around. And if you go into any tall building, like Trump Tower, and use an elevator, you can take your hat off to Alexander Miles for inventing the automatic elevator doors.

If, after the 2028 election, Trump needs a pacemaker, you can smile at the sweet irony that, for the rest of his life, a black man will live inside him. It was Otis Boykin who invented the control unit that fit into every pacemaker.

At the other end of the spectrum, we could call up the ghost of Robert Edward Lee and truly terrify him by showing what a free black man can really do. It was Moses Fleetwood ("Fleet") Walker who would patent the first artillery shell in 1891.

And finally, to the nutcases who don't believe in the Moon landings. It was Dr. George Carruthers who invented the ultraviolet camera that was taken to the Moon in 1969 to send us back the images of the Earth that proved that we'd been there[901].

Clearly, for the Confederate Taliban to acknowledge black brilliance would be to accept that the lies of the past four hundred years were just that. So it is that the far-right loves to scream 'Affirmative Action' or 'DEI' as a catch-all for any black person who has achieved anything. Of course, it's very comfortable for mediocre people to project their own inadequacies onto folks smarter than themselves.

This brings us, once again, to the toxic dumpster fire that is the life of Donald Trump. In him, we find the most persistent criminal in America. Nonetheless, until the 2024 election, this creature was finally being held to account for fifty years of deviance.

In a sight that must have occasioned some of the MAGA base to need one of Otis Boykin's pacemakers, the first person to bring a case and successfully prosecute him, for the crime of election interference, was Alvin Bragg, the black DA for Manhattan.

Also in New York, in a civil case bought by black New York Attorney General Letitia James, a jury found his crime company guilty of systematic fraud and lies and levied a fine of over $500 million in a judgement that effectively renders his 'businesses' worthless.

And in Fulton County, Georgia, a black women district attorney, Fani Wallis brought a RICO case against Trump and his multiple criminal co-conspirators in the 2020 election fraud case.

All these folks prove the point that, even on an uneven playing field, an African-American can rise as high as a European-American. These three prosecutors are brilliant legal minds who stick it to all the lies that said black people don't get there on merit.

To those who question their talents, I'd simply point this out. Trump was spending $50 million a year on his lawyers and had half the federal judiciary and the Supreme Court on his side. Yet, until the 2024 election, these three prosecutors were proving their intellectual mettle by winning.

I can show you what *real* affirmative action actually looks like. It's the unqualified rich white students admitted to Harvard—although all Ivy League universities work with similar practices—as legacy admissions (Daddy went there,) donor admissions (Daddy donates $500,000,) or on 'athletic' scholarships (Daddy donates $500,000). For Harvard alone, these make up over four out of ten white students. Suffice to say, three-quarters would have been rejected without these advantages[902].

The Confederate Taliban doesn't want you to hear this, but what makes America so successful is the infusion of the hyphenated people: Scots, Irish, English, Italian, Spanish, Swedish, German, Nigerian, Somali, Japanese, Chinese, Korean, Indian, Arab, and Greek. All fusing with the here-for-many-generations African Americans, Latinos, and Native Americans. It's all these people thrown together in a cultural salad bowl that has given us the most influential society the world has ever known.

To see what the nation would look like without people of color, especially black folks, just look to Europe, where many white immigrants came from. It's nice and sensible, but no European country lights up the world.

How about Canada, the nation most like our own? This had the same European settlers who arrived about the same time. It has similar terrain, climate, and natural resources, but very few African Americans. While Canada is a very pleasant place to live, it can't rival the USA in exporting 'WOW!' to the world.

Then, zoom the lens in and think about how boring sports were before integration. Yet, look what happened when the field was opened up. We got Muhammad Ali, Michael Jordan, Carl Lewis, Mike Tyson, and Tiger

Woods, and of course, Simone Biles, Florence Griffith Joyner, and Serena and Venus Williams?

I can't leave out football. Until 1946, the NFL was segregated and snooze-fest-sterile. Today, nearly three-quarters of the players are black and for a third of the country, football is a religion. The Super Bowl receives over one hundred million viewers, and weeknight football routinely gets an average of seventeen million viewers. That's five times as much as any TV show.

What about food? Black Cuisine has also tremendously influenced America, with many popular dishes coming from the antebellum South. There, talented but enslaved black chefs brought an African style to what would have been fairly bland-tasting European food.

Fried chicken quite possibly came from Scottish slaveholders who bought it from their native Scotland (a country that still enjoys battering and frying many things, including Mars Bars). But the chicken we know today would only come after an African-American spin. This is from the BBC;

> With years of honed experience, as well as an adeptness at seasoning and frying, African American cooks caused fried chicken to lose its Scottish identity and it became as quintessentially "Southern" as black-eyed peas, cornbread, collard greens, macaroni and cheese and sweet potato pie.[903]

In the epic Netflix show, House of Cards, Kevin Spacey's character, Frank Underwood, repeatedly visits the fictional 'Freddy's BBQ Joint' to feast on a breakfast plate of lower spares. That food came from the antebellum south, where enslaved cooks were the barbecue master chefs, creating magic marinades to make ribs taste fantastic.

As for that American staple of mac and cheese. It's true that Thomas Jefferson discovered the pasta and the cheese in Europe. However, it was his French-trained—because he was a free man in France—but enslaved chef James Hemings who put the African-American spin on it that Americans enjoy today. Mr. Hemings was also responsible for giving the nation French fries, firm ice cream, and meringue[904].

Thinking about those who want to make others' lives better brings me on to the loving faith of black Christians. Black parishioners attend Methodist, Presbyterian, or Episcopalian churches that actually expect something of their flock and that follow the Gospel of the New Testament, those being the real teachings of Jesus.

Black pastors preach against punching down and welcome all people. They also don't live in multi-million-dollar mansions or fly around in private jets because, for them, everything is about being a good Christian. This is the polar opposite of the evangelical fundamentalist churches that preach hate and license their followers to smash down on women, people of color, and LGBTQ+ folks.

Just from reading this chapter, do you see how easy it is to get positive images in your head? On that note, when people are given positive reinforcement and praise for effort, they have a higher opinion of what they can achieve. Unsurprisingly, many go on to lead more successful lives. Sociologists have a term for this: the Pygmalion Effect[905]. This reminds me of a quote from the actor Tom Hanks:

> I had a teacher for two and a half years, Mrs Castle, who told me that I was smart, and she told me that I was curious, and she told that I was good natured, and I didn't know that I was any of those things.[906]

There's a flip side to that, and it's called the Golem Effect. When someone is not offered constructive advice or praise for effort, or even worse, is demeaned, it's a predictor for a worse life.

Now, imagine that you're at school, and the teacher never offers you any constructive praise, and instead of pointing you towards a career in architecture or bio-engineering, they tell you to look for a job in manual labor or unskilled work.

That sort of thinking ties into one of the Confederate Taliban's many lies: that black folks—especially men—are both very dangerous and also very childlike. As a result, they couldn't be trusted to do the things you or I would take for granted, one of which was being able to vote.

This puts me in mind of the Louisiana Literacy Test from 1964[907]. It was supposed to 'test' whether, before they were allowed to vote, a black citizen had, at least, a fifth-grade education. Leaving aside how this contravenes the Fifteenth Amendment, there were thirty questions to be answered in ten minutes. Just one incorrect answer represented a failure, which would invalidate their ability to vote.

In 2014, a group of Harvard graduates sat the test. Bear in mind, these were some of the brightest minds in the country; indeed, the sort of folks who may end up working at NASA, winning Nobel Prizes, or saving humanity. Yet, every one of them failed the test, and none of them would be allowed to vote. Don't blame them. It was designed to be impossible to pass[908].

Combine all that with the deliberate suppression of stories of black brilliance, and one can see how easy it was for segregationists to use the fake argument about black folks lack of 'intelligence' to preclude them from loans, mortgages, or grants, or anything that could help them get ahead in life.

Those crap golem-effect style ideas about black folks not being able to be trusted to run businesses or repay loans haven't died. According to uber-capitalist investment bank, JP Morgan, black business owners are three times as likely to be rejected as white folks[909].

To keep working people divided, the powerful need to keep the biases alive. So it is that the despicable and the deplorable must always signal to people of color to 'know your place.' Through the book, you will have read about CRT and DEI. Of the latter, DEI means Diversity, Equity and Inclusion. It does exactly what it says on the tin: recruits from the widest pool of the best black, white, brown, LGBTQ, and disabled folks. From this, organizations and businesses get a wider perspective on new markets and broader ways of looking at problems.

On a grand level, imagine if the CIA had employed some clever Muslim folks before the year 2001 to analyze and understand the true threat that Osama Bin Laden represented.

If that's too expansive an example, then I can show you someone who doesn't value DEI: Mr. Donald Trump. Every fraudulent business he has managed, he has managed to bankrupt. Contrast his failures with inclusive corporate titans like Apple, Nike, or IKEA, who are wildly successful.

So it is that the far-right use 'DEI' at its basest level to substitute for the N-word but also to gaslight regular folks about an 'unqualified hire'—invariably a black person—no matter how brilliant they were, even if they were the 44th President.

Of course, no mirror exists to reflect right-wing hypocrisy, and to illustrate my point better, we have to enter the septic tank that is the mind of that demented and deranged curiosity, Mad Musk. This first-generation immigrant from apartheid South Africa, with a worldview less well shaped than a six-year-old, had words to say about DEI in 2024: "DEI is just another word for racism. Shame on anyone who uses it."[910]

To see what this meant in practice, I went to Tesla's website;

Our Diversity, Equity and Inclusion team uses a people-first and data-driven approach to champion DEI in our business and in the communities in which we operate. Tesla is a majority-minority company—with underrepresented groups as 67% of our U.S. workforce.[911]

You read that figure correctly. This diversity of people and thinking might explain why, in the Model S, X, Y, and 3, his employees have built some of the most durable and consequential passenger cars and made him a multi-billionaire in the process.

Anyway, I needed to check who these diverse employees were. The same Tesla site gives us a breakdown of the Tesla workforce: 28% Hispanic. 21% Asian. 11% black or African American. 2% Native Hawaiian. 1% American Indian. 4% two or more races, and 33% white[912].

Musk took that page down in 2024,[913] but the fragile, friendless freak didn't understand the concept of the internet archive that stores permanent copies of all web pages[914].

To end, if some fool tries this 'DEI is reverse racism' nonsense on you, just ask them this. In America, people sue McDonald's if their coffee is too hot[915]. So, if companies are hiring all these disastrously unqualified people, how come every corporation in the Fortune 500 with a DEI program isn't collapsing under the weight of all the lawsuits? And how come the federal government isn't drowning in litigation?

Of course, dear reader, you're clever enough to know the answer.

Chapter 31

Why The Right-Wing Hates Hollywood So Much.

In 2020, after the Korean masterpiece, Parasite, won the Academy Award for Best Picture, Trump's response was, "What the hell was that all about?' "Can we get like *Gone with the Wind* back please?"[916]

It was fitting for a prince of propaganda to speak about one of the greatest pieces of propaganda America has ever known. 1939's Gone With The Wind was a masterclass in gaslighting and revisionist history. Its purpose was to make Americans believe in the 'Lost Cause' myth.

Sarah Churchwell, the brilliantly insightful author of 'The Wrath to Come: Gone with the Wind and the Lies America Tells', described how the movie allowed viewers to be; "safe from having to consider either the historical, or actual, existence of Black people."[917]

In that, she also gave us a perfect fourteen-word summation of what many right-wingers really mean when they use the word 'woke.' Parenthetically, that also explains why they always flounder when asked to define what 'woke' means.

In 2024, Trump came out with, "It's politically incorrect to watch Gone With the Wind."[918] Here the felon was signalling to this audience that liberals were coming to steal their 'culture' and 'heritage.'

Personally, I don't care if people want to watch it. I merely want to illustrate the disinformation value it represented to the Confederate Taliban.

The only part of the story that needs to concern us is how, through Luciferian duplicity, it strives to paint black folks as the 'white man's burden.' Thus, with striking parallels to today's Confederate Taliban, the victims in Gone with the Wind aren't the stolen, enslaved, raped, tortured, and murdered Africans. No, instead, they're the 'honorable God-fearing Christian' white slaveholders, forced by 'northern aggression' to end their way of life.

To illustrate the indoctrination effect on the American population, Guinness World Records has the movie as the highest grossing of all time, with inflation-adjusted earnings of $3.44 billion[919].

Bear in mind that the 1930s to the 1950s were the golden age for movie-goers, with many Americans going twice a week. Of course, back then, Hollywood was a strictly black and white world with Tinseltown painting a comfortable picture of a nation 'real Americans' could easily relate to. It was a world of straight male actors like Gary Cooper, Clark Gable, and John Wayne. For actresses, all that was required was that they be demure, pretty, and straight.

As far as everyone else was concerned; blacks and browns 'knew their place', and gays were unseen, or if seen, it was only to be picked up by the cops on charges of depravity.

In truth, the entertainment industry was happy to self-censor in order to promote the patriarchal fantasy that was the SWIMPs American life. In it, men went to work, whilst their immaculately turned-out housewives were fantastically happy to stay home, looking after their respectful and exceptionally well-behaved children.

I wanted to include this section to illustrate why the far-right hates Hollywood so much today. It's because they don't make 'Lost Cause' or patriarchal propaganda anymore. This is infuriating, as the right-wing knows the power of the story. Like Hollywood, their whole communication strategy is to tell myths and stories that resonate with their follow-ers, whether "Benghazi," "Birthergate," "Pizzagate," "Hillary's Emails," "Q",

"Stop the Steal," "Kung-Flu Virus," "Hunter Biden's laptop," or "Haitians eating pets."

There's something else to note on a slight tangent. The far right loves to portray today's Hollywood as a woke liberal paradise of unpronounceable smoothies, hedonistic sex, and virtue signaling. In fact, it's a rapacious, uber-capitalist chew-em-up-and-spit-'em-out money machine.

As for the virtue signaling, it was Hollywood that seduced young women from all across America with the dream of fame and fortune. Then, for some, once they arrived, their first taste of Tinseltown was to be brought to a powerful producer's swanky office, where a sweaty old slob would introduce them to his 'casting couch' to see how much they 'really wanted the role.'

It was patriarchal power that allowed predatory men to get away with both the sexual assault and the subsequent silencing of women after the assault. And so it would remain until 2016, when women stood up and were finally heard[920]. So much for 'woke' Hollywood.

This brings us on to the polar opposite of 'woke' in part-time thief and full-time traitor Steve Bannon. Before he was Trump's first-term chief strategist, he tried to become a Hollywood producer. Thankfully for us, sloppy Steve was too lazy or too stupid to make it happen. Amazingly, though, his moronically primitive brain had the right thoughts; that movies could influence minds, and, in turn, influence society.

Thank goodness he didn't get together with some far-right billionaires and use their money to take over a studio. Then they could have pumped out their own blockbuster movies. Using some CGI, we could have had John Wayne in Beverly Hills Cop (without Eddie Murphy) and Clark Gable in Lethal Weapon (replacing Danny Glover), and Gary Cooper in Crimson Tide (goodbye Denzel Washington).

Be grateful for small mercies and even bigger imbeciles. If the Confederate Taliban had denied folks in middle America positive role models of people of color, these septic toads could have held up progress in society for decades.

This leads us on to the diverse picture of America that we see in the movies today. Let's not delude ourselves; it's primarily because Hollywood wants profits. To make them, it needs people to visit theaters to watch their latest productions. As we are no longer in the 1950s, that audience isn't just white; it's black, brown, and LGBTQ+. Studios know audiences want to see themselves reflected on the screen, so, out of self-interest, they feature diverse casts in their movies.

As to the awakenings of diversity on the screen. It was in the 1960s that America got a slight chance to see black and white folks working together with "In the Heat of the Night," where Sidney Poitier starred alongside Rod Steiger. The 1970s picked up the pace, and by 1974, the ever masterful Mel Brooks pushed the envelope of what white people would see by wrapping it in comedy. With Blazing Saddles, he brought us one of the first black cowboys (even though, in real life, a third of cowboys were people of color).

But there was more. SPOILER ALERT: The black cowboy was the sheriff, trying to save the town from bandits. Yet, all the while, the town's bigwigs were more concerned with busying themselves trying to get rid of him. Brooks' genius was that, while we were laughing, we were being educated on the idiotic poison of racism.

But it wasn't until the 1980s that things really got motoring. Here's where we got to see white and black people not just working together but forming relationships. Eddie Murphy may be known by many as Dr. Doolittle, but for me, his three totemic performances were back in the 1980s. He starred alongside Nick Nolte in Walter Hill's seminal 1982 action comedy, 48 Hrs. Then, in John Landis's exceptional Trading Places from 1983, and in 1984, we saw him in Martin Brest's sublime Beverly Hills Cop.

These movies were groundbreaking, because they showed us something that, up to that point, we hadn't seen on the big screen. White and black characters acting as equals.

To that point, many big-budget blockbusters in the 1980s or 1990s featured the lightning strike logo and the words, "A Simpson/Bruckheimer Production," before the film. This was the legendary powerhouse production team of Don Simpson (now passed away) and Jerry Bruckheimer. They were the juggernaut of Hollywood in the 80s and 90s, with anything they wanted getting greenlit and becoming box office gold. They produced, amongst many others, Bad Boys, Beverly Hills Cop, Con Air, Crimson Tide, Flashdance, Enemy of the State, and Top Gun[921].

Simpson and Bruckheimer understood middle America, as well as anyone in Hollywood, and significantly better than most Democratic politicians or strategists, even up to today.

The genius of these two was that their films featured white, black and brown characters working together to take down an evil bad guy. And by including everyone, importantly, no one felt excluded, and the movie could gain the widest audience.

The 'political' byproduct of Simpson/Bruckheimer-made blockbusters was that, whilst helping black actors break through a glass ceiling, they were doing it in a non-threatening way, without making white people feel left out or uncomfortable. Then, as those movies played in theaters across Middle America, whether by accident or design, they served as counter-programming to the right-wing propaganda of Fox, AM radio, and television shows like 'Cops.'

I'll go out on a limb and say, for voters in states like Indiana, Iowa, North Carolina, and Ohio, seeing positive images of white and black characters working together allowed them to see past the color of Barack Obama's skin and into the hope of his message, helping him win there in 2008.

It wasn't just characters in the stories who worked together; it was white and black folks working together within the studio system. In the casting of 1996's smash hit, Independence Day, Will Smith, as fine an actor as he was, needed white allies to root for him.

The studio feared that a black actor couldn't open a blockbuster. Fortunately, Smith was championed by both Dean Devlin, the movie's writer, and Ronald Emmerich, the movie's director[922]. The payoff was an $817 million box office that put paid to the notion that a black actor couldn't triumph at the box office[923].

Remember, Hollywood's self-interest is in the bottom line, so once studios saw black actors could bring in the coin, they opened up their loving arms.

Which brings us to today. The purpose of the Confederate Taliban is to persuade voters that the American experiment is broken, so the constant profitable bombardment of positive, reinforcing messages must be torture for them. Obviously, anti-'woke' patriarchal crybabies like Trump and Mad Musk are so fragile that their sensibilities are offended by seeing images of empowered women, women kicking men's asses, or any positive images of black, brown or LGBTQ+ folks. Yet, deep down, their greatest fear of Hollywood is knowing that images of men and women—whether white, black, brown, gay, or straight—working together are so much more hopeful than their broken-down dystopian vision of American carnage.

Chapter 32

What Exactly Do The Snowflakes Want To Say?

What exactly is freedom of speech? Does it mean 'free speech' for anyone to say anything they want with no consequences? Or is it 'fearless speech?'[924], where everyone—men, women, LGBTQ+ folks, white, black, or brown—can have equal access to the 'marketplace of ideas' without being abused? These are two very different concepts.

Here's a question for the ardent 'free speech' enthusiast. Imagine if someone asks on social media, "Is Elon Musk a pedophile?" That's not an accusation or allegation; it's free speech and 'just asking the question'. It's also a common right-wing trick. The mere juxtaposition of his name next to *that* word is enough to seed an idea in our brains, and if it's repeated, it will turn from people asking, 'is Elon Musk a pedophile?' into 'Elon Musk is a pedophile'. Now a question has become a statement.

Ironically, that's the world Mad Musk himself is ushering forward on his Twitter platform, where there is no distinction between fact and fiction or truth and reality.

We have previously established that he is quite dim, but he is also very transparent. As an exceedingly fragile SWIMP, he knows that true freedom of speech is the ability to question power, yet power (he) never wants to be questioned.

To ensure that doesn't happen, in his world of 'anyone being able to say anything', stupidity is elevated to sit unchallenged alongside knowledge. Once there, all it has to do is create chaos, confusion, and doubt. Ultimately, the powerful hope this leads to exhaustion and apathy. After all, anything that stops ordinary people from discussing important matters like taxes on rich people, regulation on killer corporations, gun reform, or women's healthcare means the patriarchs get to stay powerful.

Which brings us on to the far-right's love of complaining about 'cancel culture.' I wouldn't normally waste my time with this crap, as I know it is just misdirection. However, many don't and fall for their BS. So, here goes.

For the right, apparently, liberals are snowflakes who melt at the slightest wrong word. It's puzzling, as I am not aware of liberals banning one book. Indeed, anyone can still get hold of any John Wayne film, or the KKK promo video, 'Birth of a Nation,' or Mein Kampf. Yes, publishers sometimes update the language in older books to appeal to modern audiences, but that's because they want to sell books to a new customer base, and the original books are always still available.

To the point of 'cancellation,' let's visit with the forensically intelligent British author and radio host, James O'Brien, who offered us this;

> I do find in my work, the people who complain most about being cancelled are people complaining about being cancelled on their own show, or on a tour of the studios promoting their new book about how it's impossible for them to get their message out there, or they're on a chat show complaining about how they're not allowed to say what they want to say while they're saying it.[925]

Of course, we can look at some people who aren't cancelled, like Joe Rogan and Trump. Hell, just look at the aforementioned Mad Musk, the human cesspit who *owns* Twitter.

Down the food chain, those who complain about being "cancelled" are usually just using that term to gin up the far-right. Many a time, their acts or acting isn't good enough, and they can't cut it in the modern world.

Of course, how could you ever tell a snowflake that? But it's okay because their grievance game can put them on a new lane to a profitable right-wing career of doing more of the same: punching down on people weaker than them. The comedian Laurie Kilmartin offered us this on 'cancel culture'

> It's a way to make money. Before social media, if you had bad jokes, people just didn't laugh, and now they tell you that they don't like a joke, and that's their right...comedians aren't, quote, cancelled, they're just changing their audience. I think there's a kind of fan base out there that wants to identify with a grievance, and has nothing to do with stand-up comedy and the quality of jokes.[926]

You only know the words 'cancel culture' primarily because it's cheap catnip and clickbait to fill up the pages and screens of the lazy corporate news media.

If we are to believe that same media, a student can't open their mouth without offending someone. But delving into the facts shows this is mostly just another right-wing manufactured method of dividing people. Here's a newsflash: language changes.

When I was growing up in the 1980s, what is now called political correctness was called 'being diplomatic.' Before that time, it was normal to hear the N-word, as well as other slurs like chink, faggot, greaser, kike, paki, spic, wetback, wop, or yid. For receipts, go and watch any Hollywood movie from the early 1980s.

Obviously, that language, signaling for marginalized people to 'know their place,' never went away. Indeed, across whole swathes of America today, those words are in customary and continuous usage.

So it is that the people who want to use these terms are so pissed off because they can't say the words *without* consequences. However, realistically, unless you are a complete Neanderthal, how is it so hurtful to use the modern phrases?

At this point, I can hear my dear conservative friends protest, saying, 'Black men address each other as "nigga." Yes, but when that word ended in "er," it was from a time that a black man could be lynched just for looking at a white man or woman in the 'wrong' way. It's loaded with four hundred years of slavery, oppression, and violence that no other group of people in America ever experienced. So, I reckon for the goddamn hell that twenty generations of black people have gone through, they have earned the right to own that word.

All this being said, we are going to introduce two opposing thoughts into our head. Up until 1985, it's true, white people didn't need to think before they spoke, and for people over sixty years old, it might be stressful to have to weigh everything before they speak, for fear that it may cause someone offense.

We know everything is about *intent*. With more people sitting at the table—women, people of color, LBGTQ+—sometimes choosing the right phrase is difficult. Consider this: "He's black......no an African- American....no a person of color." Because it is difficult, it can make people feel stressed and anxious. Then, getting it wrong can make some people feel stupid, and stupid makes us stand out, and standing out is humiliating, and we're human, so humiliation is a painful feeling. And suddenly, it's, "Why is everything so woke!"

My mom is eighty-six years old. She was born in 1938, and in conversation, she occasionally uses words that people may find outmoded today, like "colored", but I don't stop and correct her, as I know her intent.

Remember that there are more Democrats in Texas than there are in New York. We have so many friends we've never met in places we've never been, and the last thing that we need to do is send them into the clutches of the GOP. We can either rail against them for being stupid, ignorant, racist, or all three, or we can welcome them into the Democratic big tent. Remember, the aim is to win people over.

Apart from policing language, if I could offer another small piece of advice to my liberal friends, be careful judging historical figures by today's standards. Aside from the regress of the far-right and global warming, in a lot of ways, it's a better world than the one I grew up in. Huge social advances have taken place in my lifetime. Indeed, for many people, those epitaphs you read eight paragraphs back weren't just words; they were what came before being spat on, kicked, punched, or something much, much worse.

Chapter 33

There's Only One Flag, And It Belongs To You Too.

Whether we call it 'Christian nationalism', 'white nationalism', or fascism, the creed of hate that Trump's MAGA espouses is not new. But in the new age, it has led to the Oklahoma City bombing, January 6th, and all the radicalized killers who rampage in churches, shopping centers, and schools. Down that path, America dies.

As a progressive populist, I'm also a nationalist, but don't despair, for I believe in civic nationalism. It means loving America, despite all her flaws, and wanting the future to be better than the past. Civic nationalism is for true patriots who believe in democracy and that an inclusive America can work for all her citizens, whether in red states or blue.

You will have read in this book how the patriotism of the far-right is always a fairy-tale of their own concoction. In fact, it's a horrific, debased ethnic nationalism where their opponents are "vermin", and "enemies from within."[927]

The far-right profess to love the military, but only the unquestioning 'Manifest Destiny' kind. So, they love the (never served) John Wayne character in the (fictional) 'Green Berets' and the (fictional) Rambo characters in Rambo 2, 3, and 4, waging all-out unmerciful Christian war for America.

And they positively revere General Douglas MacArthur. Indeed, he completely sums up their worldview. We can start with his murderous and treacherous treatment of the brave American veterans of the Bonus March in 1932. For simply seeking the bonuses the government promised them, MacArthur, with President Hoover's ascension, ordered American troops to fire live ammunition on these peaceful protestors in Washington[928].

Then, as murderous fools tend not to change their spots, during the Korean War, MacArthur proposed using nuclear weapons on a scale that might have ended humanity. For a receipt, we have his words: "I would have dropped between 30 to 50 tactical atomic bombs on his air bases and other depots."[929]

None of this was a problem for the SWIMPs. Indeed, it was John Wayne, who, whilst a coward, understood his role as a prop, claiming that MacArthur had told him, "You represent the American serviceman better than the American serviceman himself."[930]

Moving forward to the 1980s, we can meet retired Lt. Col. Oliver North. Here is a liar, lucky to escape prison, who secretly sold weapons to Iran, using the proceeds to fund the right-wing death squads who murdered women and children in Nicaragua[931]. Yet, in the world of the Confederate Taliban, North is a God-fearing, all-American hero.

By contrast, former Secretary of State John Kerry, the recipient of a Silver Star for his service in Vietnam as a Swift Boat Commander, is a weakling and a traitor[932], for to the Confederate Taliban, liberals are never the right kind of warrior.

However, there is a person who is even worse than a liberal, and that's a Republican who will work with liberals for the good of the nation.

Meet John McCain, a Republican who also served his country with honor in Vietnam. The war may have been wrong because it was fought against Vietnamese nationalists, rather than communists, but the young men who went over there were all brave heroes.

McCain was a Navy pilot whose job it was to protect American troops' lives during the war. He was shot down during a mission and captured, yet even after five years in a POW camp, he didn't break or betray America[933].

Then, once the war ended, he came home and gave years of solid service as a decent GOP senator. McCain was what a Republican used to look like.

Just to illustrate, I recall a town hall event in Minnesota during the 2008 election. A woman voter started reeling off the standard Rush Limbaugh, AM radio conspiracist paranoia of the sort that would mark her out as, then, a Tea Party and, now, a Trump supporter.

Her ramblings went along the lines of, she can't trust Obama because he's an 'Arab.' McCain didn't even need to think and straightaway took the microphone from her and gently corrected her, saying;

> No, ma'am, He's a decent family man and citizen, that just
> I just happen to have disagreements with on fundamental
> issues, and that's what the campaign's all about. He's not [an
> Arab].[934]

After that, people like that woman never allowed him to recover in the polls. They are the GOP's crocodiles, trained over the centuries by demonic preachers, pastors, and patriarchs, and all they want to hear is the culture-war red meat that reinforces their violent, unpatriotic hatred of modern America. It was to his credit that McCain's principles and real Christian values wouldn't allow him to indulge them.

To a coward like five-times draft deferred Trump and his disciples, Mc-Cain was a "loser," they claim, because he was shot down. However, this straight, white man's actual 'crime' was being willing to seek consensus with his opponents.

Come 2016, and Trump understood the power of the military in the eyes of the far-right. So it would be that, early in his administration, he appointed three square-jawed, battle-proven heroes. General John Kelly (Chief of Staff), General H.R. McMaster (National Security Adviser) and General Jim Mattis (Defense Secretary). These were all decorated, honorable men who, if they saw someone fall over, would be more likely to reach out a hand than step on them. They didn't last long. Their crimes? Questioning the cult leader.

Whilst thinking of what patriotism is, some words stick in my mind of the black Governor of Maryland, combat veteran, Wes Moore. When asked about his hopes for America in 2023, he offered words that few reasonable people could disagree with;

> What this country has meant to my family is that I can literally be the grandson of a man that the Ku Klux Klan ran out of (South Carolina), and also in the same breath, be a person who is about to become the first Black Governor in the history of the State (of Maryland). Both of those things are true. And we can't look at one without understanding the other.[935]

In a 2023 Gallup survey, 67% of Americans questioned were proud to be American[936]. This is one of the easiest lifts in politics that liberals fail to grasp.

Unlike almost every other country in the Western world, the Stars and Stripes adorn houses, shops, t-shirts, offices, and uniforms. Americans are patriotic. Yet, by not showing up, liberals have allowed rancid Republicans to steal the banner of the patriot, which they use as both a shield and a baton—the shield to cover up their fake patriotism and the baton to smash anyone who points out their hypocrisy.

This being so, some liberals complain that the Star-Spangled Banner contains references to slavery, which it does. Other people point to neo-Nazis using the flag, which is their right. But those same folks should understand that it was the Stars and Stripes that the Union army carried into battle against the original Confederates. Since then, soldiers of all colors and creeds have fought side by side in the muddy fields of Europe, the jungles of Asia, and the deserts of the Middle East. Brave white, black and brown troops have died for the flag and the dream that it represents.

If we don't meet ordinary patriotic Americans where they are, they won't know what we stand for. It's such an easy win. Just take back the flag for decent Americans, take back the flag to represent civility and community, and take back the flag to show a strong, proud nation that looks after all her citizens, whoever they may be.

Just returning to civic nationalism, progressive veterans have a great understanding of what a fairer America can look like because they lived it. I describe the United States Military in my book, When Coal Miners Drive Cadillacs, as the small oasis of social democracy in America. It's a place where, in exchange for service, one can receive subsidized food, housing, education, and childcare, along with universal medical care and a gold standard pension.

To make the point, we have so many progressive vets on the Democratic side. There are organizations like VoteVets and veterans like Pete Buttigieg, Tammy Duckworth, Allison Gill, Ken Harburgh, Jason Kander, Lucas Kunce, Wes Moore, Richard Ojeda, Tim Walz, and Fred Wellman. They will all make you proud to be an American and show you the best side of patriotism. They understand duty, honor, and sacrifice, and never ever punch down. As importantly, they have seen the worst that societies can be, so they understand how much better Americans' lives could be with progressive policies.

Everything that cowardly Trump and his feeble MAGA coalition aren't, these folks are, and you can use their examples in 2026 and 2028 as pathfinders to win over the other side, especially in red states.

Chapter 34

Something Else You May Enjoy Reading

If you found this book enlightening, you may wonder about practical steps to defeat the Confederate Taliban. Here's part of the opening chapter from my book When Coal Miners Driver Cadillacs.

<u>The Democratic Messenger Who May Never Have Met A Real Voter.</u>

After the 2024 election, many political consultants and pundits tried to explain what happened. However, there is no mystery. Trump won because over six million 2020 Democratic voters couldn't or didn't vote. Notwithstanding that, the media offered a narrative of a decisive victory. That's total BS. Out of around 152 million votes across the nation, just three states decided the election—Michigan, Pennsylvania, and Wisconsin. Trump's 230,000 extra votes over Kamala Harris in those states meant forty-four electoral college votes, which meant victory[937].

On a related note, I recall the seemingly curious conundrum of thousands of voters in New York's 14th Congressional District choosing representative Alexandria Ocasio-Cortez for Congress and Trump for the presidency in 2024. When asked why, one replied that they both 'cared' for the working class[938]. Leaving aside what an astounding con man Trump is, it brings us to the seemingly intractable paradox of why many people like Democratic policies yet hate Democrats. It's a notion that escapes liberals, but for many citizens, voting is about feelings more than it is facts, and everyone wants to feel that someone has their back. Allow me to present you with a story that might illustrate the point;

> Think of Democrats as a smart but meek kid with a $20 bill who, at the school fair on a scorching hot summer's day, quietly offers to buy his classmates ice-cold smoothies. However, he calls them 'nutritionally balanced appetizing beverages' and speaks so softly that no one hears him except the rich, entitled Republican bully, who, in plain view and with the acquiescence of the teacher (the news media), steals the weak Dem kids $20 and yells out to his thirsty classmates, 'Ice-Cold Smoothies On Me!'. While the class is enjoying their smoothies, the Republican bully tells them the Dem kid could have done this, but because he hates them, he deliberately wanted to keep them thirsty. And as this whole sorry saga unfolds, the meek Dem kid is just standing there, soft and quiet, never bothering to remonstrate with the teacher or to correct his classmates' misconceptions by telling them it was actually *his* idea and it was *his* money that the Republican bully stole to buy the smoothies.

Alongside never shouting about their achievements, the other reason Democrats lose, not only their own voters but also find it so hard to win over enough of the other side, is that they won't fight. To explain this fatal political misunderstanding; when we're in trouble, instinctively, we want someone to step in and stand up for us. This is a primal feeling because it's about our own survival. Even if our 'hero' gets punched in the face and knocked down, the fact they were willing to fight for us is enough to make us love them.

That readiness to make a sacrifice or fight for people is an amalgam of courage and integrity and might be the most attractive and magnetic quality a person can possess. Indeed, the willingness to punch up at power in fighting for ordinary people is part of the reason politicians like Alexandria Ocasio-Cortez, Jasmine Crockett, Maxwell Frost, and Bernie Sanders are so popular.

On a grander scale, it's the essence of why firefighters and the military are so respected. Think back to the morning of September 11th, 2001, and the images of the firefighters entering the burning World Trade Center buildings to rescue people. Or, after the terrorist attack of January 6th, 2021, to the images of the National Guardsmen protecting the seat of our democracy in Washington. On both these occasions, they were the people heading towards danger to risk themselves to protect others.

Heroism and sacrifice are points not lost on our friends in Hollywood. In the 1950s, it may have been High Noon or Bad Day at Black Rock. In modern times, we have the enormously successful Marvel and DC Studios superhero movies like Black Widow, Captain America, and Superman. Regardless of the era, the reason for these movies' popularity was that the hero was always battling to protect the 'little guy' from a powerful enemy.

"No one fucks with a Biden". Those were the words of President Biden, captured on a 'hot-mic,' spoken whilst visiting Florida in 2022.[939] He was speaking privately about the far right using the media to attack his son, Hunter, but it showed genuine emotion and fight.

The idiotic corporate media feigned shock at hearing a word I use a hundred times a day as an adverb, adjective, expletive, noun, pronoun, and verb. Hell, it's used on almost every show and movie I watch and every podcast I listen to. If the word 'fuck' concerns you more than the word 'fascism', then may I gently suggest this isn't the battle for you.

Just to the point of his words, as ever, the corporate media misinformed us by missing the point, which was that by saying it, the President sounded tough and decisive, just like a Commander-in-Chief should.

I recall another occasion when Joe turned up the heat on the media. For the whole of 2023, their pundits had been repeating Republican lies by predicting a recession. Yet, every month, the economic statistics revealed strong retail sales, manufacturing, and jobs growth[940].

By December 2023, after announcing more record low unemployment figures, Biden had reached his limit and said, "All good. Take a look. Start reporting it the right way."[941]

You will read in chapter six about how the mainstream media never carries good-news because fear is so much better for ratings; however, ever since that date, talk of recession more or less ended. That's what happens when you stand up for yourself.

History will record Joe Biden as both a phenomenal political operator in the legislative sphere and as a truly decent man. However, he was from an age of decorum and consensus and, as such, didn't understand the age he was living in, where the other side just wanted control and domination.

Unlike many in the political media, I won't castigate President Biden. Instead, look at Washington, where there are over two hundred and fifty Democrats in Congress, together with a whole political operative class of thousands. Yet, only about fifty of them fight hard. The vast majority won't fight, which makes them look scared and weak. So, for many voters, Democrat is a synonym for 'weak'. I agree, even though I don't want them to be.

At this juncture, I have to note that, with just over one hundred days of campaigning before the 2024 presidential election, Vice President Kamala Harris, together with her VP pick, Minnesota Governor Tim Walz, started doing something that Democrats wouldn't do by fighting. The hopeful and empathetic Harris/Walz ticket promised voters it would take on the fascist Project 2025 agenda, protect women's rights, have Medicare pay for sick Americans' home help[942], and guarantee the down payments for first-time home buyers.

Despite milquetoast billionaire-friendly Democratic consultants actively toning down the campaign's hopeful messaging[943], and even with the VP courting centrist billionaires like Mark Cuban, and former rabid right-wingers like Liz Cheney, this should have led to 2020 levels of voters turning out to vote[944]. But it didn't, with many potential Democratic voters either abstaining, voting third party, or even casting their ballots for a wealthy white male felon, sexual abuser, and traitor instead of a battle-tested, empathetic biracial female candidate.

Some of them were Arab-Americans and progressive young voters, furious at the Biden administration's de facto sanctioning of the Israeli government's genocidal war on Palestine, yet too naïve to see that Trump would be one thousand times worse for the Palestinians[945]. Others were the 42% of Latinos who voted for the Grand Old Party (GOP), too blind to see that MAGA Republicans see all brown folks as deportable[946]. Then there were the Teamsters and the Longshoremen's unions, who wouldn't endorse the Harris campaign even while Trump and Elon Musk laughed at stripping workers of their rights[947].

Most astonishing of all though, were the 18-29-year-old women of Gen Z. Given how Republicans had helpfully signposted a horrific Handmaid's Tale future of rape and patriarchal domination, one might have assumed that self-interest would bring them out to vote Democratic. No such luck. Six out of ten young women sat at home, and of those who bothered to vote, four out of ten went for Trump[948].

By December 2024, with Project 2025 fully revealed and the federal government set for the chopping block, reports abounded of Trump voters crying at the prospect of losing their jobs or entitlements[949]. For these people, the expression 'I never thought the leopards would eat my face'[950] was a perfect summation of their childlike mindset. 'Fuck around and find out' was a cruder, yet equally apt observation.

Perhaps the least covered yet most devastatingly effective weapon that Republicans possessed was the complicit and compliant corporate news, print, and television media, specifically the political press and pundits. These conniving and cowardly jackals spent the entire Biden presidency demeaning the president's mental competence and achievements whilst 'sanewashing' Trump and Republicans[951]. Instead of chasing down GOP lies and asking follow-up questions, these lazy corporate hacks acted as stenographers rather than journalists by regurgitating en masse the disinformation spewing out of the right-wing ecosphere, whether from Fox News or the toxic social media platforms of billionaire oligarchs Elon Musk and Mark Zuckerberg.

This being so, Trump and his circus of frenzied, fragile political freaks do put on a good 'show' of fighting. In my book, 'The Confederate Taliban,' I describe who he is 'fighting' for: his coalition of scared, fake-Christian, angry, rich, and insane voters.

Most GOP voters don't or won't see that Trump's number one interest is himself and his billionaire cronies. Still, Republicans 'confidence' has the effect of fooling both the corporate media and many normal, low-information voters that this orange creep and his toxic goons are 'competent,' 'decisive,' and 'fighting for them.'

You may have heard the expression 'It's better to beg forgiveness than ask permission.' Democrats always ask permission, and it looks so damn submissive.

> 'Please let women control their own bodies. Please ban kid-killing AR-15s. Please, can we have fair voting? Please, can the Supreme Court be nice? Please, don't murder the planet. Please, please, please.

For Republicans, saying 'NO!' to compliant, placid, and timid Democrats will always make them look tough and decisive in the eyes of the corporate media and millions of low-information voters.

Despite this, for many elite liberals, there is exasperation at the average voter for not being able to see what an existential threat to democracy the GOP has become. Indeed, coming into the election, I'm sure many of those citizens were more familiar with Project Gotham (a video game), or Project Runway (a TV show), than with Project 2025.

To explain. Most people spend their time working for a living, looking after their families, enjoying their time off work, and maintaining their relationships. Then, when they take in political information, they may get misinformed by Facebook, disinformed by Twitter, or only marginally better, watch 'The News,' with its both-sides, horse-race method of reporting politics. So, whilst voters should shoulder some of the burden of their bad decisions, a lot of our ire must land on liberal politicians who can't effectively message their own ideas.

To the point of how many people like Democratic policies, the proposed offerings in Joe Biden's original $3 trillion Build Back Better plan were all highly popular. Three months of paid family leave and three months of paid sick leave have 84% popularity[952]. The $15 minimum wage is popular with 62% of Americans[953]. Medicare for All is 57% popular (explain it better, and the figure will soar.)[954] And 79% of voters support free childcare for low-income and middle-class families. In the chapter "How to Win Every Election," I will show you how to get these policies across the line.

Chapter 35

Acknowledgements and Reading/Listening List

Writing a book is a long and sometimes frustrating process. So, I have to thank my brother Ed for reading through it and offering some constructive criticism and praise. Also, my friend John and his brother, Andrew, were kind enough to read early drafts and said they enjoyed it. Thanks also to my friend Stuart, who listened to me ramble on during our morning dog walks. I can't leave out my now-passed dad, and still-here mom. Without them and all the experiences they gave me, this never would have happened.

For the research, I had some fantastic tutors. At the end, I will list some books that really helped me:

First, though, in order to get started on the journey, I needed to supplement the critical thinking that was already inside me. There were three books that greatly helped me; The Perils of Perception by Bobby Duffy (2018). Factfulness-Ten Reasons We're Wrong by Hans Rosling (2018) and Think Like a Rocket Scientist by Ozan Varol (2020).

I will give a fuller list at the end of this acknowledgment. However, before that, it's a modern world, and, for me, podcasts have proved immeasurably useful. On that note, where listening to the Daily Wire, Joe Rogan, or Jordan Petersen can only make your dumber, the shows I recommend will make you smarter for every minute you listen to them. Also, the presenters of these podcasts are some of my favorite kinds of liberals: ones who fight.

To start, there's Tell Me Everything with John Fugelsang (it's also a daily podcast called 'The John Fugelsang Show'). John is a wise, funny, and intelligent liberal who punches up and never backs down. If you've read this far, you'll love him.

There's also The Bob Cesca Show will also ensure you are ultra-smart. Bob and his co-hosts hit you with super-insightful comments and observations.

You could also listen to The Hartmann Report, with the brilliant, empathetic fighter and patriot Thom Hartmann. It's guaranteed to expand your knowledge of politics, society, and economics.

Over in rural Illinois, we have the superb Professional Left Podcast with Driftglass and Blue Gal. A year of listening to them will give you a better education than most Ivy League political science graduates receive.

You could try "democracy-ish" with the amazing Danielle Moodie and Wajahat Ali. If you had a time machine and travelled back five years, you'd see they predicted everything that would happen. Priceless.

You have read about him in the book, but Trey Crowder also has a podcast called "Weekly Skews" co-hosted with Mark Agee. Listen, and know you will always be smarter by the end.

There are two fantastic progressive veterans who also have superb shows: F.P. Wellman's 'On Democracy' and 'Burn the Boats' with Ken Harbaugh.

And now on to the book reading list. It's not exhaustive, but it will get you started.

<u>Book Reading List:</u>

The Sum of Us by Heather McGhee.

Merge Left - Ian Haney Lopez

The Cruelty Is the Point: The Past, Present, and Future of Trump's America by Adam Serwer

Amy Chua: Political Tribes and World on Fire.

Malcolm Gladwell: Blink, David and Goliath, The Tipping Point

The Fifth Risk by Michael Lewis

Blood Gun Money: How America Arms Gangs and Cartels by Ioan Grillo

Robert E. Lee and Me: A Southerner's Reckoning with the Myth of the Lost Cause by Ty Seidule

Wajahat Ali: Go Back to Where You Came from: And Other Helpful Recommendations on How to Become American.

The Liberal Redneck Manifesto by Trae Crowder

White Trash. The 400-Year Untold History of Class in America (2016) by Nancy Isenberg

Strangers in Their Own Land: Arlie Russell Hochschild

Elie Mystal: Allow Me to Retort: A Black Guy's Guide to the Constitution

Uncomfortable Conversations with a Black Man by Emmanuel Acho

Plutocrats The Rise of the New Global Super-Rich - Chrystia Freeland

Jared Yates Sexton: American Rule How a Nation Conquered the World but Failed Its People

Evil Geniuses_ The Unmaking of America_ A Recent History by Kurt Andersen

Listen Liberal: Thomas Frank

Arguing with Zombies by Paul Krugman

Jill Lepore: These Truths: A History of the United States

How To Win Friends and Influence People by Dale Carnegie

1. Ross, D. (2022, November 3). *Essay: The Crack-Up by F. Scott Fitzgerald*. American Masters. https://www.pbs.org/wnet/americanmasters/f-scott-fitzgerald-essay-the-crack-up/1028/

2. President Wilson House. (n.d.). Wilson and Race. President Wilson House. https://woodrowwilsonhouse.org/wilson-topics/wilson-and-race/

3. Chronicle, B. K. A. (2016, December 28). This president's grandson lived remarkable life. *Augusta Chronicle*. https://eu.augustachronicle.com/story/news/2016/12/28/president-s-grandson-lived-remarkable-life/14273012007/

4. Jones, Robert P. 2023. *The Hidden Roots of White Supremacy: And the Path to a Shared American Future.*
New York, NY, Simon & Schuster.

5. Jones, Robert P. 2023. *The Hidden Roots of White Supremacy: And the Path to a Shared American Future.*
New York, NY, Simon & Schuster.

6. Pope Francis: It was a genocide against indigenous peoples - Vatican News. (2022, July 30). Www.vaticannews.va. https://www.vaticannews.va/en/pope/news/2022-07/pope-francis-apostolic-journey-inflight-press-conference-canada.html

7.
Harrold, Stanley, and Randall M. Miller. *Fugitive Slaves and Spaces of Freedom in North America*. Edited by DAMIAN ALAN PARGAS. University Press of Florida, 2018. https://doi.org/10.2307/j.ctvx06x80.

8. King, G. (2013, November 15). Where the Buffalo no longer roamed. *Smithsonian Magazine*. https://www.smithsonianmag.com/history/where-the-buffalo-no-longer-roamed-3067904/

9. *Buffalo Hunting*. (n.d.). https://thewest.harpweek.com/Sections/Buffalo/BuffaloHunting1002.htm

10. All About Bison. (2024, January 4). *History of legislation -*. https://allaboutbison.com/history-of-legislation/

11. King, G. (2013b, November 15). Where the Buffalo no longer roamed. *Smithsonian Magazine*. https://www.smithsonianmag.com/history/where-the-buffalo-no-longer-roamed-3067904/

12. King, G. (2013c, November 15). Where the Buffalo no longer roamed. *Smithsonian Magazine*. https://www.smithsonianmag.com/history/where-the-buffalo-no-longer-roamed-3067904/

13. Flatcreekindev. (2017, December 30). *The Bison: from 30 million to 325 (1884) to 500,000 (today)*. Flat Creek Inn. https://www.flatcreekinn.com/bison-americas-mammal/

14. "Kill the Indian in him, and save the man": R. H. Pratt on the Education of Native Americans | Carlisle Indian School Digital Resource Center. (n.d.). https://carlisleindian.dickinson.edu/teach/kill-indian-him-and-save-man-r-h-pratt-education-native-americans

15. *US Indian Boarding School History*. (n.d.). The National Native American Boarding School Healing Coalition. https://boardingschoolhealing.org/education/us-indian-boarding-school-history/

16. Native American Lands | Ownership and Governance | Natural Resources Revenue Data | Natural Resources Revenue Data. (n.d.). https://archive.revenuedata.doi.gov/how-it-works/native-american-ownership-governance/

17. https://www.ncsl.org/quad-caucus/an-issue-of-sovereignty

18. *Milestones: 1830–1860 - Office of the Historian*. (n.d.). https://history.state.gov/milestones/1830-1860/indian-treaties

19. Apple Podcasts. (2023, December 8). *Texas Hold 'Em Abortion Access*. https://podcasts.apple.com/us/podcast/texas-hold-em-abortion%20access/id1464094232?i=1000637986759

20. *Opioid crisis | HRSA*. (2023, December 1). https://www.hrsa.gov/opioids

21. BBC News. (2017, October 26). Trump: Opioid "national shame" a public health emergency. *BBC News*. https://www.bbc.co.uk/news/world-us-canada-41756705

22. Radcliffe, K. R. a. M. (2023, August 16). Over 100 Anti-LGBTQ+ laws passed in the last five years — half of them this year. *FiveThirtyEight*. https://fivethirtyeight.com/features/anti-lgbtq-laws-red-states/

23. Apple Podcasts. (2024b, March 5). *The John Fugelsang podcast on Apple Podcasts*. https://podcasts.apple.com/us/podcast/the-john-fugelsang-podcast/id1464094232

24. Indigenous children for sale: The money behind the Sixties Scoop. (2016, September 29). *CBC*. https://www.cbc.ca/news/canada/manitoba/sixties-scoop-americans-paid-thousands-indigenous-children-1.3781622

25. Claiborne, R. E. (2023, December 19). Indian Child Welfare Act Supreme Court case. *Deseret News*. https://www.deseret.com/2022/12/2/23465296/indian-child-welfare-act-supre me-court-case

26. Zaretsky, S., & Zaretsky, S. (2015, January 7). The Biglaw firms with the highest partner billing rates (2015). *Above the Law*. https://abovethelaw.com/2015/01/the-biglaw-firms-with-the -highest-partner-billing-rates-2015/2/

27. Barnes, R. (2023, May 20). A priceless win at the Supreme Court? No, it has a price. *Washington Post*. https://www.washingtonpost.com/politics/a-priceless-win-at-the-supreme-cou rt-no-it-has-a-price/2011/07/25/gIQAvOsPZI_story.html

28. Gibson, Dunn & Crutcher LLP. (2024, March 6). *Oil and Gas - Practices - Gibson Dunn*. Gibson Dunn. https://www.gibsondunn.com/practice/oil-and-gas/

29. *Law.com*. (n.d.). https://www.law.com/law-firm-profile/?id=119&name=Gibson-Dunn-C rutcher

30. BBC News. (2020, July 7). Dakota Access Pipeline: Judge suspends use of key oil link. https://www.bbc.co.uk/news/world-us-canada-53317852

31. file:///C:/Users/lease/Downloads/Up-in-smoke.pdf

32. Smith, H. (2023, July 28). California wildfires offset greenhouse gas reductions - Los Angeles Times. *Los Angeles Times*. https://www.latimes.com/california/story/2022-10-20/california -wildfires-offset-greenhouse-gas-reductions

33. Mexican-American War: Causes & Treaty of Guadalupe Hidalgo, HISTORY. (2022, August 10). Mexican-American War: Causes & Treaty of Guadalupe Hidalgo | HISTORY. HISTO- RY. https://www.history.com/topics/19th-century/mexican-american-war

34. Blakemore, E., & Blakemore, E. (2023, July 11). *California's Little-Known Genocide*. HIS- TORY. https://www.history.com/news/californias-little-known-genocide

35. https://www.history.com/news/californias-little-known-genocide

36. Mann, C. C., & Yüyan, K. (2020, December 17). 'There's good fire and bad fire.' An Indige- nous practice may be key to preventing wildfires. *History*. https://www.nationalgeographic .com/history/article/good-fire-bad-fire-indigenous-practice-may-key-preventing-wildfires

37. Apple Podcasts. (2024b, March 4). *Biden announces U.S. aid for desperate Palestini- ans*. https://podcasts.apple.com/us/podcast/biden-announces-u-s-aid-for-desperate-palesti nians/id1464094232?i=1000648012096

38. I'm not the first person to use this phrase. Kevin Levin, the historian, used it in a slightly different connotation back in 2008 to describe 'Lost Cause' apologists.

39. Frederick Douglass: Narrative of the life of Frederick Douglass: An American Slave

40. Kell, G. (2021, January 6). Damn the Curse of Ham: How Genesis 9 Got Twisted into Racist Propaganda. *The Gospel Coalition*. https://www.thegospelcoalition.org/article/damn-curse -ham/

41. Assembly, G. (2021, August 17). *"Negro womens children to serve according to the condition of the mother" (1662) - Encyclopedia Virginia*. Encyclopedia Virginia. https://encyclopediavirginia.org/entries/negro-womens-children-to-serve-according-t o-the-condition-of-the-mother-1662/

42. *Transcription Source:* William Waller Hening, ed., *The Statutes at Large; Being a Collection of All the Laws of Virginia from the First Session of the Legislature, in the Year 1619* (New York: R. & W. & G. Bartow, 1823), 2:170.

43. Dodds, I. (2023, December 28). Trump shares word cloud predicting 'revenge' and 'dictatorship' for second term. *The Independent*. https://www.independent.co.uk/news/world/ame ricas/us-politics/trump-word-cloud-dictatorship-b2470392.html

44. Frederick Douglass: Narrative of the life of Frederick Douglass: An American Slave

45. Read more at https://www.brainyquote.com/authors/walter-cronkite-quotes

46. Freedom's Dominion A Saga of White Resistance to Federal Power: Jefferson Cowie: Hardback (08 Dec 2022): ISBN: 9781541672802

47. *South Carolina Declaration of Secession (1860) | Constitution Center*. (n.d.). National Constitution Center – constitutioncenter.org. https://constitutioncenter.org/the-constitution/hi storic-document-library/detail/south-carolina-declaration-of-secession-1860

48. https://www.tsl.texas.gov/ref/abouttx/secession/2feb1861.html

49. *A declaration of the immediate causes which induce and justify the secession of the state of Mississippi from the Federal Union -.* (n.d.) . https://www.mshistorynow.mdah.ms.gov/issue/a-declaration-of-the-immediate-causes-w hich-induce-and-justify-the-secession-of-the-state-of-mississippi-from-the-federal-union

50. *Cornerstone Speech*. (n.d.). American Battlefield Trust. https://www.battlefields.org/learn/p rimary-sources/cornerstone-speech

51. Moreno, P. (2010). Unions and discrimination. In *Cato Journal* (Vols. 30–30, Issue 1). http s://www.cato.org/sites/cato.org/files/serials/files/cato-journal/2010/1/cj30n1-4.pdf

52. Hparkins. (2020, December 2). *Lincoln to Slaves: Go somewhere else*. Pieces of History. https://prologue.blogs.archives.gov/2010/12/01/lincoln-to-slaves-go-somewhere-else/

53. *Fourth debate: Charleston, Illinois - Lincoln Home National Historic Site (U.S. National Park Service)*. (n.d.). https://www.nps.gov/liho/learn/historyculture/debate4.htm

54. TeachingAmericanHistory.org. (2022, October 11). *Address at Cooper Union | Teaching American History*. Teaching American History. https://teachingamericanhistory.org/document/address-at-cooper-institute/

55. Statista. (2024, February 2). *Child mortality in the United States 1800-2020*. https://www.statista.com/statistics/1041693/united-states-all-time-child-mortality-rate/

56. Frederick Douglass: Narrative of the life of Frederick Douglass: An American Slave

57. *Teachinghistory.org*. (n.d.). https://teachinghistory.org/history-content/ask-a-historian/24242

58. TeachingAmericanHistory.org. (2023, May 31). *An oration in memory of Abraham Lincoln | Teaching American History*. Teaching American History. https://teachingamericanhistory.org/document/oration-in-memory-of-abraham-lincoln/

59. South to America: A Journey Below the Mason-Dixon to Understand the Soul of a Nation

60. Ross, A. (2018, April 23). How American racism influenced Hitler. *The New Yorker*. https://www.newyorker.com/magazine/2018/04/30/how-american-racism-influenced-hitler

61. Whitman, J. (2017, March 21). Why the Nazis Loved America. *TIME*. https://time.com/4703586/nazis-america-race-law/

62. Katznelson, I. (2022, May 25). What America taught the Nazis in the 1930s. *The Atlantic*. https://www.theatlantic.com/magazine/archive/2017/11/what-america-taught-the-nazis/540630/

63. *Lynching of Rubin Stacy · Textbook*. (n.d.). http://historymaking.org/textbook/items/show/263

64. Le dîner du comte de Boulainvilliers (1767): Troisième Entretien

65. *Matthew 25 (NIV)*. (n.d.). https://www.biblegateway.com/passage/?search=Matthew%2025&version=NIV;KJV

66. Reilly, K. (2016, September 10). Read Hillary Clinton's 'Basket of Deplorables' remarks about Donald Trump supporters. *TIME*. https://time.com/4486502/hillary-clinton-basket-of-deplorables-transcript/

67. "Horwitz, Tony: SPYING ON THE SOUTH." Penguin Books. 2019

68. Administrador. (2024, September 18). A Profile of Trump Voters: The Demographics of his MAGA Enthusiasts and Their Relationship to Him - OPEU. OPEU. https://www.opeu.org.br/2024/09/18/a-profile-of-trump-voters-the-demographics-of-his-maga-enthusiasts/

69. Potts, M., & Fuong, H. (2023, September 26). The biggest differences between Republican primary voters and the general electorate. ABC News. https://abcnews.go.com/538/biggest-differences-republican-primary-voters-general-electorate/story?id=103416674

70. Doran, W. (n.d.). *Donald Trump set the record for the most GOP primary votes ever. But there's another record he didn't mention.* @Politifact. https://www.politifact.com/factchecks/2016/jul/08/donald-trump/donald-trump-set-record-most-gop-primary-votes-eve/

71. Durkee, A. (2024, March 23). Trump lawyers paid nearly $50 million from political PAC since first indictment. *Forbes.* https://www.forbes.com/sites/alisondurkee/2024/03/21/trump-lawyers-paid-nearly-50-million-from-political-pac-since-first-indictment/

72. Noor, P. (2019, November 27). Trump posted a picture of himself as Rocky. No one knows what to make of it. *The Guardian.* https://www.theguardian.com/us-news/2019/nov/27/donald-trump-rocky-picture-twitter

73. https://twitter.com/WalshFreedom/status/1610647539887357959

74. Longwell, S. (2023, January 31). *Exclusive Bulwark Poll: Most Republicans Want to Move on from Trump.* The Bulwark. https://www.thebulwark.com/exclusive-bulwark-poll-most-republicans-want-to-move-on-from-trump/

75. Beast, D. (2023, July 24). *This is the only way Trump will lose his base's support.* Apple Podcasts. https://podcasts.apple.com/us/podcast/this-is-the-only-way-trump-will-lose-his-bases-support/id1508202790?i=1000622232602

76. https://www.amazon.com/FSFLAG-Double-Stitched-Polyester-Grommets/dp/B088T5YWWP

77. Beast, D. (2024, January 18). *Listen closely: Trump wants to be a 'Messiah' figure for evangelicals.* Apple Podcasts. https://podcasts.apple.com/us/podcast/listen-closely-trump-wants-to-be-a-messiah-figure/id1508202790?i=1000642178111

78. Kruger, J., & Dunning, D. (1999). Unskilled and Unaware of it: How Difficulties in Recognizing one's Own Incompetence Lead to Inflated self-assessments. Journal of Personality and Social Psychology, 77(6), 1121–1134. https://doi.org/10.1037//0022-3514.77.6.1121

79. https://www.nytimes.com/2021/04/03/us/politics/trump-donations.html

80. Levin, S. (2024b, August 22). Trump calls his supporters 'basement dwellers', says former press secretary. *The Guardian*. https://www.theguardian.com/us-news/article/2024/aug/2 0/republican-trump-dnc-speakers

81. https://edition.cnn.com/2024/04/10/politics/trump-2017-tax-cuts-rich/index.html

82. Baldwin, J. (1990). The fire next time. Penguin Classics.

83. Noah, T. (2024, March 6). *Bill Ackman's plagiarism hypocrisy is stratospheric*. The New Republic. https://newrepublic.com/article/177951/bill-ackman-plagiarism-twtter-har

84. William A. Gladstone Afro-American Military Collection: Special Field Orders, No. 15, Headquarters, Military Division of the Mississippi, by Major General W. T. Sherman, re "young and able bodied negroes must be encouraged to enlist," mentions bounties paid and locations for settlement of freed Negr. (n.d.). The Library of Congress. https://www.loc.go v/item/mss83434256/

85. Onion, A. (2024, January 24). Reconstruction - Civil War End, Changes & Act of 1867 | HISTORY. *HISTORY*. https://www.history.com/topics/american-civil-war/reconstruction

86. Apple Podcasts. (2024b, February 10). *Weekend interviews: CO Rep. Diana DeGette and historian Jefferson Cowie*. https://podcasts.apple.com/us/podcast/weekend-interviews-co-re p-diana-degette-and-historian/id1464094232?i=1000644883383

87. Wolfe, L. R. (2025, April 10). The Red Scare Roots of Today's Culture Wars | Cold War. Cold War | Events, Entertainment, and Espionage. https://coldwarstudies.com/2025/04/10/the -red-scare-roots-of-todays-culture-wars/

88. https://www.nytimes.com/1957/11/04/archives/battle-for-science-lead-an-analysis-of-differ ences-between-us-and.html

89. Domino Theory: Definition, Cold War & Vietnam War, HISTORY. (2022, November 9). Domino Theory: Definition, Cold War & Vietnam War | HISTORY. HISTORY. https://w ww.history.com/topics/cold-war/domino-theory

90. Better jobs & higher wages. (n.d.). National Civil Rights Museum. https://www.civilrights museum.org/better-jobs-higher-wages

91. Laurent, S. (2023, April 4). MLK Was an Exemplar of a Black Socialist Tradition. Ja- cobin. https://jacobin.com/2023/04/martin-luther-king-jr-mlk-socialism-class-racial-justic e-civil-rights-movement

92. *Dr. Martin Luther King, Jr. on Labor*. (n.d.). AFSCME. https://www.afscme.org/about/hi story/mlk/dr-martin-luther-king-jr-on-labor

93. Cobb, J. (2018, April 4). Even Though He Is Revered Today, MLK Was Widely Disliked by the American Public When He Was Killed. Smithsonian. https://www.smithsonianmag.com/history/why-martin-luther-king-had-75-percent-disapproval-rating-year-he-died-180968664/

94. https://www.mckinsey.com/~/media/McKinsey/Featured%20Insights/Urbanization/US%20cities%20in%20the%20global%20economy/MGI_Urban_America_Full_Report.pdf

95. Bureau, U. C. (2017, October 24). Big and Small America. The United States Census Bureau. https://www.census.gov/library/stories/2017/10/big-and-small-counties.html

96. Muro, M., & Shriya Methkupally. (2024, November 8). Trump again won counties representing a minority share of national GDP, but with notable gains. Brookings. https://www.brookings.edu/articles/trump-again-won-counties-representing-a-minority-share-of-national-gdp-but-with-notable-gains/

97. Bageant, J. (2007). Deer hunting with Jesus: Dispatches from America's class war. Crown

98. Harry S. Truman and civil Rights | Harry S. Truman. (n.d.). https://www.trumanlibrary.gov/education/presidential-inquiries/harry-s-truman-and-civil-rights

99. Brown v. Board of Education (1954). (2024, March 18). National Archives. https://www.archives.gov/milestone-documents/brown-v-board-of-education

100. Corn, David. 2022. *American Psychosis: A Historical Investigation of How the Republican Party Went Crazy.*

101. Corn, David. 2022. *American Psychosis: A Historical Investigation of How the Republican Party Went Crazy.*

Page 65

102. Brenner, M. (2017, June 28). How Donald Trump and Roy Cohn's ruthless symbiosis changed America. Vanity Fair. https://www.vanityfair.com/news/2017/06/donald-trump-roy-cohn-relationship

103. Gopnik, A. (2013, October 11). The John Birchers' Tea Party. *The New Yorker.* https://www.newyorker.com/news/daily-comment/the-john-birchers-tea-party

104. *Hillary Rodham Clinton unveils health care plan.* (n.d.). Commonwealth Fund. https://www.commonwealthfund.org/publications/newsletter-article/hillary-rodham-clinton-unveils-health-care-plan

105. Mayer, J. (2018, September 24). How Russia Helped Swing the Election for Trump. The New Yorker. https://www.newyorker.com/magazine/2018/10/01/how-russia-helped-to-swing-the-election-for-trump

106. Gross, T. (2023, May 17). A historian details how a secretive, extremist group radicalized the American right. NPR. https://www.npr.org/2023/05/17/1176662608/a-historian-details-how-a-secretive-extremist-group-radicalized-the-american-rig

107. Bringing back Birch. (n.d.). Southern Poverty Law Center. https://www.splcenter.org/fighting-hate/intelligence-report/2013/bringing-back-birch

108. Corn, David. 2022. *American Psychosis: A Historical Investigation of How the Republican Party Went Crazy.*

Page 81

109. Baugh, L. S. (2024, February 16). Southern strategy | Definition, The South, History, Republican Party, Democratic Party, & Facts | Britannica. Www.britannica.com. https://www.britannica.com/topic/Southern-strategy

110. Corn, David. 2022. *American Psychosis: A Historical Investigation of How the Republican Party Went Crazy.*

Chapter 8: Ratfucking America

111. https://www.nixonlibrary.gov/sites/default/files/virtuallibrary/documents/haldeman-diaries/37-hrhd-journal-vol02-19690428.pdf

112.
Mirisola, Alberto, et al. "Societal Threat to Safety, Compensatory Control, and Right-Wing Authoritarianism." *Political Psychology*, vol. 35, no. 6, 2014, pp. 795–812. *JSTOR*, http://www.jstor.org/stable/43783822. Accessed 19 Apr. 2024.

113. *Jurisdictions previously covered by Section 5.* (2023, May 17). https://www.justice.gov/crt/jurisdictions-previously-covered-section-5

114. Institution, S. (n.d.). *Button, Ronald Reagan, 1980 | Smithsonian Institution*. Smithsonian Institution. https://www.si.edu/object/button-ronald-reagan-1980%3Anmah_522618

115. Schwarz, J., & Schwarz, J. (2023, July 25). The murder of the U.S. middle class began 40 years ago this week. *The Intercept*. https://theintercept.com/2021/08/06/middle-class-reagan-patco-strike/

116. Elert, G. (n.d.). *Number of Billionaires - The Physics Factbook*. Hypertextbook. https://hype rtextbook.com/facts/2005/MichelleLee.shtml

117. Americans for Tax Reform. (n.d.). DeSmog. https://www.desmog.com/americans-tax-refor m/

118. Gray, D. (2024, October 6). Every Single Movie Donald Trump Was In. Yahoo Entertainment. https://www.yahoo.com/entertainment/every-single-movie-donald-trump-190014936.html

119. Zaru, D. (2018, October 11). Donald Trump's fall from hip-hop grace: From rap icon to public enemy No. 1. ABC News; ABC News. https://abcnews.go.com/Politics/donald-tru mps-fall-hip-hop-grace-rap-icon/story?id=58411276

120. https://www.washingtonpost.com/politics/2016/live-updates/general-election/real-time-fac t-checking-and-analysis-of-the-first-presidential-debate/fact-check-has-trump-declared-bank ruptcy-four-or-six-times/

121. Lopez, G. (2016, December 1). The Reagan administration's unbelievable response to the HIV/AIDS epidemic. *Vox*. https://www.vox.com/2015/12/1/9828348/ronald-reagan-hiv-a ids

122. Message to the Congress transmitting the Pro-Life Act of 1988. (n.d.). Ronald Reagan. http s://www.reaganlibrary.gov/archives/speech/message-congress-transmitting-pro-life-act-1988

123. Office of the Historian. (2019). Monroe Doctrine, 1823. State.gov. https://history.state.gov /milestones/1801-1829/monroe

124. Pai Raikar, S. (2023). Banana republic (politics) | Description, Origin, History, Examples, & Facts | Britannica. Www.britannica.com. https://www.britannica.com/topic/banana-repub lic

125. Karlin, M. (2012, June 10). The School of the Americas, the CIA and the US-Condoned Cancer of Torture Continue to Spread in Latin. Truthout. https://truthout.org/articles/the-school-of-the-americas-the-cia-and-the-us-con doned-cancer-of-torture-continues-to-spread-in-latin-america-including-mexico/

126. *Ronald Reagan Made Central America a Killing Field*. (n.d.). Jacobin.com. https://jacobi n.com/2021/05/greg-grandin-empires-workshop-latin-america

127. Saudi Arabia funds and exports Islamic extremism: The truth behind the tox- ic U.S. relationship with the theocratic monarchy. (2016, January 6). *Sa- lon*. https://www.salon.com/2016/01/06/saudi_arabia_funds_and_exports_islamic_extre mism_the_truth_behind_the_toxic_u_s_relationship_with_the_theocratic_nation/

128. The Heritage Foundation. (2023). Project 2025 PRESIDENTIAL TRANSITION PRO-JECT. https://static.heritage.org/project2025/2025_MandateForLeadership_FULL.pdf

129. *Pat Buchanan for President 1996 Campaign brochure.* (n.d.). http://www.4president.org/brochures/1996/patbuchanan1996brochure.htm

130. *The Overton Window: How Politics Change | Definition and Examples — Conceptually.* (n.d.). Conceptually. https://conceptually.org/concepts/overton-window

131.

132. Richter, P. (2019, March 5). NEWS ANALYSIS : Some Republicans showing sympathy for militias' views - Los Angeles Times. *Los Angeles Times.* https://www.latimes.com/archives/la-xpm-1995-05-15-mn-886-story.html

133. Gray, R. (2021, June 9). Trump Defends White-Nationalist Protesters: 'Some Very Fine People on Both Sides' The Atlantic. https://www.theatlantic.com/politics/archive/2017/08/trump-defends-white-nationalist-protesters-some-very-fine-people-on-both-sides/537012/

134. Shesol, J. (2020, July 17). How Newt Gingrich made nastiness a virtue. *Washington Post.* https://www.washingtonpost.com/outlook/how-newt-gingrich-made-nastiness-a-virtue/2020/07/16/1cba30c8-8a28-11ea-9dfd-990f9dcc71fc_story.html

135. https://www.nytimes.com/2007/03/09/us/politics/09brfs-GINGRICHSAYS_BRF.html

136. *Disrupting the ballot count 2000/2020.* (n.d.). THE VOLUNTOWN PEACE TRUST. https://www.voluntownpeacetrust.org/a-peace-of-history-blog/disrupting-the-ballot-count-20002020

137. Chulov, M. (2018, August 7). My son, Osama: the al-Qaida leader's mother speaks for the first time. The Guardian; The Guardian. https://www.theguardian.com/world/2018/aug/03/osama-bin-laden-mother-speaks-out-family-interview

138. The Editors of Encyclopaedia Britannica. (2019). United States Presidential Election of 2008 | United States government. In Encyclopædia Britannica. https://www.britannica.com/event/United-States-presidential-election-of-2008

139. Pengelly, M. (2023, February 9). Mitt Romney to mull Republicans' "slide toward authoritarianism" in biography. The Guardian; The Guardian. https://www.theguardian.com/books/2023/feb/09/mitt-romney-book-republicans-authoritarian-biography

140. *Romney: "No one's ever asked to see my birth certificate."* (2012, August 24). NBC News. https://www.nbcnews.com/news/world/romney-no-ones-ever-asked-see-my-birth-certificate-flna963300

141. Guignion, D. (2022, January 16). "Birtherism," Trump and anti-Black racism: Conspiracy theorists twist evidence to maintain status quo. The Conversation. https://theconversation.com/birtherism-trump-and-anti-black-racism-conspiracy-the orists-twist-evidence-to-maintain-status-quo-174444

142. Today, K. W. U. (2020, September 19). Then and now: What McConnell, others said about Merrick Garland in 2016 vs. after Ginsburg's death. USA TODAY. https://eu.usatoday.com/story/news/politics/2020/09/19/what-mcconnell-said-mer rick-garland-vs-after-ginsburgs-death/5837543002/

143. Jacobs, B. (2015, June 26). "Love is love": Obama lauds gay marriage activists in hailing "a victory for America." The Guardian. https://www.theguardian.com/us-news/2015/jun/2 6/obama-gay-marriage-speech-victory-for-america

144. Collina, T. (2024, May 7). Killing the Iran nuclear deal was one of Trump's biggest failures | Responsible Statecraft. Responsiblestatecraft.org. https://responsiblestatecraft.org/iran-nu clear-deal/

145. *Health coverage under the Affordable Care Act: Current enrollment trends and state estimates.* (2023, March 23). ASPE. https://aspe.hhs.gov/reports/current-health-coverage-under-affor dable-care-act

146. H.L. Mencken. Baltimore Sun 26 July 1920.

147. How might Trump "drain the swamp"?. (2016, October 18). BBC News. https://www.bb c.co.uk/news/election-us-2016-37699073

148. Jalonick, M., Tucker, E., Amiri, F., Colvin, J., Balsamo, M., & Merchant, N. (2022, December 23). Trump "lit that fire" of Capitol insurrection, Jan 6 Committee report says. PBS NewsHour. https://www.pbs.org/newshour/politics/trump-lit-that-fire-of-capitol-insurrection -jan-6-committee-report-says

149. Tannehill, B. (2024, March 6). *The polls prove it: many Republicans love fascism.* The New Republic. https://newrepublic.com/article/177796/polls-republicans-trump-maga-fascism

150. Cesca, B. (2024, January 17). *Rachel Bitecofer Day.* Apple Podcasts. https://podcasts.apple. com/us/podcast/rachel-bitecofer-day/id380996798?i=1000642020697

151. Dorn, S. (2023, December 18). Trump doubles down on Anti-Immigrant 'Blood' Slur—Despite widespread criticism he's quoting Hitler. *Forbes.* https://www.forbes.com/sites/saradorn/2023/12/17/trump-doubles-down-on-ant i-immigrant-blood-slur-despite-widespread-criticism-hes-quoting-hilter/?sh=70102e8878b7

152. Sainato, M. (2024, May 22). Donald Trump removes video on Truth Social with 'unified reich' reference. *The Guardian*. https://www.theguardian.com/us-news/article/2024/may/21/donald-trump-video-unified-reich

153. William F. Buckley, Father Of American Conservatism. (n.d.). NPR.org. https://www.npr.org/2011/12/17/143665421/how-william-f-buckley-fathered-american-conservatism

154. Gross, T. (2023) A historian details how a secretive, extremist group radicalized the American right, NPR. Available at: https://www.npr.org/2023/05/17/1176662608/a-historian-details-how-a-secretive-extremist-group-radicalized-the-american-rig (Accessed: 29 May 2025).

155. Goldberg, M. (2024, September 17). The Hays Code: A History of Hollywood's Self-Censorship + Its Influence on Film. Backstage.com. https://www.backstage.com/magazine/article/hays-code-rules-history-77748/

156. Hunt, K. (2018, July 27). Hollywood Codebreakers: 'Rebel Without a Cause' speaks to teens. Medium. https://medium.com/@kristinhunt/hollywood-codebreakers-rebel-without-a-cause-speaks-to-teens-782355b15ea5

157. Leal, S. R., PhD. (2022, August 1). Elvis Presley: social activist - Sheldon Rocha Leal, PhD - medium. Medium. https://medium.com/@shelrochaleal/elvis-presley-social-activist-f804d430375f

158. https://americansongwriter.com/remember-when-elvis-was-censored-from-the-waist-down-on-the-ed-sullivan-show/

159. PBS NewsHour. (2016, February 16). Column: This is what happens when you take Ayn Rand seriously. PBS NewsHour. https://www.pbs.org/newshour/economy/column-this-is-what-happens-when-you-take-ayn-rand-seriously

160. *"Understanding Trump" by George Lakoff, author of "Moral Politics: How Liberals and Conservatives Think, Third Edition."* (n.d.). University of Chicago Press. https://press.uchicago.edu/books/excerpt/2016/lakoff_trump.html

161. https://www.archives.gov/publications/prologue/2006/spring/vips-military.html

162. Elhassan, K. (2022, September 22). *These World War II Heroines Should be Household Names.* History Collection. https://historycollection.com/these-world-war-ii-heroines-should-be-household-names/14/

163. Kisken, T. (2024, April 12). WWII veteran talks about flat feet, unlearned lessons and turning 104. Ventura County Star. https://eu.vcstar.com/story/news/local/2024/04/12/world-war-ii-vet-thought-flat-feet-might-keep-him-out-of-the-war/73224245007/

164. Can You Go To The Military If You Have Flat Feet? (2016). Bilt Labs. https://biltlabs.com/blogs/blog/can-you-go-to-the-military-if-you-have-flat-feet?srslt id=AfmBOoqPIcnhSXaWg-tPfo6y5oIdyNbSWX3hyKHGTPnk_Tv5Z4oU4p-U

165. Burchell, S., & Taggart, F. (2016, September 1). Look inside John Wayne's house in California. *Architectural Digest*. https://www.architecturaldigest.com/story/john-wayne-california-ho use

166. https://www.thewrap.com/wp-content/uploads/2020/06/John_Wayne_Playboy_Int2.pdf

167. Anderson, C., Chief & The National WWII Museum. (2021). THE TUSKEGEE AIRMEN: The African American Pilots of WWII. In The National WWII Museum. The National WWII Museum. https://www.nationalww2museum.org/sites/default/files/2017-07/tuske gee-airmen.pdf

168. *African American or Black people | National Air and Space Museum*. (n.d.). https://airands pace.si.edu/explore-and-learn/topics/blackwings/tuskegee.cfm

169. VIPs in uniform | National Archives. (n.d.). https://www.archives.gov/publications/prolog ue/2006/spring/vips-military.html

170. https://foreignpolicy.com/2020/09/08/trump-mocked-us-military-troops-losers-whole-life /

171. Goldberg, J. (2020, September 3). Trump: Americans who died in war are 'Losers' and 'Suckers.' The Atlantic. https://www.theatlantic.com/politics/archive/2020/09/trump-am ericans-who-died-at-war-are-losers-and-suckers/615997/

172. Britzky, H. (2022, August 8). Trump reportedly didn't want wounded warriors in his military parade because it wouldn't 'look good.' *Task & Purpose*. https://taskandpurpose.com/news /trump-military-parade-wounded-veterans/

173. *Wounded Warrior receives Top Military Police Award*. (2023, September 26). AUSA. https ://www.ausa.org/news/wounded-warrior-receives-top-military-police-award

174. Howard, A., & Howard, A. (2017, January 30). Question and Answer with Captain Avila - Hardwood Floors Magazine. *Hardwood Floors Magazine - The magazine of the National Wood Flooring Assocation*. https://hardwoodfloorsmag.com/2017/01/30/question-answer -captain-avila/

175. Trump lost it over wounded soldier: report. (2023, September 21). Sa-lon. https://www.salon.com/2023/09/21/us-general-says-was-angered-by-invite-to-wound ed-soldier-nobody-wants-to-see-that/

176. LaChance, N. (2024, August 31). 'Suckers,' 'Losers,' jokes about medals: Trump doesn't understand the military. Rolling Stone. https://www.rollingstone.com/politics/politics-news/trump-does-not-understand-military-arlington-1235093220/

177. Yang, M. (2024, October 25). 'Fascist', 'conman', 'predator', 'cheat': what 11 former Trump staffers say about him now. The Guardian. https://www.theguardian.com/us-news/2024/oct/25/election-trump-staffers-john-kelly

178. Luce, E. (2019, June 5). James Ellroy on time warps, his new novel and Trump. *Australian Financial Review*. https://www.afr.com/life-and-luxury/arts-and-culture/james-ellroy-on-time-warps-his-new-novel-and-trump-20190604-p51u8a

179. Serwer, A. (2021). The cruelty is the point: the past, present, and future of Trump's America. First edition. New York, One World.

180. Ismail, A. (2022, January 4). A year later, we know exactly who the Capitol rioters were. The answer is not comforting. *Slate Magazine*. https://slate.com/news-and-politics/2022/01/january-6-capitol-riot-arrests-research-profile.html

181. *Opinion | Why the true identities of Trump's Capitol-attacking uber fans matter.* (2022, January 6). NBC News. https://www.nbcnews.com/think/opinion/january-6-busts-key-myth-about-trump-supporters-rioters-ncna1287105

182. Ismail, A. (2022, January 4). A year later, we know exactly who the Capitol rioters were. The answer is not comforting. *Slate Magazine*. https://slate.com/news-and-politics/2022/01/january-6-capitol-riot-arrests-research-profile.html

183. Coates, R. (2024, March 15). What is the "great replacement theory"? A scholar of race relations explains. The Conversation. https://theconversation.com/what-is-the-great-replacement-theory-a-scholar-of-race-relations-explains-224835

184. https://www.theguardian.com/us-news/2022/mar/05/putin-ukraine-invasion-white-nationalists-far-right

185. Mathers, M. (2024, April 17). Russian soldier death toll hits 50,000 in Putin's 'meat grinder' war with Ukraine. The Independent. https://www.independent.co.uk/news/world/europe/russian-soldiers-death-toll-50-000-ukraine-b2530037.html

186. FitzGerald, B. J. (2024, February 11). Trump says he would "encourage" Russia to attack Nato allies who do not pay their bills. *BBC News*. https://www.bbc.co.uk/news/world-us-canada-68266447

187. https://edition.cnn.com/videos/politics/2024/04/07/michael-mccaul-russian-propaganda-infected-gop-base-mike-turner-sotu-vpx.cnn

188. Vargas, R. A. (2024, April 9). House intelligence chair says Republicans are 'absolutely' repeating Russian propaganda. *The Guardian*. https://www.theguardian.com/us-news/20 24/apr/08/republican-mike-turner-russia-propaganda

189. Corbett, H. (2022, October 27). #MeToo Five Years Later: How The Movement Started And What Needs To Change. Forbes. https://www.forbes.com/sites/hollycorbett/2022/10/27/ metoo-five-years-later-how-the-movement-started-and-what-needs-to-change/

190. Dougherty, H. (2024, November 2). Listen To The Jeffrey Epstein Tapes: "I Was Donald Trump's Closest Friend." The Daily Beast. https://www.thedailybeast.com/listen-to-the-jef frey-epstein-tapes-i-was-donald-trumps-closest-friend/

191. *The West Coast think tank helping to orchestrate DeSantis's war on the woke | The Nation*. (2023, March 29). The Nation. https://www.thenation.com/article/politics/the-west-coast-think -tank-helping-to-orchestrate-desantis-war-on-the-woke/

192. Piper, J. (2024, February 8). *It's my state too, stand with me*. Apple Podcasts. https://podcas ts.apple.com/gb/podcast/its-my-state-too-stand-with-me/id1697256408?i=1000644619530

193. Today, R. W. M. U. (2018, March 14). "You can't buy class": A candid photo of Joe Biden and a homeless man is breaking hearts. USA TODAY. https://eu.usatoday.com/story/news/poli tics/onpolitics/2018/03/13/joe-biden-homeless-man/422097002/

194. Griffing, A. (2024, February 2). Trump Campaign Adviser Eviscerates "Fraud" Candace Owens and Charlie Kirk: Trying to Establish ... Medi-aite. https://www.mediaite.com/media/podcasts/trump-campaign-adviser-eviscerates-frau d-candace-owens-and-charlie-kirk-trying-to-establish-the-superiority-of-whites-over-blacks/

195. Hurst, E. (2023, June 12). Charlie Kirk tells fan who wants to be surgeon to consider getting pregnant and making sammiches. *Wonkette*. https://www.wonkette.com/p/charlie-kirk-tell s-fan-who-wants-to-be-surgeon-to-consider-getting-pregnant-and-making-sammiches

196. SLODYSKO, B. (2023, October 10). How Trump's MAGA movement helped activist become a millionaire. Los Angeles Times. https://www.latimes.com/world-nation/story/202 3-10-10/how-trumps-maga-movement-helped-a-29-year-old-activist-become-a-millionaire

197. Treisman, R. (2024, July 29). JD Vance went viral for "cat lady" comments. The centuries-old trope has a long tail. NPR. https://www.npr.org/2024/07/29/nx-s1-5055616/jd-vance-chi ldless-cat-lady-history

198. Adam, J. (2023, March 21). When could women open a bank account? Forbes Advisor. https://www.forbes.com/advisor/banking/when-could-women-open-a-bank-account/

199. National Domestic Violence Hotline. (n.d.). Marital Rape and Domestic Violence. The Hotline. https://www.thehotline.org/resources/marital-rape-and-domestic-violence/

200. Houghtaling, E. Q. (2024, March 7). *Trump's Christian nationalist friends have a horrifying plan for a second term*. The New Republic. https://newrepublic.com/post/179150/christia n-nationalist-second-trump-term-plans

201. https://www.youtube.com/watch?v=PWHuhI6EDdU

202. https://www.youtube.com/watch?v=n8vfBSSFxfM

203. https://twitter.com/djconn/status/1773588903879950736

204. Blazina, C. (2024, April 14). What the 2020 electorate looks like by party, race and ethnicity, age, education and religion. *Pew Research Center*. https://www.pewresearch.org/short-reads/2020/10/26/what-the-2020-electorate-look s-like-by-party-race-and-ethnicity-age-education-and-religion/

205. Potts, M., & Fuong, H. (2023, September 26). *The biggest differences between Republican primary voters and the general electorate*. ABC News. https://abcnews.go.com/538/bigges t-differences-republican-primary-voters-general-electorate/story?id=103416674

206. Corey, B. L. (2019, August 18). No, The Bible Doesn't Say The Earth Is Only 6,000 Years Old. Benjamin L. Corey. https://www.benjaminlcorey.com/no-bible-doesnt-say-earth-6000-year s-old/

207. *Rapture Doctrine invented by John Darby in 1830 AD*. (2024). Bible.ca. https://www.bible. ca/rapture-origin-john-nelson-darby-1830ad.htm

208. Randall Balmer. (2014, May 27). The Real Origins of the Religious Right. POLITICO Magazine. https://www.politico.com/magazine/story/2014/05/religious-right-real-origins-1071 33/

209. Filipovic, J. (2017, August 8). The GOP assault on women's health began with the 1976 Hyde amendment. *The Guardian*. https://www.theguardian.com/commentisfree/2013/oct/03/ hyde-amendment-abortion-gop-women

210. Frank, G., & Young, N. J. (2022, May 16). What everyone gets wrong about evangelicals and abortion. *Washington Post*. https://www.washingtonpost.com/outlook/2022/05/16/what -everyone-gets-wrong-about-evangelicals-abortion/

211. Tribune, C. (2021, August 9). CARTER OFFERS a RED-HOT TRAVELING TIP TO FALWELL. *Chicago Tribune*. https://www.chicagotribune.com/news/ct-xpm-1986-09-13 -8603080412-story.html

212. Karem, B. (2023, August 30). John Fugelsang - If you're a true Christian, how can you vote for Donald Trump's "Revenge" tour? *JATQ Podcast*. https://www.justaskthequestion.com/post/john-fugelsang-if-you-re-a-true-christian-how-can-you-vote-for-donald-trump-s-revenge-tour

213. TeachingAmericanHistory.org. (2022a, July 7). *James Madison's Memorial and Remonstrance | Teaching American History*. Teaching American History. https://teachingamericanhistory.org/document/memorial-and-remonstrance/

214. Free Speech Center. (2024, February 19). *1797 Treaty of Tripoli - The Free Speech Center*. The Free Speech Center. https://firstamendment.mtsu.edu/article/1797-treaty-of-tripoli/

215. *Churches, integrated auxiliaries, and conventions or associations of churches | Internal Revenue Service*. (n.d.). https://www.irs.gov/charities-non-profits/churches-integrated-auxiliaries-and-conventions-or-associations-of-churches

216. *Romans 13:6-7 (NIV)*. (n.d.). Bible Gateway. https://www.biblegateway.com/passage/?search=Romans%2013%3A6-7&version=NIV

217. Garcia-Navarro, L., Boyd, S. A., Arthur, D., Bacon, A., Pitkin, K., Sabouraud, C., Jones, I., Herrero, S., & McCusker, P. (2023, March 2). Opinion | Why the G.O.P.'s attack on trans rights could backfire on the party. *The New York Times*. https://www.nytimes.com/2023/03/02/opinion/trans-gender-attacks-republican-party.html

218. Culpepper, P. (2020, February 7). *The secret network that threatens democracy - Washington Daily News*. Washington Daily News. https://www.thewashingtondailynews.com/2020/02/07/the-secret-network-that-threatens-democracy/

219. *Williams County, Ohio, elections, 2023 - Ballotpedia*. (n.d.). Ballotpedia. https://ballotpedia.org/Williams_County,_Ohio,_elections,_2023

220. Kim, J. (2024, January 23). An Ohio church is suing a city over not being allowed to house homeless people. *NPR*. https://www.npr.org/2024/01/23/1226214707/an-ohio-church-is-suing-a-city-over-not-being-allowed-to-house-homeless-people

221. *Matthew 25 (NIV)*. (n.d.-b). https://www.biblegateway.com/passage/?search=Matthew%2025&version=NIV;KJV

222. Npr. (2023, August 4). Former Baptist leader sees a crisis of faith in America — but also a way forward. *NPR*. https://www.npr.org/transcripts/1192227439?ft=nprml&f=1192227439

223. Guy, C. C. (2022, June 22). *Bringing more engagement to the fight against Christian nationalism*. BJC. https://bjconline.org/bringing-more-engagement-to-the-fight-against-christian-nationalism/

224. Fields, G., Mascaro, L., & Amiri, F. (2024, May 23). *Appeal to Heaven flag: History, symbolism and controversy | AP News*. AP News. https://apnews.com/article/alito-supreme-court-flags-history-symbol-protest-a5415aeba90e21a86a50f8489fc54b7a

225. https://www.science.org/content/article/fighting-back-against-alternative-facts-experts-share-their-secrets

226. https://stock.adobe.com/uk/search?k=jesus+sitting&asset_id=619800010

227. *Opinion | How Trump became Iowa evangelicals' chosen one*. (2024, January 16). MSNBC.com. https://www.msnbc.com/opinion/msnbc-opinion/trump-iowa-caucus-win-evangelical-vote-rcna134001

228. Yang, M., & Walters, J. (2021, November 20). Kyle Rittenhouse found not guilty after fatally shooting two in Kenosha unrest. *The Guardian*. https://www.theguardian.com/us-news/2021/nov/19/kyle-rittenhouse-verdict-kenosha-shooting

229. Zurcher, N. I. &. A. (2021, November 19). Kyle Rittenhouse case: Why it so divides the US. BBC News. https://www.bbc.co.uk/news/world-us-canada-59348734

230. McCullough, J. (2024, February 6). Daniel Perry sentenced to 25 years for killing protester. Abbott has pledged pardon. *The Texas Tribune*. https://www.texastribune.org/2023/05/10/daniel-perry-murder-austin-protestor/

231. Levitz, E. (2024, May 17). Why Greg Abbott's pardon of far-right killer Daniel Perry is chilling. *Vox*. https://www.vox.com/politics/2024/5/17/24159084/daniel-perry-pardon-greg-abbott-samuel-alito-flag

232. Kim, J. (2023, May 21). Daniel Penny says he felt no shame after the NYC subway death of Jordan Neely. *NPR*. https://www.npr.org/2023/05/21/1177435414/daniel-penny-interview-nyc-subway-killing-jordan-neely

233. Smith, D. (2024, April 14). 'I am your retribution': Trump rules supreme at CPAC as he relaunches bid for White House. The Guardian. https://www.theguardian.com/us-news/2023/mar/05/i-am-your-retribution-trump-rules-supreme-at-cpac-as-he-relaunches-bid-for-white-house

234. Quoteresearch. (2020, June 25). *Puritanism — the haunting fear that someone, somewhere, may be happy – quote Investigator®*. https://quoteinvestigator.com/2020/06/25/puritanism/

235. Apple Podcasts. (2024a, January 2). *2023 year in review - The God Squad*. https://podcasts.apple.com/us/podcast/2023-year-in-review-the-god-squad/id1464094232?i=1000640372932

236. Chris Casady. (2006, February 22). *Frank Zappa On Crossfire 1986* [Video]. YouTube. http s://www.youtube.com/watch?v=B9856_xv8gc

237. Apple Podcasts. (2024f, February 15). *Multiple choice tragedies*. https://podcasts.apple.com /gb/podcast/multiple-choice-tragedies/id1464094232?i=1000645496259

238. Carter, J. (2024, January 2). 9 things You should know about the Prosperity Gospel. *The Gospel Coalition*. https://www.thegospelcoalition.org/article/9-things-prosperity-gospel/

239. Brumley, J. (2023, October 11). Belief in prosperity gospel growing among American Protestants – Baptist News Global. Baptist News Global. https://baptistnews.com/article/belief-i n-prosperity-gospel-growing-among-american-protestants/

240. Pecan Acres, TX | Data USA. (n.d.). Data USA. https://datausa.io/profile/geo/pecan-acres -tx/

241. https://www.houstonchronicle.com/news/investigations/unfair-burden/article/kenneth-co peland-wealth-pastor-tax-free-mansion-16662283.php

242. Brice-Saddler, M. (2019, June 6). A wealthy televangelist explains his fleet of private jets: 'It's a biblical thing.' *Washington Post*. https://www.washingtonpost.com/religion/2019/06/04 /wealthy-televangelist-explains-his-fleet-private-jets-its-biblical-thing/

243. Today, W. C. U. (2018, May 30). Televangelist says God told him he needs 4th private plane. *USA TODAY*. https://eu.usatoday.com/story/news/nation-now/2018/05/29/televangelist -wants-new-jet/653202002/

244. https://money.cnn.com/2017/02/06/news/economy/donald-trump-beattyville-kentucky/in dex.html

245. Fernandes, J. (2018, January 29). Why People Love "Assistance to the Poor" But Hate "Welfare." Talk Poverty. https://talkpoverty.org/2018/01/29/people-love-assistance-poor-h ate-welfare/index.html

246. Sella, O. V. (2022, January 17). The Story of American Televangelism. The Science Survey. https://thesciencesurvey.com/features/2022/01/17/the-story-of-american-televangelism/

247. Resources, L. C. (2023, May 9). As baptisms and giving increase, Southern Baptists continue slide in members - The Baptist Paper. The Baptist Paper. https://thebaptistpaper.org/as-ba ptisms-and-giving-increase-southern-baptists-continue-slide-in-members/

248. Pulpit & Pen News. (2020, May 3). SBC's National Day of Prayer Goes All-In on 'NAR's Seven Mountain Mandate' *Pulpit & Pen News*. https://pulpitandpen.org/2020/05/03/sbc s-national-day-of-prayer-goes-all-in-on-nars-seven-mountain-mandate/

249. *Yahoo is part of the Yahoo family of brands.* (n.d.). https://www.yahoo.com/lifestyle/hobby
-lobby-criticism-decorations-encourage-gun-violence-181912698.html

250. *1 John 4:20 (NIV).* (n.d.). Bible Gateway. https://www.biblegateway.com/passage/?search=
1%20John%204%3A20&version=NIV

251. Jesus and John Wayne – How White Evangelicals Corrupted a Faith and Fractured a Nation
23 Jun. 2020: by Kristin Kobes Du Mez

252. Saul, H. (2014, March 12). "Come to church, win a gun": Pastor John Ko-
letas organises giveaway at church service | The Independent. *The Indepen-
dent.* https://www.independent.co.uk/news/world/americas/come-to-church-win-a-gun-p
astor-john-koletas-organises-giveaway-at-church-service-9186235.html

253. Allen, B. (2014, March 11). *New York church giving away assault rifle – Baptist News Global.*
Baptist News Global. https://baptistnews.com/article/ny-church-giving-away-assault-rifle/

254. Salam, E. (2024, June 18). Megachurch pastor and ex-Trump adviser admits child sexual abuse.
The Guardian. https://www.theguardian.com/us-news/article/2024/jun/17/pastor-robert
-morris-sexual-abuse-trump-adviser

255. Smietana, B. (2024, September 19). SBC to Sell Nashville Headquarters to Cover Cost of
Abuse Cases - Christianity Today. Christianity Today. https://www.christianitytoday.com/
2024/09/southern-baptist-sbc-nashville-building-headquarters-sale-abuse-legal-cost/

256. Helmore, E. (2024, March 7). Liberty University fined $14m over 'culture of silence' around
sexual assault. *The Guardian.* https://www.theguardian.com/us-news/2024/mar/06/libert
y-university-fined-sexual-assault

257. Granda, G., & Ebner, M. (2022, October 24). Inside the Jerry Falwell love triangle: Pool Boy
tells all. Rolling Stone. https://www.rollingstone.com/politics/politics-features/pool-boy-je
rry-falwell-love-triangle-1234610995/

258. FitzGerald, F. (2007, May 16). Jerry Falwell's Christian Army. The New Yorker. https://ww
w.newyorker.com/magazine/1981/05/18/a-disciplined-charging-army

259. Times, N. Y. (1985, September 4). JACKSON AND FALWELL ON "NIGHTLINE." *The
New York Times.* https://www.nytimes.com/1985/09/04/arts/jackson-and-falwell-on-nigh
tline.html

260. Curry, M. S. a. L. (2023, December 27). *Doomscroll Rewind: Matt and Lisa on comedians
crying cancel culture.* Apple Podcasts. https://podcasts.apple.com/ca/podcast/doomscroll-re
wind-matt-and-lisa-on-comedians-crying/id1703361874?i=1000639848304

261. Apple Podcasts. (2024i, March 2). *Weekend Interviews: The God Squad + Jonathan Metzl*. https://podcasts.apple.com/us/podcast/weekend-interviews-the-god-squad-jonathan-metzl/id1464094232?i=1000647778366

262. https://thehill.com/homenews/campaign/4753439-heritage-leader-second-american-revolution/

263. Lerner, K. (2023b, June 9). 12m Americans believe violence is justified to restore Trump to power. *The Guardian*. https://www.theguardian.com/us-news/2023/jun/09/january-6-trump-political-violence-survey

264. *Robert Edward Lee - Arlington House, the Robert E. Lee Memorial (U.S. National Park Service)*. (n.d.). https://www.nps.gov/arho/learn/historyculture/robert-lee.htm

265. American History Central. (2024, March 16). *Battle of Cheat Mountain, Summary, Facts, Significance, 1861*. https://www.americanhistorycentral.com/entries/battle-of-cheat-mountain/

266. *Defining battles of the civil war*. (n.d.). https://education.nationalgeographic.org/resource/defining-battles-civil-war/

267. Making sense of Robert E. Lee (2003) Smithsonian.com. Available at: https://www.smithsonianmag.com/history/making-sense-of-robert-e-lee-85017563/ (Accessed: 29 May 2025).

268. Blount, R., Jr. (2013, November 17). Making sense of Robert E. Lee. *Smithsonian Magazine*. https://www.smithsonianmag.com/history/making-sense-of-robert-e-lee-85017563/

269. *Ulysses S. Grant*. (n.d.). American Battlefield Trust. https://www.battlefields.org/learn/biographies/ulysses-s-grant

270. *FACTS - The Civil War (U.S. National Park Service)*. (n.d.). https://www.nps.gov/civilwar/facts.htm

271. *Robert Edward Lee - Arlington House, the Robert E. Lee Memorial (U.S. National Park Service)*. (n.d.). https://www.nps.gov/arho/learn/historyculture/robert-lee.htm

272. Author Says Hitler Was "Blitzed" On Cocaine And Opiates During The War. (2017, March 7). NPR.org. https://www.npr.org/transcripts/518986612

273. *Collections search - United States Holocaust Memorial Museum*. (n.d.). https://collections.ushmm.org/search/catalog/irn504463

274. https://www.nytimes.com/2018/04/10/magazine/rhodesia-zimbabwe-white-supremacists.html

275. Beyer, G. (2024, October 27). What Was the Rhodesian Bush War? TheCollector. https://www.thecollector.com/what-was-rhodesian-bush-war/

276. Bloomberg - Are you a robot? (2023b, October 10). https://www.bloomberg.com/news/articles/2023-10-10/south-african-2022-census-shows-population-at-62-million

277. Censorship, C. T. (n.d.). *Saudi Arabia*. Censorship. https://censorship.fandom.com/wiki/Saudi_Arabia

278. Chulov, M. (2023, February 1). Rate of executions in Saudi Arabia almost doubles under Mohammed bin Salman. *The Guardian*. https://www.theguardian.com/world/2023/feb/01/executions-in-saudi-arabia-almost-double-under-mohammed-bin-salman

279. https://www.chron.com/culture/religion/article/christian-pastor-rape-accusations-death-19848806.php

280. Mullen, M. (2023, April 19). Oklahoma City bombing - Memorial, 1995 & Deaths | HISTORY. *HISTORY*. https://www.history.com/topics/1990s/oklahoma-city-bombing

281.

282. Wikipedia contributors. (2024, April 17). *Timothy McVeigh*. Wikipedia. https://en.wikipedia.org/wiki/Timothy_McVeigh

283.

284. Pengelly, M. (2021, July 14). Top US general warned of 'Reichstag moment' in Trump's turbulent last days. *The Guardian*. https://www.theguardian.com/us-news/2021/jul/14/donald-trump-reichstag-moment-general-mark-milley-book

285. Beaumont, P. (2020, December 15). Steve Bannon banned by Twitter for calling for Fauci beheading. *The Guardian*. https://www.theguardian.com/us-news/2020/nov/06/steve-bannon-banned-by-twitter-for-calling-for-fauci-beheading

286. Thompson, S. (2023, March 7). Arnold Schwarzenegger insists antisemites will 'die miserably' in stern address. *Indy100*. https://www.indy100.com/celebrities/arnold-schwarzenegger-antisemitism-hate-youtube

287. Beckett, L. (2020, October 16). QAnon: a timeline of violence linked to the conspiracy theory. *The Guardian*. https://www.theguardian.com/us-news/2020/oct/15/qanon-violence-crimes-timeline

288. Atske, S. (2020, October 8). *Most Americans who have heard of QAnon conspiracy theories say they are bad for the country and that Trump seems to support people who promote them | Pew Research Center*. Pew Research Center's Journalism Project. https://www.pewresearch.org/journalism/2020/09/16/most-americans-who-have-heard-of-qanon-conspiracy-theories-say-they-are-bad-for-the-country-and-that-trump-seems-to-support-people-who-promote-them/

289. Graff, G. M. (2023, November 14). Here's the Proof There's No Government Alien Conspiracy Around Roswell. Wired. https://www.wired.com/story/roswell-aliens-fermi-paradox/

290. Little, B., & Little, B. (2019, July 19). The wildest moon landing conspiracy theories, debunked. HISTORY. https://www.history.com/news/moon-landing-fake-conspiracy-theories

291. *Why has it been 50 years since humans went to the moon?* (2022, December 16). National Air and Space Museum. https://airandspace.si.edu/stories/editorial/why-50-years-since-humans-went-moon

292. Gottschall, Jonathan. The Storytelling Animal: How Stories Make Us Human. Boston: Houghton Mifflin Harcourt, 2012.

293. Poulos, G. (n.d.). *When did humans first start to speak? How language evolved in Africa*. The Conversation. https://theconversation.com/when-did-humans-first-start-to-speak-how-language-evolved-in-africa-194372

294. Gottfried, S. (2019, September 25). The Science Behind Why People Gossip—And When It can be a good thing. *TIME*. https://time.com/5680457/why-do-people-gossip/

295. Targeted online ads are the success of "surveillance capitalism." (n.d.). Magellan Financial Group. https://www.magellangroup.com.au/insights/targeted-online-ads-are-the-success-of-surveillance-capitalism/

296. Brumfiel, G. (2022, April 24). Their mom died of COVID. They say conspiracy theories are what really killed her. *NPR*. https://www.npr.org/sections/health-shots/2022/04/24/1089786147/covid-conspiracy-theories

297. Glenza, J. (2024, February 25). 'Not a disease you want to relive': why is the US seeing outbreaks of measles? *The Guardian*. https://www.theguardian.com/science/2024/feb/25/us-measles-outbreak

298. Evans, J. (2021, December 15). Nazi Hippies: When the New Age and Far Right overlap. *Medium*. https://gen.medium.com/nazi-hippies-when-the-new-age-and-far-right-overlap-d1a6ddcd7be4

432

299. *Dietrich Bonhoeffer*. (n.d.). https://encyclopedia.ushmm.org/content/en/article/dietrich-bo
     nhoeffer

300. Bonhoeffer, D. (2001). Letters and Papers from Prison. United Kingdom: SCM.

301. Bonhoeffer, D. (2001). Letters and Papers from Prison. United Kingdom: SCM.

302. Wikipedia contributors. (2024, March 4). *Dietrich Bonhoeffer*. Wikipedia. https://en.wikip
     edia.org/wiki/Dietrich_Bonhoeffer

303. History Does Not Repeat Itself, But It Rhymes – Quote Investigator. (2014, January 12).
     Quoteinvestigator.com. https://quoteinvestigator.com/2014/01/12/history-rhymes/

304. Reporter, G. S. (2021, November 18). US Capitol rioter who wore horned headdress sen-
     tenced to 41 months. *The Guardian*. https://www.theguardian.com/us-news/2021/nov/1
     7/qanon-shaman-jacob-chansley-sentenced-capitol-attack-role

305. Today, J. H. U. (2016, February 24). Donald Trump loves the "poorly educated" — and they
     love him. *USA TODAY*. https://eu.usatoday.com/story/news/politics/onpolitics/2016/02/
     24/donald-trump-nevada-poorly-educated/80860078/

306. Levin, B. (2022, January 31). Trump makes it clear he'd be an out and out dictator if reelected
     in 2024. *Vanity Fair*. https://www.vanityfair.com/news/2022/01/donald-trump-mike-pen
     ce-2020-overturned

307. Oxford essential quotations. (2017). In *Oxford University Press eBooks*. https://doi.org/10.
     1093/acref/9780191843730.001.0001

308. BBC News. (2019, September 6). Why is billionaire George Soros a bogeyman for the hard
     right? *BBC News*. https://www.bbc.co.uk/news/stories-49584157

309. *The Roman Empire: in the First Century. The Roman Empire. Jesus | PBS*. (n.d.). https://w
     ww.pbs.org/empires/romans/empire/jesus.html

310. *Why were the Jews expelled from England in 1290?* (n.d.). Faculty of History. https://www.
     history.ox.ac.uk/why-were-the-jews-expelled-from-england-in-1290-0

311. Gillingham, J., & Griffiths, R. A. (2002). 6. Wealth, population, and social change in the later
     middle ages. In *Oxford University Press eBooks* (pp. 99–112). https://doi.org/10.1093/actra
     de/9780192854025.003.0006

312. Charles BaudelaireMon cœur mis à nu1864

313. The Wiener Holocaust Library. (n.d.). Medieval Antisemitism. The Holocaust Explained. https://www.theholocaustexplained.org/anti-semitism/medieval-antisemitism/

314. Wein, R. B., & Wein, R. B. (2021, July 27). *History of Jewish money lending.* Jewish History | We Bring Jewish History to Life. https://www.jewishhistory.org/the-rothschilds/

315. Phillips, G. (n.d.). *Antisemitism: how the origins of history's oldest hatred still hold sway today.* The Conversation. https://theconversation.com/antisemitism-how-the-origins-of-historys -oldest-hatred-still-hold-sway-today-87878

316. Museum, U. H. (2021, December 15). Lessons from a Forced Reckoning with Hitler's Germany. *Medium.* https://medium.com/memory-action/lessons-from-a-forced-reckoning-wi th-hitlers-germany-95e5ddca441c

317. Aron, L. (2023, September 24). Putin is worried, so he turned to Anti-Semitism. *The Atlantic.* https://www.theatlantic.com/ideas/archive/2023/09/putin-russia-anti-semitism-sta lin/675424/

318. Harding, L. (2007, July 2). The richer they come … The Guardian. https://www.theguardi an.com/world/2007/jul/02/russia.lukeharding1

319. Aron, L. (2023, September 24). Putin is worried, so he turned to Anti-Semitism. *The Atlantic.* https://www.theatlantic.com/ideas/archive/2023/09/putin-russia-anti-semitism-sta lin/675424/

320. Schneider, T. (2023, October 8). For years, Netanyahu propped up Hamas. Now it's blown up in our faces. Www.timesofisrael.com. https://www.timesofisrael.com/for-years-netanyah u-propped-up-hamas-now-its-blown-up-in-our-faces/

321. https://www.nytimes.com/2023/11/30/world/middleeast/israel-hamas-attack-intelligence. html.

322. Haaretz. (2023, December 17). Israeli failed to act after discovering Hamas assets worth half a billion-dollars, New York Times reports. Haaretz.com. https://www.haaretz.com/israel-news/2023-12-17/ty-article/israel-failed-to-act-after-findin g-hamas-assets-worth-half-a-billion-dollars-nyt-reports/0000018c-74e3-d48b-a5ec-74f382e0 0000.

323. https://www.amnesty.org/en/latest/news/2024/12/amnesty-international-concludes-israel-is-committing-genocide-against-palestinians-in-gaza/

324. https://www.facebook.com/middleeasteye. (n.d.). Jewish "self-determination" or Jewish supremacy? Middle East Eye. https://www.middleeasteye.net/opinion/jewish-self-determination-or-jewish-supremacy

325. Who Are the Christian Nationalists? A Taxonomy for the Post-Jan. 6 World. (2023). Pulitzer Center. https://pulitzercenter.org/stories/who-are-christian-nationalists-taxonomy-post-jan-6-world

326. Reset DOC. (2024). Reset DOC. https://www.resetdoc.org/story/growing-weight-religious-zionism-israel-war-gaza/

327. https://www.facebook.com/Labourheartlands. (2024, August 12). Zionism Vs. Judaism: Why The Distinction Matters In The Israel-Palestine Debate - Heartlands. Labour Heartlands. https://labourheartlands.com/zionism-vs-judaism/

328. The Battle of Armageddon: A Prophetic View. (n.d.). Www.churchofjesuschrist.org. https://www.churchofjesuschrist.org/study/manual/old-testament-student-manual-kings-malachi/enrichment-i?lang=eng

329. Today, P. (2023, November 10). Why Do Evangelical Christians Support Israel's Genocide against Palestinians? - Politics Today. Politics Today. https://politicstoday.org/why-do-evangelical-christians-support-israels-genocide-against-palestinians/

330. https://www.facebook.com/middleeastmonitor. (2024, March 20). Young US evangelicals are refusing to be "useful idiots" for Israel. Middle East Monitor. https://www.middleeastmonitor.com/20240320-young-us-evangelicals-are-refusing-to-be-useful-idiots-for-israel/

331. Sullivan, K. (2024, March 19). Trump says any Jewish person who votes for Democrats "hates their religion" and "everything about Israel." CNN. https://edition.cnn.com/2024/03/18/politics/trump-antisemitic-jewish-people-israel-support-netanyahu

332. U.S. Jews upset with Trump's latest rhetoric say he doesn't get to tell them how to be Jewish. (2024, March 22). PBS NewsHour. https://www.pbs.org/newshour/politics/u-s-jews-upset-with-trumps-latest-rhetoric-say-he-doesnt-get-to-tell-them-how-to-be-jewish

333. https://www.facebook.com/32109457015. (2024, August 28). "Very Bad Sign for Democracy": AIPAC Has Spent Over $100 Million on 2024 Elections | Common Dreams. Common Dreams. https://www.commondreams.org/news/aipac-100-million

334. Now, D. (2024, December 17). *Alex Gibney on "The Bibi Files," Netanyahu's Corruption Case & How Endless War Keeps Him in Power*. Democracy Now! https://www.democracynow.org/2024/12/17/bibi_files

335. Coates, R. (2024, March 15). What is the "great replacement theory"? A scholar of race relations explains. The Conversation. https://theconversation.com/what-is-the-great-replacement-theory-a-scholar-of-race-relations-explains-224835

336. Rogers, K. (2021, March 4). Why QAnon has attracted so many white evangelicals. *FiveThirtyEight*. https://fivethirtyeight.com/features/why-qanon-has-attracted-so-many-white-evangelicals/

337. Rogers, K. (2021b, March 4). Why QAnon has attracted so many white evangelicals. *FiveThirtyEight*. https://fivethirtyeight.com/features/why-qanon-has-attracted-so-many-white-evangelicals/

338. https://www.cia.gov/readingroom/docs/CIA-RDP78-02646R000600240001-5.pdf

339. Dockterman, E. (2019, December 16). The True Story Behind *Bombshell* and the Fox News Sexual Harassment Scandal. *TIME*. https://time.com/5748267/bombshell-true-story-fox-news/

340. https://edition.cnn.com/2020/08/27/media/fox-news-pays-10m-tucker-carlson/index.html

341. Schnell, M. (2021, September 14). The Hill. *The Hill*. https://thehill.com/homenews/media/572224-tucker-carlson-says-he-lies-on-show-when-im-really-cornered-or-something/

342. Folkenflik, D. (2020, September 29). You literally can't believe the facts Tucker Carlson tells you. so say Fox's lawyers. *NPR*. https://www.npr.org/2020/09/29/917747123/you-literally-cant-believe-the-facts-tucker-carlson-tells-you-so-say-fox-s-lawye

343. Madarang, C. (2023, August 1). Tucker Carlson Calls Trump 'Demonic Force' in New Legal Filing. *Rolling Stone*. https://www.rollingstone.com/politics/politics-news/fox-news-disbelief-2020-election-fraud-dominion-lawsuit-1234681503/

344. Harvey, J. (2023, March 8). Tucker Carlson exposed: says he hates Trump "Passionately" in private texts. *HuffPost*. https://www.huffpost.com/entry/tucker-carlson-hates-trump-passi onately-private-texts-dominion-lawsuit_n_6407e981e4b018d7c56db8d9

345. Lange, J. (2017, April 3). *Tucker Carlson tried to join the CIA*. Theweek. https://theweek.co m/speedreads/689969/tucker-carlson-tried-join-cia

346. https://www.nytimes.com/2023/04/24/business/media/tucker-carlson-career-history.html

347. https://www.politico.com/news/magazine/2022/06/30/tim-miller-republican-campaigns-0 0043250?

348. Klein, C. (2020, August 29). Tucker Carlson claims BLM is a "Hoax" as thousands march on Washington. *Vanity Fair*. https://www.vanityfair.com/news/2020/08/tucker-carlson-claim s-blm-is-a-hoax-as-thousands-march-on-washington

349. https://www.vice.com/en/article/v7vezb/great-replacement-theory-decade-of-hate

350. Mastrangelo, D. (2021, August 5). The Hill. *The Hill*. https://thehill.com/homenews/med ia/566499-poll-vaccine-hesitancy-among-fox-news-viewers-down-10-percent-since-march/

351. Bland, A. (2020, December 19). Rupert Murdoch receives dose of Covid vaccine in UK. The Guardian. https://www.theguardian.com/media/2020/dec/18/rupert-murdoch-receiv es-dose-of-covid-vaccine-in-uk

352. https://edition.cnn.com/2020/12/17/media/tucker-carlson-fox-news-vaccine/index.html

353. Moynihan, D. (2021, December 23). Fox News is killing us: Here are the receipts. Wisconsin Examiner. https://wisconsinexaminer.com/2021/12/23/fox-news-is-killing-us-here-are-the -receipts/

354. Suderman, A., & Swenson, A. (2024, September 5). Well-known right-wing Influ- encers Duped to Work for Covert Russian operation, U.S. Prosecutors Say. PBS News. https://www.pbs.org/newshour/politics/well-known-right-wing-influencers-duped -to-work-for-covert-russian-operation-u-s-prosecutors-say

355. Reporter, G. S. (2024, February 21). FBI informant who lied about Bidens' Ukraine ties had contact with Russians – prosecutors. The Guardian. https://www.theguardian.com/us-ne ws/2024/feb/20/fbi-informant-biden-ukraine-russia

356. Pengelly, M. (2022, May 20). Tucker Carlson tried to use Hunter Biden to get his son into Georgetown. *The Guardian*. https://www.theguardian.com/us-news/2022/may/19/tucke r-carlson-hunter-biden-georgetown-emails

357. https://edition.cnn.com/2023/02/27/media/dominion-fox-news/index.html

358. Luscombe, R. (2024, February 7). Tucker Carlson confirms Russia trip and teases Putin interview. *The Guardian*. https://www.theguardian.com/us-news/2024/feb/06/tucker-car lson-russia-trip-vladimir-putin-interview

359. https://www.independent.co.uk/news/world/americas/us-politics/putin-tucker-carlson-cia -interview-b2493559.html

360. Schwarz, J., & Schwarz, J. (2022b, August 26). The origin of student debt: Reagan adviser warned free college would create a dangerous "Educated proletariat". *The Intercept*. https:// theintercept.com/2022/08/25/student-loans-debt-reagan/

361. https://www.fastcompany.com/90981774/controversial-prageru-videos-are-catching-on-in -a-handful-of-states

362. *PragerU*. (n.d.). https://www.prageru.com/

363. Noor, D. (n.d.). Inside the Republican plot to dismantle US environmental policy. Mother Jones. https://www.motherjones.com/politics/2023/07/charles-koch-heritage-foundatio n-republicans-climate-policy/

364. Google let Daily Wire advertise on "climate change is a hoax" searches. (2023, January 27). The Guardian. https://www.theguardian.com/environment/2023/jan/27/daily-wire-googl e-ads-climate-crisis-deniers

365. Stone, P. (2023, September 5). Texas fracking billionaire brothers fuel rightwing media with millions of dollars. The Guardian. https://www.theguardian.com/us-news/2023/sep/05/t exas-fracking-billionaire-brothers-prageru-daily-wire

366. https://www.vice.com/en/article/y3p33j/fracking-farris-dan-wilks-prageru-climate-crisis-de nial-shapiro

367. https://www.reuters.com/article/us-usa-election-wilks-specialreport-idUSKCN0RB0ZF20 150911

368. https://www.exposedbycmd.org/2023/12/13/bradley-funneled-86-million-to-right-wing-lit igation-policy-media-youth-groups-and-higher-education-in-2022/

369. O'Dell, Y. W. S., Rob. (2019, April 4). What is ALEC? "The most effective organization" for conservatives, says Newt Gingrich. Center for Public Integrity. https://publicintegrity.org/politics/state-politics/copy-paste-legislate/what-is-alec-the-m ost-effective-organization-for-conservatives-says-newt-gingrich/

370. Best, R. (2020, July 8). *Confederate statues were never really about preserving history*. FiveThirtyEight. https://projects.fivethirtyeight.com/confederate-statues/

371. Álvarez, B. (n.d.). *Florida's new history standard: 'A blow to our students and nation'* | *NEA*. https://www.nea.org/nea-today/all-news-articles/floridas-new-history-standard-blo w-our-students-and-nation

372. Khalil, J. (2024, January 24). United Daughters of the Confederacy could lose Virginia tax exemptions. VPM; Virginia's home for Public Media. https://www.vpm.org/news/2024-01 -24/united-daughters-of-the-confederacy-tax-exemptions-general-assembly

373. Reporter, G. S. (2018, August 10). 'The lost cause': the women's group fighting for Confederate monuments. *The Guardian.* https://www.theguardian.com/us-news/2018/aug/10/u nited-daughters-of-the-confederacy-statues-lawsuit

374. *TWISTED SOURCES: How Confederate propaganda ended up in the South's schoolbooks.* (n.d.). Facing South. https://www.facingsouth.org/2019/04/twisted-sources-how-confede rate-propaganda-ended-souths-schoolbooks

375. Gross, T. (2023) A historian details how a secretive, extremist group radicalized the American right, NPR. Available at: https://www.npr.org/2023/05/17/1176662608/a-historian-detai ls-how-a-secretive-extremist-group-radicalized-the-american-rig (Accessed: 29 May 2025).

376. https://www.facingsouth.org/2019/04/twisted-sources-how-confederate-propaganda-ende d-souths-schoolbooks

377. https://www.facingsouth.org/2019/04/twisted-sources-how-confederate-propaganda-ende d-souths-schoolbooks

378. Special to National Post. (2016, June 9). Scott Van Wynsberghe: "Gone With The Wind" — your favourite racist book. *Nationalpost.* https://nationalpost.com/opinion/scott-van-wyns berghe-gone-with-the-wind-your-favourite-racist-book

379. *Remarks upon signing Bill amending the Library Services Act* | *The American Presidency Project.* (n.d.). https://www.presidency.ucsb.edu/documents/remarks-upon-signing-bill-am ending-the-library-services-act

380. Schaub, M. (2015, October 5). Texas textbook calling slaves "immigrants" to be changed, after mom's complaint - Los Angeles Times. *Los Angeles Times.* https://www.latimes.com/book s/jacketcopy/la-et-jc-texas-textbook-calls-slaves-immigrants-20151005-story.html

381. Greenlee, C. (2019, August 26). How history textbooks reflect America's refusal to reckon with slavery. *Vox.* https://www.vox.com/identities/2019/8/26/20829771/slavery-textbook s-history

382. https://twitter.com/natsechobbyist/status/1658433415002161153

383. Bowden, J. (2023, July 26). Why Florida's new curriculum on slavery is becoming a political headache for Ron DeSantis. *The Independent*. https://www.independent.co.uk/news/world/americas/us-politics/ron-desantis-florida-schools-slavery-b2382414.html

384. Salam, E. (2024a, March 14). Book bans in US schools and libraries surged to record highs in 2023. *The Guardian*. https://www.theguardian.com/books/2024/mar/14/book-bans-us-schools-surge

385. Storynory. (2018, March 19). *Jack and the Beanstalk*. https://www.storynory.com/jack-and-the-beanstalk/

386. Gallo, A. (2021, December 12). "Where they burn books, they will ultimately burn people also." *Medium*. https://medium.com/la-mia-biblioteca/where-they-burn-books-they-will-ultimately-burn-people-also-34b835d13b7d

387. *Missouri Republican candidate torches LGBTQ-inclusive books in viral video*. (2024, February 7). NBC News. https://www.nbcnews.com/nbc-out/out-politics-and-policy/missouri-republican-candidate-torches-lgbtq-inclusive-books-viral-vide-rcna137715

388. New. (2023). New Histories - The Wall Street Crash. Sheffield.ac.uk . https://newhistories.sites.sheffield.ac.uk/volumes/2012-13/volume-4/issue-2-days-that-shook-the-world/the-wall-street-crash

389. *Reasons the support of the Nazi Party grew - End of the Weimar Republic - WJEC - GCSE History Revision - WJEC - BBC Bitesize*. (2023, January 10). BBC Bitesize. https://www.bbc.co.uk/bitesize/guides/zp34srd/revision/2

390. *Zyklon B on the US border | The Nation*. (2015, June 29). The Nation. https://www.thenation.com/article/archive/zyklon-b-us-border/

391. https://www.psychologytoday.com/gb/blog/time-travelling-apollo/201606/the-two-faces-nostalgia

392. Orwell, G. (1949). 1984. Secker & Warburg.

393. Wallace-Wells, B. (2021, June 18). How a conservative activist invented the conflict over critical race theory. *The New Yorker*. https://www.newyorker.com/news/annals-of-inquiry/how-a-conservative-activist-invented-the-conflict-over-critical-race-theory

394. *Black, Hispanic homebuyers pay higher interest rates on average, even as ownership levels hit new peaks*. (2024, February 21). Fortune. https://fortune.com/2024/02/20/black-hispanic-homebuyers-pay-higher-interest-rates-on-average-even-as-ownership-levels-hit-new-peaks/

395. Claremont Institute. (2021, June 1). *Christopher Rufo: Critical Race Theory and Woke Capital* [Video]. YouTube. https://www.youtube.com/watch?v=jQzaLwfEQdk

396. Pengelly, M. (2023, June 15). Sarah Palin denies then seems to confirm that Trumpism is a cult. *The Guardian*. https://www.theguardian.com/us-news/2023/jun/15/sarah-palin-tru mpism-cult-confirmation

397. Goodreturns. (n.d.). *Charles Koch & family: Charles Koch & family Net Worth, Biography, Age, Spouse, Children & More*. Goodreturn. https://www.goodreturns.in/charles-koch-fam ily-net-worth-and-biography-blnr16.html

398. Pilkington, E. (2023, October 26). "Get the right cases to the supreme court": inside Charles Koch's network. The Guardian; The Guardian. https://www.theguardian.com/us-news/2 023/oct/26/charles-koch-us-government-rightwing-supreme-court

399. David Corn; American Psychosis: A Historical Investigation of How the Republican Party Went Crazy. Grand Central Publishing. 13 September 2022. Page 220

400. Haberman, M., Swan, J., & Goldmacher, S. (2023, June 29). Koch Network raises over $70 million for push to sink Trump. *The New York Times*. https://www.nytimes.com/2023/06 /29/us/politics/koch-network-trump-2024.html

401. https://www.nytimes.com/2024/02/25/us/politics/haley-koch-network.html

402. *David Corn: American Psychosis*: A Historical Investigation of How the Republican Party Went Crazy. Grand Central Publishing. 13 September 2022. Page 235

403. https://quoteinvestigator.com/2018/07/31/believe-eyes/

404. Light, E. (n.d.). *Narcissistic projection: understanding the psychology behind blaming others - PERSONALITY UNLEASHED*. PERSONALITY UNLEASHED. https://personalityun leashed.com/narcissistic-projection/

405. Chow, K. (2017, April 19). "Model Minority" Myth Again Used As A Racial Wedge Between Asians And Blacks. NPR. https://www.npr.org/sections/codeswitch/2017/04/19/524571 669/model-minority-myth-again-used-as-a-racial-wedge-between-asians-and-blacks

406. Frazin, R. (2019, February 8). The Hill. *The Hill*. https://thehill.com/blogs/blog-briefing-r oom/news/429180-candace-owens-if-hitler-just-wanted-to-make-germany-great-and/

407. Parry, T. D. (2019, December 6). Why right-wing commentators distort the history of slavery and emancipation. *Washington Post*. https://www.washingtonpost.com/outlook/2019/12/ 06/why-right-wing-commentators-distort-history-slavery-emancipation/

408. Wiltz, A. (2021, December 15). Can you pass the brown paper bag test? - ILLUMINA-TION-Curated - medium. *Medium*. https://medium.com/illumination-curated/can-you-p ass-the-brown-paper-bag-test-20aeac6e93f6

409. *Loving v. Virginia, 388 U.S. 1 (1967)*. (n.d.). Justia Law. https://supreme.justia.com/cases/f ederal/us/388/1/

410. Marnin, J. (2021, March 1). Fact Check: Did Candace Owens run a liberal blog before becoming a conservative? *Newsweek*. https://www.newsweek.com/fact-check-did-candace-o wens-run-liberal-blog-before-becoming-conservative-1573008

411. Cavazos, N. (2023, December 29). Nikki Haley defends leaving slavery out as cause of Civil War after backlash. *CBS News*. https://www.cbsnews.com/news/nikki-haley-fails-to-mentio n-slavery-when-asked-about-cause-of-civil-war-new-hampshire-town-hall/

412. Cabral, S. (2024, May 22). *Nikki Haley says she is voting Trump for president*. BBC News. https://www.bbc.co.uk/news/articles/ck77rvmp8xno

413. Ramirez, N. M. (2024, May 29). Nikki Haley writes 'Finish them!' on Israeli bomb after refugee massacre. *Rolling Stone*. https://www.rollingstone.com/politics/politics-news/nikki -haley-finish-them-bomb-israel-gaza-1235028702/

414. Middle East Eye. (2024, March 31). *87-year-old Holocaust survivor says: "Stop the genocide in Gaza"* [Video]. YouTube. https://www.youtube.com/watch?v=F3xuIdVjtiI

415. Poonia, G. (2024, January 31). How did Vivek Ramaswamy respond to Babylon Bee's 7-Eleven joke? *Deseret News*. https://www.deseret.com/2024/1/20/24043264/vivek-ramas wamy-7-eleven-employee-joke-babylon-bee/

416. Ladden-Hall, D. (2024, May 9). Ann Coulter tells Ramaswamy she wouldn't vote for him 'Because you're an Indian.' The Daily Beast. https://www.thedailybeast.com/ann-coulter-t ells-ramaswamy-she-wouldnt-vote-for-him-because-youre-an-indian

417. Palantir: Why US firm up for huge NHS deal is controversial. (2023). OpenDemocra-cy. https://www.opendemocracy.net/en/palantir-nhs-federated-data-platform-peter-thiel-d ata-privacy/

418. Selyukh, A. (2016, July 22). "I am proud to be gay," tech investor Peter Thiel tells GOP Convention. *NPR*. https://www.npr.org/2016/07/21/486966882/i-am-proud-to-be-gay-t ech-investor-peter-thiel-tells-gop-convention

419. Donegan, M. (2023, November 8). Mike Johnson, the new speaker of the House, is a gender extremist. The Guardian; The Guardian. https://www.theguardian.com/commentisfree/2 023/nov/08/mike-johnson-house-speaker-republican

420. Shoaib, A. (2023, October 28). Speaker Mike Johnson explained why his "adopted" Black son is not involved in his public life. *Business Insider*. https://www.businessinsider.com/speaker -mike-johnson-explains-relationship-adopted-black-son-2023-10

421. NG, K. (2021, January 22). What is the history of the word "woke"? The Independent. https://www.independent.co.uk/news/uk/home-news/woke-meaning-word-history-b1790787.html

422. Caruso, S. (2023, July 19). Everything to know about the Bud Light controversy. People.com. https://people.com/bud-light-controversy-everything-to-know-7547159

423. Faber, D., & Javers, E. (2024, February 10). Trump's pro-Anheuser-Busch post came after UFC boss Dana White urged him to back company, source says. *CNBC*. https://www.cnbc.com/2024/02/09/trumps-pro-anheuser-busch-post-came-after-ufc-boss-dana-white-urged-him-to-back-company-source-says.html

424. Otten, T. (2024, March 13). *Florida Republican calls trans people "Mutants" and "Demons" on house floor*. The New Republic. https://newrepublic.com/post/171802/florida-republican-calls-trans-people-mutants-demons-house-floor

425. Wade, P., & Reis, P. (2023, March 6). CPAC speaker calls for eradication of 'Transgenderism' — and somehow claims he's not calling for elimination of transgender people. *Rolling Stone*. https://www.rollingstone.com/politics/politics-news/cpac-speaker-transgender-people-eradicated-1234690924/

426. Malone, C. (2023, April 22). The Gospel of Candace Owens. *The New Yorker*. https://www.newyorker.com/news/annals-of-communications/the-gospel-of-candace-owens

427. The Young Turks. (2022, November 13). *Right-Wingers STUNNED to discover women are people too* [Video]. YouTube. https://www.youtube.com/watch?v=rd8RSrmdC4s

428. https://www.forbes.com/sites/danidiplacido/2022/03/21/dave-rubin-is-being-rejected-by-his-own-audience/?sh=67d6d7464f95

429. *Judah Benjamin*. (n.d.). Copyright 2024. https://www.jewishvirtuallibrary.org/judah-benjamin

430. Gross, T. (2023) A historian details how a secretive, extremist group radicalized the American right, NPR. Available at: https://www.npr.org/2023/05/17/1176662608/a-historian-details-how-a-secretive-extremist-group-radicalized-the-american-rig (Accessed: 29 May 2025).

431. *Texas GOP's new platform calls gay people "abnormal" and rejects trans identities*. (2022, June 21). NBC News. https://www.nbcnews.com/nbc-out/out-politics-and-policy/texas-gops-new-platform-calls-gay-people-abnormal-rejects-trans-identi-rcna34530

432. We need to talk about the GOP's 'Black friends' | The nation. (2020, September 2). The Nation. https://www.thenation.com/article/politics/rnc-black-republicans/

433. Ahmed, T. (2023, August 10). GOP donor Anton Lazzaro sentenced to 21 years for sex trafficking minors in Minnesota. *The Independent*. https://www.independent.co.uk/news/world/americas/crime/anton-lazzaro-sex-trafficking-minnesota-b2390853.html

434. Dickinson, T. (2023, April 17). Stop The Steal founder Ali Alexander apologizes amid allegations of texting teens. *Rolling Stone*. https://www.rollingstone.com/politics/politics-news/ali-alexander-apologizes-inappropriate-messages-1234716609/

435. Ramirez, N. M. (2023, May 5). Here's Who Kanye West Just Picked to Manage His Campaign. Rolling Stone. https://www.rollingstone.com/politics/politics-news/kanye-west-milo-yiannopoulos-presidential-campaign-manager-1234729985/

436. Beast, D. (2023, July 16). Nick Fuentes admits his dream wife is 16 years old. *The Daily Beast*. https://www.thedailybeast.com/nick-fuentes-admits-his-dream-wife-is-16-years-old

437. Helmore, E. (2023, November 21). Moms for Liberty outreach leader exposed as registered sex offender. *The Guardian*. https://www.theguardian.com/us-news/2023/nov/21/moms-for-liberty-sex-offender

438. https://www.politico.com/news/2023/12/06/christian-ziegler-florida-rape-accusations-00130503

439. Helmore, E. (2022, June 13). US Southern Baptist churches facing 'apocalypse' over sexual abuse scandal. *The Guardian*. https://www.theguardian.com/world/2022/jun/12/southern-baptist-church-sexual-abuse-scandal

440. Kirby, J., Stewart, E., & Golshan, T. (2018, July 20). Ohio State scandal: Jim Jordan and the Ohio State sexual abuse controversy, explained. *Vox*. https://www.vox.com/policy-and-politics/2018/7/7/17542878/jim-jordan-richard-strauss-ohio

441. Pengelly, M. (2023, October 19). Ex-Ohio State wrestlers say Jim Jordan unfit for speakership for ignoring sexual abuse scandal. *The Guardian*. https://www.theguardian.com/us-news/2023/oct/11/jim-jordan-house-speaker-ohio-state-wrestlers-abuse

442. Tuerkheimer, D. (2021, October 31). How was Larry Nassar able to get away with his terrible crimes? The Guardian. https://www.theguardian.com/commentisfree/2021/oct/31/how-was-larry-nassar-able-to-get-away-with-his-terrible-crimes

443. National Archives. (2021, September 7). 15th Amendment to the U.S. Constitution: Voting Rights (1870). National Archives. https://www.archives.gov/milestone-documents/15th-amendment

444. Frey, W. H. (2018, March 14). The US will become "minority white" in 2045, Census projects. Brookings. https://www.brookings.edu/articles/the-us-will-become-minority-white-in-2045-census-projects/

445. Chang, A. (2019, October 17). The man who rigged America's election maps. *Vox*. https://www.vox.com/videos/2019/10/17/20917852/gerrymander-hofeller-election-map

446. Bybee, R. (2022, March 4). *Smoking gun: voter suppression, in their own words*. Progressive.org. https://progressive.org/magazine/smoking-gun-voter-suppression/

447. *TOP 25 QUOTES BY PAUL WEYRICH | A-Z Quotes*. (n.d.). A-Z Quotes. https://www.azquotes.com/author/15542-Paul_Weyrich

448. Karem, B. (2023, June 3). EP:187 - Author David Pepper joins us to discuss his new book "Saving Democracy" *JATQ Podcast*. https://www.justaskthequestion.com/post/ep-187-author-david-pepper-joins-us-to-discuss-his-new-book-saving-democracy

449. https://crsreports.congress.gov/product/pdf/R/R43626/15

450. *Translational Applied Demography: Packing, cracking and the art of gerrymandering around Milwaukee*. (n.d.). https://apl.wisc.edu/shared/tad/packing-cracking

451. https://constitution.congress.gov/browse/essay/amdt14-S1-8-6-4/ALDE_00013451/

452. Levitt, J. (2020). Where are the lines drawn? All about Redistricting. https://redistricting.lls.edu/redistricting-101/where-are-the-lines-drawn/

453. *List of United States Representatives from Wisconsin - Ballotpedia*. (n.d.). Ballotpedia. https://ballotpedia.org/List_of_United_States_Representatives_from_Wisconsin

454. *Partisan composition of state legislatures - Ballotpedia*. (n.d.). Ballotpedia. https://ballotpedia.org/Partisan_composition_of_state_legislatures

455. *Pass the John R. Lewis Voting Rights Advancement Act*. (2024, February 29). Brennan Center for Justice. https://www.brennancenter.org/our-work/research-reports/pass-john-r-lewis-voting-rights-advancement-act

456. *The Republican war on drop boxes continues - Democracy docket*. (2023, August 2). Democracy Docket. https://www.democracydocket.com/analysis/the-republican-war-on-drop-boxes-continues/

457. Fowler, S. (2020, October 17). Why do nonwhite Georgia voters have to wait in line for hours? Too few polling places. *NPR*. https://www.npr.org/2020/10/17/924527679/why-do-nonwhite-georgia-voters-have-to-wait-in-line-for-hours-too-few-polling-pl

458. Bickerton, J. (2023, November 8). Mississippi running out of ballots in Black-Majority areas raises questions. *Newsweek*. https://www.newsweek.com/mississippi-running-out-ballots-black-majority-areas-raises-questions-1841797

459. Herman, A., Johnson, C. N., Leingang, R., Lerner, K., Levine, S., & Pilkington, E. (2023, March 9). The election-denying Republicans who aided Trump's "big lie" and got promoted. The Guardian. https://www.theguardian.com/us-news/ng-interactive/2023/mar/09/trump-big-lie-2020-election-republican-supporters-congress

460. Weill, K. (2022, November 12). Some Republicans want to raise voting age after Gen Z's strong midterm turnout. *The Daily Beast*. https://www.thedailybeast.com/some-republicans-want-to-raise-voting-age-after-gen-zs-strong-midterm-turnout

461. The growing threat of Republican Election Vigilantes - Democracy Docket. (2023, September 14). Democracy Docket. https://www.democracydocket.com/opinion/the-growing-threat-of-republican-election-vigilantes/

462. Hartmann, T. (2024, April 15). Can voter suppression hand the 2024 election to Trump? The Hartmann Report. https://hartmannreport.com/p/can-voter-suppression-hand-the-2024-a65

463. Ramirez, N. M. (2024, December 18). Funding Bill Includes a Raise for Congress Members, Better Health Care. Rolling Stone. https://www.rollingstone.com/politics/politics-news/funding-bill-raise-congress-health-care-1235210780/

464. Barr, J. (2019, March 15). Fox News contributor Salaries revealed in financial disclosures. *The Hollywood Reporter*. https://www.hollywoodreporter.com/news/general-news/fox-news-contributor-salaries-revealed-financial-disclosures-1193630/

465. Johnson, L. (2012, January 18). Newt Gingrich praised private equity when paid $60,750 to deliver speech. *HuffPost UK*. https://www.huffingtonpost.co.uk/entry/newt-gingrich-private-equity_n_1212980

466. *Here's what happens to candidates' leftover money*. (2022, November 16). NBC News. https://www.nbcnews.com/meet-the-press/meetthepressblog/s-happens-candidates-leftover-money-rcna57340

467. Leonard, K. (2021, December 16). Reading pays for members of Congress: they just made $1.8 million in book advances and royalties. *Business Insider*. https://www.businessinsider.com/members-of-congress-made-18-million-as-book-authors-in-2020-2021-12

468. Kelly, K., Playford, A., Parlapiano, A., & Uz, E. (2022, September 15). Stock trades reported by nearly a fifth of Congress show possible conflicts. *The New York Times*. https://www.nytimes.com/interactive/2022/09/13/us/politics/congress-stock-trading-investigation.html

469. Marcos, C. M. (2024, May 21). Judge upholds $83m E Jean Carroll defamation verdict against Trump. The Guardian. https://www.theguardian.com/us-news/2024/apr/25/e-jean-carroll-trump-defamation.

470. Court, K. E. &. M. H. I. (2024, May 6). *Trump trial: Judge threatens ex-president with jail if he keeps breaking gag order*. BBC News. https://www.bbc.co.uk/news/world-us-canada-68945269

471. O'Driscoll, S. (2024, May 16). Donald Trump could face grilling over gag order notes. *Newsweek*. https://www.newsweek.com/donald-trump-gag-order-hush-money-trial-tommy-tuberville-manhattan-new-york-court-1901523

472. Apple Podcasts. (2023, December 7). *Kevin's "Home Alone" in the house*. https://podcasts.apple.com/us/podcast/kevins-home-alone-in-the%20%20house/id1464094232?i=1000637871305

473. Jeff Jackson. (2023, April 17). *Most of the angry voices in Congress are faking. - Rep. Jeff Jackson* [Video]. YouTube. https://www.youtube.com/watch?v=_PEo9U6UWdY

474. https://www.vice.com/en/article/bvn4b8/jd-vance-trump-messages

475. https://www.washingtonpost.com/local/social-issues/in-rural-america-disability-benefit-rates-are-twice-as-high-as-in-urban-areas/2017/07/22/3e600722-575c-11e7-a204-ad706461fa4f_story.html

476. Conn, B. (2024, July 25). The Myth that J.D. Vance Bootstrapped His Way to the Top. TIME. https://time.com/7002807/jd-vance-bootstrapped-myth/

477. *Yale University G.I. Bill® Tuition Assistance*. (2024, January 25). https://www.collegefactual.com/colleges/yale-university/paying-for-college/veterans/

478. TYT Sports. (2024, January 9). *Mark Cuban CRUSHES Pathetic Trump Stooge JD Vance* [Video]. YouTube. https://www.youtube.com/watch?v=xbmsWbGUSHE

479. Israel, J. (2023, April 13). *In another flip-flop, Ohio GOP Senate nominee J.D. Vance says there's no climate crisis*. American Journal News. https://americanjournalnews.com/ohio-senate-2022-election-republican-jd-vance-democrat-tim-ryan-climate-crisis-coal-electric-vehicles/

480. https://video.pbswisconsin.org/video/jd-vance-endorses-great-replacement-theory-xangpd/

481. TYT Sports. (2024b, January 9). *Mark Cuban CRUSHES Pathetic Trump Stooge JD Vance* [Video]. YouTube. https://www.youtube.com/watch?v=xbmsWbGUSHE

482. Ibrahim, N. (2024, July 30). JD Vance said of his wife, "Obviously she's not a white person"? Snopes. https://www.snopes.com/fact-check/jd-vance-wife-white-person/

483. ABC News (Australia). (2021, January 15). *Some Republicans feared they'd 'be murdered' if they voted for impeachment, Rick Wilson says | 7.30* [Video]. YouTube. https://www.youtube.com/watch?v=WjBrnm566Bk

484. Romney: A Reckoning: By McKay Coppins ·
Published Simon and Schuster, 2023.

485. Forum, R. (2024, January 31). How much does Mitt Romney spend on security? | Opinion.
Deseret News. https://www.deseret.com/opinion/2023/9/30/23894602/civility-in-politics
-mitt-romney-security

486. Lindsey Graham says he was afraid of Former President Donald Trump. (2022, June 18).
Salon. https://www.salon.com/2022/06/18/lindsey-graham-says-he-was-afraid-of_partner/

487. Choi, J. (2021, November 1). The Hill. *The Hill*. https://thehill.com/homenews/senate/5
79453-graham-told-officers-on-jan-6-to-use-their-guns-on-rioters-report/

488. Dasgupta, S. (2022, August 29). Senator Lindsey Graham warns of 'riots in the street' if
Trump is prosecuted. *The Independent*. https://www.independent.co.uk/news/world/amer
icas/us-politics/lindsey-graham-trump-riots-on-the-street-b2154793.html

489. Balevic, K. (2022, September 24). Ted Cruz said Republicans don't criticize Trump because if they do, "he turns around and punches them in the face" for it. *Business Insider*. https://www.businessinsider.com/cruz-gop-wont-criticize-trump-he-punches-them-in-f
ace-2022-9?r=US&IR=T

490. Schonfeld, Z. (2022, October 2). The Hill. *The Hill*. https://thehill.com/homenews/senate
/3671136-collins-says-she-wouldnt-be-surprised-if-a-lawmaker-is-killed-amid-rise-in-threats/

491. Fortinsky, S. (2023, October 20). The Hill. *The Hill*. https://thehill.com/homenews/house
/4265337-bacon-wife-slept-loaded-gun-ugly-phone-calls-speaker-vote/

492. Beast, D. (2024, February 22). *Wake up! Republicans really are trying to ban contraception*.
Apple Podcasts. https://podcasts.apple.com/us/podcast/wake-up-republicans-really-are-try
ing-to-ban-contraception/id1508202790?i=1000646477325

493. *Georgia's 14th congressional district - Ballotpedia*. (n.d.). Ballotpedia. https://ballotpedia.or
g/Georgia%27s_14th_Congressional_District

494. Npr. (2020, October 20). A One-Man propaganda band. *NPR*. https://www.npr.org/tran
scripts/925558235

495. https://www.adl.org/resources/blog/nicholas-j-fuentes-five-things-know

496. https://finance.yahoo.com/news/rich-marjorie-taylor-greene-123013FF7.html

497. *Controversial speaker came with $15K price*. (n.d.). https://thecourier.com/news/338251/c
ontroversial-speaker-came-with-15k-price/

498. Marcus, J. (2022, August 26). White House trolls Marjorie Taylor Greene for student loan criticism: 'She had $183k in PPP loans repaid.' *The Independent*. https://www.independent.co.uk/news/world/americas/us-politics/marjorie-taylor-greene-student-debt-ppp-b2153020.html

499. Katje, C. (2023, February 18). Here's How Much Marjorie Taylor Greene May Have Made Buying Oil And Defense Stocks Before Russia Invaded Ukraine. *markets.businessinsider.com*. https://markets.businessinsider.com/news/stocks/here-s-how-much-marjorie-taylor-greene-may-have-made-buying-oil-and-defense-stocks-before-russia-invaded-ukraine-1032107270

500. Bharade, A. (2023, June 8). Marjorie Taylor Greene, who previously called climate change a "scam," is now using it as an argument to deter migrants away from the US. *Business Insider*. https://www.businessinsider.com/marjorie-taylor-greene-using-climate-change-to-stop-migrants-coming-2023-6?r=US&IR=T

501. Hsu, A. (2019, June 24). How Georgia became a surprising bright spot in the U.S. solar industry. *NPR*. https://www.npr.org/2019/06/24/733795962/how-georgia-became-a-surprising-bright-spot-in-the-u-s-solar-industry

502. Gershon, L. (2019). When cities closed pools to avoid integration. *JSTOR Daily*. https://daily.jstor.org/when-cities-closed-pools-to-avoid-integration/

503. Allen, R. (2024, February 6). These 17 Texan lawmakers still won't say if they accept the 2020 election. *The Texas Tribune*. https://www.texastribune.org/2022/01/06/texas-congress-ted-cruz-2020-election-jan-6/

504. *Which Party Receives More Corporate Donations? | Quorum*. (n.d.). Www.quorum.us. https://www.quorum.us/blog/corporate-donations/

505. Kaplan, J. (2021, November 3). Kyrsten Sinema's hometown is about to raise the minimum wage to $15 — a measure the Arizona senator voted against. Business Insider. https://www.businessinsider.com/tucson-sinemas-birthplace-just-voted-for-a-15-minimum-wage-2021-11

506. O'Neil, L. (2021, December 7). Winemaking and marathon running: what Kyrsten Sinema does instead of her job. *The Guardian*. https://www.theguardian.com/us-news/2021/oct/16/kyrsten-sinema-senate-biden-build-back-better

507. Tindera, M. (2022, February 7). Billionaire Republican donors are now giving to Manchin and Sinema. *Forbes*. https://www.forbes.com/sites/michelatindera/2022/02/04/billionaire-republicans-are-now-donating-to-manchin-and-sinema/?sh=5603adbb1bd9

508. https://www.politico.com/news/2023/11/09/inside-the-gops-operation-to-retire-manchin-00126472

509. *Joe Manchin is a very good friend to his fossil fuel donors*. (2022, August 25). https://jacobin .com/2022/08/joe-manchin-ira-fossil-fuel-donors

510. Waxman, O. B. (2019, October 17). The History Behind *Jojo Rabbit* and What It Was Really Like to Be in the Hitler Youth. *TIME*. https://time.com/5700753/hilter-youth-jojo-rabbit/

511. Fabina, J., Hernandez, E. L., & McElrath, K. (2023). School enrollment in the United States: 2021. In American Community Survey Reports (ACS-55). https://www.census.gov/conte nt/dam/Census/library/publications/2023/acs/acs-55.pdf

512. Nwef. (2023, October 2). *Why do so many parents choose private religious schools?* Noah Webster Educational Foundation. https://noahwebstereducationalfoundation.org/why-do -so-many-parents-choose-private-religious-schools/

513. Shaw, A., & Kligler, Z. (2024, March 10). Billionaires Yass and DeVos are on a crusade to destroy US public schools. Truthout. https://truthout.org/articles/billionaires-yass-and-de vos-are-on-a-crusade-to-destroy-us-public-schools/

514. https://www.politico.com/story/2016/12/betsy-devos-education-trump-religion-232150

515. Heubeck, E. (2022, July 6). The latest perk schools are using to attract teachers: 4-Day weeks. *Education Week*. https://www.edweek.org/leadership/the-latest-perk-schools-are-us ing-to-attract-teachers-4-day-weeks/2022/06

516. *A Four-Day school week? Here are the costs and benefits*. (2023, August 31). RAND. https://www.rand.org/blog/rand-review/2023/08/a-four-day-school-week-here-ar e-the-costs-and-benefits.html

517. Greenhouse, S. (2020, November 5). Billionaires v teachers: the Koch brothers' plan to starve public education. *The Guardian*. https://www.theguardian.com/us-news/2018/sep/07/ari zona-fight-koch-brothers-school-vouchers

518. https://www.politico.com/magazine/story/2014/05/religious-right-real-origins-107133/

519. Free Speech Center. (2024b, February 19). *Zelman v. Simmons-Harris(2002) - The Free Speech Center*. The Free Speech Center. https://www.mtsu.edu/first-amendment/article/723/zelm an-v-simmons-harris

520. *Bloomberg - Are you a robot?* (2023c, December 17). https://www.bloomberg.com/opinion/articles/2023-12-17/moms-for-liberty-co-foun der-caught-up-in-sex-scandal-with-her-husband

521. Graham, E. (n.d.). *Supreme Court decision paves way for public funds to flow to religious schools | NEA*. https://www.nea.org/nea-today/all-news-articles/supreme-court-decision-paves-wa y-public-funds-flow-religious-schools

522. Seering, L. (n.d.). *Dispelling the myth of "School choice" - Freedom from Religion Foundation*. https://ffrf.org/faq/state-church/item/22744-voucherfaq

523. https://www.nytimes.com/2023/07/24/us/arizona-private-school-vouchers.html

524. Meckler, L., & Boorstein, M. (2024, June 4). Billions in taxpayer dollars now go to religious schools via vouchers. *Washington Post*. https://www.washingtonpost.com/nation/2024/06/03/tax-dollars-religious-schools/

525. *Robbing from the poor to educate the rich | The nation*. (2023, February 10). The Nation. https://www.thenation.com/article/society/vouchers-attack-public-education/

526. *School vouchers: There is no upside*. (n.d.). Shanker Institute. https://www.shankerinstitute.org/blog/school-vouchers-there-no-upside

527. Fischer, H. (2023, June 1). Arizona school vouchers program to cost $900 million. *KAWC*. https://www.kawc.org/news/2023-06-01/arizona-school-vouchers-program-to-cost-900-million

528. Cowen, J. (2023, April 19). How school voucher programs hurt students. *TIME*. https://time.com/6272666/school-voucher-programs-hurt-students/

529. Apple Podcasts. (2024l, March 7). *On Democracy with FPWellman on Apple Podcasts*. https://podcasts.apple.com/us/podcast/dirt-road-democrats-need-us-with-jess-piper/id1623863298

530. https://www.tcsmonroe.com/tuition-and-fees

531. Fung, K. (2024, February 28). Pastor who defended rapists got millions to run private school. *Newsweek*. https://www.newsweek.com/pastor-who-defended-rapists-got-millions-run-private-school-1873815

532. https://www.tcsmonroe.com/our-history

533. The Young Turks. (2024, February 26). *WHACKO pastor says he would clear men of rape if victim wore THIS* [Video]. YouTube. https://www.youtube.com/watch?v=vvoKjhTaIzg

534. JustinParmenter. (2024, February 24). *NC church whose pastor says women that wear shorts invite rape has received millions in public tax dollars for school vouchers*. Notes From the Chalkboard. https://notesfromthechalkboard.com/2024/02/24/nc-church-whose-pastor-says-women-that-wear-shorts-invite-rape-has-received-millions-in-public-tax-dollars-for-school-vouchers/

535. Greene, P. (2024, April 30). School vouchers have a transparency problem. Forbes. https://www.forbes.com/sites/petergreene/2024/04/30/school-vouchers-have-a-transparency-problem/

536. Apple Podcasts. (2024m, March 7). *On Democracy with FPWellman on Apple Podcasts*. https://podcasts.apple.com/us/podcast/dirt-road-democrats-need-us-with-jess-piper/id1623863298

537. Tennessean, C. L. (2023, January 14). The school choice movement has a voter problem | Opinion. *Knoxville News Sentinel*. https://eu.tennessean.com/story/opinion/contributors/2023/01/14/opinion-the-school-choice-movement-has-a-voter-problem/69807226007/

538. Walker, T. (n.d.). 'No accountability': Vouchers wreak havoc on states | NEA. https://www.nea.org/nea-today/all-news-articles/no-accountability-vouchers-wreak-havoc-states

539. Yang, M. (2023b, August 15). Oklahoma sued for funding US's first 'state-sponsored' religious charter school. *The Guardian*. https://www.theguardian.com/us-news/2023/aug/13/oklahoma-lawsuit-religious-public-charter-school

540. Yang, M. (2023b, August 15). Oklahoma sued for funding US's first 'state-sponsored' religious charter school. *The Guardian*. https://www.theguardian.com/us-news/2023/aug/13/oklahoma-lawsuit-religious-public-charter-school

541. https://twitter.com/Edu_Historian/status/1581006302830264327

542. Heard, H. Y. (2020, October 29). *#100 A wolf at the schoolhouse door*. Apple Podcasts. https://podcasts.apple.com/us/podcast/100-a-wolf-at-the-schoolhouse-door/id1080145136?i=1000496479210

543. Fox, J. (2014, July 30). Are Corporate Taxes Headed the Way of Prohibition? Harvard Business Review. https://hbr.org/2014/07/are-corporate-taxes-headed-the-way-of-prohibition

544. MacLean, N. (n.d.). How Milton Friedman Aided and Abetted Segregationists in His Quest to Privatize Public Education. Institute for New Economic Thinking. https://www.ineteconomics.org/perspectives/blog/how-milton-friedman-aided-and-abetted-segregationists-in-his-quest-to-privatize-public-education

545. Moukawsher, T. G. (2024, June 25). Bump-Stock ruling reveals a Supreme Court obsessed with word play | Opinion. *Newsweek*. https://www.newsweek.com/bump-stock-ruling-reveals-supreme-court-obsessed-word-play-opinion-1916914

546. Supreme Court Historical Society. (n.d.). History of the Court: The Warren Court, 1953-1969. The Supreme Court Historical Society. https://supremecourthistory.org/history-of-the-courts/warren-court-1953-1969/

547. Quoteresearch. (2017, November 30). *It is difficult to get a man to understand something when his salary depends upon his not understanding it – quote Investigator®*. https://quoteinvesti gator.com/2017/11/30/salary/

548. https://scholarship.law.georgetown.edu/cgi/viewcontent.cgi?article=2362&context=facpub

549. https://jeffersonpapers.princeton.edu/selected-documents/thomas-jefferson-james-madison

550. *The Supreme Court's faux 'Originalism.'* (2022, June 26). POLITICO. https://www.politic o.com/news/magazine/2022/06/26/conservative-supreme-court-gun-control-00042417

551. Pruitt, S., & Pruitt, S. (2018, October 29). *How Robert Bork's Failed Nomination Led to a Changed Supreme Court*. HISTORY. https://www.history.com/news/robert-bork-ronald-r eagan-supreme-court-nominations

552. Rhodes, C. (2022, June 29). The Federalist Society: Architects of the American dystopia. *Al Jazeera*. https://www.aljazeera.com/opinions/2022/6/29/the-federalist-society-architects-o f-the-american-dystopia

553. Michaelson, J. (2018b, July 24). The secrets of Leonard Leo, the man behind Trump's Supreme Court pick. *The Daily Beast*. https://www.thedailybeast.com/the-secrets-of-leon ard-leo-the-man-behind-trumps-supreme-court-pick

554. Buckley v. Valeo, 424 U.S. 1 (1976) and First National Bank of Boston v. Bellotti, 435 U.S. 765 (1978)

555. *S1, EP7 | Campaigns so successful they've landed in court*. (n.d.). Drilled. https://drilled.med ia/podcasts/drilled/1/drilleds01-e06

556. Wikipedia contributors. (2024, February 21). *Óscar R. Benavides*. Wikipedia. https://en.wi kipedia.org/wiki/%C3%93scar_R._Benavides

557. *Code of conduct for United States judges*. (n.d.). United States Courts. https://www.uscourt s.gov/judges-judgeships/code-conduct-united-states-judges

558. Schwartz, M. (2023, April 28). Jane Roberts, who is married to Chief Justice John Roberts, made $10.3 million in commissions from elite law firms, whistleblower documents show. *Business Insider*. https://www.businessinsider.com/jane-roberts-chief-justice-wife-10-milli on-commissions-2023-4?r=US&IR=T

559. https://www.npr.org/2024/06/03/nx-s1-4987590/upside-down-american-flag-protest-sym bol-history

560. Tait, R. (2024, June 11). Alito doubts US right and left can co-exist and wife criticizes Pride flag in secret recording. *The Guardian*. https://www.theguardian.com/us-news/article/202 4/jun/11/samuel-martha-ann-alito-recording

561. Zhou, L. (2023, May 5). A running list of Supreme Court Justice Clarence Thomas's ethics scandals. *Vox*. https://www.vox.com/politics/2023/5/5/23712870/supreme-court-clarence -thomas-ginni-ethics-harlan-crow-ethics-violations

562. https://x.com/TonyHussein4/status/1653426249639788545

563. Cheng, B. (2024, March 12). *Shelby County v. Holder - SCOTUSblog*. SCOTUSblog. https: //www.scotusblog.com/case-files/cases/shelby-county-v-holder/

564. Introduction to the federal court system. (2023, May 12). https://www.justice.gov/usao/ju stice-101/federal-courts

565. https://thetriallawyermagazine.com/2020/12/trump-has-placed-200-judges/

566. Hall, M. (2023, April 13). The rogue court that paved the way for Roe's demise. *Texas Monthly*. https://www.texasmonthly.com/news-politics/fifth-circuit-court-appeals-roe-wade-scot us-supreme-abortion-rights/

567. Drenon, B. (2024, June 14). *What are bump stocks? US Supreme Court lifts Trump-era ban on gun attachments*. BBC News. https://www.bbc.co.uk/news/world-us-canada-68419279

568. Aronoff, K. (2024, June 28). *This is why the Supreme Court shouldn't try to do the EPA's job*. The New Republic. https://newrepublic.com/article/183285/supreme-court-chevron-gors uch-nitrous-oxide

569. https://www.axios.com/2024/06/28/supreme-court-chevron-doctrine-ruling

570. Leingang, R. (2024, July 1). Sotomayor says immunity ruling makes a president 'king above the law.' *The Guardian*. https://www.theguardian.com/us-news/article/2024/jul/01/sonia -sotomayor-dissent-trump-immunity-case

571. *Justices 1789 to present*. (n.d.). https://www.supremecourt.gov/about/members_text.aspx

572. *The Supreme Court of the United States and the Federal Judiciary | Federal Judicial Center*. (n.d.). https://www.fjc.gov/history/courts/supreme-court-united-states-and-federal-judiciary

573. Simmons-Duffin, S. (2023, April 25). In Oklahoma, a woman was told to wait until she's "crashing" for abortion care. *NPR*. https://www.npr.org/sections/health-shots/2023/04/2 5/1171851775/oklahoma-woman-abortion-ban-study-shows-confusion-at-hospitals

574. Surana, K. (2024, September 19). Under Georgia's abortion ban, she died after delayed care. ProPublica. https://www.propublica.org/article/georgia-abortion-ban-amber-thurman-death

575. Sharf, Z. (2022, May 4). Variety. *Variety.* https://variety.com/2022/digital/news/howard-stern-slams-supreme-court-justices-abortion-1235257602/

576. *Limits of fetal viability and its enhancement.* (2001, January 1). PubMed. https://pubmed.ncbi.nlm.nih.gov/11753511/

577. Sasani, A. (2023, December 12). Kate Cox case: what led to the Texan fleeing the state for an abortion? *The Guardian.* https://www.theguardian.com/world/2023/dec/12/kate-cox-texas-abortion-case-explained

578. 26-year-old woman faces Texas murder charge for "self-induced abortion." (2022, April 9). *CBS News.* https://www.cbsnews.com/texas/news/26-year-old-woman-faces-texas-murder-charge-for-self-induced-abortion/

579. Edwards, J. (2022, April 29). Ohio lawmaker calls pregnancies from rape an 'opportunity' for victims. *Washington Post.* https://www.washingtonpost.com/nation/2022/04/29/ohio-rape-bill-opportunity/

580. Yang, M. (2023, July 10). Man gets life sentence for raping girl, nine, forced to leave Ohio for abortion. *The Guardian.* https://www.theguardian.com/world/2023/jul/06/nine-year-old-child-rape-victim-abortion-indiana-ohio-life-sentence

581. Loofbourow, L. (2019, May 30). Why society goes easy on rapists. Slate Magazine. https://slate.com/news-and-politics/2019/05/sexual-assault-rape-sympathy-no-prison.html

582. National Sexual Violence Resource Center. (2011). Statistics about sexual violence [Report]. https://www.nsvrc.org/sites/default/files/publications_nsvrc_factsheet_media-packet_statistics-about-sexual-violence_0.pdf

583. Lewis, T. (2024, February 20). *64,000 Pregnancies Caused by Rape Have Occurred in States with a Total Abortion Ban, New Study Estimates.* Scientific American. https://www.scientificamerican.com/article/64-000-pregnancies-caused-by-rape-have-occurred-in-states-with-a-total-abortion-ban-new-study-estimates/

584. Alfaro, M. (2022, April 14). Michigan GOP candidate says he tells daughters to 'lie back and enjoy it' if rape is inevitable. *Washington Post.* https://www.washingtonpost.com/politics/2022/03/08/gop-candidate-rape-2020-election/

585. Junger, Sebastian. 2017. *Tribe.* London, England: Fourth Estate.

586. Junger, Sebastian. 2017. *Tribe*. London, England: Fourth Estate.

587. Guha, N., & Guha, N. (2022, March 22). *In multiple states, rapists can sue their victims for parental custody*. Prism. https://prismreports.org/2022/03/22/in-multiple-states-rapists-can-sue-their-victims-for-parental-custody/

588. Guha, N., & Guha, N. (2022, March 22). *In multiple states, rapists can sue their victims for parental custody*. Prism. https://prismreports.org/2022/03/22/in-multiple-states-rapists-can-sue-their-victims-for-parental-custody/

589. Fear, Courage, and Cohesion. (1994, November). U.S. Naval Institute. https://www.usni.org/magazines/proceedings/1994/november/fear-courage-and-cohesion

590. Malešević, S. (2021, March 25). Emotions and Warfare: The Social Dynamics of Close-Range Fighting. Oxford Research Encyclopedia of Politics. Retrieved 4 Aug. 2025, from https://oxfordre.com/politics/view/10.1093/acrefore/9780190228637.001.0001/acrefore-9780190228637-e-1981.

591. VA.gov | Veterans Affairs. (n.d.). https://www.ptsd.va.gov/professional/treat/txessentials/psychedelics_assisted_therapy.asp

592. Bowman, E. (2022, July 11). As states ban abortion, the Texas bounty law offers a way to survive legal challenges. *NPR*. https://www.npr.org/2022/07/11/1107741175/texas-abortion-bounty-law

593. *Abortion in Muslim countries 2024*. (n.d.). https://worldpopulationreview.com/country-rankings/abortion-in-muslim-countries

594. Mat Stone. (2022, November 13). *The legend George Carlin 1996 full show - Back in town* [Video]. YouTube. https://www.youtube.com/watch?v=MK2W2cyAzLI

595. Gallman, V. (2022, November 22). Demonizing single women won't save the GOP - ILLUMINATION - medium. Medium. https://medium.com/illumination/demonizing-single-women-wont-save-the-gop-d39706b30025

596. *14th Amendment to the U.S. Constitution: Civil Rights (1868) | National Archives*. (n.d.). https://www.archives.gov/milestone-documents/14th-amendment

597. Sherman, C. (2024, March 20). States push 'fetal personhood' bills despite outrage at Alabama IVF ruling. The Guardian. https://www.theguardian.com/society/2024/mar/20/states-fetal-personhood-bill

598. https://www.pennmedicine.org/updates/blogs/fertility-blog/2018/march/ivf-by-the-numbers

599. https://www.businessinsider.com/gop-republican-ivf-support-criticism-alabama-ruling-202 4-2

600. *Alabama's IVF ruling puts Republicans in a political bind.* (2024, February 23). NBC News. https://www.nbcnews.com/politics/2024-election/alabamas-ivf-ruling-embryos-rep ublican-political-bind-rcna140070

601. Staff, T. (2024, April 30). Read the full transcripts of Donald Trump's interviews with TIME. *TIME.* https://time.com/6972022/donald-trump-transcript-2024-election/

602. Sherman, C. (2024c, November 10). 2024 US elections takeaways: how female voters broke for Harris and Trump. The Guardian. https://www.theguardian.com/us-news/2024/nov/ 06/election-trump-harris-women-voters

603. Spencer-Elliott, L. (2024, November 8). Women report rise in online misogyny following Donald Trump's victory. The Independent. https://www.independent.co.uk/life-style/tru mp-misogyny-tiktok-reproductive-rights-us-election-b2643207.html

604. PBS NewsHour. (2022, April 20). *WATCH: Michigan lawmaker says, 'We will not let hate win'* [Video]. YouTube. https://www.youtube.com/watch?v=iLWo8B1R0MY

605.

606. White women benefit most from affirmative action. So why do they oppose it? (n.d.) . USA TODAY. https://eu.usatoday.com/story/money/2023/06/29/affirmative-action-wh o-benefits-white-women/703712190007/

607. Nadeem, R. (2023, July 12). *Behind Biden's 2020 victory | Pew Research Center.* Pew Research Center - U.S. Politics & Policy. https://www.pewresearch.org/politics/2021/06/30/behind -bidens-2020-victory

608. Cronk, A. (n.d.). How Purity Balls and Purity Culture Pervert Girlhood. https://library.georgetown.edu/sites/default/files/PERVERSION%20OF%20GIRL HOOD%20EXAMINED%20VIA%20PURITY%20BALLS.pdf

609. Stuart, T. (2023, November 8). Abortion Wins Big in Kentucky, Ohio, Virginia 2023 Elections. Rolling Stone. https://www.rollingstone.com/politics/politics-features/abortion-win s-big-kentucky-ohio-virginia-2023-elections-1234872518/

610. There's nothing good about Phyllis Schlafly. (2020, May 20). https://jacobin.com/2020/05 /mrs-america-series-review-phyllis-schlafly

611. Raga, P., & Raga, P. (2020, April 29). Phyllis Schlafly Gay Son: Schlafly family dynamics in "MrS. America." Distractify. https://www.distractify.com/p/phyllis-schlafly-gay-son

612. https://www.phyllisschlafly.com/wp-content/uploads/2021/04/PSCA_PSR_05_03_1971 10-Section-2.pdf

613. Hemmer, N. (2016, September 7). How Phyllis Schlafly — grassroots activist, media innovator — remade the Republican Party. *Vox.* https://www.vox.com/2016/9/7/12837748/phyllis-schlafly-grassroots-activist-media-republican-era

614. Du Bois, W. E. B. (William Edward Burghardt), 1868-1963. Black Reconstruction in America : an Essay toward a History of the Part Which Black Folk Played in the Attempt to Reconstruct Democracy in America, 1860-1880. New York :Oxford University Press, 2007.

615. Smith, N. (2021, June 7). *America's scarcity mindset.* Noahpinion.blog; Noahpinion. https ://www.noahpinion.blog/p/americas-scarcity-mindset

616. Bennett, L. (2015, August 10). What Trump really meant when he said that Megyn Kelly had "Blood coming out of her wherever." *Slate Magazine.* https://slate.com/news-and-politics/2015/08/megyn-kelly-blood-coming-out-of-her-whereever-comment-in-cnn-don-lemon-interview-it-was-classic-trump-and-not-just-because-of-his-sexism.html

617. Forbes Breaking News. (2024, March 10). *Trump jabs Megyn Kelly during rant about media, then touts support from women at Georgia rally* [Video]. YouTube. https://www.youtube.com/watch?v=NhP4MeMrAAc

618. https://bulkmunitions.com/556x45mm-62-grain-fmj-m855-pmc-green-tip-556k-1000-rounds/

619. BulkMunitions. (2024, April 9). 9mm 124gr FMJ American Eagle (AE9AP) 1000 | Bulk Ammo For Sale. https://bulkmunitions.com/9mm-124-gr-fmj-federal-american-eagle-ae9ap-1000-rounds/

620. Winkler, A. (2011, November 9). Did the Wild West Have More Gun Control Than We Do Today? HuffPost. https://www.huffpost.com/entry/did-the-wild-west-have-mo_b_956035.

621. The Guardian. https://www.theguardian.com/us-news/2023/feb/09/missouri-rejects-ban-children-carrying-guns-in-public

622. Loh, M. (2022, May 30). America has 20 million AR-15 style rifles in circulation, and more guns than people in the country. Business Insider. https://www.businessinsider.com/us-20-million-ar-15-style-rifles-in-circulation-2022-5

623. Gallup.com. https://news.gallup.com/poll/264932/percentage-americans-own-guns.aspx

624. Food Industry Facts. (n.d.). Www.fmi.org. https://www.fmi.org/our-research/food-industry-facts

625. Geiger, A. (2024, April 14)

626. Pew Research Center. https://www.pewresearch.org/short-reads/2023/04/26/what-the-da
ta-says-about-gun-deaths-in-the-u-s/

627. CDC Provisional Data: Gun Suicides Reach All-time High in 2022, Gun Homicides
Down Slightly from 2021. (2023, August 15). Johns Hopkins Bloomberg School of Public
Health. https://publichealth.jhu.edu/2023/cdc-provisional-data-gun-suicides-reach-all-tim
e-high-in-2022-gun-homicides-down-slightly-from-2021.

628. Pew Research Center. (2023, April 26). What the data says about gun deaths in the U.S. | Pew
Research Center. https://www.pewresearch.org/short-reads/2023/04/26/what-the-data-sa
ys-about-gun-deaths-in-the-u-s/. For the 32%Gallup. (2024, February 7).

629. Dickinson, T. (2019, August 5). All-American Killer: How the AR-15 became mass shooters'
weapon of choice. Rolling Stone. https://www.rollingstone.com/politics/politics-features/
all-american-killer-how-the-ar-15-became-mass-shooters-weapon-of-choice-107819/

630. Law&Crime Network. (2023, April 27). *'He's Got a Rifle!': Texas Cops Face Off with Armed
Suspect Rapidly Firing AR-15 in Wild Shootout* [Video]. YouTube. https://www.youtube.c
om/watch?v=qAuPY2oIgp0.

631. PoliceActivity. (2023, April 12). *Police bodycam footage of Louisville Bank shooting* [Video].
YouTube. https://www.youtube.com/watch?v=UMZVSjUoEVM.

632. https://s3.documentcloud.org/documents/2859676/ARPA-AR-15.pdf

633. https://s3.documentcloud.org/documents/2859676/ARPA-AR-15.pdf

634. Andersen, J. (2022, June 2). *The AR-15 is for mass killing — ban it | Opinion*. Minnesota
Reformer. https://minnesotareformer.com/2022/05/31/17232/.

635. Mickeviciute, R., & Mickeviciute, R. (2024, February 14). *Revealed: Top 10 world's fastest
fighter jets in 2024*. AeroTime. https://www.aerotime.aero/articles/top-10-worlds-fastest-fi
ghter-jets

636. Wikipedia contributors. (2024, May 5). *AIM-9 Sidewinder*. Wikipedia. https://en.wikipedi
a.org/wiki/AIM-9_Sidewinder

637. Roth, E. (2024, May 24). Activision and Meta sued by families of Uvalde school shooting
victims. *The Verge*. https://www.theverge.com/2024/5/24/24164311/activision-meta-laws
uit-call-of-duty-uvalde-shooting.

638. *Texas school shooter bought 2 rifles after turning 18, carried out Robb Elementary attack days later.* (2022, May 25). ABC7 Los Angeles. https://abc7.com/elementary-school-shooting-texas-shooter-salvador-ramos-uvalde-tx/11893076/

639. Despart, Z. (2024, February 6). "He has a battle rifle": Police feared Uvalde gunman's AR-15. The Texas Tribune. https://www.texastribune.org/2023/03/20/uvalde-shooting-police-ar-15/

640. Jacobo, J., & El-Bawab, N. (2022, December 14). Timeline: How the shooting at a Texas elementary school unfolded. *ABC News.* https://abcnews.go.com/US/timeline-shooting-texas-elementary-school-unfolded/story?id=84966910

641. Dickinson, T. (2019, August 5). All-American Killer: How the AR-15 became mass shooters' weapon of choice. Rolling Stone. https://www.rollingstone.com/politics/politics-features/all-american-killer-how-the-ar-15-became-mass-shooters-weapon-of-choice-107819/

642. Us, P. W. W. (2015, December 3). *How Ronald Reagan learned to love gun control.* Theweek. https://theweek.com/articles/582926/how-ronald-reagan-learned-love-gun-control

643. *Think you know the NRA? Guess again! | Brady.* (n.d.). Brady. https://www.bradyunited.org/blog/think-you-know-the-nra-guess-again?

644. Mikkelson, D. (2013, January 10). *Ronald Reagan on AK-47s.* Snopes. https://www.snopes.com/fact-check/true-arms-talks/

645. Schwarz, J., & Schwarz, J. (2022, June 24). Right-Wing Supreme Court continues its "Great fraud" about the Second Amendment. *The Intercept.* https://theintercept.com/2022/06/24/supreme-court-gun-second-amendment-bruen/

646. https://en.wikipedia.org/wiki/Gun_control_policy_of_the_Bill_Clinton_administration

647. *A Brief history of guns in the U.S. | Hopkins Bloomberg Public Health Magazine.* (n.d.). Hopkins Bloomberg Public Health Magazine. https://magazine.jhsph.edu/2021/brief-history-guns-us

648. Busse, Ryan. 2021. Gunfight: My Battle against the Industry That Radicalized America. Public Affairs. Page 102

649. https://www.usatoday.com/in-depth/news/investigations/2022/08/18/ftc-gun-ads-deceptive-marketing-mass-shootings/10347606002/

650. https://www.nytimes.com/2018/03/03/us/politics/ar-15-americas-rifle.html

651. {{meta.pageTitle}}. (n.d.). {{Meta.siteName}}. https://www.oyez.org/cases/2007/07-290

652. *DISTRICT OF COLUMBIA v. HELLER*. (n.d.). https://www.law.cornell.edu/supct/html/07-290.ZS.html.

653. The "Gun Dude" and a Supreme Court case that changed who can own firearms in the U.S. *NPR*. https://www.npr.org/2022/08/14/1113705501/second-amendment-supreme-court-dick-heller-gun-rights

654. Onion, A. (2023, December 20). Fourteenth Amendment: Simplified Summary, text & Impact | HISTORY. *HISTORY*. https://www.history.com/topics/black-history/fourteenth-amendment)

655. *S3E33 / #Vets4GunReform / Joseph Plenzler, Kyleanne Hunter, Peter Lucier, Steven Kiernan - Just Human Productions*. (2021, October 13). Just Human Productions. https://www.justhumanproductions.org/podcasts/e33-gun-violence-in-america-vets4gunreform

656. {{meta.pageTitle}}. (n.d.-b). {{Meta.siteName}}. https://www.oyez.org/cases/2021/20-843

657. https://www.houstonchronicle.com/local/gray-matters/article/She-took-a-bullet-for-a-Republican-Does-her-life-11233871.php

658. Marcos, C. (2017, October 3). The Hill. *The Hill*. https://thehill.com/homenews/house/353714-scalise-shooting-fortified-view-on-gun-rights/

659. 2nd Amendment | Congressman Steve Scalise. (2022, August 24). Congressman Steve Scalise. https://scalise.house.gov/issues/2nd-amendment

660. Bipartisan Safer Communities Act of 2022 - Ballotpedia. (n.d.). Ballotpedia. https://ballotpedia.org/Bipartisan_Safer_Communities_Act_of_2022

661. https://www.houstonchronicle.com/local/gray-matters/article/She-took-a-bullet-for-a-Republican-Does-her-life-11233871.php

662. Gunman pointed rifle at local officer before firing at Trump during rally, sources tell AP. (2024, July 14). PBS News. https://www.pbs.org/newshour/politics/gunman-pointed-rifle-at-local-officer-before-firing-at-trump-during-rally-sources-tell-ap

663. Sullum, J. (2019, September 10). When the NRA opposed open carry. *Reason.com*. https://reason.com/2014/06/17/when-the-nra-opposed-open-carry/

664. Goldstick, J. E., Cunningham, R. M., & Carter, P. M. (2022). Current causes of death in children and adolescents in the United States. *New England Journal of Medicine/the New England Journal of Medicine, 386*(20), 1955–1956. https://doi.org/10.1056/nejmc2201761

665. https://capitol.texas.gov/tlodocs/86R/billtext/html/HB00496F.htm

666. What We Don't Know about School Shooter Drills. (2023). New England Journal of Medicine, 389(13). https://doi.org/10.1056/nejmp2308309

667. Swofford, A. (2018, February 24). Opinion | I was a marine. I don't want a gun in my classroom. *The New York Times*. https://www.nytimes.com/2018/02/24/opinion/sunday/marine-gun-classroom.html

668. *A Brief history of guns in the U.S. | Hopkins Bloomberg Public Health Magazine*. (n.d.-b). Hopkins Bloomberg Public Health Magazine. https://magazine.jhsph.edu/2021/brief-history-guns-us.

669. Today, K. K. U. (2023, February 17). Florida 3-year-old dies after shooting himself with gun he found in parents' nightstand, officials say. *The Daytona Beach News-Journal*. https://eu.usatoday.com/story/news/nation/2023/02/17/florida-3-year-old-shooting-fathers-gun/11279703002/.

670. *ABC News*. https://abcnews.go.com/US/4-year-shot-killed-3-year-houston-sheriff/story?id=97819873

671. Associated Press & By Associated Press. (2023, January 7). 6-year-old shoots teacher in Virginia classroom, police say - Los Angeles Times. *Los Angeles Times*. https://www.latimes.com/world-nation/story/2023-01-06/6-year-old-shoots-teacher-in-virginia

672. https://edition.cnn.com/2023/04/20/us/neighbor-child-shooting-basketball-singletary/index.html .

673. Treisman, R. (2023, April 19). 2 Texas cheerleaders were shot after 1 tried to get in the wrong car after practice. *NPR*. https://www.npr.org/2023/04/19/1170823978/texas-cheerleaders-shot-car-parking-lot-practice

674. Willard, L. (2023, April 18). A woman was shot to death in a car as it turned around in a rural New York driveway. *NPR*. https://www.npr.org/2023/04/18/1170709922/a-woman-was-shot-to-death-in-a-car-as-it-turned-around-in-a-rural-new-york-drive

675. https://edition.cnn.com/2023/04/18/us/woman-shot-wrong-driveway-upstate-new-york/index.html
.

676. Rios, E. (2023, May 1). Texas shooting suspect still at large as father says family called 911 five times. *The Guardian*. https://www.theguardian.com/us-news/2023/may/01/texas-mass-shooting-suspect-cleveland-family-fbi..

677. Hill, M. (2024, March 1). Man sentenced for killing woman who wound up in his driveway after wrong turn | AP News. *AP News*. https://apnews.com/article/wrong-driveway-shooting-new-york-gillis-monahan-cdca1723c6ba7afb89102a1e1aaa3fe0

678. *Obituary of Kaylin A. Gillis | Flynn Bros. Inc - Schuylerville.* (n.d.). https://flynnbrosinc.com/tribute/details/3933/Kaylin-Gillis/obituary.html

679. Chmielewski, Kenny, Ray, & Michael. (2025, April 23). Mass shooting | Definition, Statistics, Weapons, & Locations. Encyclopedia Britannica. https://www.britannica.com/topic/mass-shooting

680. BulkMunitions. (2024, April 9). *9mm 124gr FMJ American Eagle (AE9AP) 1000 | Bulk Ammo For Sale.* https://bulkmunitions.com/9mm-124-gr-fmj-federal-american-eagle-ae9ap-1000-rounds/..

681. *Prosecutors argue Ethan Crumbley had been* "sending his mother disturbing texts about his state of mind," and his parents "were made aware, in graphic form, of the serious risk posed by their son prior to the shooting."James David Dickson, The Detroit News. (2021b, December 24).

682. Drenon, B. (2024, April 9). Ethan Crumbley: Parents of Michigan school gunman sentenced to at least 10 years. BBC News. https://www.bbc.co.uk/news/world-us-canada-68773119

683. Sokmensuer, H. (2023, November 30). A football player, bowler, freshman and an artist: Remembering the Oxford school shooting victims 2 years later. *Peoplemag.* https://people.com/crime/michigan-school-shooting-remembering-victims/

684. https://www.politico.com/news/magazine/2022/05/27/stopping-mass-shooters-q-a-00035762

685. Illing, S. (2022b, March 12). America's frozen gun debate. *Vox.* https://www.vox.com/vox-conversations-podcast/22933212/vox-conversations-america-gun-rights-second-amendment-stephen-gutowski

686. *S3E3 / Guns & Honor / Dov Cohen, Eric Ruben, Ryan Brown, Rory Miller - Just Human Productions.* (2021b, October 13). Just Human Productions. https://www.justhumanproductions.org/podcasts/e3-gun-violence-in-america-guns-honor

687. Rosenberg, S. (2024, April 14). A closer look at police officers who have fired their weapon on duty. *Pew Research Center.* https://www.pewresearch.org/fact-tank/2017/02/08/a-closer-look-at-police-officers-who-have-fired-their-weapon-on-duty/

688. Official online fishing & Hunting license sales. (n.d.). https://tpwd.texas.gov/business/licenses/online_sales/#

689. https://www.usnews.com/news/best-states/texas/articles/2022-07-20/no-indictment-in-shooting-death-of-girl-during-atm-robbery

690. Kenny-Stancil. (2023, May 6). "The future the GOP wants for all of America": Texas gun law unleashes deadly mayhem. *Common Dreams*. https://www.commondreams.org/news/202 2/10/27/future-gop-wants-all-america-texas-gun-law-unleashes-deadly-mayhem

691. *No indictment for robbery victim who allegedly killed 9-Year-Old girl by mistake*. (2022, July 20). Law & Crime. https://lawandcrime.com/crime/no-indictment-for-robbery-victim-wh o-allegedly-killed-9-year-old-girl-by-mistake.

692. *S3E33 / #Vets4GunReform / Joseph Plenzler, Kyleanne Hunter, Peter Lucier, Steven Kiernan - Just Human Productions*. (2021, October 13). Just Human Productions. https://www.justh umanproductions.org/podcasts/e33-gun-violence-in-america-vets4gunreform

693. S3E4 / Gun Culture 2.0 / Chris Marvin, David Yamane, Kevin Creighton - Just Human Productions. (2021, October 13). Just Human Productions. https://www.justhumanprod uctions.org/podcasts/e4-gun-violence-in-america-gun-culture-2-0. .

694. Hoffman, B. (2024, August 1). The curse of knowledge: what it is and how to overcome it. Forbes. https://www.forbes.com/sites/brycehoffman/2024/07/27/the-curse-of-knowledge -what-it-is-and-how-to-overcome-it/

695. S3E4 / Gun Culture 2.0 / Chris Marvin, David Yamane, Kevin Creighton - Just Human Productions. (2021, October 13). Just Human Productions. https://www.justhumanprod uctions.org/podcasts/e4-gun-violence-in-america-gun-culture-2-0

696. Sands, B. L. (2022, May 30). Handguns: Canada proposes complete freeze on ownership. BBC News. https://www.bbc.co.uk/news/world-us-canada-61641543

697. On gun violence, the United States is an outlier. (n.d.). Institute for Health Metrics and Evaluation. https://www.healthdata.org/news-events/insights-blog/acting-data/gun-violen ce-united-states-outlier.

698. Saric, I. (2023, April 28). Fox News poll finds voters overwhelmingly want restrictions on guns. Axios. https://www.axios.com/2023/04/28/fox-news-poll-voters-want-gun-control

699. Suciu, P. (2020, July 2). Yes, machine guns are "Legal" (But here comes all the catches). The National Interest. https://nationalinterest.org/blog/reboot/yes-machine-guns-are-legal-her e-comes-all-catches-163921.

700. https://www.newsfromthestates.com/article/insurance-questions-remain-bill-arming-schoo l-staff-advances

701. Hall, S. (2024, February 20). *Exxon Knew about Climate Change Almost 40 Years Ago*. Scientific American. https://www.scientificamerican.com/article/exxon-knew-about-climate-cha nge-almost-40-years-ago/

702. *First Paper to Link CO2 and Global Warming, by Eunice Foote (1856)*. (n.d.). The Public Domain Review. https://publicdomainreview.org/collection/first-paper-to-link-co2-and-global-warming-by-eunice-foote-1856

703. Resilience. (2019, July 30). *A "Foote-Note" on the Hidden History of Climate Science: Why You Have Never Heard of Eunice Foote*. Resilience. https://www.resilience.org/stories/2019-07-30/a-foote-note-on-the-hidden-history-of-climate-science-why-you-have-never-heard-of-eunice-foote/

704. *With his seminal paper 75 years ago, Bell Labs icon Claude Shannon ushered in the digital age*. (2023, July 6). Nokia Bell Labs. https://www.bell-labs.com/institute/blog/with-his-seminal-paper-75-years-ago-bell-labs-icon-claude-shannon-ushered-in-the-digital-age/

705. Eschner, K. (2017, March 13). The World's First Solar-Powered Satellite is Still Up There After More Than 60 Years. *Smithsonian Magazine*. https://www.smithsonianmag.com/smart-news/worlds-first-solar-powered-satellite-still-there-after-59-years-180962510/

706. scudchasers. (2015, August 9). *The Unchained Goddess 1958 - Bell Science Hour (Discusses Weather / Climate Change)* [Video]. YouTube. https://www.youtube.com/watch?v=x1ph_7C1Jq4

707. Dockrill, P. (2019, May 15). *One Oil Company Expertly Predicted This Week's CO2 Milestone Almost 40 Years Ago: ScienceAlert*. ScienceAlert. https://www.sciencealert.com/exxon-expertly-predicted-this-week-s-nightmare-co2-milestone-almost-40-years-ago

708. Climate-Admin. (2021, February 4). *Exxon Confirmed Global Warming Consensus in 1982 with In-House Climate Models - Inside Climate News*. Inside Climate News. https://insideclimatenews.org/news/22092015/exxon-confirmed-global-warming-consensus-in-1982-with-in-house-climate-models/

709. Biello, D. (2024, February 20). *Where did the Carter White House's solar panels go?* Scientific American. https://www.scientificamerican.com/article/carter-white-house-solar-panel-array/

710. Weilbacher, M. (2023, July 10). James Hansen, whose Senate testimony made waves in 1988, was right about climate change. *https://www.inquirer.com*. https://www.inquirer.com/opinion/climate-change-james-hansen-testimony-35-years-20230710.html

711. https://www.nytimes.com/1988/06/24/us/global-warming-has-begun-expert-tells-senate.html

712. Hall, S. (2024b, February 20). *Exxon Knew about Climate Change Almost 40 Years Ago*. Scientific American. https://www.scientificamerican.com/article/exxon-knew-about-climate-change-almost-40-years-ago/

713. Goldenberg, S. (2021, August 25). Rush Limbaugh goes the extra mile in rant about New York Times reporter. *The Guardian.* https://www.theguardian.com/environment/2009/oct/21/rush-limbaugh-andy-revkin

714. DeSmog. (2020, April 13). *Drilled S1EP5: aggressive think tanks, shouty pundits, and a new religious argument - DeSmog.* https://www.desmog.com/aggressive-think-tanks-shouty-pundits-and-new-religious-argument/

715. Nerger, M. (2022, December 8). *6 Claims made by climate change skeptics—and how to respond.* Rainforest Alliance. https://www.rainforest-alliance.org/everyday-actions/6-claims-made-by-climate-change-skeptics-and-how-to-respond/

716. Oreskes, N., & Supran, G. (2023, December 7). The forgotten oil ads that told us climate change was nothing. *The Guardian.* https://www.theguardian.com/environment/2021/nov/18/the-forgotten-oil-ads-that-told-us-climate-change-was-nothing

717. So, K. (2024, July 18). Climate Deniers of the 118th Congress. Center for American Progress. https://www.americanprogress.org/article/climate-deniers-of-the-118th-congress/

718. Burkeman, O. (2021, August 25). Memo exposes Bush's new green strategy. *The Guardian.* https://www.theguardian.com/environment/2003/mar/04/usnews.climatechange

719. https://www.edmunds.com/toyota/prius/2024/mpg/

720. Michaelson, R. (2022, November 11). 'Explosion' in number of fossil fuel lobbyists at Cop27 climate summit. *The Guardian.* https://www.theguardian.com/environment/2022/nov/10/big-rise-in-number-of-fossil-fuel-lobbyists-at-cop27-climate-summit

721. Carrington, D., & Stockton, B. (2023, December 4). Cop28 president says there is 'no science' behind demands for phase-out of fossil fuels. *The Guardian.* https://www.theguardian.com/environment/2023/dec/03/back-into-caves-cop28-president-dismisses-phase-out-of-fossil-fuels

722. Watts, J. (2024, April 4). Just 57 companies linked to 80% of greenhouse gas emissions since 2016. *The Guardian.* https://www.theguardian.com/environment/2024/apr/04/just-57-companies-linked-to-80-of-greenhouse-gas-emissions-since-2016

723. *Fossil fuel subsidies surged to record $7 trillion.* (2023, August 24). IMF. https://www.imf.org/en/Blogs/Articles/2023/08/24/fossil-fuel-subsidies-surged-to-record-7-trillion

724. Coleman, C., & Dietz, E. (2019, July 29). Fact Sheet: Fossil Fuel Subsidies: A Closer Look at Tax Breaks and Societal Costs | White Papers | EESI. Environmental and Energy Study Institute. https://www.eesi.org/papers/view/fact-sheet-fossil-fuel-subsidies-a-closer-look-at-tax-breaks-and-societal-costs

725. Cost of electricity by country 2024. (n.d.). https://worldpopulationreview.com/country-rankings/cost-of-electricity-by-country

726. Myllyvirta, L. (2024, July 10). Analysis: China's clean energy pushes coal to record-low 53% share of power in May 2024. Carbon Brief. https://www.carbonbrief.org/analysis-chinas-clean-energy-pushes-coal-to-record-low-53-share-of-power-in-may-2024/

727. Shield, C. (2024, November 27). Pakistan's surprise solar surge shocks experts and grid. Dw.com; Deutsche Welle. https://www.dw.com/en/pakistan-solar-power-renewable-energy-power-grid-v2/a-70885544

728. *Executive Summary – CO2 emissions in 2023 – Analysis - IEA*. (n.d.). IEA. https://www.iea.org/reports/co2-emissions-in-2023/executive-summary

729. Aronoff, K. (2024, March 16). *Trump's fire sale of public lands for oil and gas drillers*. The New Republic. https://newrepublic.com/article/159290/trumps-fire-sale-public-lands-oil-gas-drillers

730. https://www.texasmonthly.com/news-politics/texas-republican-war-on-renewable-energy/

731. *Texas leaders threaten wind and solar boom with legislative push*. (n.d.). Financial Times. https://www.ft.com/content/f0f38eec-6cec-49bc-9390-ed4ac4402525

732. Words Matter: How the language of climate change has changed | USDA Climate Hubs. (n.d.). https://www.climatehubs.usda.gov/hubs/northeast/news/words-matter-how-language-climate-change-has-changed

733. Cusick, D. (2024, February 20). *Miami is the "Most vulnerable" coastal city worldwide*. Scientific American. https://www.scientificamerican.com/article/miami-is-the-most-vulnerable-coastal-city-worldwide/

734. https://edition.cnn.com/2018/11/17/politics/gillum-concedes-florida-governors-race-desantis/index.html

735. https://www.axios.com/local/miami/2024/02/02/desantis-campaign-cost

736. Florida's election police come up empty. (2024, July 29). Brennan Center for Justice. https://www.brennancenter.org/our-work/analysis-opinion/floridas-election-police-come-empty

737. Levine, S. (2022, April 21). Florida Republicans pass congressional map severely limiting Black voter power. *The Guardian*. https://www.theguardian.com/us-news/2022/apr/21/florida-republicans-pass-map-limits-black-voter-power

738. *Florida Supreme Court - Ballotpedia*. (n.d.). Ballotpedia. https://ballotpedia.org/Florida_Supreme_Court

739. Ray, M. (2016, August 8). *Orlando shooting of 2016 | Timeline, Motive, Deaths, & Facts*. Encyclopedia Britannica. https://www.britannica.com/event/Orlando-shooting-of-2016

740. https://edition.cnn.com/2018/02/15/us/florida-school-shooting-timeline/index.html

741. Woodward, A. (2022, May 9). What is Florida's Don't Say Gay bill? *The Independent*. https://www.independent.co.uk/news/world/americas/us-politics/dont-say-gay-bill-florida-desantis-b2074720.html

742. Stuart, T. (2023, May 19). Inside the fight to keep a Florida college queer. *Rolling Stone*. https://www.rollingstone.com/culture/culture-features/ron-desantis-takeover-florida-queer-new-college-1234732975/

743. Waxman, O. B. (2023, February 1). The real reason Florida wants to ban AP African-American studies, according to an architect of the course. *TIME*. https://time.com/6251733/ap-african-american-history-professor-florida-interview/

744. DeLuca, A., & Finkel, T. (2023, October 17). Updated list: Every known Florida School District book ban, July 2021 through June 2023. *Miami New Times*. https://www.miaminewtimes.com/news/more-than-350-books-banned-in-florida-schools-since-last-july-16817328

745. Billson, C., & Billson, C. (2023, January 22). *Stephen King shares advice for young people whose schools are banning books*. PinkNews | Latest Lesbian, Gay, Bi and Trans News | LGBTQ+ News. https://www.thepinknews.com/2023/01/22/stephen-king-books-bans/

746. Greve, J. E. (2023, April 12). 'People will die': why is Ron DeSantis loosening gun laws that most Floridians support? *The Guardian*. https://www.theguardian.com/us-news/2023/apr/11/ron-desantis-florida-gun-control-permitless-carry

747. Izaguirre, A. (2023, April 15). DeSantis signs Florida GOP's 6-week abortion ban into law | AP News. *AP News*. https://apnews.com/article/florida-abortion-ban-approved-c9c53311a0b2426adc4b8d0b463edad1

748. Rentoul, J. (2017, August 26). The top 10: misattributed quotations | The Independent. The Independent. https://www.independent.co.uk/voices/the-top-10-misattributed-quotations-a7910361.html

749. Hyatt, J. (2023, December 22). This Self-Made Wall Street billionaire has never read a single investment book. *Forbes*. https://www.forbes.com/sites/johnhyatt/2023/12/22/this-self-made-wall-street-billionaire-has-never-read-a-single-investment-book/

750. *Bloomberg - Are you a robot?* (n.d.). https://www.bloomberg.com/features/2021-palm-beach-mansions-sea-level/?leadSource=uverify%20wall

751. Mazzei, P. (2023, June 22). A 20-Foot sea wall? Miami faces the hard choices of climate change. *The New York Times*. https://www.nytimes.com/2021/06/02/us/miami-fl-seawall-hurrican es.html

752. Mulligan, M., & Chesnes, M. (2023, April 3). Hurricane Ian costliest storm in Florida history, reached Cat 5, new report states. *Tampa Bay Times*. https://www.tampabay.com/hurrican e/2023/04/03/hurricane-ian-florida-landfall-damage-estimate-total-deaths/

753. Milman, O. (2023, May 28). DeSantis accused of 'catastrophic' climate approach after campaign launch. *The Guardian*. https://www.theguardian.com/us-news/2023/may/28/ron-d esantis-climate-crisis-campaign

754. Rahman, K. (2024, October 4). Full list of Republicans who voted against FEMA funding before Helene hit. Newsweek. https://www.newsweek.com/republicans-voted-against-fem a-funding-1963980

755. Moon, E. (2024, January 3). "It's really a crisis:" Florida state leaders unpack rising homeowners insurance costs. *FOX 13 Tampa Bay*. https://www.fox13news.com/news/florida-home-i nsurance-crisis-cost-price-premium-institute-rates

756. Gelfman-Randazzo, J. (2024, February 7). *Florida insurance crisis spells mortgage disaster - Environmental, Social and Governance (ESG) initiative*. Environmental, Social and Governance (ESG) Initiative. https://esg.wharton.upenn.edu/homepage/florida-insurance-crisis-s pells-mortgage-disaster/

757. https://magicguides.com/disney-world-statistics/
https://floridareview.co.uk/useful-resources/florida-tourism-numbers

758. *Disney World Tickets | Orlando, Florida | Walt Disney World® Official site*. (n.d.). https:// www.disneyholidays.co.uk/walt-disney-world/tickets/

759. Mir, A. (2023, August 15). Two Years Under the Taliban: Is Afghanistan a Terrorist Safe Haven Once Again? United States Institute of Peace. https://www.usip.org/publications/ 2023/08/two-years-under-taliban-afghanistan-terrorist-safe-haven-once-again

760. House, W. (2021, August 31). *Remarks by President Biden on the end of the war in Afghanistan*. The White House. https://www.whitehouse.gov/briefing-room/speeches-rem arks/2021/08/31/remarks-by-president-biden-on-the-end-of-the-war-in-afghanistan/

761. https://www.cia.gov/readingroom/docs/DOC_0000515454.pdf

762. *Statement on the fourth anniversary of the Soviet invasion of Afghanistan | The American Presidency Project*. (n.d.). https://www.presidency.ucsb.edu/documents/statement-the-four th-anniversary-the-soviet-invasion-afghanistan

763. *Operation DESERT STORM | U.S. Army Center of Military History*. (n.d.). https://histor y.army.mil/html/bookshelves/resmat/desert-storm/index.html

764. Think Again: Nation Building. (2024). Carnegie Endowment for International Peace. http s://carnegieendowment.org/posts/2002/10/think-again-nation-building?lang=en

765. Waxman, O. B. (2022, August 30). Mikhail Gorbachev championed 'Glasnost' and 'Pere- stroika.' Here's how they changed the world. *TIME*. https://time.com/5512665/mikhail-g orbachev-glasnost-perestroika/

766. Quoteresearch. (2015, August 28). *Give a man a fish, and you feed him for a day. Teach a man to fish, and you feed him for a lifetime – quote Investigator®*. https://quoteinvestigator.com /2015/08/28/fish/

767. Chrystia Freeland, Plutocrats: The Rise of the New Super-Rich and the Fall of Everyone Else. Penguin (2012).

768. Isaqzadeh, M., Giustozzi, A., & Integrity Watch Afghanistan. (2013). On Afghanistan's Roads: Extortion and Abuse against Drivers. In Integrity Watch Afghanistan. https://www.baag.org.uk/sites/default/files/resources/attachments/IWA%20 On_afghanistans_roads_extortion.pdf

769. BBC News. (2021, November 10). Afghanistan's ghost soldiers undermined fight against Taliban - ex-official. *BBC News*. https://www.bbc.co.uk/news/world-asia-59230564

770. Reporter, G. S. (2022, October 19). Afghanistan's corruption epidemic is wasting billions in aid. *The Guardian*. https://www.theguardian.com/global-development-professionals-netw ork/2016/nov/03/afghanistans-corruption-epidemic-is-wasting-billions-in-aid

771. https://www.reuters.com/world/asia-pacific/profits-poppy-afghanistans-illegal-drug-trade-b oon-taliban-2021-08-16/

772. Gault, M., & Gault, M. (2024, July 27). Afghanistan's opium business boomed under US occupation. VICE. https://www.vice.com/en/article/afghanistans-opium-business-boome d-under-us-occupation/

773. Menon, S. (2022b, July 8). Afghanistan earthquake: What foreign aid is getting in? BBC News. https://www.bbc.co.uk/news/world-asia-59518628

774. Writer, S. (2023, June 20). *Afghanistan's opium tragedy persists despite Taliban cultivation ban*. Nikkei Asia. https://asia.nikkei.com/Spotlight/The-Big-Story/Afghanistan-s-opium-traged y-persists-despite-Taliban-cultivation-ban

775. Kumar, R. (2022, June 29). Afghan officials fled to luxury homes leaving millions to suffer. Al Jazeera. https://www.aljazeera.com/news/2022/6/29/afghan-officials-escaped-to-luxury-con

776. Team, B. V. J. (2021b, August 31). Afghanistan: What was left behind by US forces? *BBC News*. https://www.bbc.co.uk/news/world-58393763

777. http://tf.com.vn/uploaded/1/492_HIIDE_Datasheet.pdf

778. https://www.mrt.com/news/article/Afghan-Girls-Return-to-School-7849395.php

779. https://www.eurasiareview.com/25062024-afghanistans-lithium-treasure-chinas-key-to-ev-d ominance-oped/

780. *The Taliban's Successful Opium Ban is Bad for Afghans and the World*. (n.d.). United States Institute of Peace. https://www.usip.org/publications/2023/06/talibans-successful-opium -ban-bad-afghans-and-world

781. Yong, N. (2023, December 12). Myanmar overtakes Afghanistan as top opium producer. BBC News. https://www.bbc.co.uk/news/world-asia-67688413

782. Crisp, E. (2023, November 8). The Hill. *The Hill*. https://thehill.com/homenews/campaig n/4299354-santorum-ohio-results-pure-democracies/

783. Swan, J., & Haberman, M. (2023, April 20). Heritage Foundation makes plans to staff next G.O.P. administration. *The New York Times*. https://www.nytimes.com/2023/04/20/us/p olitics/republican-president-2024-heritage-foundation.html

784. https://www.reuters.com/world/us/us-2024-hopeful-desantis-targets-three-federal-departm ents-elimination-2023-06-29/

785. Swan, J., Savage, C., & Haberman, M. (2023, July 18). Trump plans to expand presidential power over agencies in 2025. *The New York Times*. https://www.nytimes.com/2023/07/17 /us/politics/trump-plans-2025.html

786. *DocumentCloud*. (n.d.). https://www.documentcloud.org/documents/24088042-project-2 025s-mandate-for-leadership-the-conservative-promise

787. Woodward, A. (2024, February 23). Far-right influencer calls for 'end of democracy' at CPAC as Republicans downplay January 6. *The Independent*. https://www.independent.co.uk/ne ws/world/americas/us-politics/posobiec-democracy-cpac-january-6-b2501566.html

788. Sommerlad, J. (2024, February 24). Who's speaking at CPAC? All the scheduled presen- ters. *The Independent*. https://www.independent.co.uk/news/world/americas/us-politics/c pac-2024-conference-speakers-schedule-trump-b2501874.html

789. Elliott, A. P. K. (2022, August 23). Barre Seid donated $1.6 billion to conservative Marble Freedom Trust. *ProPublica*. https://www.propublica.org/article/dark-money-leonard-leo-b arre-seid

790. Treisman, R. (2023, December 4). Democracy is at stake if Trump is reelected, Liz Cheney warns in her new book. TPR. https://www.tpr.org/2023-12-04/democracy-is-at-stake-if-tr ump-is-reelected-liz-cheney-warns-in-her-new-book

791. EU. (n.d.). Hungary– EU country profile | European Union. European-Union.europa.eu. https://european-union.europa.eu/principles-countries-history/eu-countries/hungary_en

792. White, L. (2022, June 27). *"Goulash Authoritarianism": Hungary's informational autocracy - Democracy Digest*. Democracy Digest. https://www.demdigest.org/goulash-authoritarianis m-hungarys-informational-autocracy/

793. Transparency International. (2019, November 19). *Hungary's elections: free but not fair - News*. Transparency.org. https://www.transparency.org/en/news/hungarys-elections-free-but-not -fair

794. White, L. (2022b, June 27). *"Goulash Authoritarianism": Hungary's informational autocracy - Democracy Digest*. Democracy Digest. https://www.demdigest.org/goulash-authoritariani sm-hungarys-informational-autocracy/

795. Bucsky, P. (2022, March 29). Hungarian businesses as EU rentiers. Social Europe. https:// www.socialeurope.eu/hungarian-businesses-as-eu-rentiers

796. Bayer, L. (2023, December 21). Hungary's 'draconian' new law can be used to punish Orbán critics, US warns. The Guardian. https://www.theguardian.com/world/2023/dec/21/hung ary-draconian-new-law-can-be-used-to-punish-orban-critics-us-warns

797. Bátorfy, A., & Urbán, Á. (2019). State advertising as an instrument of transformation of the media market in Hungary. *East European Politics*, *36*(1), 44–65. https://doi.org/10.1080/2 1599165.2019.1662398

798. White, L. (2022d, June 27). *"Goulash Authoritarianism": Hungary's informational autocracy - Democracy Digest*. Democracy Digest. https://www.demdigest.org/goulash-authoritariani sm-hungarys-informational-autocracy/

799. Bayer, L. (2023, December 21). Hungary's 'draconian' new law can be used to punish Orbán critics, US warns. The Guardian. https://www.theguardian.com/world/2023/dec/21/hung ary-draconian-new-law-can-be-used-to-punish-orban-critics-us-warns

800. Amnesty International. (2024, February 28). Hungary: Propaganda Law has "created cloud of fear" pushing LGBTI+ community into the shad- ows. https://www.amnesty.org/en/latest/news/2024/02/hungarypropaganda-law-has-crea ted-cloud-of-fear-pushing-lgbti-community-into-the-shadows/

801. Bayer, L. (2023, March 13). Viktor Orbán's battle for EU funds reveals existential clash. *POLITICO*. https://www.politico.eu/article/viktor-orban-battle-eu-funds-reveal-existential-clash/

802. Busquets, A. (2023, February 16). POLITICO Poll of Polls — Hungarian polls, trends and election news for Hungary. *POLITICO*. https://www.politico.eu/europe-poll-of-polls/hungary/

803. Daniels, J. (2023, December 19). *How Viktor Orbán wins | Journal of Democracy*. Journal of Democracy. https://www.journalofdemocracy.org/articles/how-viktor-orban-wins/

804. Hogg, R. (2024, August 19). Hungary offered €30,000 to couples having 3 kids—but its birth rate has still fallen to a record monthly low. Fortune Europe; Fortune. https://fortune.com/europe/2024/08/19/hungary-offered-e30000-to-couples-having-3-kids-but-its-birth-rate-has-still-fallen-to-a-record-monthly-low/

805. Pogue, J. (2022, April 20). What Peter Thiel, J.D. Vance, and others are learning from Curtis Yarvin and the New Right. *Vanity Fair*. https://www.vanityfair.com/news/2022/04/inside-the-new-right-where-peter-thiel-is-placing-his-biggest-bets

806. Shephard, A. (2024, July 31). Read J.D. Vance's Violent Foreword to Project 2025 Leader's new book. The New Republic. https://newrepublic.com/article/184393/jd-vance-violent-foreword-kevin-roberts-project-2025-leader-book

807. Mehrara, M. (2024, August 22). JD Vance appears to suggest Democrats "Tried to kill" Donald Trump. Newsweek. https://www.newsweek.com/jd-vance-suggests-democrats-tried-kill-donald-trump-1942849

808. *How big business bailed out the Nazis*. (n.d.). Brennan Center for Justice. https://www.brennancenter.org/our-work/analysis-opinion/how-big-business-bailed-out-nazis

809. https://www.businessinsider.com/wbd-david-zaslav-biden-trump-election-regulation-sun-valley-2024-7

810. Lange, J., Erickson, B., & Heath, B. (2024, November 6). Trump's return to power fueled by Hispanic, working-class voter support. Reuters. https://www.reuters.com/world/us/trumps-return-power-fueled-by-hispanic-working-class-voter-support-2024-11-06/

811. Yang, J. (2024, July 29). Republicans cheer for "mass deportation" – a dark new chapter in America's history of othering "them." The Guardian; The Guardian. https://www.theguardian.com/us-news/article/2024/jul/29/republicans-trump-mass-deportation-immigration

812. Martin Niemöller: "First they came for the Socialists. . ." (n.d.). https://encyclopedia.ushmm.org/content/en/article/martin-niemoeller-first-they-came-for-the-socialists

813. Bayne, B. (2023, August 25). *Hollywood & The March on Washington: When Fame Overcame Fear | Features | Roger Ebert.* Roger Ebert. https://www.rogerebert.com/features/hollywoo d-and-the-march-on-washington-when-fame-overcame-fear

814. Smith, D. (2023, March 21). 'He was certainly a racist': J Edgar Hoover and a history of white nationalism. *The Guardian.* https://www.theguardian.com/books/2023/mar/21/the-gosp el-of-j-edgar-hoover-lerone-martin

815. Ohtadmin. (2023, August 2). An imaginary interview with Tony Bennett. *Queens Gazette -.* https://www.qgazette.com/articles/an-imaginary-interview-with-tony-bennett/

816. Ohtadmin. (2023b, August 2). An imaginary interview with Tony Bennett. *Queens Gazette -.* https://www.qgazette.com/articles/an-imaginary-interview-with-tony-bennett/

817. Treisman, R. (2022, November 2). Martin Luther King Jr. paid the bill for Julia Roberts' birth. Here's the backstory. *NPR.* https://www.npr.org/2022/11/01/1133121228/julia-ro berts-mlk-birth

818. Oladipo, G. (2023, February 18). Nearly 1,000 contributors protest New York Times' coverage of trans people. The Guardian. https://www.theguardian.com/us-news/2023/feb/17 /new-york-times-contributors-open-letter-protest-anti-trans-coverage

819. Schillace, B. (2024, February 20). *The forgotten history of the world's first trans clinic.* Scientific American. https://www.scientificamerican.com/article/the-forgotten-history-of-the-world s-first-trans-clinic/

820. https://edition.cnn.com/election/2024/results/oklahoma

821. Death of Nex Benedict. (2024, February 25). Wikipedia. https://en.wikipedia.org/wiki/De ath_of_Nex_Benedict

822. Twitter activist behind far-right "Libs of TikTok" revealed to be US Orthodox Jew. (2022, April 22). The Times of Israel. https://www.timesofisrael.com/twitter-activist-behind-far-r ight-libs-of-tiktok-revealed-to-be-us-orthodox-jew/

823. McHardy, M. (2024, February 27). Republican state lawmaker slammed after referring to LGBTQ+ community as 'filth.' *The Independent.* https://www.independent.co.uk/news/ world/americas/us-politics/tom-woods-oklahoma-lgbt-nex-benedict-b2503412.html

824. TYT Investigates. (2023, June 14). School board president DESTROYS homophobic protestors [Video]. YouTube. https://www.youtube.com/watch?v=vYvt8IIwC2s

825. *Murder in the U.S.: number of offenders by gender 2022 | Statista.* (2024, February 13). Statista. https://www.statista.com/statistics/251886/murder-offenders-in-the-us-by-gender/

826. The Williams Institute at UCLA School of Law. (2023, July 20). *More than 40% of transgender adults in the US have attempted suicide - Williams Institute*. Williams Institute. https://williamsinstitute.law.ucla.edu/press/transpop-suicide-press-release/

827. https://www.instagram.com/p/BopoXpYnCes/?hl=en

828. Biden's vow of Black justice a nod to his most loyal voters. (2022, January 28). PBS News. https://www.pbs.org/newshour/nation/bidens-vow-of-black-justice-a-nod-to-his-most-loyal-voters

829. https://www.netflix.com/gb/title/81028336

830. Spangler, T. (2024, September 15). Donald Trump Rages at Taylor Swift: "I Hate Taylor Swift!" Variety; Variety. https://variety.com/2024/music/news/donald-trump-i-hate-taylor-swift-truth-social-1236144531/

831. Ritschel, C. (2021, November 12). People are appalled by video of millennials trying Cracker Barrel for the first time. *The Independent*. https://www.independent.co.uk/life-style/cracker-barrel-millennials-video-b1956699.html

832. https://twitter.com/WalshFreedom/status/1735353062540062741

833. Presidential election in Texas, 2020 - Ballotpedia. (n.d.). Ballotpedia. https://ballotpedia.org/Presidential_election_in_Texas,_2020

834. Race Relations Act 1976 (Repealed). (2025). Legislation.gov.uk. https://www.legislation.gov.uk/ukpga/1976/74/england/2000-07-28

835. Mellett, K. (2024, May 6). *"No Irish, No Blacks, No Dogs": Irish Times readers recall seeing notorious signs in Britain*.
The Irish Times.
https://www.irishtimes.com/ireland/social-affairs/2024/05/06/no-irish-no-blacks-no-dogs-irish-times-readers-recall-encountering-notorious-signs-in-britain/

836. Otte, J. (2025, February 5). 'What a circus': eligible US voters on why they didn't vote in the 2024 presidential election. The Guardian. https://www.theguardian.com/us-news/2024/dec/13/why-eligible-voters-did-not-vote

837. The development of agriculture. (n.d.). https://education.nationalgeographic.org/resource/development-agriculture/

838. https://www.psychologytoday.com/gb/blog/singular-perspective/202105/why-the-human-brain-is-so-good-detecting-patterns

839. Mobbs D, Hagan CC, Dalgleish T, Silston B, Prévost C. The ecology of human fear: survival optimization and the nervous system. Front Neurosci. 2015 Mar 18;9:55. doi: 10.3389/fnins.2015.00055. PMID: 25852451; PMCID: PMC4364301.

840. Chekroud AM, Everett JA, Bridge H, Hewstone M. A review of neuroimaging studies of race-related prejudice: does amygdala response reflect threat? Front Hum Neurosci. 2014 Mar 27;8:179. doi: 10.3389/fnhum.2014.00179. PMID: 24734016; PMCID: PMC3973920.

841. *The life that shaped Mark Twain's Anti-Slavery views.* (2023, August 16). American Federation of Teachers. https://www.aft.org/periodical/american-educator/fall-2002/life-shaped-mark-twains-anti-slavery-views

842. Rothman, L. (2016, June 1). Marilyn Monroe's forgotten radical politics. *TIME.* https://time.com/4346542/radical-politics-marilyn-monroe/

843. Bregman, Rutger. 2020. Humankind. London, England: Bloomsbury Publishing PLC. Page 354

844. Groypers. (2024, February 3). Institute for Strategic Dialogue. https://www.isdglobal.org/isd-explainer/groypers/

845. David Pakman Show. (2024, February 21). *Neo-Nazis try marching, LEAVE when confronted* [Video]. YouTube. https://www.youtube.com/watch?v=p19KfcJXldc

846. *Yale University G.I. Bill® Tuition Assistance.* (2024, January 25). https://www.collegefactual.com/colleges/yale-university/paying-for-college/veterans/

847. Kamali, S. (2022, July 13). Former Oath Keeper reveals racist, antisemitic beliefs of white nationalist group – and their plans to start a civil war. The Conversation. https://theconversation.com/former-oath-keeper-reveals-racist-antisemitic-beliefs-of-white-nationalist-group-and-their-plans-to-start-a-civil-war-185006

848. Wendling, B. M. (2022, November 29). Stewart Rhodes' son: 'How I escaped my father's militia.' *BBC News.* https://www.bbc.co.uk/news/world-us-canada-63709446

849. Wendling, B. M. (2022, November 29). Stewart Rhodes' son: 'How I escaped my father's militia.' *BBC News.* https://www.bbc.co.uk/news/world-us-canada-63709446

850. Hall, R. (2024, April 4). Son of Oath Keepers militia leader explains why he's running for office as a Democrat: 'I saw the bullsh*t.' *The Independent.* https://www.independent.co.uk/news/world/americas/us-politics/stewart-rhodes-dakota-adams-oath-keepers-b2522881.html

851. Wendling, B. M. (2022b, November 29). Stewart Rhodes' son: 'How I escaped my father's militia.' *BBC News.* https://www.bbc.co.uk/news/world-us-canada-63709446

852. Picciolini, C. (n.d.). *My descent into America's neo-Nazi movement -- and how I got out* [Video]. TED Talks. https://www.ted.com/talks/christian_picciolini_my_descent_into_america_s_ neo_nazi_movement_and_how_i_got_out

853. Cineas, F. (2021, January 18). Why the FBI is vetting the National Guard ahead of Biden's inauguration. *Vox*. https://www.vox.com/2021/1/18/22237128/fbi-vetting-national-guar d-ahead-of-biden-inauguration

854. France, D. (2018, March 9). *Combat: It was the best of times, it was the worst of times.* . . https://www.linkedin.com/pulse/combat-best-times-worst-duane-france-ma-ncc?trk=mp -author-card

855. World Population Review. (2024). New York City, New York Population 2024. Worldpop ulationreview.com. https://worldpopulationreview.com/us-cities/new-york/new-york

856. *NYPD announces December 2023, End-of-Year Citywide crime statistics.* (2024, January 4). The Official Website of the City of New York. https://www.nyc.gov/site/nypd/news/p0009 8/nypd-december-2023-end-of-year-citywide-crime-statistics

857. Wilkinson, A. (2019, July 8). When They See Us: why Central Park 5 prosecutor Linda Fairstein faced fallout. *Vox*. https://www.vox.com/the-highlight/2019/6/27/18715785/lin da-fairstein-central-park-five-when-they-see-us-netflix

858. Central Park Five: Crime, Coverage & Settlement, HISTORY. (2019, September 23). Central Park Five: Crime, Coverage & Settlement | HISTORY. *HISTORY*. https://www.history.co m/topics/1980s/central-park-five

859. PBS NewsHour. (2016, August 16). The origin of "white trash," and why class is still an issue in the U.S. *PBS NewsHour*. https://www.pbs.org/newshour/show/origin-white-trash-class -still-issue-u-s

860. Marshall, S. (2019, July 18). Tonya Harding Part 1. Listen Notes; Sarah Marshall. https://w ww.listennotes.com/podcasts/youre-wrong-about/tonya-harding-part-1-34XVnYSr6xu/

861. *Understanding Adverse Childhood Experiences (ACES) | Kaiser Permanente*. (n.d.). Kaiser Permanente. https://healthy.kaiserpermanente.org/health-wellness/health-encyclopedia/h e.understanding-adverse-childhood-experiences-aces.acm1444

862. Stein, E. (2021, November 20). What's fact and what's fiction in King Richard. *Slate Magazine*. https://slate.com/culture/2021/11/king-richard-movie-accuracy-will-smith-ric hard-williams.html

863. Gaur, A. (2023, December 29). Venus and Serena Williams' ex-mentor makes no qualms about expending funds on their talent – 'It was not a long shot.' EssentiallySports. https://www.essentiallysports.com/wta-tennis-news-venus-and-serena-williams-ex-mentor-makes-no-qualms-about-expending-funds-on-their-talent-too-many-to-count/

864. How Serena and Venus Williams' father helped push the sisters to tennis stardom. (2024, February 22). *Biography*. https://www.biography.com/athletes/richard-williams-serena-venus-williams-father

865. Nier, C. L., III. (2012, April 1). *Racial predatory lending and African American wealth accumulation*. Race, Racism and the Law. https://racism.org/articles/basic-needs/economic-issues-and-race/1189-housing06-1

866. Center for Responsible Lending, & Bocian, D. G. (2012). *The State of Lending in America and its Impact on U.S. Households*. https://www.responsiblelending.org/sites/default/files/uploads/3-mortgages.pdf

867. *Owning the Consequences: Clinton and the repeal of Glass-Steagall | Demos*. (2015, September 11). Demos. https://www.demos.org/blog/owning-consequences-clinton-and-repeal-glass-steagall

868. Provost, N. (2023). Mixing: A History of Anti-Miscegenation Laws in the United States. History in the Making, 16, 7. https://scholarworks.lib.csusb.edu/cgi/viewcontent.cgi?article=1284&context=history-in-the-making

869. Kalomiris, M. (2022, February 3). Unfit to Breed: America's Dark Tale of Eugenics | NIH Intramural Research Program. Irp.nih.gov. https://irp.nih.gov/catalyst/29/4/unfit-to-breed-americas-dark-tale-of-eugenics

870. Jhangiani, R., & Tarry, H. (2022, January 26). *5.3 Biases in attribution*. Pressbooks. https://opentextbc.ca/socialpsychology/chapter/biases-in-attribution/

871. https://collider.com/kerry-washington-django-unchained-interview/

872. Uncomfortable Conversations with a Black Man. Emmanuel Acho : Flatiron Books, 2020.

873. Booker, B. (2021, January 13). Former Michigan Gov. Rick Snyder Charged In Flint Water Crisis. NPR.org. https://www.npr.org/2021/01/13/956592508/new-charges-in-flint-water-crisis-including-former-michigan-gov-rick-snyder

874. Bailey, C. C. I. M. M. &. C. (2022, September 4). *Jackson water crisis: A legacy of environmental racism?* BBC News. https://www.bbc.co.uk/news/world-us-canada-62783900

875.

876. https://www.politico.com/magazine/story/2018/01/28/lbj-great-society-josh-zeitz-book-21
6538/

877. https://untappedcities.com/2020/07/31/the-controversial-history-of-levittown-americas-fir
st-suburb/

878. https://genius.com/Randy-newman-rednecks-lyrics

879. Kitossa, T. (2018, October 17). "Thugs" is a race-code word that fuels anti-Black racism.
The Conversation. https://theconversation.com/thugs-is-a-race-code-word-that-fuels-anti
-black-racism-100312

880. Demby, G. (2013, December 20). The truth behind the lies of the original "Welfare
Queen." *NPR*. https://www.npr.org/sections/codeswitch/2013/12/20/255819681/the-tr
uth-behind-the-lies-of-the-original-welfare-queen

881. Bouie, J. (2014, November 26). Michael Brown wasn't a superhuman demon to anyone but
Darren Wilson. *Slate Magazine.*
https://slate.com/news-and-politics/2014/11/darren-wilsons-racial-portrayal-of-michael-br
own-as-a-superhuman-demon-the-ferguson-police-officers-account-is-a-common-projection
-of-racial-fears.html

882. How the term 'super-predator' shaped the criminal justice system. (2020, November 28).
[Video]. NBC News. https://www.nbcnews.com/news/us-news/analysis-how-media-creat
ed-superpredator-myth-harmed-generation-black-youth-n1248101

883. Pryor, W. H., Jr., Barkow, R. E., Breyer, C. R., Reeves, D. C., Bolitho, Z. C., Wilson Smoot,
J. P., UNITED STATES SENTENCING COMMISSION, Office of Research and Data,
Schmitt, G. R., Schmitt, G. R., Reedt, L., & Blackwell, K. (2017). *Demographic Differences in
sentencing: An update to the 2012 Booker report* [Report]. United States Sentencing Commission. https://www.ussc.gov/sites/default/files/pdf/research-and-publications/research-publ
ications/2017/20171114_Demographics.pdf

884. https://www.dea.gov/drug-information/drug-scheduling

885. https://www.vox.com/2014/6/17/5818402/rand-paul-wants-the-us-to-stop-jailing-black-an
d-brown-kids-for-drugs

886. https://edition.cnn.com/2014/07/02/politics/rand-paul-civil-rights-act/index.html

887. https://usafacts.org/articles/how-much-do-states-spend-on-prisons/

888. Salganicoff, A., Sobel, L., Gomez, I., & Ramaswamy, A. (2024, March 13). *The Hyde Amendment and coverage for abortion services under Medicaid in the Post-Roe era | KFF.* KFF. https://www.kff.org/womens-health-policy/issue-brief/the-hyde-amendment-and-co verage-for-abortion-services-under-medicaid-in-the-post-roe-era/

889. Race And Country Music Then And Now. (n.d.). NPR.org. https://www.npr.org/section s/therecord/2013/08/23/213852227/race-and-country-music-then-and-now

890. Chow, A. R. (2019, September 11). Black artists helped build country Music—And then it left them behind. TIME. https://time.com/5673476/ken-burns-country-music-black-artists/

891. Rauchway, E. (2021, October 6). President Trump's 'America First' slogan was popularized by Nazi sympathizers. *Washington Post.* https://www.washingtonpost.com/posteverything/wp/2017/01/20/president-trump s-america-first-slogan-was-popularized-by-nazi-sympathizers/

892. Institution, S. (n.d.). *The American axis : Henry Ford, Charles Lindbergh, and the rise of.* Smithsonian Institution. https://www.si.edu/object/american-axis-henry-ford-charles-lind bergh-and-rise-third-reich-max-wallace%3Asiris_sil_1094433

893. Sister Rosetta Tharpe - Topic. (2015, February 21). Up above my head I hear music in the air [Video]. YouTube. https://www.youtube.com/watch?v=y-Jr-W6A5rs

894. Yaniz, R., Jr. (2023, April 13). Jimi Hendrix was deeply inspired by this gospel legend. *Showbiz Cheat Sheet.* https://www.cheatsheet.com/entertainment/jimi-hendrix-was-deeply-inspired -by-this-gospel-legend.html/

895. *Ringo Starr reveals impact black music had on Beatles sound.* (2020, July 8). Female First. https://www.femalefirst.co.uk/music/musicnews/ringo-starr-reveals-impact-black-m usic-beatles-sound-1249405.html

896. Hermes, W. (2018, June 25). Why sister Rosetta Tharpe belongs in the Rock and Roll Hall of Fame. *Rolling Stone.* https://www.rollingstone.com/music/music-features/why-sister-ro setta-tharpe-belongs-in-the-rock-and-roll-hall-of-fame-123738/

897. Hermes, W. (2018b, June 25). Why sister Rosetta Tharpe belongs in the Rock and Roll Hall of Fame. *Rolling Stone.* https://www.rollingstone.com/music/music-features/why-sister-ro setta-tharpe-belongs-in-the-rock-and-roll-hall-of-fame-123738/

898. https://open.spotify.com/show/5fmqWs23wlbAAXYa49HwsO

899. https://www.blackpast.org/african-american-history/jones-frederick-mckinley-1893-1961/

900. Shaylyn.Duong. (2024, February 1). *Top 10 inventions by Black Inventors - COUNTRY 107.1*. COUNTRY 107.1. https://www.country1071.com/2023/01/30/top-10-inventions-by-bla ck-inventors/

901. *African-American Inventors III*. (n.d.). https://education.nationalgeographic.org/resource/ african-american-inventors-20th-and-21st-century/

902. Cineas, F. (2023, July 25). The Supreme Court didn't end affirmative action for white people. *Vox*. https://www.vox.com/politics/2023/6/30/23778906/affirmative-action-white-applica nts-legacy-athletic-recruitment

903. *Love mac and cheese? You should thank James Hemings, the enslaved chef of Thomas Jefferson, for the dish*. (2022, November 23). TODAY.com. https://www.today.com/food/people/ja mes-hemings-mac-and-cheese-enslaved-chef-thomas-jefferson-rcna58226

904. Staff, B. (2022, November 18). *Meet James Hemings, the first French-Trained Black chef who introduced these 4 popular dishes to Americans*. Because of Them We Can.

905. *Business Psychology: Golem Effect vs. Pygmalion Effect – Brescia University – Owensboro, Kentucky*. (2017, December 14). https://www.brescia.edu/2017/12/golem-effect-vs-pygmalion -effect/

906. https://www.nytimes.com/2023/07/14/podcasts/ezra-klein-podcast-transcript-tom-hanks.h tml

907. Jones, J. (2016b, November 8). Take the near impossible literacy test Louisiana used to suppress the Black vote (1964). Open Culture. https://www.openculture.com/2014/07/lit eracy-test-louisiana-used-to-suppress-the-black-vote.html

908. Annear, S. (2016, December 8). Even Harvard students failed the 1964 Louisiana Literacy Test. Boston Magazine. https://www.bostonmagazine.com/news/2014/11/07/harvard-stu dents-failed-the-1964-louisiana-literacy-test/

909. Morgan, J. (2021, October 12). *Black Women Entrepreneurs: Growth and Headwinds | J.P . Morgan*. https://www.jpmorgan.com/insights/business/business-planning/black-women -are-the-fastest-growing-group-of-entrepreneurs-but-the-job-isnt-easy

910. https://edition.cnn.com/2024/02/01/business/tesla-dei-elon-musk/index.html

911. http://web.archive.org/web/20230824214119/https://www.tesla.com/en_gb/impact/peo-ple

912. https://www.tesla.com/en_gb/impact/people

913. Bloomberg - Are you a robot? (2024b, January 29). https://www.bloomberg.com/news/art icles/2024-01-29/tesla-drops-minority-worker-language-after-musk-s-dei-rants

914. http://web.archive.org/

915. Hernandez, J. (2023, September 28). A woman is suing McDonald's after being burned by hot coffee. It's not the first time. NPR. https://www.npr.org/2023/09/28/1201421914/a -woman-is-suing-mcdonalds-after-being-burned-by-hot-coffee-its-not-the-first-ti

916. White, A. (2020, February 21). Donald Trump's Parasite rant was a snap- shot of his blinkered, ludicrous worldview | The Independent. *The Indepen- dent.* https://www.independent.co.uk/arts-entertainment/films/features/trump-parasite-o scars-gone-with-the-wind-bloodsport-colorado-rally-a9349211.html

917. Sarah Churchwell, *The Wrath to Come*: Gone with the Wind *and the Lies America Tells* (London: Head of Zeus, Bloomsbury, 2022),

918. Leingang, R. (2024, April 6). Trump's bizarre, vindictive incoherence has to be heard in full to be believed. *The Guardian.* https://www.theguardian.com/us-news/2024/apr/06/donal d-trump-speech-analysis

919. Highest-grossing film at the global box office (inflation-adjusted). (2014). Guinness World Records. https://www.guinnessworldrecords.com/world-records/highest-box-office-film-g ross-inflation-adjusted

920. Brittain, A. (2023, March 27). Me Too movement. Encyclopedia Britannica; Britannica. https://www.britannica.com/topic/Me-Too-movement

921. *Advanced search.* (n.d.). IMDb. https://www.imdb.com/search/title/?companies=co01027 70

922. Sharf, Z. (2021, July 2). IndieWire. *IndieWire.* https://www.indiewire.com/features/gener al/independence-day-studio-refused-will-smith-racism-1234648383/

923. *Independence Day (1996) 7.0 | Action, adventure, Sci-Fi.* (1996, July 3). IMDb. https://ww w.imdb.com/title/tt0116629/

924. https://www.hachettebookgroup.com/titles/mary-anne-franks/fearless-speech/9781645030 539/?lens=bold-type-books

925. The Loop. (2024, March 7). *"Does cancel culture really still exist?" James O'Brien speaks to Sienna Wilson | THE LOOP* [Video]. YouTube. https://www.youtube.com/watch?v=owt b5AN0pWw

926. Beast, D. (2024, February 10). *Guardian Angels' thug tactics get exposed in Times Square*. Apple Podcasts. https://podcasts.apple.com/us/podcast/guardian-angels-thug-tactics-get-exposed-in-times-square/id1508202790?i=1000644908208

927. Desk, T. W. (2024, October 31). Garbage Row: 15 times Donald Trump used dehumanising language. The Times of India; Times Of India. https://timesofindia.indiatimes.com/world/us/garbage-row-15-times-donald-trump-used-dehumanising-language/articleshow/114816892.cms

928. *Bonus Expeditionary Forces march on Washington (U.S. National Park Service)*. (n.d.). https://www.nps.gov/articles/bonus-expeditionary-forces-march-on-washington.htm

929. Gnam, C. (2022, October 4). *Douglas MacArthur's Plan to Win The Korean War*. Warfare History Network. https://warfarehistorynetwork.com/douglas-macarthur-atomic-bombs-will-win-the-korean-war/

930. Grenier, R. (2015b, September 3). *John Wayne's image*. Commentary Magazine. https://www.commentary.org/articles/richard-grenier/john-waynes-image/

931. Byrne, M. (2018, May 17). Long before Trump, Oliver North was incredibly dishonest—and beloved. Newsweek. https://www.newsweek.com/2018/05/25/oliver-norths-929613.html

932. *John Kerry - recipient -*. (n.d.). https://valor.militarytimes.com/hero/23625

933. Daugherty, G., & Daugherty, G. (2018, September 10). *John McCain in the military: From Navy brat to POW*. HISTORY. https://www.history.com/news/john-mccain-navy-career-timeline-vietnam-pow

934. Stewart, E. (2018, September 1). Watch John McCain defend Barack Obama from a voter calling him "Arab" in 2008. *Vox*. https://www.vox.com/policy-and-politics/2018/8/25/17782572/john-mccain-barack-obama-statement-2008-video

935. Ball/Easton, M., MD. (2023, February 14). Where Wes Moore comes from. *TIME*. https://time.com/6250784/wes-moore-interview/

936. Brenan, B. M. (2024, February 7). Extreme pride in being American remains near record low. *Gallup.com*. https://news.gallup.com/poll/507980/extreme-pride-american-remains-near-record-low.aspx

937. https://www.nytimes.com/interactive/2024/11/05/us/elections/results-president.html

938. Dorman, J. L. (2024, November 12). AOC asked voters why they backed her candidacy and Trump's reelection. Instagram users pointed to the economy and Gaza. Business Insider. https://www.businessinsider.com/aoc-trump-harris-democrats-economy-gaza-split-ticket-voters-2024-11

939. " *Biden Caught on Hot Mic: "No one f—s with a Biden."* The Associated Press, 2022, https://www.youtube.com/watch?v=Mpk210Ee1Sg

940. Yang, Z. (2024, October 16). The Biden-Harris Macroeconomic Record Is Getting a Bum Rap. American Enterprise Institute - AEI. https://www.aei.org/economics/the-biden-harris-macroeconomic-record-is-getting-a-bum-rap/

941. Lane, S. (2023, December 25). The Hill. *The Hill.* https://thehill.com/homenews/administration/4375922-biden-rips-media-for-economy-coverage-start-reporting-it-the-right-way/

942. Luhby, T., & Davis, E. (2024, October 8). Harris proposes Medicare pay for home health care for first time. CNN. https://edition.cnn.com/2024/10/08/politics/harris-home-health-care-medicare-proposal

943. Geevarghese, J. (2024, November 14). Now is the time for finger-pointing. Democratic elites must own their loss. The Hill. https://thehill.com/opinion/campaign/4988643-democratic-party-challenge-harrison/

944. "Everyone is taking their skim": How Democratic consultants cashed in on Harris' losing campaign. (2024, November 24). Salon. https://www.salon.com/2024/11/24/everyone-is-taking-their-skim-how-democratic-consultants-cashed-in-on-harris-losing-campaign/

945. Farivar, M. (2024, November 7). In historic shift, American Muslim and Arab voters desert Democrats. Voice of America. https://www.voanews.com/a/in-historic-shift-american-muslim-and-arab-voters-desert-democrats/7854995.html

946. Gerbaud, G., Harrison, C., & Robertson, K. (2024, November 6). How Latinos Voted the 2024 U.S. Presidential Election. AS/COA. https://www.as-coa.org/articles/how-latinos-voted-2024-us-presidential-election

947. Trump and Musk discussed firing striking workers. The UAW is now seeking an NLRB investigation. (2024, August 13). PBS News. https://www.pbs.org/newshour/politics/trump-and-musk-discussed-firing-striking-workers-the-uaw-is-now-seeking-an-nlrb-investigation

948. Young voters shifted toward Trump but still favored Harris overall. (2024, November 12). Tufts Now. https://now.tufts.edu/2024/11/12/young-voters-shifted-toward-trump-still-favored-harris-overall

949. Thompson, S. (2024, December 8). 2024 Election Donald Trump voter regrets stories. BuzzFeed. https://www.buzzfeed.com/sarathompson1/donald-trump-voters-regrets-flipped

950. Leopards Eating People's Faces Party - Wiktionary, the free dictionary. (2022). Wiktionary. https://en.wiktionary.org/wiki/Leopards_Eating_People%27s_Faces_Party

951. https://link.motherjones.com/public/36678690

952. Svirnovskiy, G. (2021, June 7). Paid leave is incredibly popular — even with Republicans. *Vox*. https://www.vox.com/2021/6/7/22380427/poll-paid-leave-popular-democrats-republicans-covid-19

953. Schaeffer, K. (2024, April 14). Most Americans support a $15 federal minimum wage. Pew Research Center. https://www.pewresearch.org/short-reads/2021/04/22/most-americans-support-a-15-federal-minimum-wage/

954. Brenan, B. M. (2024, February 7). Majority in U.S. still say gov't should ensure healthcare. *Gallup.com*. https://news.gallup.com/poll/468401/majority-say-gov-ensure-healthcare.aspx